MW00812617

UNDERSTANDING RHETORIC

UNDERSTANDING RHETORIC

A Guide to Critical Reading and Argumentation

Eamon Cunningham

BrownWalker Press
Irvine • Boca Raton

Understanding Rhetoric: A Guide to Critical Reading and Argumentation

Copyright © 2018 Eamon Cunningham
All rights reserved. No part of this publication may be reproduced,
distributed, or transmitted in any form or by any means, including
photocopying, recording, or other electronic or mechanical methods,
without the prior written permission of the publisher, except in the case
of brief quotations embodied in critical reviews and certain other
noncommercial uses permitted by copyright law.

BrownWalker Press / Universal Publishers, Inc.
Irvine • Boca Raton
USA • 2019
www.BrownWalkerPress.com

978-1-62734-705-1 (pbk.)
978-1-62734-706-8 (ebk.)

Typeset by Medlar Publishing Solutions Pvt Ltd, India
Cover design by Ivan Popov

Publisher's Cataloging-in-Publication Data

Names: Cunningham, Eamon M., author.
Title: Understanding rhetoric : a guide to critical reading and argumentation /
Eamon M. Cunningham.
Description: Irvine, CA : BrownWalker, 2019. | Includes bibliographical
references.
Identifiers: LCCN 2018952253 | ISBN 978-1-62734-705-1 (pbk.)
| ISBN 978-1-62734-706-8 (ebook)
Subjects: LCSH: English language--Rhetoric--Handbooks, manuals, etc. |
Composition (Language arts)--Study and teaching. | Academic writing--
Study and teaching. | Reading. | Critical thinking. | BISAC: LANGUAGE
ARTS & DISCIPLINES / Rhetoric. | LANGUAGE ARTS &
DISCIPLINES / Composition & Creative Writing.
Classification: LCC PE1408 .C86 2019 (print)
| LCC PE1408 (ebook) | DDC 808/.042--dc23.

CONTENTS

Unit 2: Argument

Unit 3: Synthesis

Additional Resources

PREFACE

*U*nderstanding Rhetoric: A Guide to Critical Reading and Argumentation* is a composition textbook that outlines three essential skills – rhetoric, argument, and source-based writing – geared towards newcomers and advanced students alike. The book was conceptualized as an alternative to the typical experience of many first-year composition students, namely a course centered around a textbook comprised mostly of contemporary non-fiction readings with a heavy emphasis on writing in four primary modes – exposition, description, narration, and analysis. In place of this approach, this text offers a theory-based, rhetorical approach to composition that stresses the interrelation between the act of reading, writing, and image analysis. Though comprehensive in its coverage, the book's focus is a simple one: how to move beyond a "gut reaction" while reading to an articulation of what is effective and what is not, while explicitly answering the most important question of "Why?" This text gets at this central concern in two fundamental ways.

First, the text teaches composition as a cumulative process, coaching you *how* to question, challenge, and expand on not just the readings you hold in your hands, but also *how* to interrogate the internal processes of writing and thinking. The blend of composition methods in this book attempt to detail the cross-point of product and process in the act of writing (cognitivist theory), note the profound effect of social and historical realities upon our interpretations (social-constructionist theory), and expand the notion of rhetoric beyond mere writing to any act of communication, image, music, film, and so forth (post-structural theory). Such an approach breaks with the long-standing mode of composition instruction known as "current-traditional rhetoric," a widespread pedagogical stance that reduces writing to its lowest common-denominators: prescriptive rules and technical correctness. While these are not wholly unimportant, this book will work counter several of current-traditional rhetoric's central assumptions: 1) the emphasis on product over process, 2) the privileging of arrangement over invention, 3) the characterization of grammatical and mechanical correctness as (often) the sole concern of the teacher, 4) and the artificial reduction of writing into basic modes (exposition, description, narration, and analysis) devoid of any explicit theoretical basis for doing so. By challenging you to consider where your responses come, this text transforms reading and writing from a matter of coming up with answers to questions to learning what type of questions need to be asked in the first place. The "right" questions, the text argues, are fundamentally rhetorical in nature.

Second, the content of the practice-based chapters is framed into a larger mesh of intellectual history to provide a general introduction to the great minds of our collective heritage. Countering the popular notion that tradition somehow locks our wrists to the past, this book highlights the rich (and often very fascinating) body of rhetorical scholarship by presenting the writing and thinking you are doing today as being continuous with a long history of writing instruction that goes back to the ancient world. Since the 1960s, higher education has increasingly rediscovered the wisdom of the ancient rhetorical traditions and has worked to restore the ties between theory and practice, an idea which had largely fallen out of fashion in the 19th and early 20th century. A theory-based model of instruction assumes rhetoric to be a teachable technique available to anyone with an open mind and a decent work ethic. This book provides equal representation from classical and contemporary theory with the recognition that theory cannot be fully grasped without practice, and practice cannot be fully understood without its theoretical antecedent. After all, you can't write "outside the box" until you know where the box is and what it looks like.

To meet these goals, the text will, foremost, emphasize your role as an active responder to what you read. This approach owes a great debt to Christina Hass and Linda Flower's "Rhetorical Reading Strategies and the Construction of Meaning" (1988), a work which argues that reading is a constructive (rather than merely receptive) process where "meaning" does not exist *in* a text but in readers and the representations they build *from* a text. The "constructive" metaphor makes the process, Haas and Flower say, sound "tidy, rational, and fully conscious," and you may well be thinking that this "left-brain" approach may sterilize what many students cherish about their time spent in English classrooms. But, I would argue, that seeing how writing can work from the inside-out, as if you were an anatomist examining a text's inner organs and its workings, is arguably the most productive and generative way to engage in a study of communication, both within the borders your classroom and beyond.

Upon conclusion, you will learn how to construct meaning in new ways – to see even the most familiar of texts anew – while continuously emphasizing the context of a discourse situation which includes, as Haas and Flower note, the writer of the original text, other readers, the rhetorical context for reading, and the history of the discourse itself. This notion should challenge some of your preconceptions about a text as merely content and information in favor of the understanding that "a piece of writing is a result of someone's intentions, part of a larger discourse world, that has real effects on real readers." This basic assumption of what a text is should dispel the idea of "rightly" and "wrongly" responding to it while pushing you in achieving coherence and clarity in your thinking and analysis, so that *your* ideas, *your* meanings, *your* insights are built and communicated.

If the lessons of this book are undertaken with an open mind, you will begin to step apart from the crowd, and your reading, writing, and thinking will stand out. You will become an active participant in the writings you examine and begin to bring whatever thoughts and experiences you have into dialogue with the world around you. You will learn to pay attention to how good writing works, to its internal logic and governing ideas, in order to join the very few who can actually look closely at a piece of writing, dissect it, and write sensibly about it.

Eamon Cunningham

UNIT 1

RHETORIC

CHAPTER ONE

A BRIEF HISTORY OF RHETORIC

"We will no longer accept politicians who are all talk and no action, constantly complaining but never doing anything about it. The time for empty talk is over. Now arrives the hour of action."

—Inaugural Address, Donald J. Trump, January 20, 2017

Whether he knew it or not, Donald Trump's inaugural address re-cast an age-old skepticism towards rhetoric into a modern context: language is used not to reveal the truth but to conceal it. Check "rhetoric" in a thesaurus, and you'll find its synonyms are universally negative: bombast, grandiloquence, pomposity, and so on. Turn on the T.V. and you'll hear things like "actions speak louder than words" and "that's just empty rhetoric" as insults aimed to slash at credibility and character. For Trump, and for most of contemporary culture, language is seen as the tool by which ambitious politicians weasel their way into public office, weenie out of an accusation, or work around public interest. Language is the weapon of the liar to reverse the order of reality and illusion. If language is the weapon, rhetoric is often thought to be the battle plan for its strategic deployment. But Trump's incredulous stance towards rhetoric – trotted out before the nation on January 20, 2017 – is as old as the subject itself. What is the origin of this skepticism and has this attitude changed over time? Let's find out.

Rhetoric in the Classical Period

It's the 5th century B.C., and two men are locked in a heated debate inside a Sicilian courtroom. The case: an old man has brought suit against his protégé for refusing to pay him the arranged fee for instruction he provided in a new art, rhetoric. This dazzling new technique – a systematic method to convince others of your point of view – is powerful, pragmatic, and (as this case illustrates) prone to potential misuse. Each man pleads their case to the judge. The young man defends his refusal to pay his teacher, citing a loss in his first court case after his program of instruction in the rhetorical arts. This is *prima facie* evidence, he argues, of his teacher's lousy instruction and, thus, a violation of the original agreement. The old man comes back. He turns the young man's argument around, claiming that if he used oratory in the first place, even unsuccessfully, that merely shows a defect in the young man's use of the skill, not that it wasn't taught to him. Things grind to a stalemate. Fed up with the bickering, the jury drops the case and jeer both out of the courtroom, κακοῦ κόρακος κακὸν ᾠόν (a bad egg from a bad crow). So goes the legend of Corax ("the crow"), history's first rhetorician, and his pupil, Tisias (the "egg," as it were).

Most popular accounts of rhetorical history begin with the doings of the shadowy Corax and his pupil, Tisias. Everything about these two men is steeped in mystery and legend. The little bit we do confidently know about Corax comes from a number of one-off mentions scattered over approximately one thousand years of fragmented writing. Plato mentions Tisias's rhetorical art in the *Phaedrus* (370 B.C.) but only roundaboutly suggests the existence of a Corax-like teacher. Aristotle mentions Corax by name in *The Art of Rhetoric* (350 B.C.) but does so with careful qualifications regarding his existence. In his commentaries on Plato's *Phaedrus*, Hermias of Alexandria suggests that Corax was the teacher of Tisias, though later scholia on the same text, notably P. Couvreur's *Hermia Alexandrini in Platonis, Phaedrum Scholia* (1901), argues it was the other way around. Accounts of Corax continued into the Roman world. Sextus Empiricus, Marcus Tullus Cicero, Ammianus Marcellinus all make consistent claims to Corax as the father of rhetoric, though these assertions were recorded almost a millennium after his death. What we can know for sure about him is that Corax is mysterious, to say the least.

From 485 – 465 B.C., in the generation before Corax, Syracuse – a region in southeastern Sicily – came under the control of a succession of tyrannical rulers: Gelon I, Hieron I, and Thrasybulus. Known to history collectively as the Deinomenids, these royals were best known for wresting private property away from the landed aristocracy through a kind of early (tyrannical) form of eminent domain. When Thrasybulus assumed the throne in 466 B.C., enough was enough, and he was quickly overthrown in a popular uprising among the landowners that ushered in a period of democracy that lasted until 405 B.C. Deposing Thrasybulus, however, raised one big question for the citizens of Syracuse: how should all the seized land be rightfully redistributed back into the hands of its rightful owners? This question was to be hashed out in courts of law, but the average citizen had no means to effectively represent himself in such a context, effectively setting the stage for Corax and the democratizing force of his speech. This story is derived almost entirely from Cicero's *Brutus or History of Famous Orators; also His Orator, or Accomplished Speaker* (46 A.D.), where the author retells Corax's story as it was originally laid down by Aristotle.

> Aristotle, therefore, informs us, that when the Tyrants were expelled from Sicily, and private property (after a long interval of servitude) was determined by public trials, the Sicilians Corax and Tisias (for this people, in general, were very quick and acute, and had a natural turn for controversy) first attempted to write precepts on the art of Speaking. Before them, he says, there was no one who spoke by method, and rules of art, though there were many who discoursed very sensibly, and generally from written note.

Notice the implications of Cicero's account. First, it concedes that Corax was by no means the first person to speak rhetorically, but he was the first to systematize rhetoric as a *techne*, a skill or art that can be taught and learned. Thus, Corax is the first rhetorician, one who teaches others *how* to persuade on their own behalf: how to seize attention (the "proem"), how to advance a proposition (the "demonstration"), and how to close things out (the "epilogue"). This structure as a model for argumentation is common practice now, but that is only because Corax's early teachings presumably formed the core of what the great Greek thinkers – Socrates, Plato, Aristotle – eventually had to say on the subject.

The legacy of Corax has had an enduring mark on the history of rhetoric, since it is credited as the foundation for two of the three branches of rhetoric which are still recognized today. One set of scholars maintain

Corax was instrumental in the development of "forensic" or "judicial" rhetoric (the type of speech used to discuss past action especially in legal contexts), where others argue him as a key figure in the early development of "deliberative" or "political" rhetoric (the type of speech used in deliberative political bodies, often in service of power). The credit for the third branch, "epideictic" or "display" rhetoric, often goes to Gorgias, a rhetorical giant whom we'll see much more about later on. Exactly which of these branches Corax had the most influence on and exactly how this occurred has been a longstanding matter of scholarly squabble.

Students of Corax saw the practical application of his brand of rhetoric in judicial and political contexts, and it wasn't long before this skill proliferated into all realms of public life. Teachers of persuasion, "Sophists," soon began popping up all over the Mediterranean basin to educate anyone on how to argue, given that they had a little extra money on hand to pay for the skill. The greatest transmitter of this practice was a Sicilian named Gorgias (485 B.C. – 380 B.C.), who took Corax's skills off the island of Sicily and into the big city, Athens.

Less shadowy than Corax, but no less important to the history of rhetoric, was Gorgias of Leontini, Sicily. He was rumored to have known Corax and Tisias personally, and it's pretty clear from his four extant writings (*Athenian Funeral Oration, Palamedes, Encomium on Helen*, and *On Nature or Not-Being*) that the general principles of his rhetoric follow from this earlier tradition, particularly the belief of rhetoric as a *techne* and the preference of probabilities to immutable truth. He has a compelling personal life, perhaps the most interesting man in the world of his day. In 427 B.C., he was sent as an ambassador by his native city to Athens, and the Athenians liked him so much he never came home. He stayed as an itinerant teacher of rhetoric, traveling from city to city on the Greek mainland, pitching his skill to anyone with a few extra bucks. Never married and with no children, he lived to be 105 years old and made a pretty good living as history's first successful Sophist. His oratory was truly something to behold, more akin to magic than public speaking. Look no further than the reaction to his *Athenian Funeral Oration*. Gorgias must have been on his game that night since, following the ceremony, a gold statue of him was erected in the temple of Apollo at Delphi to commemorate the event. He was a regular fixture at festival celebrations (an unusual honor for visitors to the Greek mainland) and his performances became the stuff of legend. His speaking style relied heavily on sonic features – alliteration, assonance, antithesis, parallelism – and his manner of delivery resembled that of a poetic rhapsode or dramatic performer. Some historical accounts describe his ability to "take requests" from the audience to produce an off-the-cuff speech in nearly any oratorical style to the delight and astonishment of those in attendance. Gorgias could lift his audience up and carry them away, turning oration into a rapturous experience that no listener would soon forget. In short, he was good at what he did.

For Gorgias, speech *is* the attraction, not outcome of it. Deliberative rhetoric may pass laws and judicial rhetoric may mete out justice, but these styles have a common limitation: the speaker must be careful to not call attention to the speech *as* an act of artifice, elsewise it will blow their cover as a disinterested and selfless rhetor appealing to the greater good. Shakespeare knew this balancing act well. Hamlet makes this point directly in the play that bears his name, yet this hidden gem of a monologue, sitting in the shadow of the "To Be or Not to Be" soliloquy from the previous scene, is often overlooked. In Act III, scene ii, Hamlet is backstage speaking to the traveling players. Just before the curtain goes up, Hamlet runs down what makes a convincing performance:

> Be not too tame neither, but let your own discretion/be your tutor:
> suit the action to the word, the/word to the action; with this spe-
> cial o'erstep not/the modesty of nature: for anything so overdone is/
> from the purpose of playing, whose end, both at the/first and now,
> was and is, to hold, as 'twere, the/mirror up to nature…

Don't be overblown. Don't be too dull. Above all, he says, act natural and the audience will eat from the palm of your hand. This is sound advice for the deliberative and judicial rhetorician: call too much attention to the showiness of the performance and the jig is up. Not so with Gorgias. He reveled in the showmanship and his highly stylized speech doubled as a living billboard for what he was selling. Rhetoric that is conscious of itself *as* rhetoric – known as "epideictic" or "display" rhetoric – became Gorgias's stock-in-trade and history remembers him as the founding figure of rhetoric's third major branch.

Plato (428 B.C. – 348 B.C.), the great searcher of Truth in the Ancient world, didn't take the word games of the Sophists lying down and, in fact, a primary theme of the Platonic dialogues at large is both Socrates's and Plato's hostility towards the Sophists. Both viewed them as corrupt teachers who taught young men to argue only for victory and money, and many of Plato's works contain strong criticisms of the Sophistic project: *Euthydemus, Protagoras, Parmenides, Republic, Sophist, Statesman, Ion,* and *Phaedrus.* His greatest head-on attack against this practice appeared in his dialogue *Gorgias* (380 B.C.), which contains the first appearance of the term "rhetoric" in published literature. Socrates, the main character of Plato's dialogues, saw Gorgias as a corrupter of the young men who studied rhetoric with him since he propagated a Coraxian form of persuasion to his students: "Rhetoric is the art of persuading an ignorant multitude about the justice or injustice of a matter, without imparting any real instruction." Plato saw this as the mere appearance of wisdom, a façade for deception through gestures of pseudo-cleverness in the way one speaks. What's more, whether one's argument is virtuous or wicked, true or false, is beside the point. For Gorgias, being able to speak well is both a lucrative skill and an end in itself. Eloquence isn't just for those with a knack for it; Gorgias believed it is teachable skill that can be used by anyone – a "rhētorikè téchnē" or *skill of speaking* – for any reason, at any time. More troubling yet, Gorgias's clientele, the young nobility of Athens training for careers in politics and law, would take these skills into positions of power and authority, thus perpetuating what Plato saw as one of the all-time great evils done against the Greek people. For Plato, to mis-educate society's leaders on a program of rhetorical deception is to poison the very heart of the state. For a lighthearted and comedic example of rhetoric in the hands of the stupid and incompetent, check out Plato's lesser known dialogue *Euthydemus* (384 B.C.). This dialogue illustrates Plato's distrust of democracy in a nutshell – nitwits egging on halfwits, none of whom have the faintest idea of the higher ideals required for civic life to flourish. And, for Plato, if mob rule is the disease of democracy, rhetoric is the contagion through which it spreads.

Plato's pupil, Aristotle (384 B.C. – 322 B.C.), was foremost in the revival of rhetoric's academic respectability. He defined rhetoric as "the faculty of observing in any given case the available means of persuasion" in the ur-text of composition studies *The Art of Rhetoric.* Aristotle thought the truth of things could be found here in this world – unlike the ethereal and transcendent world of Forms put forth by Plato – and, as such, thought language itself could contain some degree of truth. Like Gorgias, Aristotle conceded that rhetoric was a skill that could be taught, and teachers forever-after have used his highly pedagogical system outlined in *The Art of Rhetoric* as a baseline for rhetoric and composition instruction in classrooms all over the world. Aristotle's *The Art of Rhetoric* has no equal in its importance to the discipline. It is split into two major parts: a first portion on *lexis* (style in rhetoric) and second portion on *taxis* (types of rhetoric). And among this work's many lasting contributions to the study of composition is a smooth reworking of Corax and Gorgias's modes of discourse (deliberative, judicial, and epideictic), the means of persuasion (ethos, logos, and pathos), and the underlying logical structures of argument formulation (dialectic, syllogism, and enthymeme).

Aristotle's brand of rhetoric is the child of two fathers: the Sophistic tradition (Corax and Gorgias) and the philosophical tradition (Socrates and Plato). Though he rightly conceded the probabilistic nature of rhetoric, he nonetheless maintained it as an exercise in logic, not merely bravado and stagecraft. To this end, Aristotle insisted upon the fact that rhetoric always be delivered in the "plain" style, a direct style of communication that stresses clarity, focus, precision, and logical soundness. Such a recharacterization of the discipline spurned a newfangled focus on the academic applications of rhetoric, particularly in the practice of critical reading, critical writing, and the other dozens of academic activities which form the basis of any good English class today. As the English philosopher Alfred North Whitehead may have put it, the future of rhetorical studies is but a series of footnotes to Aristotle.

If Aristotle gave us the great gift of structure, then Marcus Tullus Cicero (106 B.C. – 46 B.C.) gave us the great gift of showmanship. Cicero, described by Quintillian as "not the name of a man, but of eloquence itself" in *Institutio Oratoria* (95 A.D.), was the most pre-eminent speaker in the Roman Republic, and his legacy has cast a long shadow into the subsequent centuries of rhetorical studies and scholarship. Cicero was also an accomplished politician, philosopher, and linguist and is often described as having one of the greatest minds in the Classical world (so much so that he was posthumously labeled a "Virtuous Pagan" by the Catholic tradition in the Middle Ages). He is most well-known for his writing about rhetoric, producing a total of six books, which are still studied and utilized today. Among his most famous contributions to the field are the "five canons of rhetoric" which appear in *Rhetorica ad Herennium* (circa 80 B.C.), an anonymous work often attributed to Cicero or at least derived from his direct teachings. The five canons were, and still are, the foundational principles of effective public speaking. From salesmen to CEOs, politicians to professional wrestlers, anyone in a public speaking engagement will likely find themselves talking in Ciceronian terms. The five canons are:

1. Invention: Coming up with something to say and deciding on a rhetorical strategy.
   - *Who is the audience? What do they value? How can I target these values?*

2. Arrangement: Sequencing the parts of the speech into the most effective order.
   - *How can attention be seized? How much context does the audience need? What counterarguments may be raised and how can they be refuted?*

3. Style: Presenting the speech with eloquence and emotion.
   - *How can I appeal to the audience's emotion? What makes a phrase memorable and how can this be integrated into the speech? What type of language will appeal to the morals and principles of the audience?*

4. Memory: Committing a speech to memory as if to perform it.
   - *How can I present without hesitation or omission? How much rehearsal is necessary to make the speech appear as if it is off the cuff?*

5. Delivery: Using voice, gestures, and performance elements effectively.
   - *How can vocal tone and pace affect the perception of the speech? What body gestures can be used to reinforce the content of the message? How can the auditory and visual elements of a speech coalesce effectively?*

Think of all the great speeches in recent history: Winston Churchill's "We Shall Never Surrender," Franklin Roosevelt's "The Only Thing We Have to Fear is Fear Itself," Dwight D. Eisenhower's "Message to the Invasion Troops," John F. Kennedy's "Ask Not What Your Country Can Do for You," Martin Luther King's "I Have a Dream," George W. Bush's "Address to the Nation on the Night of 9/11." Now try to think of any one of these that doesn't pattern itself upon Cicero's rhetorical structures. You'll find that you simply can't do it. We approach public speaking the way we do because Cicero systematized and articulated the five canons of rhetoric two millennia ago. Contemporary rhetoric is saturated in these Ciceronian themes. He's one of us.

Rhetoric from the Medieval Period to the Renaissance

Beginning with the crowing of Otto the Great as Holy Roman Emperor in 962, Europe enjoyed one of the most magnificent flourishings of culture the world has seen, and the study of rhetoric took several more steps forward. Contrary to the popular imagination, the Middle Ages were not an age of religious tyranny that purged the pagan legacy of Greece and Rome down the memory hole. In fact, the great scholars of the Middle Ages had long been curious about the Classical past, and the proliferation of Classical ideas now joined forces with the institutional reach of the Catholic Church. This synthesis was seen most prominently in the crowning achievement of the Middle Ages: the establishment of the university. Central to the education of students in the medieval university were the rhetorical works of Aristotle and Cicero, thus cementing the canonical status of these two great Classical thinkers. The medieval university was built from a curricular model known as the "Trivium": a three-part course of study comprised of grammar (needed to understand language), logic (needed to process language), and rhetoric (needed to produce language to others). Broken into its two roots, *tri* and *via*, Trivium translates to "the place where three roads meet." The three roads of all education – the input (grammar), process (logic), and output (rhetoric) of language – meet at the destination of Truth, a metaphor which aptly captures the teleological worldview so central to the medieval education. To the Trivium, add arithmetic, geometry, music, and astronomy (the "Quadrivium"), and you have the seven classical "Liberal Arts." This type of education – a systematic program with rhetoric at its center – produced some of the greatest writers and thinkers in history: St. Dominic, Albertus Magnus, Thomas Aquinas, St. Augustine, Adelard of Bath, Duns Scots, and William of Ockham.

In essence, rhetoric became the mode of communication at the center of all academic disciplines – not just those classified in the humanities – to express real thought, real truth, in the most effective possible way. And for the first time, written, not just spoken, discourse took on a much more central role. Students in the medieval universities would often be presented with a text for investigation – a selection from Aristotle, assorted Papal bulls, various theological letters – to be read critically, followed with a written task designed to focus the subsequent discussion. This newfangled focus of written rhetoric from the Middle Ages would not realize its full implications until the Early Modern period of Western Culture. Meet Martin Luther.

The Middle Ages were essentially ended in the early 16th century by Martin Luther (1483–1546), a German monk best known for his leading role in the theological upheaval which undid the distinction between the spiritual classes and the secular classes (in favor of a "priesthood" of all believers) known as the Protestant Reformation. According to Luther, all the faithful should have access to Scripture and the idea of restricting access by an authoritative and self-appointed group of clerics interfered with Luther's understanding of authentic spirituality. It is true to say that the Protestant Reformation is a largely theological question, but the change in the technology of communication – the printing press – concurrent with an idea as ignitable as Luther's resulted in one of the greatest quantum leaps in the history of rhetoric.

Luther was far from the first person to challenge perceived corruptions of the Roman Catholic Church when he nailed his 95 theses to the door in Wittenberg in 1517, but he was the first to publish these arguments in an era of mass print production. Before, where heretical ideas had to be copied longhand and distributed in manuscript form, the church was very effective at finding theological troublemakers and eliminating them. Though the church could have eliminated Luther with ease, they could never silence the 300,000 printed copies of his writing which had proliferated Europe from 1518–1520 alone. What's more, the Lutheran credo of *Sola Fide, Sola Scriptorium* ("by faith alone, by scripture alone") placed a new-found emphasis on the individual and literacy – to thoughtfully read and interpret the writing of others – as a necessary credential to participate in theological life. The focus on "individualism" subsequently became a driving force in all aspects of cultural development in the following centuries: the artistic emphasis on "humanism" in the Italian Renaissance, the scientific advances in the Age of Enlightenment which placed man at the center of the natural world, the political revolutions of America and France that transferred civic authority to the individual citizen, the literary strand of "rugged individualism" in the early literary production of the United States, the power-driven philosophy of Friedrich Nietzsche and the existentialism of Jean-Paul Sartre. No aspect of Western Culture was untouched by Luther's upheaval, rhetoric included.

Rhetoric in the Modern Period

Rhetoric in the modern period, the 19th century to the present day, increasingly became characterized by a strong emphasis on pluralism, the inclusion of as many perspectives as possible in the formation of written and spoken discourse. Dialogue-based rhetoric or "dialogism" is a strand of rhetorical scholarship most commonly attributed to the work of Mikhail Bakhtin (1895–1974), a Russian literary theorist. Bakhtin argued in *The Dialogic Imagination* (1981) that meaning, knowledge, and even reality itself are conventionally constructed through the use of language and in the social relations among individuals in a common culture. Consistent with Post-Structural ideologies of the late 20th century, Bakhtin maintained that an individual can relate to the world only as far as that individual's linguistic resources will allow; that is, our understanding of the world and our interaction with it is ultimately bounded by the limits of language. And if language is a social convention, and if the construction of knowledge is circumscribed by the limits of language, Bakhtin argued that meaning exists insofar as an individual's culture and related institutions will allow for at that particular period of historical development. Add to this the fact that social realities are not static and change over time, and you have the Bakhtinian paradigm in a nutshell: a given text can have one meaning to a reader in one culture but be loaded with an entirely different meaning for another reader in a different time and place. A writer doesn't simply produce a text in the void, nor does its reader comprehend it unmediated by social and historical realties. In other words, both production and reception of text is actually process of *response* to the social context that generated it. In composition classrooms, this is often referred to as the "conversation" or "social-constructionist" model of writing.

Bakhtinian scholarship is wide-reaching, even inescapable, in its influence. Elements of dialogism have seeped into every major area of academic inquiry in the 20th century – literary criticism, history, philosophy, sociology, anthropology, psychology, linguistics – thus transforming the way that the modern world constructs knowledge. Examples will help. Take Shakespeare's eponymous character Hamlet. For readers in the 18th and 19th century, Hamlet's agony over his father's revenge and subsequent theorizing and philosophizing about his actions make him the paragon of the Renaissance courtier, poet, and philosopher. Readers in the 20th century tend to see this very same character as a beautiful but ineffectual soul, a good man who has been psychically and morally fractured by the circumstances of the play. When I read *Hamlet* with my own students – 21st century American teenagers – they see something else entirely: a middle-aged man in arrested adolescence asserting himself brashly in an adult world that he knows very little about. Who's got the "right" interpretation? On whose authority can we settle this question? How is it that the very same text, the very same words, generate such diverging interpretations? This example shows how central historical context is in the production of analytic speech and writing about a text. It also illustrates the dialogic stance that all texts are polyvocal; that is, a text can speak with several voices to several audiences, often simultaneously. This frustration of how exactly to navigate the plurality of perspectives offered by a text is not new. One of the first recorded instances of this irritation is from Plato's middle dialogue, *Protagoras* (380 B.C.). Plato lampoons literary critics when the dialogue's main character, Socrates, offers three brilliant, yet incoherent and contradictory, ways to interpret the poetry of Simonides and Pittacus to a crowd of onlookers.

Dialogism works on the assumption that meaning is inextricably bound to language and that each word has its own discrete history of definitions and uses (the "diachronic" meaning) and connotations and associations (the "synchronic" meaning). To say that an author definitively means "x" when the author says "y" is a bogus assertion under a dialogic understanding of rhetoric since reliable truth claims would require an author to unpack all of the associations, both diachronic and synchronic, of a given word to authentically wield its "full" meaning. Consider the word "lamb." Typically, this word refers to a small sheep, but our colloquial usage in day-to-day conversation ignores this word's history of meanings that go all the way back to the days of Old English and beyond. More than this, "lamb" carries along with it a whole set of associations: tender, passive, weak, peaceful, sacred, sacrificial, blood, spring, frisky, pure, innocent and so on. Of course, we don't mean to suggest all this each time we speak, but this doesn't negate the fact that when we use language we subconsciously bring some of the word's meaning to the table while actively ignoring others. This is why some modern linguists have gone so far as to describe all language use as an act of repression. Whatever intelligible meaning there is with a given word is only derived relationally from the word to the historical, cultural, and linguistic contexts of its speaker. Words mean nothing in and of themselves. They only "mean" in a mesh of a much larger system.

If you can accept this premise, it's easy to see how even a single word becomes an endless hall of mirrors and any real type of communication breaks down. Whenever an author uses words, those words often carry far more meaning than any single writer would want to communicate. In a sense, as Jacques Derrida suggested in famous lecture "Structure, Sign and Play in the Discourse of the Human Sciences" (1966), meaning is out of the author's control. It's propagative. Even as your eyes pass over this page, each word refers to more words, which themselves refer to more words, a process which could be iterated indefinitely. It is this "polysemous" nature – the ability of a text to convey a vast array of meaning to an audience – that is often the source of resistance to Derrida's ideas. Any reader, or author for that matter, could never possibly hope to encapsulate *all* the meanings of a commonly used word. Writing, for Derrida, is unique because it is the inscription of lasting symbols which exist independent of the presence of the author.

Roland Barthes, in his 1968 essay "The Death of the Author," takes Derrida's rhetorical theory a few steps further. In the domain of fourteen words, his closing line – "the birth of the reader at the cost of the death of the author" – effectively supplants the author (the producer of the message) as the primary source of meaning with the reader (the receiver of the message). Think of it this way: Whenever we read a piece of writing, be it literature, a historical document, an email, a tabloid magazine, and so forth, the author is always absent. Though the writer is absent in a physical sense, his meaning persists, even after his own death. This idea becomes a central theme of Barthes's work: once thoughts are recorded in writing, the author is no longer in control of those sentences and ideas. Readers one week, one year, or one century later will understand the text in ways that have little to do with an author's original intentions. This is the keystone of dialogism. Dialogic reading, in a sense, "deauthorizes" the author: the reader, not the author, becomes the ultimate source of meaning. It is the reader who is free to interact with the plurality of ideas that a text has to offer, to get lost in the play of its "heteroglossia," as Bakhtin may have put it.

Believe it or not, text messaging, Tweeting, and status updating are fundamentally dialogic activities. When I give my introductory lectures on the importance of dialogism in the construction of knowledge, I start by telling students to envision a scenario. You are home at night. Your phone buzzes.

You get a text from a good friend you haven't heard from in a few days. The message reads, "Hey...". I then have students jot a note to themselves which explains the implied or suggested meaning of this cryptic text. I then ask them why they drew the conclusion they did. Inevitably, this leads to a discussion of how past experience – direct or indirect – shapes and ultimately dictates meaning or purpose behind words. I sometimes follow by hypothesizing various iterations of the original – "hey.," "heeeeey," "Hey!" – to reinforce the main point that even seemingly innocuous changes in capitalization, punctuation, and spelling can greatly alter a reader's interpretation. This scenario – though both low-stakes and non-literary – highlights several of the main strands of dialogism as outlined in Kay Halasek's *A Pedagogy of Possibility* (1999): 1) human communication involves a plurality of perspectives, all of which come from a unique historical, cultural, and linguistic context, 2) meaning of language use can, and often does, vary between participants in communication, and 3) that each participant in a communication is, to some degree, prompted by, and preparing for, what others have to say.

Look around any good classroom and you'll see dialogic rhetoric at work. Under the influence of modern scholars such as James Kinneavy, Kenneth Bruffee, Patricia Bizzell, James Berlin, Charles Bazerman, and Greg Myers, it's not uncommon (in fact, it's often promoted) to observe teachers encouraging students to work together as they compose and revise their work. The operative belief is that cooperative activities will not only improve the texts under review but lead students to a more complete and thorough understanding of the text as a whole. The "truth" of things only begins to emerge when we have as many perspectives as possible thrown into the mix. A good dialogic classroom takes this cultural belief, writ small, and pushes its potential to the boundaries. It's easy to see with the renewed interest in social learning theory, collaborative learning, and multiculturalism how Bakhtinian dialogism underwrites the curriculum taught in composition classrooms across the country. It's important to stress here that dialogism isn't just ivory tower stuff; this stance towards reading, writing, and thinking has some very real and very practical benefits for teachers and students alike. It is, indeed, intellectually fulfilling to say while reading, "I've got it; I see this connection" and that in itself is a wonderful thing, but dialogism has no place for passive readers. Dialogism calls on you to be an active participant in the text, bringing whatever thoughts and experiences you have to the table. Dialogism will help you to learn to pay attention to *how* good writing works, to its internal logic and governing ideas. In turn, dialogic instruction will help you to habitually read closely, think critically, and write sensibly about your insights.

It is, at this point, where we enter the ongoing, dynamic history of rhetoric. John Locke once said, "Reading furnishes the mind only with materials of knowledge; it is thinking that makes what we read ours." As you begin to expand, intensify, or challenge your own thinking, you are doing something quite special in an English classroom: you are taking your first steps in self-generating insight into a text through a process where *you* must come up with the main insights, and *you* must develop these insights in light of the evidence that you've gathered. But more than this: it's a way for you to take the first steps in the direction of a dialogic stance toward rhetoric – a stance that acknowledges that everything is prompted by and prepares for some other utterance – in a non-threatening way. Once you leave the border of a classroom, you're on your own as a reader, writer, and thinker. The mountain stands in front of you, so to speak, and all I have given you here is a pickaxe and a small wheelbarrow, but moving any mountain begins by carrying away a few small stones.

CHAPTER TWO

RHETORICAL ANALYSIS – A GUIDED METHODOLOGY

When I was in college, a professor of mine once told me, "If you think you have everything figured out on the first reading, something must be wrong. Either you are not reading good writing, or you are not reading carefully enough." I loved the readings in my English classes – from Plato to Postmodernism – even before I had much of a clue about what these writers really meant. As a student, I was too often taken by the hand to the "right" answer, thinking in ways that had been mapped out for me, and writing in ways that did little for my own curiosity and sense of investigation. It took me a long time to understand what my professor really meant by that comment, but once I developed the thoughtful and patient approach to reading he described, things changed. I became the maker of my own meaning, turning from a passive receiver of a text to an active unraveler. I gained the authority to question, challenge, and expand on not only the texts from class, but also my own writing and thinking: where my responses came from, the process by which I constructed knowledge, and how these processes might be expanded, intensified, or challenged. Reading (and writing in response to what I had read) turned from a matter of coming up with answers to questions about a text to learning what type of questions needed to be asked in the first place. The "right" questions, it turns out, are fundamentally rhetorical in nature.

Most composition scholars agree about the fluid relationship between reading and writing, so why is it that students so often struggle to "deeply" read a text, let alone translate that reading into crisp, coherent writing? "I don't know what the author means" is a line that comes drumming into teachers' ears, all the time and from all directions. If you have ever found difficulty in generating material for critical discussion or analytical writing, rhetorical reading will suit you well. As Mary Goldschmidt's "Marginalia: Teaching Texts, Teaching Readers, Teaching Writers" (2010) says, rhetorical analysis "has been an important undercurrent in the past three decades of composition scholarship" and has been increasingly placed at the center of the writing process at the college level. In other words, rhetorical reading *is* a means of invention: if you can get yourself reading rhetorically, then you will have something worthwhile to say about whatever text you hold in your hands.

In a rhetorical analysis, a reader is trained to become a sort-of meta-reader, a self-conscious, analytic reader who demonstrates, as Goldschmidt says, the "very kinds of critical reading habits that [instructors] routinely use but too infrequently verbalize or model except through the kinds of questions we ask in class." The method contained in this chapter, grounded in both Classical and contemporary rhetorical theory, will get you to start asking the right questions of a text by working with an easy-to-follow, three stage process. A contemporary speech – as well as a series of hypothetical rhetorical scenarios – will be used as running examples in this chapter to show these strategies and concepts in operation. Hopefully, you will see that rhetorical analysis is a portable skill, and this process can be easily applied to historical documents, informational texts, essays, speeches, and various other forms of print and digital media found in college classrooms. Each stage in the process is broken down by subheading, complete with an explanation of how these strategies can be pulled off, and why we should do them at all. By dissecting writing in this way, like an anatomist who peels back layer after layer of an organ to examine its intricate workings, you should stretch your own sense of options as a writer, and the effects that you see in action should be available to you the next time you sit down and compose your own work.

Let us go then to the night of September 11, 2001. At 8:30 p.m., President George W. Bush went live to the nation, addressing the country about the terrorist attacks that unfolded earlier in the day against the World Trade Center, the Pentagon, and the crashed plane in Shanksville, PA. Citizens across the United States anxiously watched these attacks unfold in real-time, and it was at this moment of national crisis that the eyes of the country turned to its leader in the Oval Office. President Bush, not known to history for his public speaking ability, answered the call and delivered one of the most memorable Presidential addresses in modern American history. Coming in at just over four minutes in length, the speech was clear, succinct, and, as we will see in this chapter, rhetorically powerful.

Address to the Nation

George W. Bush
September 11, 2001

Good evening. Today, our fellow citizens, our way of life, our very freedom came under attack in a series of deliberate and deadly terrorist acts. The victims were in airplanes, or in their offices; secretaries, businessmen and women, military and federal workers; moms and dads, friends and neighbors. Thousands of lives were suddenly ended by evil, despicable acts of terror.

The pictures of airplanes flying into buildings, fires burning, huge structures collapsing, have filled us with disbelief, terrible sadness, and a quiet, unyielding anger. These acts of mass murder were intended to frighten our nation into chaos and retreat. But they have failed; our country is strong.

A great people has been moved to defend a great nation. Terrorist attacks can shake the foundations of our biggest buildings, but they cannot touch the foundation of America. These acts shattered steel, but they cannot dent the steel of American resolve.

America was targeted for attack because we're the brightest beacon for freedom and opportunity in the world. And no one will keep that light from shining.

Today, our nation saw evil, the very worst of human nature. And we responded with the best of America – with the daring of our rescue workers, with the caring for strangers and neighbors who came to give blood and help in any way they could.

Immediately following the first attack, I implemented our government's emergency response plans. Our military is powerful, and it's prepared. Our emergency teams are working in New York City and Washington, D.C. to help with local rescue efforts.

Our first priority is to get help to those who have been injured, and to take every precaution to protect our citizens at home and around the world from further attacks.

The functions of our government continue without interruption. Federal agencies in Washington which had to be evacuated today are reopening for essential personnel tonight, and will be open for business tomorrow. Our financial institutions remain strong, and the American economy will be open for business, as well.

The search is underway for those who are behind these evil acts. I've directed the full resources of our intelligence and law enforcement communities to find those responsible and to bring them to justice. We will make no distinction between the terrorists who committed these acts and those who harbor them.

I appreciate so very much the members of Congress who have joined me in strongly condemning these attacks. And on behalf of the American people, I thank the many world leaders who have called to offer their condolences and assistance.

America and our friends and allies join with all those who want peace and security in the world, and we stand together to win the war against terrorism. Tonight, I ask for your prayers for all those who grieve, for the children whose worlds have been shattered, for all whose sense of safety and security has been threatened. And I pray they will be comforted by a power greater than any of us, spoken through the ages in Psalm 23: "Even though I walk through the valley of the shadow of death, I fear no evil, for You are with me."

This is a day when all Americans from every walk of life unite in our resolve for justice and peace. America has stood down enemies before, and we will do so this time. None of us will ever forget this day. Yet, we go forward to defend freedom and all that is good and just in our world.

Thank you. Good night, and God bless America.

The Rhetorical Situation: Exigence and the Rhetorical Triangle

The "rhetorical situation," a term derived from Lloyd Bitzer's 1968 essay of the same name, is where rhetorical reading begins. In his essay, Bitzer argues that every instance of communication consists of two fundamental elements: 1) An "exigence," an inciting incident that "calls forth a text" and 2) a "rhetorical triangle," a scenario which involves the interaction between a speaker, a subject, and an audience. Though Bitzer gives us an accessible, up-to-date discussion of these ideas, he doesn't claim credit for these ideas, nor does he wish to; they are essentially reworkings of concepts drawn from Aristotle's *The Art of Rhetoric* (350 B.C.) and *Topics*

(350 B.C.), as well as Cicero's *De Oratore* (55 B.C.), and Quintilian's *Institutio Oratoria* (85 A.D).

Exigence

Bitzer defines exigence as "a need, [or] a gap ... that can be met, filled in, or supplied *only* by a spoken or written text." Perhaps better understood as the "reason," "cause," or "source" of a text (or really any instance of communication – image, film, speech – for that matter), Bitzer's concept rests on the social-constructionist assumption that all texts are inseparable from the linguistic and cultural group that generates it. Despite its technical feel, this idea is actually quite simple. Could, for example, *1984* (1949) ever have come to be had George Orwell not experienced the propagandistic power of mass media in his time spent at the BBC? Could Melville have written *Moby Dick* (1851) had he not seen the dread and majesty of a God who can smash our tightest-rigged ships to matchsticks by wind and whale? Could Dante's *Divine Comedy* (1320) have so precisely captured the despair of spiritual dislocation had the author not been treacherously exiled from his home city of Florence in 1300? In each of these examples, the text is brought into being by an event (either internally generated by the author or externally imposed upon the author), a situation that is somehow addressed – reflectively, therapeutically, didactically – in the production of a text. The act of formulating a text in response to its exigence is referred to as *kairos* in both Classical and contemporary rhetorical teaching. *Kairos*, a Greek work which resists smooth translation to English, refers to the "timing" of a text that responds to an issue at the opportune moment. *Kairos*, the invented time of a text, is often discussed in tandem with another Greek term, *chronos*, which refers to the *chrono*logical point in history in which a text is produced. Of course, social and historical constraints influence an audience's assessment of how well a text executes the response to its exigence, but it is undeniable that a *timely* response bears nearly equal importance to the very content of that response. The above examples illustrate Bitzer's theory of exigence in relation to writing, but how may this idea manifest in day-to-day life? Consider the following:

- A pot-holed road *calls forth* a complaint letter to the local highway department.

- A job posting *calls forth* a letter of recommendation in support of an applicant.
- A prolonged drought *calls forth* legislation proposing a local water ban.
- A budget crunch *calls forth* a persuasive speech to retain staff in light of recommended cutbacks.
- A required assignment *calls forth* a term paper in English class.

Each of these hypotheticals illustrate the key relationship between a text and the wider world: an inciting event calls forth a text, an act of communication prompted by and preparing for some other utterance (to borrow the dialogic language from Chapter 1). If you have not heard of exigence, it's likely that you are familiar with two related terms – context and purpose – that function in more-or-less the same way for a rhetorical reader as exigence does. The purpose (what the author is attempting to accomplish through an act of speech or writing) links to the context (the set of elements in which speech or writing occurs that helps promotes an understanding of its message) in ways which are very difficult to separate. Let's return to the initial example above.

- Exigence: A pot-holed road calls forth a complaint letter to the local highway department.
  - Purpose: to seek repairs
  - Context: ongoing danger to pedestrians and drivers

In this instance, the exigence becomes the mitigating factor for a number of writerly choices the author of the complaint letter must eventually make. If the author is writing to seek repairs (purpose) because of the perceived danger a pot-holed road poses to drivers and pedestrians (context), then the tone of the text must be both respectful of the efforts of the highway department employees while maintaining a firm assertion that the roads must be fixed. The letter may frame this request as a service owed to taxpayers, an appeal to the

Questions to ask about purpose:

Is the text

- Explaining a process?
- Drawing comparisons?
- Persuading us to do something?
- Describing causes and effects?
- Memorializing a person/event?
- Narrating a personal story?
- Garnering emotional support?
- Raising awareness?

Figure 1 How to Consider a Text's Purpose.

safety of local drivers, or in more aggressive tones of threatened legal action should the repairs not be made. Whatever the choice, each style would go on to generate further considerations to be made by the author: What pattern of organization is best? How should I organize the evidence? Which rhetorical appeals would best suit my needs? As this hypothetical situation shows, slight variations in the exigence have tremendous implications. Had the exigence of the situation been slightly different (say, the potholes were caused from vandalism by a particular resident on the street), the chain of rhetorical choices take an entirely new trajectory. Consider Figures 1 and 2 as you read to determine both purpose and context.

Questions to ask about context:

Is the text

- Referential to a social movement, religious principle, or political ideology?

- Composed in a moment of rapid choice, dislocation, peril, or urgency?

- Reliant on the audience's background knowledge?

- Allusive to a time period (archaic language, outdated worldviews)?

Figure 2 How to Consider a Text's Context.

Though the above examples make the identification of exigence seem like a neat and orderly process, questions of exigence are not always so clean-cut. Think of the never-ending deliberations tied up in the practice of literary criticism for something like Shakespeare's *Hamlet*. An event (the death of Shakespeare's son, Hamnet, in 1596) gives rise to a text (the play *Hamlet* published in 1609) which then becomes the exigence of subsequent writing (literary criticism about the play) which then is responded to by a new text (a critique of the criticism), and so on. All of the competing points of view surrounding *Hamlet* – the coexistence of, and conflict between, diverse types of speech and thought within the responses – is where Bakhtin's theory of "heteroglossia" begins to take effect.

Case Study in Classical Argumentation: George W. Bush's "Address to the Nation" 9/11/01

Exigence, Kairos, Context, and Purpose

The events of 9/11 – the attack on the World Trade Center, The Pentagon, and the downed plane in Shanksville, PA – were the exigence that called forth Bush's national address on the night of 9/11. In the aftermath of such an event, a perplexed nation needed, even required, the clear and articulate speech of its leader to make sense of the apparent chaos that unfolded in front of the American public earlier that morning. As Denise Bostdorff noted in "George W. Bush's Post September 11 Rhetoric of Covenant Renewal" (2003), "September 11 called for a definition and understanding of what had happened. The aftermath of the terrorist attacks also brought a need for creating and sharing community." In other words, the event of 9/11 called forth a rhetorical response to give order to the day's relentless chaos, offer solace to the traumatized, and reorganize a frightened public around a common cause – all things, by the way, Bush accomplishes in his address. In this moment, words *did* speak louder than actions.

One particularly noteworthy feature of the Bush's speech is its keen attention to the *kairos* of the situation. World Trade Center 7 collapsed at 5:21 P.M., giving Bush and his team of speech writers just a matter of hours to prepare before he went live to the nation at 8:30 P.M. No event in recent American history has demanded such a timely act of speech under such trying circumstances. This was a one-of-a-kind opportunity for any president, and Bush seized it. 9/11 became the rhetorical moment that defined his early presidency, due in large part to his skillful response at the opportune moment – not too soon, not too late, but just right. Consider the great many number of things Bush pulls off in the first sentence of the address:

> "Today, our fellow citizens, our way of life, our very freedom came under attack in a series of deliberate and deadly terrorist acts."

In the domain of twenty-three words, Bush provides exposition on the event, acknowledges its magnitude and wide-ranging effects, makes a moral judgement against the attacks, and establishes credibility with the audience – all things a panicked citizenry would both need and want in the immediate aftermath of such a spectacular tragedy.

Let's see how he does this. On a surface level, these lines provide exposition on the events of the speech by acknowledging what had transpired on the morning on 9/11. Bush simultaneously defines the event as he describes it, casting moral judgements on the attackers and an air of righteousness upon the innocent victims. In doing so, Bush sets up the speech's primary contrast between American citizens and the terrorist attackers, a theme that reappears in several forms over the course of the address: justice vs. injustice, good vs. evil, us vs. them. By doing this, Bush also touches on the magnitude of 9/11 by acknowledging the attack's wide-reaching effects. Not only has it had a personal effect on individual "citizens," but Bush describes the attack as an affront to American culture ("our way of life") and Western democratic political ideology ("our very freedom"). By defining the event in such momentous terms, Bush implicitly establishes himself as the individual to guide the United States, under his leadership, into this post-9/11 world. All these rhetorical details would be for naught had Bush not also forged a connection to his audience. The repetition of "our" in the opening three phrases ("our fellow citizens, our way of life, our very freedom") works to establish a *eunoia*-style credibility with the audience by characterizing himself as standing in solidarity with the country to create a sense of shared plight and tragedy. This opening sentence only lasted about five seconds, but each moment informs, comforts, reassures, and demands justice – a diagram of the speech's overall purpose. As Bush said in his memoir, *Decision Points* (2010), the address was an attempt to "express comfort and resolve—comfort that we would recover from this blow and resolve that we would bring the terrorists to justice." Later in this chapter, we'll see how he develops this purpose through a number of rhetorical techniques.

The Rhetorical Triangle

The second component of Bitzer's "rhetorical situation" is the rhetorical triangle (see Figure 3), a framework that analyzes the interactions between the three participants of a rhetorical scenario: a speaker (producer of the message), an audience (receiver of the message), and a subject (the focus of the discourse). This triangulated relationship provides a pre-established template to assess and understand the dynamics of any act of communication, spoken, written, or otherwise. Astute readers (and skilled writers) are always attuned to the subtleties and variances within the dynamics of the rhetorical triangle (speaker-to-subject, speaker-to-audience, audience-to-subject) to analyze (or build) rhetorically effective prose and speech. Consider our hypothetical complaint letter to the highway department in terms of the rhetorical triangle.

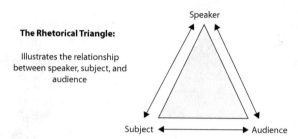

Figure 3 The Three "Participants" of a Rhetorical Situation.

- Exigence: A pot holed road calls forth a complaint letter to the local highway department.
  - Purpose: to seek repairs
  - Context: ongoing danger to pedestrians and drivers
  - Rhetorical triangle: speaker (town resident), audience (highway department), subject (pot-holed roads)

Speaker to Subject

The strength of the speaker/subject relationship derives from the speaker's authoritative relationship to the subject (see Figure 4). Known as "ethos" in the Classical tradition, the strength of this relationship is central to a message's acceptability to the audience. This seems obvious – and it is – in large part

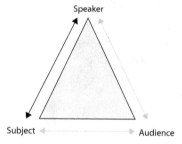

Figure 4 Relationship of Speaker to Subject.

because this speaker/subject evaluation is one of the most fundamental elements of human communication. Even those with no rhetorical education intuitively recognize and evaluate the trustworthiness and reliability of the speaker. In our imagined letter to the highway department, how could the speaker, a concerned local resident, demonstrate authority to speak on this subject? It could come in many forms. Perhaps this resident is a retired town employee with twenty years of highway department experience. Perhaps this resident is a geological engineer who has developed a road sealant that reduces normal deterioration in pavement. Perhaps this resident is a litigator who knows the legal ramifications of unkempt roads. Perhaps this resident is earnestly concerned by the physical danger posed by the lack of maintenance. To these hypotheticals we could add many more, but the point is this: a speaker must have a strongly forged relationship to the subject if he wishes to be taken seriously. Whatever the source this relationship, an ethos-laden text, built from a speaker's focused orientation towards the subject, is a crucial element for anyone who wishes to have an audience seriously consider what they have to say.

Speaker to Audience

"Audience," a term on loan from contexts of live theatre, originally referred to a group of assembled individuals with two defining characteristics: 1) the audience is a communal entity (i.e. there is only one audience) and 2) the audience is essentially passive (i.e. they are recipients of the message and take no part in its delivery or production) (see Figure 5). This definition makes perfect sense for much of rhetorical history since one's message was often delivered through oratorical means. This traditional sense of audience still applies today, of course, but the definition of this term has greatly expanded over the last 2500 years. Its evolution corresponds smoothly with developments in recording technology, from handwriting to high-definition videos, which has dramatically altered the way an audience receives and interacts with a speaker's message. In our modern world of digital publication, "audience" has become such an all-encompassing term that it is near impossible to provide a single, comprehensive definition. Below are some of the most prevailing ways "audience" is understood.

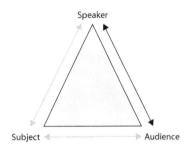

Figure 5 Relationship of Speaker to Audience.

An <u>immediate audience</u> is a group of individuals that interact with a speaker without any mediation or media. An immediate audience experiences a speech in real-time, allowing the speaker to have some control over the rhetorical situation, some of which can be prepared for ahead of time, some of which needs to be adapted to on the fly. A good speaker should align the text to the character of the audience and states of mind of the collective group, insofar as it's possible. A good audience should respond to a speaker's ideas, claims, or calls to action in light of their own understandings and interpretations.

A mediated audience is a group of individuals that experience a message via some mediating technology that acts as a go-between to the producer and receiver of that message. This can include an audience who interacts with a message through radio, television, internet, or print media. There is no way a speaker can account for all the members of these audiences, since mediated texts can easily be archived and read at any point in history. Add to this the complication of the potential mixing of mediums (reading a transcript of a spoken speech, seeing a filmic adaptation of a written narrative, listening to an audiobook of a written text, translating a text from one language to another, and so forth) and it's no wonder why those in the contemporary world may find themselves a bit skeptical of speech and the media that presents it.

A primary audience is the intended recipient of a speaker's message. This definition of audience is confined mostly to written texts, and there is a high degree of cross-over to what was mentioned above about an immediate audience. When authors write, they always compose for a particular demographic, however narrow or broad, and the features of the writing attempt to match the audience's needs, abilities, and prior knowledge. For example, Shel Silverstein aims his poetry collection *A Light in the Attic* (1981) at his childhood readers with the appropriate caricatures, archetypes, and sing-songy style to meet his readers where they are. Martin Luther King Jr., on the other hand, writes "A Letter from Birmingham Jail" (1963) with a more mature readership in mind, one who understands the implications of systemic racism, acknowledges the Christian virtues of forgiveness and charity, and has the requisite education to derive meaning from its high style. A good author will match the diction, sentence structure, level of abstraction, and so forth, to attend to the primary audience's need for maximum rhetorical effect.

A secondary audience is an auxiliary readership which the author has not directly addressed in the construction of a text. Like we said in Chapter 1, texts often outlive their authors and can therefore be theoretically read at any point in history. As social, linguistic, and cultural forces evolve, texts take on new meanings to different audiences at different points in history. For example, Martin Luther King Jr.'s "A Letter from Birmingham Jail" was ostensibly addressed to the primary audience of "My Dear Fellow Clergymen," though its status as a classroom standard for studying the civil rights movement has meant that many more readers beyond these six clergymen from Alabama in 1963 have made meaning from King's letter. In a related way, an adult who happens to pick up *A Light in the Attic* will construct meaning on a totally different level (since they are coming at the text from a more mature adult perspective) than members of Silverstein's primary audience of children and young adults. This shift in audience doesn't change the text itself, but it does affect the meaning derived from it.

A self-deliberative audience is when the speaker and audience are one and the same with the text functioning as the sounding board for the speaker's internal deliberations. Sometimes, a self-deliberative audience is used for dramatic effect. Think of something like Macbeth's soliloquy in Act I, scene vii of *Macbeth* (1606) where he debates with himself the pros and cons of killing King Duncan. The best visualization of this audience technique is the "Angel" and "Devil" manifestations of a character on each shoulder seen most often in modern cartoons, a hold-over from medieval morality plays. Access to these deliberations gives the viewing audience a vicarious insight into the inner turmoil over Macbeth's decision to kill a king out of envy. You may also think of something like *Meditations* (167 A.D.) by the Roman Emperor Marcus Aurelius. This twelve-book work was originally written as a series of private notes on Stoic philosophy, never meant to read by other readers. It was published posthumously, and in the act of reading a text whose audience was self-deliberative, a new set of meanings and rhetorical reactions emerge, none of which could have been anticipated by (or even intended at all) by the author.

A discourse community audience is a group of readers who share a set of characteristics, beliefs, or assumptions. Coined in Martin Nystrand's *What Writers Know: The Language, Process, and Structure of Written Discourse* (1982) and developed most prominently in the work of James Kinneavy and Stanley Fish, this conceptualization of audience asserts that a text's meaning is merely the product of assumptions that an interpretive community brings to the text. Most discourse communities are drawn along the lines of race, class, and/or gender: Westerners vs. Easterners, middle class people vs. poor people, men vs. women. The assumption behind this interpretive theory claims that a text, when read from any one of these perspectives, will have an entirely new set of meanings to its readers, and texts only *mean* within the confines of a specific discourse community. Think, for example, to the different meanings that can be derived from "A Letter from Birmingham Jail" from the point of view of two different groups of readers: 1) wealthy, Anglo-Saxon Protestants who are deeply entrenched in the racist culture of the mid-20th century American South and 2) poor, African-Americans who are, themselves, trying to assert a newfangled independent identity in the face of systemic racism. Many modern critical schools derive from the discourse-community based understanding of audience. New Historicism and Multiculturalism tend to focus on issues of race, Marxism and Post-Colonial stances stress class struggle, while Feminism and Queer Theory emphasize the role and function of gender in everyday affairs. Discourse community theory is one of the strongest strands of Postmodern thought and criticism. Since the interpretive communities can theoretically be iterated forever, the resulting assumption is that no authoritative interpretation of a text can logically exist. There is no Truth, but lots of truths – a series of competing perspectives, all of which are equally arbitrary and none of which are necessarily wrong.

The variables at play with how to define an audience are complicated and many. Let's reconsider our hypothetical letter to the highway department about the pot-holed road for clarity. Think of the different variables our speaker (the town resident) may need to consider about his audience. Would it make the most sense to deliver this speech in person, thereby making the highway department an immediate audience who would need to respond on the spot? Would it better to write a letter and have the highway department read the plea through a much more formalized, mediated form? Should the speaker characterize both himself and the audience as members of the same discourse community (those concerned with local well-being) for maximum persuasive effect? Answers to these questions, and dozens just like them, go back to a reader's effective consideration of the rhetorical situation.

Audience to Subject

A subject is the focus of a text. Subjects can be concrete (information on a scientific discovery) or abstract (the nature of beauty). Texts can have a singular subject (a policy decision) or multiple subjects (steps in a process). As writers begin to compose, they need to consider what an audience already knows about the subject, what information must be sup-

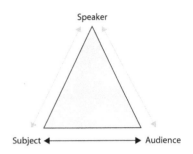

Figure 6 Relationship of Audience to Subject.

plied, and what can be taken for granted (see Figure 6). This is a matter of decorum on the part of the author and, as anyone who has been a part of a captive audience knows, respecting the intelligence of the audience sometimes makes all the difference.

In our hypothetical example, the audience (highway department) knows something about the subject (pot-holed roads). To account for this need, the speaker should assume an established familiarity within the audience/subject relationship and respect that existing knowledge unless he plans to lose the audience altogether. Imagine a highway worker reading something like, "a pothole is a depression or hollow in a road surface caused by wear or subsidence" and not meeting this letter with both an eye roll and a toss to the garbage bin. Well-intentioned, but malformed, attempts to provide information about a subject can easily come off as irreverent and condescending, thus undermining the goal of the text itself. Speakers must not pile on what can be assumed, nor should they withhold what needs to be said. It's all about knowing your audience.

Whether you are planning to write or critically read the writing of others, consider how the three points of the rhetorical triangle interact within the context of the occasion and the intended purpose of the text (Can you begin to see how all the steps are related?). Think about some, or all, of the following questions: What does the audience know about your subject? What is the audience's attitude towards it? Are there biases that must be addressed? Is there a common ground upon which you can begin your argument? How can that common ground be emphasized? In each rhetorical situation, there is a new audience, and this requires you to use different information to shape your argument effectively: that is, to borrow the words of Aristotle, to use "the best available means of persuasion."

Case Study in Rhetorical Analysis: George W. Bush's "Address to the Nation" 9/11/01

The Rhetorical Triangle

Speaker to Subject

In the years that followed the address, there has been much scholarly debate surrounding the speaker-subject dynamic, specifically how (or if) Bush used his rhetorical moment to define the events of 9/11 in a way that was politically advantageous to his administration. In "The Rhetor as Hero and the Pursuit of Truth: The Case of 9/11" (2005), Michael Hyde suggests that Bush's handling of 9/11 was largely free of political machinations. He suggests Bush used the moment of the address to provide much needed definition and clarification of 9/11 for an audience overrun by feelings of chaos and disorder: "People in a state of crisis and anxiety are in need of discourse that can help them make sense of the horror and chaos at hand and that can also lessen the trauma of their not feeling at home with their environment." For critics like Hyde, Bush's handling of the event in this speech was just right; he intervened as a clarifying voice to bring a chaotic subject under control. Other criticisms, such as John Murphy's "Our Mission and Our Moment" (2003), saw Bush's handling of the speech's subject in a different light. Rather than bringing order to chaos, Murphy contends, "President Bush has done a remarkable job of defining the attacks of September 11 to his advantage and that his rhetoric is a key factor in his success … to dominate public interpretation of the events." Murphy's stance is unarguably true to some degree – all rhetoricians attempt to align an audience's interpretation of a subject to their own – but the degree to which political motivations underlie this feature of the address is highly debatable. In any case, the speaker-subject dynamic often fosters critical debate and interpretation, a solid reminder that should counter the notion of the rhetorical triangle as a mere exercise in identification of the rhetorical players.

Speaker to Audience

What makes 9/11 unique as a rhetorical event is the way in which both speaker (Bush) and audience (American public) have equal stake in the speech's subject (the 9/11 attacks and the American response). Though some critics contend that Bush "created" his audience, using this moment to garner public support for the war on terror, his speech certainly handles the speaker-audience relationship with tremendous savviness and great care. Political criticisms notwithstanding, consider how the following line works to align the speaker and audience into a single unified entity, one which rallies around a mutual response to 9/11.

"A great people has been moved to defend a great nation."

Read this line aloud and you should notice that it sounds a little funny. Detractors of this speech may chalk the apparent subject/verb disagreement "A great people has been moved" up to one of Bush's well-known verbal gaffes, but there is much more going on here than meets the eye. The overarching theme of Bush's address is a call for national unity in the face of terrorist aggression, and this theme is writ small into the (faulty) grammar of this statement. The proper subject-verb agreement should read "A great people *have* been moved" where the plural verb "have" suggests movement of separate individuals acting on a coordinated effort. Instead, Bush opts for the singular verb "has" as if to say the citizens of the United States are not just one people, but one person. Consider the way he extends this notion of unification a bit later in the speech:

"America and our friends and allies join with all those who want peace and security in the world, and we stand together to win the war against terrorism."

When Bush says, "America and our friends and allies join with all those who want peace and security in the world," he increasingly widens the audience to capture the universal outrage of the terrorist attacks within incrementally larger discourse communities. He moves from the most immediate and specific victim of the attacks ("America"), to countries on a civilian relationship with the United States ("our friends"), to those with military ties ("allies"), to those who simply share a peaceful ideology not bound to borderlines of a nation ("join with all those who want peace and security in the world"). In doing so, Bush implies several things: those who are opposed to the US are not "friends" but adversaries; they are not "allies" but enemies; they are not "those who want peace and security" but those who want violence and terror.

Audience to Subject

In a 2012 poll reported by CBS News, Sony Electronics and Nielsen television research company conducted a study that ranked the most impactful television moments of the last fifty years. 9/11 came in as the head-and-shoulders winner, outpacing other high-profile events such as Hurricane Katrina (2005), the OJ Simpson murder verdict (1995), the Challenger space shuttle disaster (1986), and Obama's announcement of the death of Osama bin Laden (2011). Never has there been a larger tele-visual event in recent American history than 9/11, a circumstance which makes the rhetorical response to such an event a daunting task for any speaker. Think, by contrast, to Obama's announcement of Bin Laden's death in 2011. Obama spent a majority of his time explaining the basic events surrounding the top-secret raid on Bin Laden's Pakistani compound since this was a classified operation for which the audience had no context or knowledge. The rhetorical dynamics demanded Obama to spell out the subject for his audience in great detail. Not so with 9/11. The entire nation watched the events unfold in real-time and such a pre-established familiarity with the subject (9/11) for an audience (American public) presented an unusual rhetorical situation for the speaker (Bush). Instead of providing a detailed rundown of what happened, Bush instead focused on series of scattered images (perhaps to replicate the fragmented, tele-visual experience his audience had of the events). He says:

> "And no one will keep that light from shining. Today, our nation saw evil – the very worst of human nature – and we responded with the best of America. With the daring of our rescue workers, with the caring for strangers and neighbors who came to give blood and help in any way they could."

Notice how each of the three sentences use repeated breaks in the syntax to emphasize individual images and ideas in the same style of fast-paced television coverage. The first sentence ("And no one will keep that light from shining") could easily have been attached to the previous sentence. Bush, however, offsets it into its own standalone statement to bring focus and emphasis to the idea that no terror attack will ever extinguish the light of "freedom and opportunity." The second sentence ("Today, our nation saw evil – the very worst of human nature – and we responded with the best of America") is artificially fragmented by Bush's use of dashes. Bush constructs this sentence around the antithesis of evil and good, with each occupying a parallel location in the syntax. The phrase within the dashes ("the very worst of human nature") emphasizes just how heinous the terror attacks were. The third sentence ("With the daring of our rescue workers, with the caring for strangers and neighbors who came to give blood and help in any way they could") is not actually a sentence; it is a pair of prepositional phrases followed by a long adjective clause. Why the fragment, then? Instead of describing the charity and heroism of the rescue worker and neighbors in an elaborate rhetorical construction, Bush provides verbal "snap-shots" of these acts, short-staccato statements which emphasize the individuals themselves. You'll notice there is no main verb in this sentence; the individual human beings (the nouns), not their actions (the verbs), are the primary focus of these lines. Just as the audience experienced the events on television news coverage, Bush's rhetoric replicates and reinforces this experience in textual form to meet the audience where they are at.

Means of Persuasion: Ethos, Logos, and Pathos

Rhetoric is all about probability. Aristotle recognized this fact and rightly understood that there are two broad categories of evidence that will get arguers where they need to go. The first, what he called "inartistic proofs," support arguments with matter-of-fact phenomena: testimony, authoritative texts, demonstrable cause and effect, and so forth. The second, what he called "artistic proofs," derive from a speaker's ability to wield the "means of persuasion," techniques used to move an audience in the intended direction. In *The Art of Rhetoric*, Aristotle referred to the means of persuasion collectively as *pisteis*, a triad of argumentation strategies comprised of *ethos* (derived from the character of the speaker), *pathos* (derived from the emotion awakened in the audience) and *logos* (derived from the logic of the argument itself). He showcased the magic of *pisteis* in the context of a courtroom, noting how a successful attorney must do three things to win a case: 1) convince the jury that they and their client are trustworthy (ethos) 2) argue rationally for the intended outcome through use of evidence (logos) and 3) get the jury to sympathize with the perspective of their client (pathos). Skilled rhetoricians know that a convincing argument must contain a judicious mixture of all three appeals, and this principle was as true in Ancient Greece as it is today. To change minds and shape attitudes, a speech must be convincing and persuasive. By utilizing ethos, logos, and pathos, a writer is using some of the most basic (and powerful) tools in the rhetorical tool belt.

Ethos

In *The Art of Rhetoric*, Aristotle emphasized the primacy of ethos. Ethos, an argument by character, forges a connection between the speaker and audience. Ethos is everywhere in skillful speaking and writing, yet it's often difficult to explicitly identify since it appears in so many varied and nuanced forms. So, what are some of the basic moves a speaker can do to build bridges to the audience? Aristotle says there are three: *phronesis, arete*, and *eunoia*.

Phronesis refers to practical wisdom or "street smarts," the ability to know what to do in any given situation. Sometimes, *phronesis* is a function of one's natural talents. Think of the leadership of 2nd Ranger Battalion company commander John Miller (Tom Hanks) in the World War II film *Saving Private Ryan* (1998). Why is it that his squad of soldiers hang on his every word? It's not because of learned military strategies from a West Point education (he was a Midwestern schoolteacher in the film), but because he knows exactly what to do in any given situation. He retreats when he should retreat. He attacks when he should attack. He holds his position when he should hold his position. His men are never in undue danger and in the end, they get the job done under the direction of Miller's leadership. "He's a good leader," we may say as we exit the theater. But, he is a good commander precisely because of his *phronesis*-derived trustworthiness.

How can speakers and writers command the same type of reverence in rhetorical situations that John Miller did on the battlefield? Nine times out of ten, *phronesis* results from the author's due diligence and a demonstration that they've done their homework. Before a writer can survey the available options of how to speak on a topic, they must know what these options are (and somehow communicate to the audience that this selection is the most considered course of action). Have you ever wondered why writers, particularly those for academic publications, litter their texts with citations that point towards huge bibliographies? Citations signify the author's *phronesis* (in the context of academic writing) to the audience through a public display of the author's wide-reaching research, and these notes suggest the argument ought to be taken seriously. They, in other words, elbow the reader in the side as if to say, "This guy knows what he's talking about. Listen to what he has to say."

Arete, translated as "virtue" or "excellence," is often understood as a quality of character that makes a person worth admiring or following. The Classical literary tradition is diffuse with examples of *arete*. Look to the ancient world and you'll find its epic heroes invariably representing the standard by which we judge an excellent and virtuous man from that culture: The *Iliad's* Achilles is a superior Greek warrior; The Bible's David is a paragon of a Hebrew king; *Beowulf's* eponymous hero is an example of a great medieval warrior. To have *arete* is to have credibility with your followers. And to have credibility among your followers is the first step to getting them to do what you want them to do.

Arete also has use on the battlefield of words. Probably the most common way this form of ethos shows up in everyday communication is in a speaker's reputation or credentials. If a speaker is generally a respected authority in the field, credibility has already been built in the minds of the audience (consider the practice of placing "Dr." in front of one's name as a visible sign of expertise). Take, for example, William Faulkner's "Nobel Prize Acceptance Address" from Stockholm, Sweden on December 10, 1950. He makes no mention of his own accolades or writerly accomplishments in the address. His reputation precedes him; there's no need to list these things out, and Faulkner appropriately never trots out his credentials. He doesn't have to. The audience is already aware of his *arete* in the context of writing, and it is this "excellence" that invests him with the authority to speak about "the writer's duty."

Consider a different example. You are about to read a series of essays on Plato by a man named Frank McArthur. As a preface to the essays, you see this:

> *Dr. Frank McArthur is Professor of Philosophy at Yale University. A graduate of the Honors program, he earned his B.A. in Philosophy from the Harvard University and his M.A., M.Phil., and Ph.D. in Philosophy from Columbia University. Prior to taking his position at Yale University, Professor McArthur taught at Princeton University, University of Chicago, Columbia University, Providence College, and*

Oxford University. He served as the Mellon Postdoctoral Fellow at Johns Hopkins University from 2000 to 2002.

In the context of academia, these credentials are tantamount to Professor McArthur's "virtue" on the topic of Classical philosophy. Audiences need to know that a speaker is worth listening to and credentials like these – degrees from prestigious universities, professorships at Ivy League institutions, several teaching awards and grants – lets an audience know that this speaker means business. *Arete* is not reserved only for academia's elite. If you think about it, what is a cover letter or a resume – everyday writing tasks done by those with no rhetorical training – if not a showcase for one's *arete* in a particular field?

Eunoia is best understood as the "good will," "selflessness," or "disinterest" of the speaker. With *eunoia*, a speaker builds credibility with the audience by acting (maybe authentically, maybe not) as if he is one of them. Rhetorician Kenneth Burke articulates this concept of identification in his book *A Rhetoric of Motives* (1945), "You persuade a man only insofar as you can talk his language by speech, gesture, tonality, order, image, attitude, idea, identifying your ways with his." Donald Trump's 2016 bid for president is a masterful example of *eunoia*'s mass effect. Trump showcased a surprisingly keen sense on the campaign trail of presenting political issues to the average American in understandable terms. An antithesis to Barack Obama's polished rhetorical style and even demeanor, Trump's political incorrectness and plain style resonated with large chunks of country's blue-collar population whose local economies and industry had been blown to pieces in the second half of the 20th century. His vow to restore the waning coal and steel industries to their former glory was seen as entirely selfless and disinterested. He ostensibly stood to gain nothing except to "Make America Great Again," and his rhetoric continually located the interests of his audience at the dead-center of proposed policies. Trump's White House victory was due in large part to the support he garnered during his campaign stops in the Rust Belt States. Such is the power of *eunoia* when strategically wielded.

An audience will be most receptive to a persuasive plea when they feel that the speaker doesn't have anything to directly gain from the proposal. When dealing with issues of *eunoia*, the audience must keep their bias detector on high alert. Speakers who have a vested interest in the subject matter (say, they want to reduce carbon emissions because their hybrid car company stands to profit), or have some personal stake in the issue, (say, they want to reduce carbon emissions because, if they don't, they will be fired from their job as Chair of the Alliance for Climate Protection), need to be treated with an appropriate skepticism.

Our hypothetical letter to the highway department would do well to include some ethos-based maneuvers. Perhaps the speaker could outline a proposal based on research of how surrounding municipalities have handled similar pothole problems (a *phronesis*-based move which illustrates the degree of focused thought the speaker has devoted to the issue). Maybe he could characterize himself as a regular citizen with a moral obligation to preserve the local roadways through regular, tax-funded upkeep (an *arete*-based strategy which foregrounds the ideal morals and ethics of a model citizen). Or, the speaker could talk plainly as a concerned parent, interested only in the well-being and safety of local drivers and children playing nearby (a *eunoia*-based move that establishes common ground and shared interests with the audience). These rhetorical strategies, either alone or in combination, are the first step to forging a connection between speaker and audience, a connection that will have bearing on the use of the other rhetorical appeals, logos and pathos.

Logos

Logos is a word that has a long and complicated history. Translated from the original Greek most often as "word" or "reason," logos has been a central concept in the history of Western philosophy and religion used to identify nothing short of the organizing force of the universe. Christianity adopts this concept most visibly in the New Testament (originally written in Greek) by often using "the Logos" as a conventional name for Christ, "In the beginning was the Logos, and the Logos was with God, and the Logos was God…. And the Logos became flesh and dwelt among us" (John 1:1, 14). The idea of the Logos is a central strand of medieval theology (Aquinas), though it is not proprietary to Christianity. Materialists (Heraclitus), dualists (Plato), stoics (Zeno), and even psychologists (Jung and Lacan) all acknowledge in one way or another this rational, organizational principle. Indeed, the central drive of Postmodernism is the focused dismantling of "logo-centrism" in Western thought, a fight that continues to rage in both academia and popular culture.

In the context of rhetoric, logos is sometimes narrowly misunderstood as its cognate, "logic," and this confusion often derives from our exposure to formal logic, a discipline that relies on the immutable principles of mathematics as its underlying model of knowledge. Take the Pythagorean theorem. How is it that every new crop of 10th graders who calculates $A^2+B^2=C^2$ always end up with the same answer? Once deduced, Pythagoras's theorem never changes, and if you don't get the right answer, the problem is with you, not with the theorem. Mathematical knowledge is incredibly stable like that and that's why Plato found it so attractive. In his dialogue *Meno* (380 B.C.), Plato attempts to transfer the logic of mathematics into language use to show that propositions, like mathematical axioms, can be demonstrably true if logically supported. Socrates (always the main character of the Platonic dialogues) asserts that words can communicate completely logical ideas – free from ambiguity – so long as they can be defined in "every/only" structures. In the dialogue, he considers the question, "What is a triangle?" The "every/only" answer he gives goes something like this: "every triangle has three sides, and only triangles have three sides." This type of crystalline logic is neat and orderly, but day-to-day events rarely present themselves in every/only terms. Enter Aristotle.

Aristotle rightly understood that Platonic logic is only a shard of a much larger way of understanding logos in the context of rhetoric. He broadly defined logos as an author's use of patterns, conventions, and modes of reasoning that an audience finds convincing and persuasive. The best logos appeals are so tightly rigged that an audience can draw the conclusion for themselves without the speaker having to explicitly tell them (a doubly persuasive tactic which also flatters the audience's sense of self-efficacy). As Aristotle said, "the audience takes pleasure in themselves for anticipating the point." Logic, for Aristotle and rhetoricians forever after, doesn't provide ultimate proof, but it does move things beyond a reasonable doubt.

Effective logos appeals begin by grounding a topic in a foundational premise from which subsequent premises and conclusions can be reasonably inferred. Aristotle, in *Topics* (350 B.C.), referred to these starting points as the "common *topoi*," a piece of shared wisdom or common knowledge held by both speaker and audience. In contemporary usage, "topic" refers to a subject – the person, place, or thing – the speaker will elaborate upon for his audience, but Aristotle understood this term to mean something a bit different. For him, a topic was a heuristic for discovering what arguments can be made (a predecessor, perhaps, to Cicero's canon of Invention).

Once identified, Aristotle explained how all subjects can be argued in one of four ways: 1) whether a thing has occurred, 2) whether it will occur, 3) whether things are bigger or smaller than they seem, and 4) whether a thing is or is not possible. Aristotle's *topoi* evolved over time, particularly through the work of Renaissance rhetoricians in England, to take on the more recognizable label of "commonplaces." Speakers and writers need to be savvy as they identify commonplaces since conventional wisdom is just that, a convention, which shifts with location and time. Statements like "it's always darkest before the dawn," "absolute power corrupts absolutely," or "the pen is mightier than the sword" are common-sense assumptions that most members of contemporary American culture would agree to be true. By having a commonplace as the operational logic of all that's said in speech or writing, the speaker can establish a workable common ground (and here is the mesh point of logos and ethos) from which they can marshal along other proofs.

Aristotle also discussed a second group of *topoi* – twenty-eight to be exact – which the speaker can use as a ready-made launch pad for how ideas can be organized and coordinated. Some of these *topoi* have survived into the contemporary composition classroom, forming the basic structure of both spoken and written discourse. Among the most recognizable are definition, comparison, relationship, and testimony.

- *Definitional rhetoric* involves the interpretation of word meanings. Definitional claims place concepts into categories and provide perspective on these categorizations. This can be powerful mode of discourse since definitions give identity to things; it says what things are and what they are not.
- *Comparative rhetoric* measures the value of one thing relative to another. Often these comparisons are supported by measurable data or observable phenomena, the hard facts which any member of an audience could theoretically authenticate for themselves.
- *Relational rhetoric* involves the relationship of events. These claims relate past to the present, present to the past, or present to the future. Events in this mode are often rigged together according to some recognizable plan (chronological, general to particular, particular to general, ascending weightiness, and so forth) and concern matters that, in theory, can be corroborated and verified independently by any member of an audience.

- *Testimonial rhetoric* makes its case by relying on authoritative sources of information. Speakers in this mode often outsource their authority to others by citing authoritative texts, legal precedent, or expert testimony.

It's easy to see how a speaker of our hypothetical letter could easily settle on any number of commonplace assumptions shared by his highway department audience: "tax dollars ought to be used for the public good," "preventative maintenance pre-empts greater long-term costs," "investment in infrastructure has long term benefits," "manual laborers perform a much-needed public service." Depending on which one of these the author goes with, it's easy to see how the author can extend this assumption into a pattern of development (see Table 1).

Table 1 Relationship of Commonplace to Mode of Development.

Commonplace	Mode of development
"tax dollars ought to be used for the public good"	<u>Definitional</u> – The speaker may define what he means by "public good" and then frame the act of repairing the potholes in terms of this definition.
"preventative maintenance circumvents greater long-term costs"	<u>Comparative</u> – The speaker may juxtapose the small cost of the pothole repair to the potential long-term cost of auto repair, personal injury, and legal fees caused by unrepaired potholes.
"investment in infrastructure has long term benefits"	<u>Relational</u> – The speaker may explain the causes of the potholes and predict what may happen to motorists and residents if the potholes are not fixed.
"manual laborers perform a much-needed public service"	<u>Testimonial</u> – The speaker may invoke testimony from town officials on the value that a highway department brings to civic life and leverage this trust towards a promise of repair.

Pathos

While logos targets the mind of an audience, pathos goes for the heart. Appeals to pathos, or the emotions of the audience, attempt to tap into the feelings of the audience in order to move them from a state of apathy to a pathetic, sympathetic, or empathetic state (notice all four of those words derive from the same Greek root, *pathos*). If your first thought of emotionally-based rhetoric is that it's little more than a cheap pop to get the audience to act quickly before their rational side thinks better of it, think again. If you think about what *really* motivates the big decisions in life – who to date, where to live, how to raise kids, what to do with a sick pet – odds are there is a significant emotional dimension motivating the final decision. In the hands of a skilled rhetorician, pathos appeals are just as effective than ethos and logos. And like ethos and logos, pathos must work in conjunction with – not apart from – these other means of persuasion.

Aristotle believed that an effective pathos appeal fits the text to the character types and states of mind that make up the audience. In other words, he believed that certain groups of people tend to be emotionally moved by the same things. If a speaker can correctly identify this commonplace (a logos/pathos crossover), then he can appeal to these special interests via connotative diction, figurative language, personal anecdotes, human interest stories, and so forth. For example, an argument built on nostalgia may motivate the old, while tones of rebellion may motivate an adolescent audience. The joy of philanthropic charity may excite an audience of wealthy donors, whereas the exhilaration of overcoming the odds may spur on an audience of the poor. Stereotyping notwithstanding, Aristotle's ideas have survived into the modern day, forming some of the basic assumptions and techniques of modern print and television advertising. Mountain Dew ads, fueled on by rock music and adrenaline pumping-extreme sports, are hardly aimed at those in the nursing home.

Which pathos appeal to use in a given situation is somewhat of a guessing game. Aristotle gives us a useful heuristic, but, of course, there is no way any speaker could account for all the rhetorical constraints – biases, presuppositions, and ideologies – that frame the worldview an audience brings to the table in each and every rhetorical situation. The effect of an emotional appeal is largely determined by individual audience members in the same way that ethos appeals are determined subjectively. Speakers can try their best to build credibility and move the audience emotionally, but there's no guarantee these strategies will pay off. Consider a speech opposed to abortion where the speaker treats the subject from a Christian framework (ethos) supplemented by a number of heart-warming stories of babies who were brought to term and went on to live healthy and productive lives (pathos). Whereas one audience member may think the ethos and pathos choices of the speaker are highly convincing, a pro-choicer, sitting right by their side, may not. Remember the expression "One man's terrorist is another man's freedom fighter" when trying to determine the effectiveness of character and emotional appeals. Pathos, though highly influential, isn't brainwashing. Its strength is ultimately the call of the audience.

The pathos options for the author of our hypothetical complaint letter to the highway department are vast. Images of twisted cars crashes, mangled passengers, and endless litigation from unkempt potholes would certainly stir a whirlpool of emotions in the highway department audience. An aggressive tone may work, hoping that the highway department may act swiftly to diffuse the temper of an angry citizen. Our author could also soften the blow, couching his emotional appeals into contexts of patriotism and civic duty: to fix these holes is to align with deeply held emotions we commonly ascribe to our national identity. A guilt angle could work here, too. The longer the holes are ignored, the greater the risk to personal and public safety in the town, thus characterizing the repairs as an urgent priority.

Case Study in Rhetorical Analysis: George W. Bush's "Address to the Nation" 9/11/01

The Means of Persuasion – Ethos, Logos, Pathos

Ethos

The sheer gravity of 9/11 set the stage for a grand rhetorical response, one that required its speaker to have every inch the *arete* of a battlefield leader guiding those under his command. In some ways, the event itself produced the need for a strong leader, an individual to confidently step forward to provide clarification on what happened and recommendations for what to do about it. As Michael Hyde notes in his essay "The Rhetor as Hero and the Pursuit of Truth: The Case of 9/11" (2005), "...the extensive literature on 9/11 is filled with narratives detailing the courageous acts of all sorts of people: firefighters, police officers, physicians and nurses, clergy, airline personnel and passengers, construction workers. The list could go on. In adding the rhetor to this list, I subscribe to the argument that the events of 9/11 defined a monumental occasion..." In his "Address to the Nation," Bush embodied the virtues of this strongminded leader and defined himself as the rhetorical hero of the day. Consider the transition from what *happened* to what *will happen* as an example of Bush's clear-sighted *arete* amidst this moment of national panic:

"Today, our nation saw evil, the very worst of human nature. And we responded with the best of America – with the daring of our rescue workers, with the caring for strangers and neighbors who came to give blood and help in any way they could.

Immediately following the first attack, I implemented our government's emergency response plans. Our military is powerful, and it's prepared. Our emergency teams are working in New York City and Washington, D.C. to help with local rescue efforts.

Our first priority is to get help to those who have been injured, and to take every precaution to protect our citizens at home and around the world from further attacks.

The functions of our government continue without interruption. Federal agencies in Washington which had to be evacuated today are reopening for essential personnel tonight, and will be open for business tomorrow. Our financial institutions remain strong, and the American economy will be open for business, as well."

As the speech moves from paragraphs one and two to paragraphs three and four, its tone also transitions from reactive to proactive. Look closely and you'll notice this tonal transition is written onto the shifting verb tense – from past to present to future – over the course of these short paragraphs. Let's look at how this happens. The first paragraph speaks almost exclusively in the past tense to describe the national reaction to 9/11: "our nation *saw* evil," "we *responded*," "neighbors who *came* to give blood." The following two paragraphs snap to the present tense – "military *is* powerful," "emergency teams *are* working," "first priority *is* to get help" – before moving into a future-tense discussion of what proactive steps will be taken: "government *will* continue without interruption," "[Washington] *will* be open for business tomorrow," "economy *will* be open for business." In doing so, Bush sends a clear message that he understood what happened, that he knows what's occurring in the moment, and that America will resolutely move forward in the face of even the most overwhelming tragedy.

Bush also showcases several *eunoia*-based maneuvers designed to inspire the trust and confidence of his audience. For any act of speech to be effective, a speaker must somehow get the audience to effectively identify with himself and his motives. It's only once the audience sees themselves in the speaker – as sharing their plight and speaking their language – that the content of the message can start to set in. From the very first tricolon of the address ("*our* fellow citizens, *our* way of life, *our* very freedom") Bush brings the idea of national unity to the forefront. It's no mistake, then, that the last pronoun of the speech is "our," a symbolic gesture to reinforce the speech's overarching theme of national unity. It's not "me," not "you," but all of "us" jointly working towards the restoration of a just, moral order. He ends the speech by defining the event as a shared trauma but one that will be overcome through collective effort and resolve ("None of *us* will ever forget this day, yet *we* go forward to defend freedom and all that is good and just in *our* world"). This strategy is by no means unique to Bush. Nearly all the great wartime speeches of the 20th century have an echo of Bush's line "None of us will ever forget this day." Think perhaps to Franklin Delano Roosevelt's "A Date Which Will Live in Infamy" (1941) given on the night of another surprise attack on American soil, Pearl Harbor in Hawaii. Like Bush, FDR vowed to never let the pain of that day fade away into memory, an idea which itself is an iteration of Abraham's Lincoln's famous one-liner from the "Gettysburg Address" (1863), "... we here highly resolve that these dead shall not have died in vain."

Logos

Aristotle understood the persuasive power of the commonplace, and this tactic is used to its full effect in the address on the night of 9/11. Bush's speech is seeded allover with images from a collective American heritage, thus exploiting the patriotic power of these deeply held archetypes possessed in his audience's collective (un)consciousness. The first of these commonplaces appears when Bush says,

> "America was targeted for attack because we're the brightest beacon for freedom and opportunity in the world. And no one will keep that light from shining."

The United States as a "beacon" is not a randomly chosen metaphor; it has deep roots in the Christian tradition as well as American political rhetoric. The metaphor of the beacon-upon-a-hill is a paraphrase of a famous line from Jesus's Sermon on the Mount, "You are the light of the world. A city that is set on a hill cannot be hidden" (Matthew 5:14). This deeply held archetype from Scripture has been a mainstay in American political rhetoric, dating all the way back to John Winthrop's reference to the Puritan settlement in Massachusetts as a "Shining City upon a Hill." This very same image has cycled through the rhetoric of John F. Kennedy (Address to the General Court of Massachusetts in 1961), Ronald Reagan (Election Eve Address in 1980), and Barack Obama (Commencement

Address at UMASS-Boston in 2006), just to name a few notable examples. By tapping this commonplace, Bush unites his audience under the canopy of a mutual understanding: America's beacon has not yet been successfully extinguished, and even in the face of something like 9/11, America will remain atop that hill.

In the final paragraph, Bush invokes his second commonplace, one which utilizes a familiar spiritual saying that is equally recognizable for religious and non-religious folks alike. He says,

> "And I pray they will be comforted by a Power greater than any of us, spoken through the ages in Psalm 23: 'Even though I walk through the valley of the shadow of death, I fear no evil for you are with me.'"

Psalm 23 is one of the most recognizable verses from the Old Testament, partially because of its heavy presence in popular media (from Duke Ellington to Jay-Z), partially because of the regular role it plays in funeral liturgies. This verse is so often quoted because of its aphoristic quality (a concise statement that illustrates a widely held truth of belief), and Bush exploits this feature to its full effect. To paraphrase, the line reads something like, "Even in our darkest times, one need not worry if they have faith in the Lord." It doesn't need explaining how the energy of this quote can be applied to the context in which Bush delivered his address, the night of 9/11 only twelve hours removed from the falling of the Twin Towers. While no quote can heal the wounds of that morning, the allusion to Psalm 23 does provide a point of shared common ground upon which Americans can begin to reestablish their footing.

Pathos

A tragedy on the scale of 9/11 demands a pathos-laden response. Bush's audience, already in an emotional state, no doubt expected – even needed – an emotional dimension to the speech delivered in response to an event of this magnitude. It is appropriate, then, that the speech was presented in what rhetoricians describe as the "grand" or "high" style, a mode of delivery which relies on formal rhetorical structures and figures of speech to evoke an emotional response from the audience. How does he do this? Look to his lead-off paragraph for a prime example. He says,

> "The pictures of airplanes flying into buildings, fires burning, huge – huge structures collapsing have filled us with disbelief, terrible sadness, and a quiet, unyielding anger."

For those who watched 9/11 unfold minute by minute, even the lightest of reminders would likely cause the painful images from the day to come rushing back. He reminds his audience, yes, yet does so with a tactful abstractness. But, this line is noteworthy for another reason. To many first-time readers, it may seem a bit odd that the prepared transcript contains the double repetition of "huge – huge" when describing the World Trade Center buildings. This apparent stylistic aberration is not accidental. Grammatically, this repetition can almost be read as an adverb/adjective pairing as if to say the "hugely huge" structures. Among the hulking pieces of architecture that make up the New York City sky-line, the Twin Towers were the biggest of the big. And, by highlighting the sheer physical size, Bush's imagery of the destruction-of-what-seemed-indestructible naturally leads to the emotional mish-mash of "disbelief, terrible sadness, and a quiet, unyielding anger." This emotional wave gains momentum as it flows into the following paragraph:

> "Terrorist attacks can shake the foundations of our biggest build-
> ings, but they cannot touch the foundation of America. These acts
> shatter steel, but they cannot dent the steel of American resolve."

Here, diction and syntax are the delivery systems of Bush's pathos appeal. Repetition, the use of similar patterns of words or grammatical forms, help speakers present ideas clearly and concisely all while developing rhythm and balance in the delivery. Bush uses repetition throughout the address, but it's the specific repetition of "foundation" and "steel" that should grab the audience's attention here. Reread the sentences above one more time and notice how Bush alternates between the denotational and connotational meanings of each word to drive home the thematic point. "Foundation" and "steel" are initially used denotatively to signify the physical materials from which the World Trade Center was constructed. The "attack" on 9/11 destroyed the physical material yet could not rattle the connotational "foundation of America" and "steel of American resolve" (lines 17–18). In doing this, Bush plays on the literal and figurative to a rousing effect. He yokes The World Trade Center and the American public together using these shared words, thus implying that an attack on one is an attack on the other. The literal, physical material of both may be destroyed (the collapse of buildings and loss of human life), but the abstract spirit behind what each of these represent can never degrade or deteriorate. At once, Bush identi-fies the deep emotional pain the attacks have caused while inspiring a deter-mined and focused response to such an unparalleled act of aggression.

Developing the Lines of Inquiry for a Text: Structure, Syntax, and Diction

Once you've settled on the rhetorical situation and the means of persuasion, it's time to roll up your sleeves, reach into the text, and grab the words. Doing so should illustrate how individual parts of a text mesh together into a larger, unified whole. Such a style of inquiry asks that readers self-consciously identify and internalize the moves they have made while reading that will, in turn, help them to become more intentional, rhetorical readers. While you are certainly encouraged to throw your thoughts and experiences into the mix as you read, there are some general guidelines to rhetorical analysis-based inquiry. The simplest rule of thumb is this: every rhetorical observation should consist of two parts 1) a "where-in-the-text-do-I-see-this" part (that ties the observation to the text) and 2) a "why-does-this-observation-matter" part (that extends the textual observation into an interpretive or evaluative inquiry).

Most students are adept at answering questions about a text, but few are expert at asking them. This tends to be the most difficult step for students with rhetorical analysis because to ask probing questions, as Anthony Petrosky says in "From Story to Essay: Reading and Writing" (1982), "means making public what is private – a process dependent on explication, illustration, and critical examination of perception and ideas." Asking good questions begs you to engage and explore both your own knowledge and the purposes of the text, and it's this participative element which highlights the generative effects of rhetorical analysis can have for a reader. After reading a text, if you say to yourself, "I don't know what to ask," consider Table 2 (below) to get you moving in the right direction.

Knowing how to ask the right questions is a good start. The natural companion exercise to asking questions is to answer them, and here is where readers will give voice to their developing rhetorical insight of the text. To answer, at least provisionally, the rhetorical questions you've posed is to flesh out what you know, establish the limits of what you don't know, and open up new pathways for further inquiry. As Mary Goldschmidt says, by answering these initial questions, you make "visible the thinking that is often invisible…as [you] grapple with the writer's writing, the reader's reading, and the mediating contexts that shape both. [By doing so], students are trained to be more intentional and rhetorically sophisticated writers themselves."

Table 2 Linking Textual Observation to Rhetorical Inference.

The "Where-in-the-Text-Is-This" question	The "Why-Does-This-Observation-Matter" question
Where does the main point of the passage show up?	Why do you think it shows up at the beginning? Why does it delay until the middle? What's gained by waiting until the end?
Where does the author/character show us that he's worth listening to? Where does he connect with you emotionally? Where does he provide hard proof?	Why are these important to your understanding of what the author/character has to say? How do these either draw you in or push you away from what's said?
Where does the author/character's proof or examples appear in the passage?	Why do you think they're in the order they are? Why may it start with a shock and work back? Why may it begin with broad claims and follow with specifics?
Where do you see the author/character making an assumption?	Why does this assumption matter to what they are saying? Why is it biased? Why does it seem honest?
Where do you see any usually long sentences? Short sentences? Fragments?	Why would the author place these sentences where he does? How do they emphasize, or de-emphasize, the point being made?
Where do you think the author/character may not be telling us everything they know? Where do they seem genuinely confused?	Why would the author/character not be forthright? What is gained or lost by this move?
Where do you see patterns in the writing? Where does the author/character repeat things?	Why do you think these patterns are meaningful? What is the point of using the same verbs over and over again? Adjectives? Nouns? Something else?

The approach to rhetorical inquiry and analysis detailed in this chapter will no doubt come more naturally to "experienced readers [who understand] that both reading and writing are context-rich, situational, and constructive acts," an idea noted by Christina Haas and Linda Flower in "Rhetorical Reading Strategies and the Construction of Meaning" (1988). Though more sophisticated readers already have in their mind's ear the "sounds" of thought, such a process can be both generative and constructive for readers doing this type of work for the first time. Whether you are "right" is neither here nor there. Rhetorical analysis, if approached with an open mind and heart, will help you to facilitate the dialogic relationship that exists between any text and its reader. Reading rhetorically will help you figure out *how* to find a productive focus, craft an engaged response to a text, develop a coherent and organized line of thought, work carefully with source materials, and support interpretations using apt examples and quotations. But more than this, it shows that complex texts are problems with which to engage; they're meant to be complex – not just a thing to demonstrate one's mastery or to declare ready-made opinions. What you produce is what you see, and you see it because it is really there for you, and when your teacher reads what you've written, they should nod and say, "Yes, there is truth in that. It may not be the only truth, but this student has seen and has told me honestly what he has seen."

CHAPTER THREE

ESTABLISHING A WRITTEN DIALOGUE WITH A TEXT

I've always noted on my course syllabi that "we will emphasize critical reading and creativity as much as possible," but it was only until the last few years of my career that I began to reflect on how this stated goal (mis)matched up to the student reality. I try to emphasize these things as much as possible, telling my students to think analytically not only about the ideas of our authors but also about the way they can throw their own thoughts and experiences into the mix. "You have ideas," I often lead with on the first day, "but you should always want to think further about them, to improve them – partly so that you can share them with others, partly so you can live as a conscientious consumer of information." In other words, I have always urged students to search for the "higher meaning" in a text or to read "more deeply" into their own experience, but as the years have gone by, I've had a growing suspicion that students tended not to work well away from my leading hand. But I've taught them to read and write critically, haven't I? What went wrong?

Rhetorical reading is only as good as the written record you keep of it. The English classroom experience I described above relegated reading and writing to passive activities, requiring little more than this fact here, that quote there, and "voila," a fully-grown paper ready for submission. When I asked my students to establish a written dialogue with a text – a process habitual to mature readers but generally lacking in school-age students – things began to change. I saw how jet-skiing across the surface of texts, rather than diving into their deep backwaters, kept understanding, motivation, and investment in the material at bay. Rhetorical reading, as we noted in Chapter 2, is a busy process that asks a reader to keep several elements in balance – the rhetorical situation, the means of persuasion, concerns at the line and word level. The natural outgrowth of *understanding* the rhetorical sub-structure of a text is to *write* about it.

But, we are not talking here about writing in any formalized, "essayish" sense of the word. That type of writing is what composition scholars call Writing-to-Show-Learning (WTSL), written evidence of a student's mastery of a text that is communicated with a high degree of formality. Traditional analytical essays, term papers, research writing, even graded homework all fit this description and part of the frustration students have with these modes of writing is they find themselves at a loss with how to generate content for A-level work. Not knowing how to do this – or not being taught how to do this – is when all the stock problems of student papers rush in to fill the void: ambiguity, repetitiveness, lazy clichés, bombastic overwriting, outright gibberish.

Annotations – short, informal notes about a text – are the interlocutor between the language of reading and the language of writing. Annotations are profoundly different than most text-based writing students are used to because they are built on the principle of Writing-to-Learn (WTL), a formative writing task designed to help students think through key concepts or ideas presented in a text without the pressure of grades, judgement, or evaluation. But make no mistake about it: just because annotations are informal and low-stakes, it does not mean that what you produce is not purpose driven and highly generative. WTL and WTSL, though made to be mutually exclusive by some composition instructors, are rather fluid and one can, and should, transfer into the next. Exercises within this chapter will emphasize the development of the writer's voice in academic discourse through several different forms of annotation, each with their own niche focus and emphasis.

Knee-Jerk Annotations

Without clear definition, informal annotations are often a frustrating experience on both sides of the desk. Teachers tend to have an idealistic conception of what student annotations should look like. The hope is that students will be able to transform their pristinely bare texts into an annotation-covered treasure map, full of lines, X's, and detailed marginal commentary that point towards the analytical pay dirt. I think to myself sometimes, "Why shouldn't a student be able to connect 'transparent eyeball' from Emerson's *Nature* to the 'eye' of the pond in Thoreau's *Walden* or see how Aristotle's *Poetics* informs the plot sequence of Sophocles's *Antigone*?" But rather than rich analysis and insightful annotations, the only thing many students have on the due date is "the look." The look of frustration, the look of confusion. Part of this frustration lies in the fact that many students are unclear as to what is expected in annotations, however informal they may be. A few stars, underlines, or highlights (or sometimes fully highlighted documents!) just won't do. Annotations are that isthmus of communication between the audience, the author, the text, and the words and ideas beyond the borders of the page. Knee-Jerk annotations provide an outlet for those "lightbulb moments" that fade out of your mind as quickly as they come in (see Figure 1). The beauty of these notes is that they are not necessarily bound to any structural framework; they freely flow along as a text unfolds and ideas pop into your head. Maybe it's best to think of this as the analog of brainstorming in the formal writing process. Like brainstorming, promising ideas are there – however rough and raw – which should provisionally get you noticing patterns and recognizing things that are not there with a passive reading.

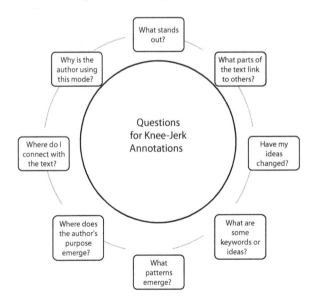

Figure 1 Considerations for Initial Reactions to a Text.

Of course, what is produced in these notes will vary from person to person, and the authors you will read have many tricks in their bag. This makes Knee-Jerk annotations a more challenging endeavor than it may initially seem. Rest assured that you won't be able to find more examples of every literary device in a single passage, and it's likely you won't see everything the author is attempting to do. You should, however, attempt to connect images,

---

Extended metaphor of morning and awakeness. Perhaps can be thought of as a kind-of spiritual awareness.

Cascading numbers highlight the rarity of an individual who chooses a "poetic or divine life."

To him whose elastic and vigorous thought keeps pace with the sun, the day is a perpetual morning. It matters not what the clocks say or the attitudes and labors of men. Morning is when I am awake and there is a dawn in me. Moral reform is the effort to throw off sleep. Why is it that men give so poor an account of their day if they have not been slumbering? They are not such poor calculators. If they had not been overcome with drowsiness, they would have performed something. The millions are awake enough for physical labor; but only one in a million is awake enough for effective intellectual exertion, only one in a hundred million to a poetic or divine life. To be awake is to be alive. I have never yet met a man who was quite awake. How could I have looked him in the face?

Throughout the opening paragraph, Thoreau's tone seems accusatory. Is there a particular "man" to whom these criticisms are directed? Or is this a broader swipe at all "men" around him?

Aphorism that builds from the opening metaphor. Seems to be intended as a reminder to both himself and his reader.

Heavy alliterative pattern with the use of "w" words give the prose a lyrical quality just at the moment of Thoreau's deepest insights in the passage.

Allusions to "Spartan" life show up elsewhere in *Walden*. Why is that? Is Thoreau's stripped-down life a modern-day version of Spartan discipline?

I went to the woods because I wished to live deliberately, to front only the essential facts of life, and see if I could not learn what it had to teach, and not, when I came to die, discover that I had not lived. I did not wish to live what was not life, living is so dear; nor did I wish to practise resignation, unless it was quite necessary. I wanted to live deep and suck out all the marrow of life, to live so sturdily and Spartan- like as to put to rout all that was not life, to cut a broad swath and shave close, to drive life into a corner, and reduce it to its lowest terms, and, if it proved to be mean, why then to get the whole and genuine meanness of it, and publish its meanness to the world; or if it were sublime, to know it by experience, and be able to give a true account of it in my next excursion. For most men, it appears to me, are in a strange uncertainty about it, whether it is of the devil or of God, and have somewhat hastily concluded that it is the chief end of man here to "glorify God and enjoy him forever."

This is ironic since Thoreau was a well-known vegetarian. The metaphor of "marrow" is interesting: it is the source of red blood cells, the essence of a living organism. To eat marrow is to consume life at its most essential level, or to "live deliberately."

Thoreau identifies, and exposes, what he believes to be a common fallacy (hasty generalization) of those who surround him.

Emerson, in *Nature*, uses this same term: "Nature never wears a mean appearance." "Meanly" means "stingy" or "miserly," and the man he describes is the antithesis of Thoreau's nature which is generous and magnanimous.

Still we live meanly, like ants; though the fable tells us that we were long ago changed into men, like pygmies we fight with cranes; it is error upon error, and clout upon clout, and our best virtue has for its occasion a superfluous and evitable wretchedness. Our life is frittered away by detail. An honest man has hardly need to count more than his ten fingers, or in extreme cases he may add his ten toes, and lump the rest. Simplicity, simplicity, simplicity! I say, let your affairs be as two or three, and not a hundred or a thousand; instead of a million count half a dozen, and keep your accounts on your thumb-nail. In the midst of this chopping sea of civilized life, such are the clouds and storms and quicksands and thousand-and-one items to be allowed for, that a man has to live, if he would not founder and go to the bottom and not make his port at all, by dead reckoning, and he must be a great calculator indeed who succeeds. Simplify, simplify. Instead of three meals a day, if it be necessary eat but one; instead of a hundred dishes,

The short, simple syntax of Thoreau's guiding credo is placed central among much more complicated sentence structure. In some ways, these sentences work to "simplify" the cluttered and needlessly complicated prose that surround it on all sides.

The sarcastic tone is built off the juxtaposition and use of "internal" and "external."

five; and reduce other things in proportion. Our life is like a German Confederacy, made up of petty states, with its boundary forever fluctuating, so that even a German cannot tell you how it is bounded at any moment. The nation itself, with all its so-called internal improvements, which, by the way are all external and superficial, is just such an unwieldy and overgrown establishment, cluttered with furniture and tripped up by its own traps, ruined by luxury and heedless expense, by want of calculation and a worthy aim, as the million households in the land; and the only cure for it, as for them, is in a rigid economy, a stern and more than Spartan simplicity of life and elevation of purpose. It lives too fast. Men think that it is essential that the Nation have commerce, and export ice, and talk through a telegraph, and ride thirty miles an hour, without a doubt, whether they do or not; but whether we should live like baboons or like men, is a little uncertain. If we do not get out sleepers, and forge rails, and devote days and nights to the work, but go to tinkering upon our lives to improve them, who will build railroads? And if railroads are not built, how shall we get to heaven in season? But if we stay at home and mind our business, who will want railroads? We do not ride on the railroad; it rides upon us. Did you ever think what those sleepers are that underlie the railroad? Each one is a man, an Irishman, or a Yankee man. The rails are laid on them, and they are covered with sand, and the cars run smoothly over them. They are sound sleepers, I assure you. And every few years a new lot is laid down and run over; so that, if some have the pleasure of riding on a rail, others have the misfortune to be ridden upon. And when they run over a man that is walking in his sleep, a supernumerary sleeper in the wrong position, and wake him up, they suddenly stop the cars, and make a hue and cry about it, as if this were an exception. I am glad to know that it takes a gang of men for every five miles to keep the sleepers down and level in their beds as it is, for this is a sign that they may sometime get up again.

Thoreau's stance towards the technological development of his day, the railroad, is quite negative. Is Thoreau opposed to the idea of progress, technological or otherwise, altogether?

Interesting syntax pattern in these lines. Thoreau includes four questions, but slides his conclusion in between the third and fourth.

Extended metaphor with references to "sleepers" and "sleep." As a whole, the passage moves from being awake at the beginning to a state of sleep at the end. Perhaps it is technology that creates man's "sleepiness" because he is busied by constant work.

notice word play, recognize motifs, and synthesize meaning with whatever thoughts and experiences you're bringing to the table, whenever you can. Below is an example of Knee-Jerk annotation on a short passage from the second chapter of Henry David Thoreau's *Walden* (1854) to give some sense of what these notations should look like in both scope and content.

The above annotations focus on a variety of concerns: author's purpose, emergent patterns, underlying ideas, key words and phrases. None of these notes are codified or systematized, yet they are still performing a vital role in the task of rhetorical reading. Knee-Jerk annotations give space to the reader to expand, intensify, or interrogate a text – to make the text one's own. The real gain of this method is element of self-generation involved; the insights into the text come through a process which *you* must come up with the main insights, and *you* must develop these insights in light of the text at hand. But more than this: Knee-Jerk annotations are a way to take your first steps in the direction of a dialogic stance toward writing – a stance that acknowledges, as Bakhtin may have said, "everything is prompted by and preparing for some other utterance" – in a non-threatening way. These notes are the ice-breaker in the conversation. To flesh this dialogue out, let's look to our next model of annotation.

Four-Fold Marginalia

The procedure below – adapted from Mary Goldschmidt's "Marginalia: Teaching Texts, Teaching Readers, Teaching Writers" (2010) – asks you to balance far more rhetorical variables than Knee-Jerk annotations by adding some structure and focus. As the left-to-right flow of the chart below indicates, Goldschmidt's system compartmentalizes annotations into "types" which are both multi-dimensional (reading with different purposes in mind) and scaffolded (where comprehension leads to evaluation, which leads to extension, which leads to rhetorical analysis), letting you focus on a text with discrete analytical purposes in mind each time you read (see Table 1).

Below is an example of Four-Fold Marginalia annotation performed on William Faulkner's "Nobel Prize Address" delivered in Stockholm, Sweden (1950).

Where students respond to the text should tell the teacher – and themselves – something about the way they have oriented themselves towards the reading. What's neat about this method is that while two (or more) readers may focus on the same portion of a text, their responses to

Table 1 Categorized Concerns for Four-Fold Marginalia.

On a first read, make	Using your comprehension notes, make	Using your comprehension and interactive/evaluative notes, make	Using your comprehension, interactive/evaluative, and extending notes, make
Comprehension Notes which are marginal comments that summarize or paraphrase:	**Interactive/ Evaluative Notes** which are marginal comments that question, analyze, criticize, praise, agree or disagree with:	**Extending Notes** which are marginal comments that go beyond the text and:	**Rhetorical Notes** which are marginal comments that examine:
– The main argument/ thesis – An example the author uses – Patterns in the type of evidence (reliance on anecdotes/ scientific findings/ historical fact, etc.) – What makes a particular line/ passage important – A contradiction or contrast that you've noticed	– The author's idea(s) – The author's writing style/structural decisions in the text – The author's word choice – The author's logic, examples, or evidence – The author's analysis – The author's assumptions – The author's methodology	– Offer an alternative explanation/updated example/analogy to ones stated in the passage – Offer additional or contradictory evidence – Pose new questions that the text doesn't directly address – React emotionally to the author's style, tone, or substance – Make a connection with your extra-textual knowledge (experience)	– How the author attends to, or fails to attend to, the audience's needs – The effect of the text of the immediate vs. mediated audience – The author's ethos ("good will,""good sense," and/or "virtue") – The author's patterns of reasoning in the text (logos) – The author's appeal to the audience's emotions (pathos) – The exigence which brought forth the text – The rhetorical constraints held by the author/audience

the text (via the Marginalia categories) will likely be dramatically different, allowing for a totally new dimension of the text to open up. The quotes you choose, and how your respond to them, are essential to your developing inquiry since, as Don Bialostosky says in *Liberal Education: Writing and the Dialogic Self* (1991), "quotation is the very act in which one voice creatively absorbs another and defines it in relation to that second voice. When we interrupt the quoted text, interrogate it, clarify its point, or expose its ambiguities, we make an opening for our own utterances and give it shape to our own roles in the conversation." You will likely discover meanings or allusions that other readers have missed – it happens all the time – and such a perception of oneself as a reader is empowering and will contribute to how you may make up your mind about the text you hold in your hands.

Interactive/evaluative: These lines contain a metaphorical representation of the subject matter for enduring art which is presented in a very Faulknerian sentence, a style that notoriously trips up even the most careful of readers who've had even a momentary lapse in attention. Readers must trust that in Faulkner's prose, there's always there's a subject doing doing it to some object. So, the question here becomes, "what is 'created out of the materials of the human spirit'?" The answer is "work," Faulkner's literary art, and once the reader tracks down this sentence's subject. Good art is figured from those things in the human experience that are ever-true, ever-relevant, or as Samuel Johnson may have said, "things that are not for an age but for all time."

Extending: In context, Faulkner's quotation "there are no longer problems of the spirit" is saying that spirituality - while crucially important to the production of enduring art and a fulfilling human life - has been subverted by basic fears for survival. Faulkner is living in the early years of the Nuclear Age and the relentless threat of being "blown up" has rendered art and the artist into a useless state. Would you rack your brain to compose contemplative and reflective art if you may die at any second? Faulkner recognizes this to be not just a crisis for the artist, but as an existential threat for all of humanity. To be preoccupied with just trying to get by to the next day is, for Faulkner, no different than living like an animal.

I feel that this award was not made to me as a man, but to my work - a life's work in the agony and sweat of the human spirit, not for glory and least of all for profit, but to create out of the materials of the human spirit something which did not exist before. So this award is only mine in trust. It will not be difficult to find a dedication for the money part of it commensurate with the purpose and significance of its origin. But I would like to do the same with the acclaim too, by using this moment as a pinnacle from which I might be listened to by the young men and women already dedicated to the same anguish and travail, among whom is already that one who will someday stand here where I am standing.

Our tragedy today is a general and universal physical fear so long sustained by now that we can even bear it. There are no longer problems of the spirit. There is only the question: When will I be blown up? Because of this, the young man or woman writing today has forgotten the problems of the human heart in conflict with itself which alone can make good writing because only that is worth writing about, worth the agony and the sweat. He must learn them again. He must teach himself that the basest of all things is to be afraid; and, teaching himself that, forget it forever, leaving no room in his workshop for anything but the old verities and truths of the heart, the old universal truths lacking which any story is ephemeral and doomed - love and honor and pity and pride and compassion and sacrifice. Until he does so, he labors under a curse. He writes not of love but of lust, of defeats in which nobody loses anything of value, of victories without hope and, worst of all, without pity or compassion. His griefs grieve on no universal bones, leaving no scars. He writes not of the heart but of the glands.

Until he relearns these things, he will write as though he stood among and watched the end of man. I decline to accept the end of man. It is easy enough to say that man is immortal simply because he will endure: that when the last dingdong of doom has clanged and faded from the last worthless rock hanging tideless in the last red and dying evening, that even then there will still be one more sound: that of his puny inexhaustible voice, still talking. I refuse to accept this. I believe that man will not merely endure: he will prevail. He is immortal, not because he alone among creatures has an inexhaustible voice, but because he has a soul, a spirit capable of compassion and sacrifice and endurance. The poet's, the writer's, duty is to write about these things. It is his privilege to help man endure by lifting his heart, by reminding him of the courage and honor and hope and pride and compassion and pity and sacrifice which have been the glory of his past. The poet's voice need not merely be the record of man, it can be one of the props, the pillars to help him endure and prevail.

Comprehension: At the beginning of this speech, Faulkner suggests that art supersedes the artist, a powerful statement about the role art plays in society. Art (literature in Faulkner's case) is so important in shaping direction of human affairs that even the producer of the art becomes inconsequential to what's produced. For Faulkner, literature is important - indispensable, really - in the development of the entire individual (micro) and society (macro) because it reminds us what is right, true, and eternal. The opening line foregrounds this idea clearly by deemphasizing himself (artist) in comparison to his work (art).

Rhetorical Analysis: Faulkner only asks one pathos-laden question in the entire address, "When will I be blown up?" and this line succinctly captures the anxiety of what it must have been like to live at the dawn of the Nuclear Age. Faulkner's personal uneasiness can be clearly inferred from these lines, but he's not just talking about himself. The emotion of this line is presented from the perspective in the manner of a "royal we," a style where the pronouns represent more than the speaker who uses them. His anxiety is the anxiety of the average man in the modern world and it's not mistake that this emotion I couched in the form of a question, a locution which suggests uncertainty and the unknown. More than this, the question is placed in the central paragraph of the three in the speech, thereby suggesting this bit of pathos is of central concern to his contemporaries.

This Marginalia exercise is also useful as a bridge to class discussion about a text. Discussing the varied and nuanced readings that each reader brings to the table invites the group to "assimilate new ideas, to accommodate others' opinions and experiences, and to develop deeper, fuller perspectives from which to examine what they read and write, and this subsequent talk will help the knowledge to flow in new directions," a concept noted in Hephzibah Roskelly's *Breaking (into) the Circle* (2003). In other words, such a conversation may stoke further ideas and give the reader a more perspectival view of the text itself disavowing the idea that there is one set, stable answer that you ought to have decoded. Here is where dialogue and the dialogic begin to overlap.

Text Travelogue

Another useful WTL inquiry exercise comes from composition scholar Paul Heilker's *The Essay: Theory and Pedagogy for an Active Form* (1996). This adapted version of Heilker's free-writing "travelogue" exercise assumes prior knowledge in Four-Fold Marginalia terminology but takes the level of articulation a few steps further. This method, couched in accessible metaphors of travel and tourism, gives space for objective ("objective snapshots") and subjective ("subjective snapshots") observations of a text on a first read. Heilker notes that this method is instrumental in his own classroom research practices since it creates "a script for each student that documents how his or her thinking developed over time in dialogic interaction and integration with other voices." Consider some of the guiding questions

Table 2 Guidelines for "Travelogue" Annotations.

Take an objective "Snapshot"	Take a subjective "Snapshot"
For five minutes, free-write on what you learned about the topic that was presented in the text.	For five minutes, free-write on what you think and feel about what you've learned about the topic that was presented in the text.
You should want to think in terms of "Comprehension Notes" and "Interactive/Evaluative Notes" from the "marginalia" activity.	You should want to think in terms of "Extending Notes" and "Rhetorical Notes" from the "marginalia" activity

Objective snapshot: Carnegie's personal wealth is well-known, but what's less well-known is the position he takes on how wealth can be used for social good. In the opening line, he acknowledges that the wealthy elite have used wealth as the instrument of oppression and personal indulgence ("The problem of our age is the proper administration of wealth") but asserts that basic human bonds – from one person to another – should be the glue that forms the basis of a functional society. The assumption in the opening line, then, is that human connections are the foundation of any functional society.

In a piece titled "The Gospel of Wealth," it makes sense that the way in which Carnegie measures a good life is by "commodities." It's easy to misread this position as an advocacy for blind consumerism or even greed. He justifies his picture of societal progress along the lines that, what's benefits the greatest number of individual's basic needs – food, clothing, shelter – is what is good and proper for society.

In the final two paragraphs of his piece, Carnegie moves from messages of promise to ones of caution. After a string of optimistic statements about how "The poor enjoy what the rich could not before afford" and "what were the luxuries have become the necessaries of life," Carnegie follows with a thunderous transition in the opening line of paragraph 4: "The price we pay for this salutary change is, no doubt, great" (line 59). In the subsequent lines, he details a variety of cautions – income inequality, class warfare, etc. – and concludes his piece on a note of trepidation.

The problem of our age is the proper administration of wealth, that the ties of brotherhood may still bind together the rich and poor in harmonious relationship. The conditions of human life have not only been changed, but revolutionized, within the past few hundred years. In former days there was little difference between the dwelling, dress, food, and environment of the chief and those of his retainers. The Indians are to-day where civilized man then was. When visiting the Sioux, I was led to the wigwam of the chief. It was like the others in external appearance, and even within the difference was trifling between it and those of the poorest of his braves. The contrast between the palace of the millionaire and the cottage of the laborer with us to-day measures the change which has come with civilization. This change, however, is not to be deplored, but welcomed as highly beneficial. It--is well, nay, essential, for the progress of the race that the houses of some should be homes for all that is highest and best in literature and the arts, and for all the refinements of civilization, rather than that none should be so. Much better this great irregularity than universal squalor. Without wealth there can be no Maecenas. The "good old times" were not good old times. Neither master nor servant was as well situated then as to-day. A relapse to old conditions would be disastrous to both-not the least so to him who serves-and would sweep away civilization with it. But whether the change be for good or ill, it is upon us, beyond our power to alter, and, therefore, to be accepted and made the best of. It is a waste of time to criticize the inevitable.

To-day the world obtains commodities of excellent quality at prices which even the preceding generation would have deemed incredible. In the commercial world similar causes have produced similar results, and the race is benefited thereby. The poor enjoy hat the rich could not before afford. What were the luxuries have become the necessaries of life. The laborer has now more comforts than the farmer had a few generations ago. The farmer has more luxuries than the landlord had, and is more richly clad and better housed. The landlord has books and pictures rarer and appointments more artistic than the king could then obtain. The price we pay for this salutary change is, no doubt, great.

We assemble thousands of operatives in the factory, and in the mine, of whom the employer can know little or nothing, and to whom he is little better than a myth. All intercourse between them is at an end. Rigid castes are formed, and, as usual, mutual ignorance breeds mutual distrust. Each caste is without sympathy with the other, and ready to credit anything disparaging in regard to it. Under the law of competition, the employer of thousands is forced into the strictest economies, among which the rates paid to labor figure prominently, and often there is friction between the employer and the employed, between capital and labor, between rich and poor. Human society loses homogeneity.

Subjective snapshot: From his belief that the social inequality is "inevitable" to statements like "much better this great irregularity [in wealth] than universal squalor" and "a relapse to old conditions would be disastrous," it is interesting to see how Carnegie, for all his philanthropic messages, is a proponent of social hierarchy and division. In other words, Carnegie argues (or rationalizes?) how social inequality is a marker of progress, and why such progress should be seen as universally beneficial. He thinks that if aristocrats go from 10 to 11 while commoners only go from 1 to 2, everyone is still better off than they were before. Of course, since Carnegie is speaking from a position of power, he supports this "progress" insofar as it doesn't disrupt the status quo of his own power and authority.

Carnegie characterizes the progress of society as inexorable – "beyond our power to alter" – and that we can only hope to make the best of the hand we are dealt. Carnegie's sociological determinism (a fancy way of saying that social progress is fated to happen) is the assumption that holds together the closing line of paragraph 1.

This idea is furthered when he refers to competition as a "law." Carnegie's diction choice of "law" suggests that competition fostered by Capitalism – with all of its consequences – is a fixed a predictable system. The paragraph in which this phrase appears is all written in the affirmative mode without any qualifiers whatsoever. This style choice reflects Carnegie's assuredness that society does indeed experience consequences – to the benefit of some and to the destruction of others – for its competitive economic system, yet these outcomes are both knowable and able to be anticipated. And if these complex processes are knowable by him, Carnegie implies that he can somehow see what the rest of us cannot, an affirmation of his social superiority.

that you may use as you walk over the landscape of a text in Heilker's terms (see Table 2).

The previous page contains an example of a Text Travelogue exercise in response to an excerpt from Andrew Carnegie's essay "The Gospel of Wealth" (1889) which was originally published in *North American Review*.

Text Travelogue writing is tied to the text, but not to the degree of the other two models seen so far in this chapter. Quoting is the salt and pepper of composition, and I've found as a teacher that many composition students tend to have a one-track mind when it comes to quotes, thinking of them as little more than backup for what's said in the paper and unable to work outside this paradigm. As such, annotation exercises which cut the reader off from the text a bit more tend to cause frustration. Since the handling of quotes in the Text Travelogue is only part of it, perhaps think of your responses, noted by Joseph Harris's *Rewriting* (2006), as "recirculating the author's writing, highlighting parts of the texts for the consideration of others" as a way to put a personal stamp on the ideas presented by the author.

Some students enjoy this method of response since it allows a reader to freely play with the ideas and write more fully and coherently about what's been read. Ann Berthoff clarifies this notion in *Forming, Thinking, Writing* (1989), referring to this type of work as "forming activities." On student-driven WTL exercises, she notes, "to observe carefully, to think cogently, to write coherently, these are all forming activities. If you consider the composing process as a continuum of forming, then you can take advantage of the fact that you are born a composer...You can discard the faulty notice that when you compose you 'figure out what you want to say before you write', and accept instead this more helpful slogan: you can't know what you mean until you hear what you say."

The P.A.P.A. (Parallel Analytical Paraphrase Annotation)

A P.A.P.A. (Parallel Analytical Paraphrase Annotation) is another form of annotation, one that draws a sharp distinction between the content and the form of a text. In this type of analysis, you must always consider what the author's words are *doing* and the strategies the author uses to achieve this effect (see Figure 2). It demands that you think about how language functions, a dimension that is distinct from what language says, as you separate the content of a text (what is being said) from the form of a text (how is it being said) to write about what you see. Grappling with the difference between the content and the function/form of a text as represented by its language is one of the deepest critical thinking exercises a reader can engage in. While distinguishing between form and content may seem daunting, it is a useful tool during close reading and analysis of text that becomes easier with practice.

But here's the added challenge. In a P.A.P.A., you need to be as equally aware of what your own words are doing as you are of the author's. Each action verb you decide to include in your annotation must

Words to describe what an author is *doing:*	
indicts	cites
provides	contradicts
describes	exemplifies
underscores	develops
elevates	introduces
repeats	concludes
narrates	transitions
highlights	supports
acknowledges	synthesizes
clarifies	satirizes

Figure 2 Action Verbs for P.A.P.A. Analysis.

reflect a rhetorical move that is being made in the writing. This means that you, the annotator, must be very careful with how things are said, paying very close attention to your own diction and syntax choices. You'll find that annotations in this form will be as long, if not longer, than the piece you are putting under scrutiny. As in any good piece of writing, there should no wasted words in these types of annotations. Each verb should be mindfully selected and deliberately placed into the architecture of the write-up. Take a look at the example P.A.P.A below. These entries represent a P.A.P.A. analysis for four paragraphs of Anthony Esolen's short essay "Dog Eared Pursuits" (2005). Each paragraph of text is accompanied by a P.A.P.A. entry.

The highlighted terms in the below P.A.P.A. entries demonstrate how the annotator perceives what Esolen's words are doing. In all sentences of the entry paragraphs, you should notice how each and every verb reflects a rhetorical move of the author. The annotator pays close attention to how the language in the source text functions, and these example entries should demonstrate how a P.A.P.A. can focus a reader into ideas that are deeply submerged in a text. An author's language is always related to *how* they convey his/her thesis, central idea, claim or proposition. So, as you read, think to yourself, "what is the author's central idea and what specific moments in the text contribute to this argument"? When performing a P.A.P.A., you may want to utilize some of the words from the Figure 2 above to describe what the author is *doing* with his language choices.

Source Text	P.A.P.A. Entry

When I was a boy, if you read at age four, you were a genius, but there were things more important than reading. You could poke a stick in the sand of a ditch. You could crush a rock against the concrete to draw pictures. Recess was the heart of school, as play and not work is the heart of life. I'm a man now, surrounded by books, sentenced to sentences, yet the rebellious boy in me rises up now and then to whip them back to their dens. Why should that rebel read? What is the point?

The author initially *acknowledges* the importance of reading but *concedes* that other activities exceed its importance. His examples *contradict* his initial claim; they are simple activities that include simple objects, a stick and a rock. The author *asserts* his claim in the center of this paragraph: "play and not work is the heart of life" which *clarifies* to the opening paradox. He *shifts* verb tense to the present and *explains* a tension, "I'm a man now, surrounded by books, sentenced by sentences" while "the rebellious boy in me rises up now and then." He *concludes* his introduction with a series of questions. These questions *generate* interest for the information in the following paragraphs.

We have assumed that unless you read, you are not intelligent, you are not educable, you are not college material, you will not be well paid, you are not worth paying attention to. So it is that our effeminate silliness dances merrily along with an iron and unappeasable snobbery.

The author *includes* himself with the reader, through the collective pronoun "we," into a common assumption, "that unless you read, you are not intelligent." He *provides* examples of this misconception and then *illustrates* them with a string of parallel syntactic arrangements ("you are not…" is *repeated* five consecutive times). He then *equates* this thinking to "silliness" and "unappeasable snobbery."

No one burns books nowadays. Burning books is an exciting and public thing, providing a great bonfire and opportunities for brawling. We do things in a more civilized way. Libraries themselves purge books; they quietly deposit them on a cart, twenty-five cents apiece, and, after a week or two, send them down the memory hole: that is, throw them into a dumpster, whence they will go to have their pages pecked at by seagulls at the landfill. Then we replace them with the readerly equivalent of padded cells and leashes, nice books that say whatever moronisms happen to be popular.

The author *contrasts* past forms of censorship against modern ones. He *elevates* the old style of book burning and *indicts* modern methods of book removal. The exciting imagery of book burning ("providing a great bonfire and an opportunity for brawling"), alongside the unceremonious disposal of books from modern libraries, *highlights* the author's feelings on the issue. He, then, *equates* modern literature to "padded cells and leashes," both symbols of confinement and restraint. He *coins* the word "moronisms"; this *underscores* his tone towards modern writing.

We replace them with gaudy picture books about a character on a television show for children, a large effete grape named Bernie or Benny or whatever, or about a girl who hits home runs in the major leagues, or a witch who was a good witch despite the mean old people who thought she was bad; or, for older kids, about Mindy in the boutique with Chad, or about some narcissistic troubled teenager and his more appalling mother. There is no prison like a book.

The author *constructs* this paragraph into only two sentences. The first sentence *exemplifies* modern examples of bad literature through intentionally vague language. This *veils* the allusion. He *references* well known icons such as Barney ("a large effete grape named Bernie or Benny") and Gregory Maguire's parallel novel *Wicked* ("a witch who was a good witch despite the mean old people who thought she was bad") to *cite* examples of worthless literature. The short length of the second sentence, in contrast to the first, *highlights* the prominence of its message. It *underscores* the overarching idea of the previous two paragraphs.

Trying any of these notation systems, alone or in combination, will help to reveal the rhetorical underpinnings of a text which often go unnoticed by a reader's eyes. Knowing how to properly establish a dialogue with a text is to know how to, in your mind's ear, hear the "sounds" of thought, its swift attacks, its stately progresses, its cuts and turns, its imposing stands.

CHAPTER FOUR

WRITING AN ANALYTICAL ESSAY

In her essay "Teaching Writing as Process" (2002), Davida Charney notes that even though "academic writing is seldom easy and there is no one right way to write, some approaches are more reliable than others. Many students who have serious problems with analytical writing rely on overly-rigid processes, ones that focus attention on low-level concerns at inappropriate times. Nothing is wrong with the approaches in-and-of-themselves, except that they have been transformed from helpful hints (or heuristics) into what composition scholar Mike Rose has termed 'rigid rules.'" Charney cites three of the most common false-starts in her classroom. In her words:

- Some students adopt a "perfect first draft strategy," believing that the text must emerge grammatically and in order from first sentence to last. They paralyze themselves agonizing over the first sentence or paragraph and then pull an all-nighter before the paper is due. If they are tired and desperate enough, sometimes the muse appears, and several pages spill out. Because the text finally "flows easily," it must be good.
- Some students strain to make their essays conform to some idealized structure (e.g. "the five-paragraph essay"), leaving out ideas that don't fit and adding filler if they don't have three text-based examples to round out this pre-fabricated mold. When thoughts are poured into a mold

like this, the writing often turns to cardboard: predictable, bland, and characterless.

- Some students treat the texts they read as absolutely authoritative and understand their role to be a mere compiler and reporter on this received wisdom. If they find conflicting accounts in their reading, they artificially harmonize them rather than engaging in interpretation or critique. When asked to defend a position to an audience that might disagree with them, they find it difficult to establish shared values or to treat alternative values as legitimate.

Charney's essay articulates something that most student-writers already know: the two biggest concerns at the heart of writing – *what* to say and *how* to say it – are tough intellectual work. Reading rhetorically, a skill covered in the previous three chapters, is a tried-and-true means of invention that addresses the former. The situation that calls forth a text (exigence), the interaction between speaker, subject, and audience (the rhetorical triangle), the way writer establishes tone and credibility (ethos), the text's pattern of development (logos), the arousal of feelings in the hearts of the audience (pathos), word choice (diction), and sentence structure (syntax) are all generative places to kick off the eventual essay you plan to write. But once you've figured of *what* to say (invention), you must now consider *how* you are going to say it (arrangement). This chapter's method follows from what's known as the Stage-Model theory, a dominant concept of writing that breaks the composing process into sequential stages: prewriting, writing, rewriting. Having dominated the composition classroom since the 1960s, its simple, three-part schema is accessible to both novice and experts alike, while still open-ended enough to remain adaptable for a variety of writing tasks. The chapter's running example illustrates these virtues by highlighting the crosswalks between the receptive (reading) and productive (writing) processes that are so essential to college-level writing.

Invention for an Analytical Essay

Any rhetorical analysis essay worth reading must be underwritten by three foundational questions:

What is the author trying to accomplish? How does he accomplish it? What is the effect of these choices?

Whatever process of pre-writing takes place (Knee-Jerk Annotations, Four-Fold Marginalia, Text Travelogue, PAPA Analysis, or something else), you must square yourself with answers to these questions before any writing can begin. Doing so will cultivate a thoughtful and patient approach to critical reading that will make visible the multiple forms, viewpoints, and tactics present in complex texts to help you gather perspective prior to arriving at your own writing, writing that is now more situated in the discourse of the subject. Let's take an example to see how this works. Consider the following pair of passages from Jonathan Edwards's "Sinners in the Hands of an Angry God" (1741) and James Van Tholen's "Surprised by Death" from *Where all Hope Lies* (2003). In each, the speaker outlines his relationship towards God and how their respective congregations can come to gain spiritual knowledge and self-understanding through his personal experiences. As you read, see how each author uses rhetorical strategies to communicate their respective understanding of God while noting the dramatically different effect of these strategies on the audience.

"Sinners in the Hands of an Angry God" Jonathan Edwards, 1741	"Surprised by Death" from *Where All Hope Lies* James Van Tholen, 2003
The use may be of awakening to unconverted persons in this congregation. This that you have heard is the case of every one of you that are out of Christ. That world of misery, that lake of burning brimstone is extended abroad under you. There is the dreadful pit of the glowing flames of the wrath of God; there is hell's wide gaping mouth open; and you have nothing to stand upon, nor anything to take hold of: there is nothing between you and hell but the air; 'tis only the power and mere pleasure of God that holds you up.	This is a strange day – for all of us. Most of you know that today marks my return to this pulpit after seven months of dealing with an aggressive and deadly form of cancer. Now, with the cancer vacationing for a little while, I am back. And of course, I'm glad to be back. But I can't help feeling how strange this day is – especially because I want to ignore my absence, and I want to pretend everybody has forgotten the reason for it. But we can't do that. We can't ignore what has happened. We can rise

You probably are not sensible of this; you find you are kept out of hell, but don't see the hand of God in it, but look at other things, as the good state of your bodily constitution, your care of your own life, and the means you use for your own preservation. But indeed these things are nothing; if God should withdraw his hand, they would avail no more to keep you from falling, than the thin air to hold up a person that is suspended in it.

Your wickedness makes you as it were heavy as lead, and to tend downwards with great weight and pressure towards hell; and if God should let you go, you would immediately sink and swiftly descend and plunge into the bottomless gulf, and your healthy constitution, and your own care and prudence, and best contrivance, and all your righteousness, would have no more influence to uphold you and keep you out of hell, than a spider's web would have to stop a falling rock. Were it not that so is the sovereign pleasure of God, the earth would not bear you one moment; for you are a burden to it; the creation groans with you; the creature is made subject to the bondage of your corruption, not willingly; the sun don't willingly shine upon you to give you light to serve sin and Satan; the earth don't willingly yield her increase to satisfy your lusts; nor is it willingly a stage

above it; we can live through it; but we can't ignore it. If we ignore the threat of death as too terrible to talk about, then the threat wins. Then we are overwhelmed by it, and our faith doesn't apply to it. And if that happens, we lose hope.

We want to worship God in this church, and for our worship to be real, it doesn't have to be fun, and it doesn't have to be guilt-ridden. But it does have to be honest, and it does have to hope in God. We have to be honest about a world of violence and pain, a world that scorns faith and smashes hope and rebuts love. We have to be honest about the world, and honest about the difficulties of faith within it. And then we still have to hope in God.

So let me start with the honesty. The truth is that for seven months I have been scared. Not of the cancer, not really. Not even of death. Dying is another matter – how long it will take and how it will go. Dying scares me. But when I say that I have been scared, I don't mean that my thoughts have centered on dying. My real fear has centered somewhere else. Strange as it may sound, I have been scared of meeting God.

How could this be so? How could I have believed in the God of grace and still have dreaded to meet him? Why did I stand in this pulpit for your wickedness to be acted upon; the air don't willingly serve you for breath to maintain the flame of life in your vitals, while you spend your life in the service of God's enemies. God's creatures are good, and were made for men to serve God with, and don't willingly subserve to any other purpose, and groan when they are abused to purposes so directly contrary to their nature and end.

And the world would spew you out, were it not for the sovereign hand of him who hath subjected it in hope. There are the black clouds of God's wrath now hanging directly over your heads, full of the dreadful storm, and big with thunder; and were it not for the restraining hand of God it would immediately burst forth upon you. The sovereign pleasure of God for the present stays his rough wind; otherwise it would come with fury, and your destruction would come like a whirlwind, and you would be like the chaff of the summer threshing floor.

The wrath of God is like great waters that are dammed for the present; they increase more and more, and rise higher and higher, till an outlet is given, and the longer the stream is stopped, the more rapid and mighty is its course, when once it is let loose. 'Tis true, that judgment against your evil works has not been executed hitherto; the floods of God's

and preach grace to you over and over, and then, when I myself needed the grace so much, why did I discover fear where the grace should have been?

God comes to us before we go to him. John Timmer used to say that this is God's habit. God came to Abraham when there was nothing to come to, just an old man at a dead end.

But that's God for you. That's the way God likes to work. He comes to old men and to infants, to sinners and to losers. That's grace, and a sermon without it is no sermon at all.

So, I've tried to preach grace, to fill my sermons up with grace, to persuade you to believe in grace. And it's wonderful work to have – that is, to stand here and preach grace to people. I got into this pulpit and talked about war and homosexuality and divorce. I talked about death before I knew what death really was. And I tried to bring the gospel of grace to these areas when I preached. I said that God goes to people in trouble, that God receives people in trouble, that God is a God who gets into trouble because of his grace. I said what our Heidelberg Catechism says: that our only comfort in life and in death is that we are not our own but belong to our faithful Savior, Jesus Christ.

vengeance have been withheld; but your guilt in the meantime is constantly increasing, and you are every day treasuring up more wrath; the waters are continually rising and waxing more and more mighty; and there is nothing but the mere pleasure of God that holds the waters back that are unwilling to be stopped, and press hard to go forward; if God should only withdraw his hand from the floodgate, it would immediately fly open, and the fiery floods of the fierceness and wrath of God would rush forth with inconceivable fury, and would come upon you with omnipotent power; and if your strength were ten thousand times greater than it is, yea ten thousand times greater than the strength of the stoutest, sturdiest devil in hell, it would be nothing to withstand or endure it.

Thus are all you that never passed under a great change of heart, by the mighty power of the Spirit of God upon your souls; all that were never born again, and made new creatures, and raised from being dead in sin, to a state of new, and before altogether unexperienced light and life (however you may have reformed your life in many things, and may have had religious affections, and may keep up a form of religion in your families and closets, and in the house of God, and may be strict in it), you are thus in the hands of an angry God; 'tis

I said all those things, and I meant them. But that was before I faced death myself. So now I have a silly thing to admit: I don't think I ever realized the shocking and radical nature of God's grace – even as I preached it. And the reason I didn't get it where grace is concerned, I think, is that I assumed I still had about forty years left. Forty years to unlearn my bad habits. Forty years to let my sins thin down and blow away. Forty years to be good to animals and pick up my neighbors' mail for them when they went on vacation.

So please don't be surprised when in the days ahead I don't talk about my cancer very often. I've told a part of my story today, because it seemed right to do it on the first day back after seven months. But what we must talk about here is not me. I cannot be our focus, because the center of my story – our story – is that the grace of Jesus Christ carries us beyond every cancer, every divorce, every sin, every trouble that comes to us. The Christian gospel is the story of Jesus, and that's the story I'm called to tell.

I'm dying. Maybe it will take longer instead of shorter; maybe I'll preach for several months, and maybe for a bit more. But I am dying. I know it, and I hate it, and I'm still frightened by it. But there is hope, unwavering hope. I have hope not in something I've done, some purity nothing but his mere pleasure that keeps you from being this moment swallowed up in everlasting destruction.

I've maintained, or some sermon I've written. I hope in God – the God who reaches out for an enemy, saves a sinner, dies for the weak.

That's the gospel, and I can stake my life on it. I must. And so must you.

Step 1: What is the author trying to accomplish?

This first step answers the question of "*What* is the author writing about?"

Each author essentially writes about the same subject, God, yet the understanding of and relationship towards this shared subject is fundamentally different for each speaker in almost every regard. The God of Edwards's sermon metes out justice to the hard-hearted sinners of his congregation in typical Great Awakening, "fire-and-brimstone" fashion. The grim, oppressive majesty of this God is presented in the most inventive conceivable way – Edwards is not working from any type of tradition but rather generates these pathos-laden images from some well deep within his own imagination. James Van Tholen paints quite a different picture. His God is not wrathful, but loving; not transcendent, but imminent; not punitive, but enlightening. It is through his own brush-with-death – an aggressive course of chemotherapy for cancer in his chest wall – that Van Tholen comes to understand the fragility of life and the transcendent mercy of God.

Step 2: How does he accomplish it?

This second step addresses the question of "*Where* in the text does the author support his purpose?"

Edward's highly charged message is delivered through several rhetorical moves:

- ○ Ethos: Edwards levels accusations *at* his congregation and, thus, does not include his own transgressions into his pathos-laden speech. This distinction is expressed through Edwards's use of second person pronouns ("you") scattered throughout the sermon:

- Paragraph 2: "<u>You</u> probably are not sensible of this; <u>you</u> find <u>you</u> are kept out of hell, but don't see the hand of God in it, but look at other things, as the good state of <u>your</u> bodily constitution, <u>your</u> care of your own life, and the means <u>you</u> use for <u>your</u> own preservation."

- Paragraph 3: "<u>Your</u> wickedness makes <u>you</u> as it were heavy as lead, and to tend downwards with great weight and pressure towards hell; and if God should let you go, <u>you</u> would immediately sink and swiftly descend and plunge into the bottomless gulf, and your healthy constitution, and <u>your</u> own care and prudence, and best contrivance, and all <u>your</u> righteousness, would have no more influence to uphold <u>you</u> and keep <u>you</u> out of hell"

  ○ <u>Repetition:</u> Edwards calls up images of hell – and the sinner's proximity to it – through the syntactical repetition of "that"/"there"/"you" clauses. These reverberate through the entire sermon:

  - Paragraph 1: "<u>That</u> world of misery, <u>that</u> lake of burning brimstone is extended abroad under you. <u>There</u> is the dreadful pit of the glowing flames of the wrath of God; <u>there</u> is hell's wide gaping mouth open; and <u>you</u> have nothing to stand upon, nor anything to take hold of: <u>there</u> is nothing between <u>you</u> and hell but the air; 'tis only the power and mere pleasure of God that holds you up."

  ○ <u>Unqualified/absolute diction:</u> Through the confident use of the verbs "is" and "are," Edwards speaks with a sure-footed conviction of Hell's existence and the sinner's eventual residency there should they not amend their behavior:

  - Paragraph 3: "There <u>are</u> the black clouds of God's wrath now hanging directly over your heads."

  - Paragraph 4: "…the waters <u>are</u> continually rising and waxing more and more mighty; and there <u>is</u> nothing but the mere pleasure of God that holds the waters back that <u>are</u> unwilling to be stopped."

- Paragraph 5: "you <u>are</u> thus in the hands of an angry God; 'tis nothing but his mere pleasure that keeps you from being this moment swallowed up in everlasting destruction."

Van Tholen patterns his sermon along a similar set of strategies but with some degree of variance in how they are expressed:

- <u>Ethos:</u> Van Tholen's sermon is built upon a strong speaker/ audience foundation. He consistently identifies and includes himself with his audience through first person plural pronouns:
  - Paragraph 2: "But <u>we</u> can't do that. <u>We</u> can't ignore what has happened. <u>We</u> can rise above it; <u>we</u> can live through it; but we can't ignore it. If <u>we</u> ignore the threat of death as too terrible to talk about, then the threat wins. Then <u>we</u> are overwhelmed by it, and our faith doesn't apply to it. And if that happens, <u>we</u> lose hope."
  - Paragraph 10: "I cannot be <u>our</u> focus, because the center of my story – <u>our</u> story – is that the grace of Jesus Christ carries <u>us</u> beyond every cancer, every divorce, every sin, every trouble that comes to <u>us</u>."
- <u>Repetition:</u> Van Tholen's sermon has a number of sonic features, chief among them is the use of anaphora (repetition at the beginning of successive phrases or clauses) to drive home the central ideas:
  - Paragraph 9: "And the reason I didn't get it where grace is concerned, I think, is that I assumed I still had about forty years left. <u>Forty years</u> to unlearn my bad habits. <u>Forty years</u> to let my sins thin down and blow away. <u>Forty years</u> to be good to animals and pick up my neighbors' mail for them when they went on vacation."
- <u>Abstract and concrete diction:</u> Van Tholen's sermon transitions between abstract reflections and concrete experiences signaled by the coordinating conjunction "but":
  - Paragraph 1: "<u>But</u> I can't help feeling how strange this day is – especially because I want to ignore my absence, and I want to pretend everybody has forgotten the reason for it."

- ▪ Paragraph 2: "<u>But</u> we can't do that. We can't ignore what has happened."
- ▪ Paragraph 9: "I said all those things, and I meant them. <u>But</u> that was before I faced death myself."

Step 3: *What is the effect of these choices?*

This third step addresses the question of *"How* do these rhetorical choices create an effect?"

The following observations drive at the "why" and "how" concerns of the observations above, moving the intellectual work from a realm of identification to one of analysis and commentary.

- ○ <u>Ethos:</u> Coercive and aggressive in his delivery, Edwards does not borrow from the "shared plight" angle of Van Tholen but instead establishes himself as an unquestionable authority on the subject of God's wrath. By repeatedly referring to his audience as "you," he sets himself outside of his indictments, thereby annihilating the "everyman" ethos that Van Tholen so heavily relies upon. Van Tholen's soft-spoken and humble tone is due in large part to the way he handles the speaker-audience relationship. Through the use of plural pronouns, Van Tholen illustrates the wider implications of his direct experience to that of the congregation, thus joining their experience with his own. Jonathan Edwards also speaks with passion, but one that is markedly different from Van Tholen's.
- ○ <u>Repetition:</u> Edwards uses repetition to stress the urgency of his message. His syntax – specifically in the alternations of "that," "there," "you" clauses – calls up an immediate vision of hell and its proximity to the unconverted. God is wrathful, yes, but not merciless. In fact, Edward's repeated references to God's mercy ("you find you are kept out of hell, but don't see the hand of God in it" and "the sovereign pleasure of God for the present stays his rough wind; otherwise it would come to fury") stresses the urgency of his message of repentance. Van Tholen's repetition also suggests urgency, but to a much different end. He admits to quasi-hypocrisy in his pre-cancer life – through

the anaphoric repetitions of "forty years" in paragraph 3 – of why he didn't understand the urgency of making oneself right with God because he had "forty years" to do it (a kind of "I'll-take-the-trash-out-later" attitude). In the biblical tradition, "forty" typically signifies a period of testing and probation (i.e. The Jews wandering in the desert for forty years; Jesus's temptation in the desert for forty days). Van Tholen taps the energy of this allusion to suggest that his own introspection in the face of death must happen all of the sudden without a period of tribulation to make gradual sense of it all. In the process, he synthesizes his personal story with familiar schemas found in scripture.

○ <u>Diction:</u> Edwards's assuredness of his audience's transgressions is written on the back of the various forms of the auxiliary verb "is." His syntax is definite, leaving no room for possibilities of 'might' and 'maybe'. "That lake of burning brimstone" and "the dreadful pit" *are* there, and they *are* waiting for the unrepentant. Such is the image of Edwards's God, a wrathful and angry being who will exact brutal reprisal upon those who do not conform to His will. The abstractions in Van Tholen's sermon are often juxtaposed with quick and abrupt transitions, specifically the coordinating conjunction "but." The word "but" appears in every paragraph and is the fulcrum upon which Van Tholen propels his discussions from ignorance about God's grace to a position of understanding it. Even on the day of his sermon, Van Tholen hasn't lost what experience has taught him. He speaks with poise and patience about what his battle with cancer has revealed to him about human life, all couched in qualified statements which acknowledge a merciful God who understands and accepts human folly.

For more visual pre-writers, organizing these observations into a short-hand graphic is useful.

As Sharon Crowley argues in *Teaching Invention* (2002), "invention is perhaps the most difficult part of rhetoric to teach. Novice writers are generally unaware that professional writing is a product of many drafts. Modern students typically do not understand that good arguments must be

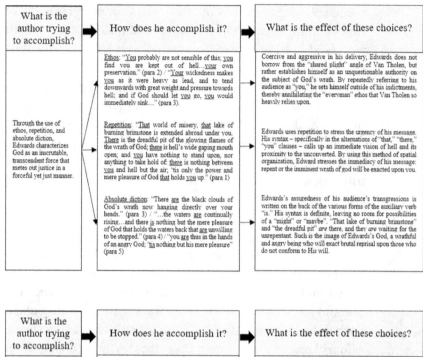

What is the author trying to accomplish?	How does he accomplish it?	What is the effect of these choices?
James Van Tholen describes a God that is not wrathful, but loving; not transcendent, but imminent; not punitive, but enlightening. It is through his own brush-with-death – an aggressive course of chemotherapy for cancer in his chest wall – that Van Tholen comes to understand the fragility of life and the transcendent mercy of God.	Ethos: "…We can rise above it; we can live through it; but we can't ignore it…Then we are overwhelmed by it, and our faith doesn't apply to it. And if that happens, we lose hope." (para 2) / "I cannot be our focus, because the center of my story—our story—is that the grace of Jesus Christ carries us beyond every cancer, every divorce, every sin, every trouble that comes to us." (para 3) Repetition: "And the reason I didn't get it where grace is concerned, I think, is that I assumed I still had about forty years left. Forty years to unlearn my bad habits. Forty years to let my sins thin down and blow away. Forty years to be good to animals and pick up my neighbors' mail for them when they went on vacation." (para 3) Abstract and concrete diction: "But I can't help feeling how strange this day is…" (para 1) / "But we can't do that. We can't ignore what has happened." (para 2) / "I said all those things, and I meant them. But that was before I faced death myself." (para 9)	Van Tholen's soft-spoken and humble tone is due in large part to the way he handles the speaker-audience relationship. Through the use of plural pronouns, Van Tholen illustrates the wider implications of his direct experience to that of the congregation, thus joining their understandings with his own. Van Tholen's repetition suggests urgency but to a much different effect than Edwards. He admits to quasi-hypocrisy in his pre-cancer life – through the anaphoric repetitions of "forty years" in paragraph 3 – of why he didn't understand the urgency of making oneself right with God because he had "forty years" to do it (a kind of "I'll-take-the-trash-out-later" attitude). This lackadaisical stance towards God is counterbalanced with the insights brought on by his brush with death. The abstractions in Van Tholen's sermon are often juxtaposed with quick and abrupt transitions, specifically the coordinating conjunction "but." The word "but" appears in every paragraph and is the fulcrum upon which Van Tholen propels his discussions from ignorance about God's grace to a position of understanding it. Even on the day of his sermon, Van Tholen hasn't lost what experience has taught him. He speaks with poise and patience about what his battle with cancer has revealed to him about human life, all couched in qualified statements which acknowledge a merciful God who understands and accepts human folly.

searched for, that finding arguments appropriate to a given situation is hard intellectual work. Nor do they see the need to produce more arguments than they plan to use on a given assignment. Indeed, students typically use arrangement as their sole means of invention, thinking in terms of composing an introduction, a thesis statement, proofs, and a conclusion-in that order." Thus far in this chapter, we've seen how rhetorical reading propels the initial stages of invention. We'll now consider how invention works hand-in-hand with arrangement to help writers produce reader-friendly, logic-driven analyses.

Arrangement for an Analytical Essay

The role of arrangement in the writing process is sometimes misunderstood. Most students are taught that good writers will first invent, then arrange, and follow up with style – always in that order. This linear approach is problematic for two reasons. For one, each act of writing operates under a unique set of rhetorical conditions. The purpose, the audience, the author's experience and background, the medium of publication, are just a few of the conditions which shift from one writing project to the next. One-size-fits-all patterns of arrangement (i.e. the "five-paragraph-essay") tend to overwhelm novice writers and encumber mature ones since they prescribe that the reading-based insights must fit into predetermined slots. Students and teachers alike often see the five-paragraph-essay as the ideal form (and often the only form), though this type of writing rarely appears in contexts outside English classrooms. It is a "form" of sorts, but its rote instruction as writing dogma often does more harm than good in the long run for developing writers. Its greatest damage to students is done by inhibiting the growth of what composition scholars refer to as "form consciousness," an awareness that different rhetorical situations call for some variation in an essay's structure. In the five-paragraph-essay myopia, writers don't see arrangement so much as a choice to made but as an obligation to be met. Second, it's important to remember that invention and arrangement are not mutually exclusive. The best critical readers annotate with an eye to how the insights will eventually coalesce, consciously (or unconsciously) understanding invention and arrangement to be part of the same prob-lem-solving process. Where invention answers the question of "*What* am I going to write about?," arrangement makes the writer consider "*How* am I going to write about it?" Think of what follows as a general set of strategies – adaptable to your specific circumstances as a writer – to be used as you see fit. In other words, these suggestions will help get things off the ground, but once the paper is up and running, you must take the controls.

The best essays are generally considered to be "whole" or "unified," an idea traceable back to Aristotle's *Poetics* (335 B.C.): "A whole is that which has a beginning, a middle, and an end." Though Aristotle largely applied this now-obvious insight to drama and poetry in *Poetics*, this marks the earliest record of a theoretical stance on arrangement in the Western tradition. Aristotle adapted his dramatic theory to contexts of speech and argument in *The Art of Rhetoric* (4th Century B.C.) in large part to counter the free-flowing, shape-shifting rhetoric of the Sophists. Aristotle's recommendations, both highly structured and easily learned, caught on in the academy, and students forever-after have used Aristotelian patterns of arrangement for nearly all modes of writing, save narration and description. Sometimes referred to as the "three-part-structure" in contemporary composition, Aristotle recommends that any piece of writing worth reading should adhere to a basic structure: an introduction, a body, and a conclusion.

The engine of the introduction is the thesis statement, and Aristotle recognized its primacy in spoken discourse in *The Art of Rhetoric*: "The most essential function and distinctive property of the introduction is to show what the aim of the speech is." Though Aristotle was more concerned with speech than writing, nearly all rhetoricians who have handled the idea of the written thesis did not sway far from Aristotle's general idea of the role it should play. Hugh Blair (1718–1800), a Scottish rhetorician most known for his theorizing on written rhetoric, provided a famous take on Aristotle's insistence on the controlling role played by the thesis in *Lectures on Rhetoric and Belles Lettres* (1783). Adopted as the standard writing textbook at Yale (1785), Harvard (1788), and Dartmouth (1822), Blair's ideas laid the groundwork for the modern thesis statement whose traits we all recognize. It should be explicit, outline the main argument, and (upon recommendation of the twentieth century author Sheridan Baker) appear toward the end of the introduction for emphasis. The thesis must not be vague, nor should it be just a topic. It is insufficient to write, "This paper is about Henry David Thoreau and Transcendentalism in *Walden*." That is a statement of case, but it is not sharp, not explicit. The thesis is the rational element in the argument, and it governs the entire paper. Always remember that a thesis, like a sword, should have an edge and come to a point.

Aristotle recognized that the thesis can't do it all; it must be paired with developmental sections which deliver on the promises made in the introduction. Body paragraphs have two distinctive features: a controlling idea and supporting details. Though Aristotle acknowledged the necessity of supporting detail in public oration, *The Art of Rhetoric* had surprisingly little to say on the topic. Classical rhetoric, which was largely composed and delivered orally, placed little emphasis on such matters as "controlling ideas," but current-traditional rhetoric recognizes the centrality of organization in effective written discourse. Most of what we know about the modern body paragraph comes from *English Composition and Rhetoric* (1866) written by Scottish logician and educator Alexander Bain (1818–1903). Bain's "organic paragraph" model – the heart of nearly all American composition courses – is the prevailing structure of how ideas should be ordered and arranged in writing. Bain felt so strongly about paragraph level coherence that he recorded "seven laws" for effective body paragraphs in his 1866 work:

1. Distribution into Sentences: The consideration of the Unity of the individual Sentence leads up to the structure of the Paragraph, as composed of sentences properly parted off.
2. Explicit Reference: The bearing of each sentence of a Paragraph on the sentences preceding needs to be explicit.
3. Parallel Construction: When several consecutive sentences iterate or illustrate the same idea, they should, as far as possible, be formed alike.
4. Indication of the Theme: The opening sentence, unless obviously preparatory, is expected to indicate the scope of the paragraph.
5. Unity: Unity in a Paragraph implies a sustained purpose and forbids digressions and irrelevant matter.
6. Consecutive Arrangement: The first thing involved in Consecutive Arrangement is, that related topics should be kept close together: in other words, Proximity has to be governed by Affinity.
7. Marking of Subordination: As in the Sentence, so in the Paragraph, Principal and Subordinate Statements should have their relative importance clearly indicated.

It's not accidental that the fourth law, the central of the seven, focuses on a paragraph's controlling idea. What we could now call a "topic sentence," Bain understands this statement to be the paragraph's point of origin from which everything else emanates. Topic sentences play a crucial role in this hierarchical paragraph theory and, he implies, they should be understood as a paragraph-level analog to the thesis statement. Brilliant writers can get away without them, but even they will not try it too often. As the thesis is to the essay, so the topic sentence is to the paragraph. Somewhere in your paragraph – towards the beginning in deductive models or at the end with inductive models – you should state explicitly what point you are trying to prove or what illustrations will (or have) been made. A paragraph should have good reason for being a distinct unit within your essay; beware of overlong paragraphs overloaded with ideas.

Once the topic sentence has been sufficiently linked to the thesis, Bain suggests that the writer must develop the idea according to some recognizable plan, the focus of his remaining six rules. Deciding on a pattern of development is often one of the most daunting tasks in college-level writing. Sharon Crowley's *Teaching Invention* (2002) points out that Aristotle's famous "topics" (*topoi* or "places") of how writing can be organized are a useful starting point. These foundational concepts – once a shortcut in the inventional process for speakers who delivered orally – have evolved over time into matters of arrangement, or "the 'modes' of expository writing": description, narration, analogy, process analysis, cause and effect, comparison and contrast, and so forth. By calling on these modes to pattern your paragraph, you help a reader see how your sentences hang together in a purpose-driven way. Consider the benefits of a comparison and contrast model. In most cases, "the writer who goes beyond the most obvious similarities between two objects to make comparisons at increasingly specific levels," Crowley says, "will discover details about both objects which might not be obvious if they were considered separately. Considering these specific details leads, in turn, to the discovery of general principles of similarity and difference which help organize the final essay, an arrangement of details based on comparison." The choice of how to organize subsidiary sentences in a body paragraph is both a question of utility and style, but Bain's general rules of thumb about their characteristics are a useful check: 1) the information must be tied to the topic sentence and not wander, 2) each sentence must cohere with those around it, and 3) the subtopics in the individual paragraph should be more or less the same length in development.

Once the body of the essay has been developed, a paper needs some type of closure. Aristotle's discussion of the conclusion in *The Art of Rhetoric* outlines four general recommendations to wrap things up: 1) Summarize the main facts and arguments 2) Emphasize your position on the topic while downplaying that of the opponent 3) Leave a favorable impression of your character (ethos) 4) Stir the audience's emotions one final time (pathos). It's easy to see how these strategies can quickly become unwieldy for novice writers, and since they were originally intended for oral discourse, they don't translate all that well to a written essay. That being said, there are some useful adaptations of these structures that writers can use to be sure the paper doesn't simply run out of gas after the final body paragraph.

Summarize while chasing the implications of your strongest points. It's a good idea not to simply repeat your thesis and call it a day. Try to find one professional article or essay that does so. Expert writers do, however, often recapitulate the main points, but they do so in a way that stresses the implications of the thesis. "Were I to accept this thesis," a reader may ask, "what would be the effect or why would it matter?" It's here that a writer can step in and answer the elusive "so what?" question which is central to any piece of writing.

Strategically lead the reader to a final, staccato statement. This strategy stresses the style of the conclusion as much as the content. Yes, you may well suggest that you have proved even more than your thesis promised but ending the conclusion with a small phrase or even a single word will often leave the reader well-disposed to your topic and emotionally stirred. To do this well, the writer must understand how a periodic sentence works. Periodic syntax has the main clause or predicate at the end. Writers can use this style to both summarize and persuade since the subordinate reasons and ideas are placed before the ultimate point. By carrying an effect of mystery, tension, suspense, or surprise – all desired effects when you're trying to rouse the pathos of the audience one final time before you sign off – a periodic sentence will make your final insights crack like a whip. Read that last sentence again, carefully, and notice its periodic style.

Situate your insights into a larger historical context. If, for example, you have discussed how a passage illustrates the corrosive effects of social media on a culture's religious institutions, you may suggest that Friedrich Nietzsche was the first thinker to sense the implications of the movement from god-to-self over a century ago. In other words, you might move from a discussion of contemporary popular culture to retrieve an idea from late 19ᵗʰ century philosophy.

Suggest that your paper's insights may be complicated by competing points of view. By recognizing that few issues can be understood in reductive, "yes/no" terms, this strategy emphasizes the writer's thoughtful nature (ethos) while handling complex topics. For example, to say that Shakespeare presents Hamlet as the archetypal Renaissance figure means that you must accept Shakespeare acknowledgement of humanity's dark side. For instance, he implies it is perfectly acceptable for Hamlet to consciously deceive those around him. Or while sent away for his own execution, it is somehow just for Hamlet to deflect his own death sentence onto his two childhood friends, Rosencrantz and Guildenstern. By highlighting Hamlet's less desirable qualities, you communicate to the reader that you understand this character – a mix of virtue and vice – as a living example of a full human being. You might then conclude the paper with a discussion of what a "hero" is and suggest a way to synthesize these conflicting traits, if there is a way, to close on a final portrait of this character.

With all the considerations of invention and arrangement in mind, it's time to take a look at a finished product. What follows is an analytical essay based on the excerpts from "Sinners in the Hands of an Angry God" and "Surprised by Death" from *Where All Hope Lies*. Notice how the essay draws on the annotations from earlier in this chapter to illustrate how an author can effectively transfer scattered notes into a final, polished product.

God – what He is and the nature of His existence – is one of the central mysteries of the Christian faith that can't be comprehended by human reason alone. Yet, preachers and lay-people alike have tried to render this highly complicated, highly inaccessible idea into terms that fit the limited capacity of our finite intellect. Jonathan Edwards in "Sinners of the Hands of an Angry God" takes one approach to describe God to his listeners: he scares the hell out his congregation by, well, scaring them out of hell via a metaphor-fueled image of a wrathful God. James Van Tholen's "Surprised by Death" takes another road. He speaks emotionally to his congregation by way of his own experience, a terrifying near-visit with God from terminal cancer. His story demonstrates, first-hand, a merciful God who has bestowed His grace on him for another shot in this world, if only for a little while. Though totally divergent in tone and approach, each sermon is ultimately effective at imparting the respective preacher's conception of God to his congregation.

As John 14:2 may have put it, these sermons illustrate the "many rooms in the house of Ethos." That is, each speaker effectively deploys ethos strategies to speak authoritatively on the matter of God, but the manifestation of that ethos appeal is a major point of divergence between the two sermons. Van Tholen's soft-spoken and humble tone is a function of his experiences, a battle with cancer that allowed him to realize his own transition from theoretical preaching to preaching that's invested with first-hand experience. In paragraph 1, he recognizes his own shortcomings and misgivings quite candidly and Van Tholen's use of concession is a central feature of his rhetorical strategy. The acknowledgement of his own pretending ("I want to ignore my absence, and I want to pretend everybody has forgotten the reason for it") is contrasted with the raw reality of his situation ("We can't ignore what has happened. We can rise above it; we can live through it; but we can't ignore it"). This juxtaposition establishes a sermon-wide pattern of moments where theory clashes with experience to emphasize just how dramatically his near-visit with God affected him. He admits to quasi-hypocrisy in his pre-cancer life – through the anaphoric repetitions of "forty years" in paragraph 3 – of why he didn't understand the urgency of making oneself right with God because he had "forty years" to do it (a kind of "I'll-take-the-trash-out-later" attitude). In the biblical tradition, "forty" typically signifies a period of testing and probation (i.e. The Jews wandering in the desert for forty years; Jesus's temptation in the desert for forty days). Van Tholen taps the energy of this allusion to suggest that his own introspection in the face of death must happen all of the sudden without a period of tribulation to make gradual sense of it all. In the process, he synthesizes his personal story with familiar schemas found throughout scripture. The transition from personal to collective hangs on this use of the word "but." This conjunction appears in every paragraph and is the fulcrum upon which Van Tholen propels his discussions from ignorance about God's grace to a position of understanding it. Even on the day of his sermon, Van Tholen hasn't lost what experience has taught him. He speaks with poise and patience about what his battle with cancer has revealed to him about human life, all couched in qualified statements which acknowledge a merciful God who understands and accepts human folly.

Jonathan Edwards also speaks with passion, but one that is markedly different from Van Tholen's. Coercive and aggressive in his delivery, Edwards does not borrow from the "shared plight" angle of Van Tholen, but rather establishes himself as an unquestionable authority on the subject of God's wrath. Rhetorically, Edwards sets himself outside of his own congregation through the use of second person pronouns (it's not "we," it's "you") to cast judgement on those in front of him. Edwards's syntax – specifically in the alternations of "that," "there," "you" clauses – calls up an immediate vision of hell and its proximity to the unconverted. Moreover, by repeatedly referring to his audience as "you," he sets himself outside of his indictments, thereby annihilating the "everyman" ethos that Van Tholen so heavily relies upon. And where the rhetorical force of Van Tholen is sourced in his colloquial style, Edwards's speech finds its energy as a pathos-laden tirade, an invective against a congregation presented with almost no qualifications whatsoever. Edwards's assuredness of his audience's transgressions is written on the back of the verb "is." His syntax is definite, leaving no room for possibilities of 'might' and 'maybe'. "That lake of burning brimstone" and "the dreadful pit" *are* there, and they *are* waiting for the unrepentant. Such is the image of Edwards's God, an inscrutable force who will exact brutal reprisal upon those who do not conform to His will. God is wrathful, yes, though He is not merciless. In fact, Edward's repeated references to God's mercy ("you find you are kept out of hell, but don't see the hand of God in it" and "the sovereign pleasure of God for the present stays his rough wind; otherwise it would come to fury") stress the urgency of his message of repentance in ways not unlike Van Tholen's sermon.

The language used by each preacher is deeply reflective of how each understands their own God. Van Tholen's language deals in specifics and is highly concrete, a strategy which allows a listener easy access to the image of his God he's communicating in his sermon. The "everydayness" of his language contributes to the universality of his message; we all confront our own misgivings somewhere in Van Tholen's story. Van Tholen's invites to identify with his plight and realize, alongside him, that God (though not always with the strutting and roaring of Edwards's God) is ever-present in everyday affairs. Edwards language contains very few concrete moments and the level of abstraction in the diction – presented in a string of imaginative metaphors – aptly corresponds to Edwards's God who is, himself, abstract, transcendent and expressible only an imaginative, even literary, style. Edwards can't talk about God directly; he only has recourse to these powerful metaphors, but the fantastical images of "dreadful pit of the glowing flames" and "bow of God's wrath" work every bit as much on a listening audience as Van Tholen's personal story. Though each take different paths, one thing is certain for both men. All rhetorical choices lead to the same destination: God.

If "prewriting" and "writing" equate to Aristotle's "beginning and "middle," then "rewriting" is the "end" that brings ultimate unity to the essay. Rewriting, or revision, divides into two broad categories: "local" revision which focuses on sentence-level concerns (diction, syntax, grammar, mechanics, and so forth) and "global" revision which examines a text's structural features (organization, development of ideas, tone, style, and so forth). Students tend to place an outsized emphasis on "local" revision – the type of stuff spelling and grammar software will catch – likely because it doesn't involve much guesswork. "Local" revision has its value but reducing rewriting to sentence-level corrections shortchanges the full generative value of revision. "Global" revision presents greater challenges to the novice writer since it requires a rigorous examination of the internal processes of how prewriting and writing occurs. Sometimes referred to as the Recursive and Cognitive-Process theory, this rewriting strategy asks you to revisit the three parts of the Stage-Model theory (prewriting, writing, rewriting) but this time as a rhetorical reader of your own work to determine its overall efficacy. It may seem counterintuitive, but once the initial writing has concluded there still remains an ongoing role of *invention* to offer solutions to

Table 1 Questions for Global and Local Revision.

Questions for Global Revision	Questions for Local Revision
– Do I mention anything in the introduction that doesn't appear in the paper's body? Vice-versa?	– Do I notice any issues with spelling or grammar?
– Do I order my paragraphs in an intelligible way? Would it make sense to rearrange them according to some recognizable plan (chronological, general to particular, ascending weightiness and so forth)?	– Do I have any mechanical errors in my sentences (sentence fragments, comma splices, apostrophe errors, dangling modifiers, and so forth)?
	– Do I write with nouns and verbs that are appropriately specific and concrete?
– Do I provide effective transitions from one sentence to another and one paragraph to another?	– Do I need to edit my pronouns to be sure they all have clear antecedents?
– Do I have any overlong paragraphs? Any underdeveloped paragraphs?	– Do I need to delete any extraneous words or phrases?
	– Do I vary the word order and length of my sentences?
– Do my concluding points aptly punctuate the essay's overall argument with both force and style?	– Do I have a good reason for placing each sentence where it appears?

discovered problems in the essay. Consider Table 1 as you revisit your work along the lines of global and local concerns.

Revising is more than fixing a paper for mere grammatical correctness; each round of revision should bring you, the writer, to higher levels of articulation and understanding through a sustained process of inquiry. Through revision, you develop a stronger understanding of how to see a writing project at the college level and to how to make a mark with your writing. Be sure that your revisions reflect substantive changes to the content: clarifying ideas, tightening wordiness, drawing more explicit connections, explicating a quote more fully, or sometimes a complete overhaul of both words and ideas. After all, to "revise" literally means to "re-see."

CHAPTER FIVE

VISUAL RHETORIC – IMAGE AS TEXT (AND TEXT AS IMAGE)

I have always been struck by Rafael's painting *School of Athens* (see Figure 1). It is a paradox; at once, it's simple but complex, orderly yet chaotic, static and dynamic. It is a snapshot that works as a photo album, telling the complete history of Western thought in a single image. This fresco, still in the Stanze di Raffaello of the Vatican's Apostolic Palace, has two central subjects in the foreground: the classical philosopher Plato (left) and his pupil, Aristotle (right). At first glance, they appear quite similar: both hold a book, both have sturdy posture, both wear a toga, each is looking at the other. But look a little closer and notice

Figure 1 Plato and Aristotle, the central figures in Raphael's School of Athens.

the contrasts. Plato points up, Aristotle down. Their hands tell a story. Plato, pointing upwards towards the World of the Forms, reflects his philosophy that non-material forms – essential ideas – are the most fundamental form of reality. Aristotle, holding his palm parallel to ground beneath him, showcases his empiricist views that asserts reality begins with what comes to us through the senses. Moreover, this fresco – hanging in the world's most famous church – brings together the Classical and Religious world into a harmonious whole that reflects the spirit of the High Renaissance.

I bring up this brief analysis to make the point that images can be "read" much in the same way that texts can, so why is it that print texts seem to get all the attention in classroom work? Schools often advertise themselves as the place that gets students "ready for the real world." This claim should strike you as odd given that schools (who, like us, exist in a culture saturated with visual imagery) often deride images the way they do: guilty pleasures which offer a break from the "real work" of reading and writing. As Moe Folk notes in "Graphic Writing: Visual Rhetoric, Student Production, and Graphic Novels" (2017), the basic assumption here is that seeing-is-simple: people can gaze upon an image and immediately grasp it, which has led to the popular assumption that images within academic contexts are for children (e.g. the use of pictures in children's books in the first stages of reading). If the ability to see an image is a natural and physical process, then reading must necessarily be the opposite, intellectual and learned, thereby endowing it with an academic "prestige" not found in pictures. This privileging of print text in the classroom – "print bias" it's sometimes called – reflects an outmoded understanding of composition that defines writing merely as words on the printed page. In this chapter, we'll see how we can expand on the notion of "text" to include all modes of communication: print, visual, or some combination of the two.

In 2004's *Picturing Texts*, Lester Faigley says it's undeniable "most of us have some response to everything we see, [but] in order to account for how an image conveys a message or evokes a response, you need to understand how different elements come together as a visual language." Consider this statement next time you sit down at your computer. Think about how text and image converge into a unified act of composition on some of the internet's most popular web pages.

It's useful to think of images *as* texts, observable things composed with a rhetorical sensibility that are worthy of analysis and deconstruction. With texts, as we've seen in Chapters 1–4, the reader acts as code-breaker, studying and making connections in order to answer the most important question to ask of anything in an English classroom, "What is *that* doing *there?*"

If you've ever stared long enough at your keyboard, you'll see its letters (signs for sounds), numbers (signs for quantities), and punctuation

The "Single-Visual" Composition

This layout emphasizes visual simplicity, a graphic metaphor for the ease and efficient functionality of the web service. Websites using this compositional layout often will have lot of unused space that surrounded a central image. Like the center of a bullseye, one's eye can't help but be drawn to the webpage's central attraction, thus pulling its users right to the primary service, idea, or message.

The "E" Composition

This layout caters to the way that our eyes naturally scan material online, namely in the shape of a capital "E." In other words, our eyes move in the natural motion of reading print texts from left-to-right, jump down a bit on the webpage, and repeat the process. By composing the visuals and text in such a way, this method allows the website to emphasize key points within the way we graze the information online.

The "Rule of Thirds" Composition

A long-standing rule of thumb in the production of photography and film, this method promotes balance and equilibrium in the visual information a reader takes in. The principle behind this is parallelism. Our eye is drawn to the image at the top of each column in the hopes that we'll work our way down to the related stories. Each column, in parallel fashion, gives its reader a new "starting" point.

marks (signs which mediate the act of writing) are more related to images than we initially give them credit for. It should come as no surprise that the academic study of images, known as semiotics, began as an outgrowth of linguistics. Its two principal founders, Ferdinand de Saussure (1857–1913) and Charles Sanders Peirce (1839–1914), worked from the same basic assumption: a word (a 'signifier,' or the sound of a word) refers to a thing in the observable world (a 'sign,' or the concept we associate with the word). This symbolic understanding of language was formalized most notably by C.K. Ogden and I.A. Richards (1893–1979) in stylishly meta-titled work *The Meaning of Meaning* (1923). Ogden and Richards argue that meaning exists neither in words or objects but rather in the perceptions and experiences of the reader who draws connections between the two (see Figure 2). For example, there is no necessary reason that we must refer to those things growing out of the ground as "trees" any more than another word (i.e. *arbre* in French, *arbol* in Spanish, בוים in Yiddish, and so forth) in the same way one tree could be painted from three different angles. In other words (or is it images?), all text merely signifies a referent in the external world, and the meaning of that sign resides in the mind of the reader. So, how is it that we can derive meaning from texts at all? Richards, in *Philosophy of Rhetoric* (1936), proposes the principle of the "interinanimation of words" which says that our understanding of a word is bound up with a cluster of related words. Similar to our discussion synchronic meaning in Chapter 1, Richard's theory of language says

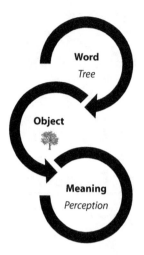

Figure 2 Visualization of Ogden and Richard's Theory of Word Meaning.

that "tree" simply points to the concept of a "tree," which then is subsequently imaged by other words – "branch," "leaf," "trunk," and so forth – all of which can never capture the theoretically full meaning of "tree." Moreover, words often suggest various meanings to different individuals: some may associate a tree with childhood nostalgia, others with environmental devastation, others with bountiful harvests, etc. If you really think about it, a picture isn't worth a thousand words. A word is worth a thousand pictures.

Claude-Levi Strauss (anthropology), Jacques Lacan (psychoanalysis), and Roland Barthes (literary criticism) expanded the application of semiotics to the business of everyday life in the second half of the 20th century. Barthes, in particular, focused on the process of meaning making and analysis in the non-linguistic realm of daily living. He showed that everyday objects – something as innocuous as pencil, for example – convey a full range of meaning beyond mere utility (it can represent creativity, education, the need for mistakes, childhood nostalgia, etc.). It is in this "polysemous" nature – the ability of an image to convey a vast array of meanings to audience at the same time – that images are thought to have a comparative sloppiness to the perceived precision of words. In his essay "The Rhetoric of the Image" from *Image, Music,*

Text (1977), Barthes focuses on the way viewers can understand images on both "linguistic" and "symbolic" levels, using a print advertisement for Panzani dried pasta as his running example (see Figure 3).

The "linguistic" level of meaning is comprised of all the words, however few, which can be understood at denotational (literal) and connotational (suggestive) levels. In Figure 3, there are two linguistic elements: the name of the product itself, Panzani, and the French caption "Pates – Sauce – Parmesan: A L'Italienne de Luxe" in the lower right-hand corner. Barthes makes specific note of the marketing slogan, pointing out "the captions… and the label…the code from which this message has been taken is the

Figure 3 Print Advertisement for Panzani Pasta referred to in Roland Barthes The Rhetoric of the Image (1977).

French language; the only knowledge required to decipher it is a knowledge of writing and French." But even if you don't speak French, that doesn't mean there is no meaningful communication going on. Consider the company's name, Panzani. He notes "…*Panzani* gives not simply the name of the firm but also, by its assonance, an additional [meaning], that of 'Italianicity.'" It certainly *sounds* Italian, and that's enough, he implies, to convince the average consumer of the product's authenticity. In other words, the ad's connotative level suggests an image of refined Italian cuisine, even if it's only just dried pasta sitting on the bottom shelf of a French grocery store.

The "symbolic" level of meaning is comprised of the all associations a viewer of the image makes to its collection of objects. These meanings vary from person to person and are a composite of the message, the viewer, and the experiences that links the two, and Barthes would argue language and culture are the two biggest mediators. Consider the image again and take inventory of what's there. In "The Rhetoric of the Image," Barthes focuses on four objects (see Table 1).

Table 1 Relationship between the visual image and its connotative meaning for Panzani Pasta ad.

The visual information	What this visual signifies
The netted bag	A more refined palate than that of a mechanical, refrigerator-based culture
The produce (tomatoes, mushrooms, peppers)	The colors of the Italian flag, another sign of the product's "Italianicity"
The total collection of objects	A total culinary service; the Panzani company has provided everything for a full meal
The overall composition of the image	The notion of a still life painting which, thereby, signifies refinement and high culture

Your interpretation of this image may differ greatly from Barthes's, and it is in this "play of meaning" where interesting, sometimes clashing perspectives, make contact. You are reading this image in the 21st century not the 20th; you are approaching the image via American culture, not European culture; your understanding is mediated through the English language, not French. To this list we could add many others, but the point is this: Barthes's theory places total authority onto the receiver, not the producer, of the message in the process of meaning-making from visual sources. It is here that the echo of dialogism reverberates into semiotics.

Strangely, visual literacy has a remarkably low status in the English classroom, being neither taught or practiced regularly. But, if schools are responsible for preparing students to deal intelligently with dominant modes of communication in our culture, it seems odd to belittle visual analysis, while extolling all things textual. In *The New Literacy* (1979), author Harry Foster notes that the average college freshman has viewed more than five hundred movies, twenty times the number of novels he or she has read in their lifetime. And that's just movies; what about all the other time spent with television, mobile devices, and the hundred other things that proliferate every waking second of nearly all 21st century citizens? In emphasizing the relationship between visual and textual language, you can broaden your options in learning and communication styles which can be deployed in a variety of rhetorical situations. In other words, thoughtful consumption of visual images has never been more important.

There is an enormous amount of meaningful information that can be gleaned from an image when properly approached, but gathering information from old drawings and paintings can sometimes be tough. However, as a regular consumer of visual information, you're already quite adept at this type of examination, and if you are working within an analytical process like we have in this chapter, all the better. Think back to *School of Athens* and imagine it gets projected onto a screen in your class. The teacher tells you to reflect on it for a minute. Eager hands go up and out come the reaction responses: "The guy on the left is pointing up while the other guy is pointing down." "One's old and one's young." "The bald guy looks wise." The teacher asks them to explain *why* they think these bits of evidence are meaningful, precisely spelling out the terms of their reaction. At this point, there is only silence.

Images can be great storytellers, and just like their written counterparts, they can be annotated, dissected, and analyzed, but students must first know how to answer the "why?" question. Image analysis does not require new skill sets but rather a transference of pre-existing abilities. You can stand on the shoulders of what you already know about textual analysis since images, like written texts, share a similar set of rhetorical principles. The components of the image – and the arrangement of those components – highlight the meaning that lies underneath the colors and lines that comprise the picture in the same way that words and sentences work jointly to create large scale meaning in a text. With increasing calls for proficiency with information presented in diverse formats and media in both school and work settings, a need for visual literacy – that is, the ability to interpret images with an analytical eye – is more urgent than ever for students. To help reach into the image to find out what's happening inside borders of the frame, let's break out Barthes's concerns into familiar categories of the rhetorical analysis process from Chapter 2, the rhetorical situation and the means of persuasion, to suggest useful parallels between textual and visual analysis:

The Rhetorical Situation:
Exigence:
Questions to ask of the *Context*:

1. Does the image make reference to a historical time period, social movement, or political ideology?
2. Does the image require prior knowledge about the situation presented or can it stand on its own?
3. Is there anything in the image that alludes to the time period in which it is set such as clothing style, archaic language or gestures, or outdated technology?

4. How was the image published? Does that publication push a certain agenda?

Questions to ask of the *Purpose*:

1. What is the purpose? Is meant to motivate the audience to action? To educate? To persuade? To dissuade?
2. Does the artist tell a story in the image? What is the story and how is it "told"?
3. From what point of view is the image presented? Is the camera meant to be the "eye" of the audience? Are you set outside the action? Is there an omniscient quality to the perspective?
4. Can text be found anywhere in the image? How does the text contribute to the central message? Denotatively? Connotatively?

The Rhetorical Triangle
Questions to ask of the *Speaker*:

1. Can something about the artist be learned by the subject that is depicted?
2. Do you think the artist is trying to be objective? Push an agenda? Be comical? Be sarcastic?
3. Is there anything in the image that indicates bias?

Question to ask of the *Audience*:

1. What is the intended audience for the image? Children? Adults? Men? Women? A particular ethnic group?
2. Does the artist assume the audience has prior knowledge about the image?
3. What is the intended reaction of the audience? Pity? Sympathy? Guilt? Anger? Action?
4. Is the audience wide? Specific? How can you tell and does that matter?

Questions to ask of the *Subject*:

1. Are some subjects emphasized more than others? What is important about those subjects?

2. Does the artist draw your eye to parts of the image through visual techniques such as a vanishing point, "spotlighting" effects, or geometrical patterns?
3. Are any of the subjects obscured or falling outside the border of the frame? Why may this be done?
4. How would the image's argument change if the setting were different?
5. Is the setting a metaphor for the message (i.e. a morning scene to represent hopefulness)?

The Means of Persuasion:

1. Is the artist attempting to gain credibility with the audience?
2. Is the artist trying to elicit an emotional response? Humor? Anger? Something else?
3. Is the artist appealing to the logic of the audience somehow?
4. Is there anything that is conspicuously absent from the image? Is this absence meaningful to what the artist is trying to express?
5. What is the style of the image? Is it overblown and cartoony? Realistic and sentimental? Fantastic and dreamlike? Why would the artist choose this style to convey their ideas?
6. Consider the overall setting of the image. For example, is it an urban street scene, a room in a private residence, a factory, a peaceful countryside, etc.? What is the time of day, the season, or the ambiance or mood of the scene? How might the needs of the artist and the restrictions of the medium have affected the choice of setting?
7. Finally, analyze the image for what is not there (the issues it does not raise, the objects and people that are not included) as much as for what is included. Does the image raise questions that are left unanswered by the scene?

This is by no means an exhaustive list, but rather it serves as the starting point to build literacy beyond the printed word, while scaffolding off the habits of mind that students already possess. Of course, images are as subtle and varied as texts, but reading images with a concrete method will help you to begin to see what's not readily apparent, to see things in a new way, to see what most of us miss.

In the summer of 2010, when I began to take in interest in visual literacy, I was searching for that perfect teachable example. Since the internet moves at the speed of thought, it wasn't long before artistic reactions emerged in response to the most widely covered event of the summer, the BP oil spill in the Gulf of Mexico. This event was the largest accidental oil spill in world history. Crude oil

Figure 4 Vlad Lazerian's BP Execution.

leaked into the gulf uninterrupted for over three months until the flow was finally capped in mid-September of that year. Almost five hundred miles of coastline, running from Louisiana to Florida, were affected. I searched for something that would artistically capture the energy of this event while offering an opportunity for visual analysis (see Figure 4).

Before the lesson began, I offered a quick orientation to the class about the importance of visual literacy and how it can help them to become a more conscientious consumer of information in their daily lives outside the borders of my classroom. The lights went off. The image was projected. Students had a minute or two to catalog their private observations. Then, as a class, we adapted the line of questions (outlined above) to give our discussion some structure. Here is a paraphrase of the discussion that took place.

Who is the *speaker*?

Vlad Lazerian, a free-lance graphic artist from Chicago, IL.

What is the *audience*?

The viewership of Yahoo!'s free photo hosting service, Flickr. Although part of a personal collection, the image has been published as a part of digital art gallery. The audience for the image is seemingly aimed at adults who have some knowledge of the event.

What is the *subject*?

The 2010 BP Gulf of Mexico oil spill, a well-known event to both the American public and the international community. The setting of the image is digitally altered to have the foregrounded action of the silhouetted figures set against the backdrop of BP's logo.

What is the *context?*

The image alludes to the high-profile oil spill from early spring of 2010. Prior knowledge of the event is helpful, but not prohibitive, to analyzing this image.

What is the *purpose?*

To argue that the unchecked flow of BP's crude oil into the Gulf of Mexico, and the collateral damage the spill caused to local ecosystems, economies, and way of life, is tantamount to the immorality of a cold-blooded execution.

What *rhetorical elements* does the speaker use to support purpose?

3 central objects (2 men and BP logo) all appear on the same plane, about 2/3 of the way up the photo at eye level.

Shoulder position is calmer than the other figure. Indicates eerie calmness, given the situation.

Brightness of BP logo's center draws attention to central subject.

A gas pump handle seems to be substituted for a pistol.

Shoulders are tensely shrugged. Hands are not shown; they are most likely bound.

The image has only three objects set against a plain white background with no accompanying text or captions. The visual effects are minimal, and the camera position seems to be straight on, perhaps reinforcing the seriousness of the subject. The focal point of the image is the white center of the BP logo. It is placed slightly off-center in the image in order to give prominence to the action taking place between the two silhouetted figures in the foreground. The pose struck by the man on the left is one of an executioner, but rather than a pistol, he holds a gas pump aimed at the head of the victim. The artistic choice to use silhouetted figures, where their specific identity is unknown, makes the image more allegorical and less a specific commentary on a singular instance. The victim, whose arms appear to be bound, is helpless and totally subject to the whim of the man on the left. The BP logo, which fans around his head, draws the viewer's eye to his head, with the "gun" just a few inches away. The tone is threatening and suggests either imminent execution or prolonged torture. Upon some further investigation, this image is a take on Eddie Adam's famous photograph entitled *Saigon Execution 1968* (see Figure 5). By utilizing this visual arrangement, Lazerian's image attempts to tap into the emotion of this source image which, itself, played a role in garnering public support against the Vietnam War by exposing and illuminating the brutality and crimes against humanity. With hopes of transference, Lazerian seems to be expecting that his image will spark similar public outcry against BP's brutality and crimes against humanity.

Figure 5 Comparison of Eddie Adam's Saigon Execution (1968) to Vlad Lazerian's BP Execution (2010).

By using a concrete methodology, this discussion showed students the first steps of moving beyond a "gut reaction" approach to image analysis. This process involved an effort to understand what the artist or photographer was "saying" in the work, to understand that when an artist draws something, or a photographer takes a picture, he is not simply recording a visual image, but sending a message to anyone who looks at the work. We saw and discussed what's effective, what's not, while explicitly answering that most fundamental question, "Why?" In essence, we "read" the image together for the first time.

Today, we find ourselves living in a deeply transformed world, one where globalization has forced a new rhetoric upon all of us. Development in the technology of communication has fundamentally altered what it means to "compose," and we increasingly speak, as Moe Folk notes, to one another in ways that require the composition, consumption, and distribution of imagistic texts on the World Wide Web. As a result, the idea of multi-literacies – to be literate in all forms of text, not just print – is critical for healthy citizenship in the modern world. Images are like essays in miniature. They sometimes tell stories. They sometimes push an agenda. They sometimes explain a viewpoint. They may do more than one of these things or something else entirely. Knowing how to handle these compositions – to read these images with a rhetorical eye – will expose the narratives that live inside the borders of these visuals and help you articulate those findings in a thoughtful, cogent way. And without this keen eye for the visual, you can never fully be a self-confident and conscientious consumer of information in the 21st century.

CHAPTER SIX

RHETORIC IN FILM

Any advanced composition course should closely examine the ways in which information is transmitted from the producer to the receiver of the message. We've done that in Chapters 1–5 by looking at the rhetorical choices an author makes as he puts pen to paper or the compositional choices a photographer makes as he snaps his photo. To this, we'll now throw a new medium into the mix: film.

Film is indebted to writing, but it has developed its own techniques for expressing information to its audience. By examining some of the principal elements shared by both, we can better understand the unique features of each. How, for instance, does film create a point-of-view, whether omniscient or limited? How does it visually represent metaphor, metonymy, and synecdoche found in textual sources? What can it do to show us worlds of inner experience like writing does? Because film is at once an art form, an economic establishment, a social and cultural creation, and a case-study in technology, entire classes (and even whole courses of study) focus of how this artform evolved from its primitive beginnings to the industrial colossus we know today. By studying film in such a way, it's easy to see how a film you may see in theaters tomorrow is heavily influenced by what has come before it (in some ways, this is the "dialogic" element of film studies). Though the historical context of the film is part of its "rhetoric," this will not be our primary focus in this chapter.

What we will do is focus on film aesthetics to understand how this artform is every inch as rhetorical as text or image, subject to same methods of analysis and deconstruction. Texts and images are somewhat limited in their expressive outlets: texts rely solely on the verbal while must images must use color and line to get things across. Film combines these two expressive forms (and after *The Jazz Singer* in 1927, audio elements were introduced as well) in all sorts of interesting and creative ways. To keep focus on the rhetoric of film, we'll refer to the principles of Chapters 1–5 in order to suggest useful parallels between textual analysis and filmic analysis and highlight the chapter's main idea: film is a fundamentally rhetorical art form.

In some senses, this will be a meta-study of film; that is, we will not be looking at what goes on inside of the film per se (plotlines, characters, dialogue, etc.) but rather the rhetorical choices that take place outside the film that lead to its composition. Viewers trained to understand film with a rhetorical sensibility are much more likely to see what the rest of the audience will miss: an off-kilter camera to suggest psychological disorder, a back-lit silhouette to define a character as an "everyman," a disjointed flow of time meant to challenge our basic notions of cause and effect, a bizarre juxtaposition of action and sound. The language of film is ultimately rhetorical. Being attuned to the conventions and techniques will not only help you understand film more deeply, it will propel you into the ongoing dialogue with how and why others may interpret the same film in completely different ways.

The Rhetorical Triangle of Film

Remember from Chapter 2 that any instance of communication requires a speaker, a subject, and an audience to occur. There is much overlap between text and film in terms of the rhetorical triangle, but there are a few things specific to the discourse created by film that we'll discuss here.

A central debate in film studies centers on questions of "authorship." In the mid-20th century, a theoretical stance towards this question known as "auteur theory" emerged. Generated by the French director Francois Truffaut (1932–1984) and popularized by the American film critic Andrew Sarris (1928–2012), auteur theory asserts that the director of the film has complete authorial control over the final cut of the film. As such, film is understood the external expression of a single governing intellect much in the same way its literary cognate, the "author," conceives of and produces a text. The English director Alfred Hitchcock, known for his meticulous storyboarding and obsession with every technical element of a film's production, is often the archetypal image of the auteur director. His most well-known films – *Rear Window* (1954), *North by Northwest* (1959), and *Psycho* (1960) – are generally regarded as high filmic art (these three often rank among the greatest films of all time) and can be deconstructed and analyzed along the same lines as any complex piece of literature. Orson Welles's *Citizen Kane* (1941), Michelangelo Antonioni's *Blow Up* (1966), Luchino Visconti's *Death in Venice* (1971), and Nicholas Roeg's *Don't Look Now* (1973) all fall into the category of auteur filmmaking where the director is filmic analog to the literary author.

As dialogic stances towards literature took hold in the 1970's and 1980's (think to theoretical contributions of Roland Barthes and Jacques Derrida mentioned in Chapter 1), attitudes towards filmic authorship began to shift as well. In contemporary film theory, the idea of the auteur director has largely fallen out of fashion. Because of the move to digitalization – so much of film now is done of green screens and computers – films are increasingly understood as the product of collaborative enterprises between multiple agencies who come together to develop a single product. This complicates the idea of "speaker" in a rhetorical sense, but, just like contemporary rhetorical understandings of authorship in texts, this advance in theory places increased responsibility onto the audience as a source or creator of meaning.

Film, by definition, is a recorded media, a notion loaded with complications when it comes to questions of audience. As we discussed in Chapter 2, recording technology tremendously complicates any singular notion of audience for a text or speech. Film, like any written text, can be viewed and interpreted by any individual at any point in history making it nearly impossible to reliably describe the identity of a film's audience. Film is unique in the sense that it can *only* be experienced in recorded form – a live-acting accompaniment to *Rocky Horror Picture Show* (1975) or a live orchestra synched with *Back to the Future* (1985) may be rare exceptions – so it's useful to broadly refer to the audience of a film in the following categories: mediated, subsidiary, and discourse-community. Look back to Chapter 2 for clarification on these concepts.

A helpful heuristic for understanding questions of subject in film is to consider it in terms of genre. Films are often classified by genre, a form of categorization where the filmmaker and the audience will recognize enough shared commonalities between its subject and conventions to put them into groups. Among some of the most recognizable genres of fictional films are comedy, suspense, horror, and drama (which themselves can be further sub-categorized into more specific groupings such as *screwball* comedy, *action*-suspense, *slasher*-horror, *period*-drama). Non-fiction films can be broken out into their own genres as well: documentary, biographical film, actuality film, direct cinema, and so forth. There are also films which blur the lines between fantasy and reality. Italian Neorealism in the 1940's–1950's and French New Wave Cinema of the 1960's fit this category both use real subjects (not actors) in invented circumstances to give a touch of authenticity to a manufactured story. By focusing on genre, it becomes a bit easier to provisionally understand how a film appeals (or doesn't appeal) rhetorically to its intended audience. Aristotle never could have anticipated the spectacle of a Hollywood production, but he would be likely to agree that a good film fits its appeals to the character types and states of mind that make up the audience, or at least the filmmaker's best guess of it.

The Elements of Film Composition

Writing and film composition are massively complex projects that involve strategic and creative choices about a number of elements: story structure, narrational voice, perspective, conflict, the passage of time, just to name a few. Authors make choices when choosing rhetorical techniques, creating their worlds, and deciding how to reveal this world across the unfolding of a plot. Filmmakers are no different, though the worlds they create are primarily formed, not by pen, but by the camera. Below we'll discuss some of the key rhetorical decisions at play in the production of film to give you a set of perspectives through which you can begin to rhetorically "read" a film's "macro" and "micro" elements. This will be followed by an example essay of how a writer may talk about these filmic techniques, thus crosswalking analysis of a text to analysis of film.

The Macro Elements of Film – The Diegesis

The *diegesis* of a film refers to the world in which a film is set. In fictional films, the diegesis may be a facsimile of reality (the stark realism of WWII in *Saving Private Ryan* (1998)), a fantasy realm with its own laws and logic (Middle Earth in the *Lord of the Rings* films (2001–2003)), an imagined world which exists inside a character's mind (the imagined "reality" of the unnamed narrator of *Fight Club* (1999)), or any combination of these. Of course, the diegesis has bearing on the way a viewer makes sense of what's on screen. Think of the concept of betrayal and how the diegetic difference in the science-fiction setting of *Star-Wars* (1977) treats this subject versus the gritty, neo Film-Noir depiction given to audiences in *Mystic River* (2003). Non-fiction films are not immune to the influence of a filmmaker's choice in diegesis. Think of something like Al Gore's *An Inconvenient Truth* (2006). The film's main arguments take place in an academic-looking lecture hall, associating his message of man-made global warming to research, seriousness, and respectability – and here is where the semiotics of the objects in the setting (Chapter 5) begin to take effect. Choices in diegesis are analogous to writerly choices of logos. If you remember from Chapter 2, writers must decide which pattern of development is best suited for a concept, claim, or idea. The ultimate choice of the world of a film's diegesis will have tremendous bearing on the meaning an audience makes of it. Below are a few terms to add a layer of nuance to this concept.

An *intradiegetic* detail describes any feature of a film that pertains to the fictional world in which the situations and events are told. It could be the sound effect of a character dropping pen onto a concrete floor; it could be the natural shadows that a high-noon sun casts down onto a character's face; it could be the free direct discourse – the flow of dialogue without narrational mediation – of a character's lines. All these things happen within the created world of the film and are consistent with the logic and observable qualities of that world. Intradiegetic details allow characters in the film (and the viewing audience of that film) to see and hear what's going on around them and are often used as a tool in the development of filmic tone. Think of the suspense that's created by the intradiegetic rumbling of an approaching T-Rex's footsteps in the Costa Rican jungle in *Jurassic Park* (1993). The thick, low rumble certainly is intimidating on its own, but this intradiegetic sound effect is also intended to connote the rumble of thunder, associating the dinosaur with the chaos of the tropical storm that hits the island while defining the T-Rex itself as veritable a force of nature. Just like a text, what you can directly see (or hear) isn't always the final word on what's really going on.

An *extradiegetic* detail describes any feature of a film that originates from a source outside the space in which the situations and events within the film occur. This could be an orchestral score running over the opening credits; this could be a mood-generating sound effect; this could be a voice-over of narrator's commentary; this could be a visual effect to distort the image on screen. All of these things are not subject to the logic and observable qualities of the filmed world; in fact, they usually operate independently, if not antithetically, from it. Extradiegetic details are never directly acknowledged by the characters on screen since they exist in a realm outside of the filmic present, though the audience is fully aware of and often heavily influenced by its usage. Leitmotifs, a recurrent musical theme throughout a filmic composition that's associated with a particular person, idea, or situation, are a clear example of an extradiegetic detail in action. Think to *Star Wars: A New Hope* (1977). Is there a better musical symbol for the evil authoritarianism of Darth Vader than John William's iconic score, *The Imperial March*? Every time Vader makes a big appearance in the film, his musical theme follows, signaling to the audience that the Dark Side is afoot. How does this work? Those with a background in orchestration may hear how composer John Williams has both the pitched and non-pitched instruments playing at or near the very bottom of their range to replicate the aura of Vader's imposing presence. What's more, the parallelism of the opening nine beats (sound it out in your head) are an apt musical symbol for both his poise and power. This theme occurs throughout the trilogy of *Star Wars* films to extradiegetically remind the viewer of Vader's traits in a way that only an orchestral score could. Or, maybe think about the menacing two-note leitmotif that signals the coming of *Jaws* (1975). Director Steven Spielberg said that the effect of the score was "half of the film's success."

Homodiegetic structures in film – where the narrator is also a character in the situations and events recounted – is where the intradiegetic and extradiegetic converge. *Stand by Me* (1986), where Gordie Lachance is both the narrator of the story and main character in the story, allows for both real-time action to occur on-screen concurrent with reflection and perspective offered from the narrative voice. Homodiegetic methods are a favorite of American director Stanley Kubrick; his adaptation of Anthony Burgess's *A Clockwork Orange* (1972) and his Vietnam film *Full Metal Jacket* (1987) both contain a coming-of-age main character that comments on their own on-screen experiences as a disembodied narrator.

In fact, the Bildungsroman genre – the coming-of-age story – is a useful written analog to understand this filmic style since the narrative structure often vacillates between action and perspectival commentary. Documentary films will often put homodiegetic structures to use as well. Nearly every Michael Moore film relies on this choice in diegesis. In films such as *Bowling for Columbine* (2002), *Fahrenheit 9/11* (2004), and *Where to Invade Next* (2015), Moore plays a dual role in the film. He is both the conductor of on-screen interviews and the voice of off-screen voiceovers that provide sidebar comments and asides to the audiences (often to shape the information that's presented on-screen with his familiar left-leaning slant).

Like homodiegetic films, *metanarratives* also resist easy classification within the binary categories of intradiegetic or extradiegetic. A metanarrative is a self-referential film that explores its main ideas often by drawing attention to its own artificiality. Metanarratives have a complicated relationship with the idea of Postmodernism, a critical theory of literature, film, and culture that is skeptical of the traditions of the past. "Meta" is a Greek prefix which means "to go beyond, behind, or transcend" so, a metanarrative goes beyond traditional forms of storytelling (those with a master narrative and logical structure) by bucking its formulas. The result is often stories which are incoherent (antithetical to the smooth narrative logic of the Classical and Renaissance traditions) and those which deploy effects to constantly remind the audience they are watching an artificial production (antithetical to the "willing-suspension-of-disbelief" notion crucial to literary and dramatic productions of previous periods in history).

To get an idea of what a metanarrative is, it's useful to consult an example from contemporary live theatre. The staging of the rock-musical *Spring Awakening* (2006), based on the German drama by Frank Wedekind, provides a nice visual of what metanarratives are all about. In live performances, the viewing audience is positioned in the main house of the theater, but on the visible stage there are high rise seats on both sides containing a sort of "meta-audience" to constantly remind the primary audience members that they are indeed watching a play. Actors acknowledge both audiences throughout the performance while moving among, and sometimes utilizing, obviously artificial objects (microphone stands, lighting rigs, and boom mics are all intentionally visible to the audience) that stylishly remind the audience they are watching an artificial production. Such a choice in staging is a visible symbol of the play's primary insight: the self-discovery and self-reflection that occurs during one's teenage sexual awakening. The characters in the play, through this choice in the staging, can't help but be watched from all angles, an apt symbol for the anxiety and awkwardness of sexual discovery and burgeoning adolescent independence which develops under parental surveillance and supervision.

How does film put the metanarrative technique to use and to what effect? *Ferris Bueller's Day Off* (1986) is diffuse with this technique. Throughout the film, Ferris regularly speaks directly to the viewing audience. Other characters on screen are unaware of these aside-like interludes, effectively allowing the main character to enter and exit the film's main diegesis on the fly. Such a rhetorical move on the part of the filmmaker is reflective of Ferris's general whimsy in the film, freely flowing between all sorts of social situations with the greatest of ease. By periodically acknowledging the fact that what's being watched is an artificial construct while maintaining the attention of his diegetic audience – his girlfriend Sloan and friend Cameron – Ferris illustrates a unique ability to the command attention of everyone he encounters through his charisma and social grace. After the closing credits, he not only speaks to the camera, but acknowledges that he is an actor speaking to a room full of movie-goers, "You're still here? It's over. Go home." In effect, the metanarrative form is elements of Ferris's character, writ large.

Director Mel Brooks, best known for his spoofing style of filmmaking, also makes heavy use of metanarrative techniques. In *Spaceballs* (1987), a parody of the original *Star Wars* films, Brooks includes a scene where the two principal characters are speaking to the audience while simultaneously watching a video tape of themselves, unsure of how the dead-air will affect a progression of the film's main diegesis. The scene carries on for nearly three minutes, driving home the film's tone of absurdity and the fact that this satire is not meant to be taken too seriously. Here, the metanarrative form doesn't focus on character; it is used as a method to communicate elements of the film's overall tone and feel.

The "Micro" Elements of Film – The Camera as Narrator

Before photography and film, the human artist was the mediating force between the world and the art that was produced; in other words, any artistic endeavor (writing, speech, sculpture, acting, etc.) gets funneled through a human perception and comes out the other side as an artistic product, which itself could be objective, expressive, pragmatic, and so on. Once the camera lens got introduced into this equation things began to change. Film theorist Andre Bazin argues in *What is Cinema?* (1965) that film fundamentally marginalizes the human being in the process of artistic production. For Bazin, there is the subject, the lens, and what's produced. The artist is pushed outside of that relationship. He's no longer functions as a channel between the two things, and Bazin imagines that cameras could one day work on their own without human intervention, thereby capturing the world through a strictly mechanical or technological process of interpretation. Perhaps here is the embryo of the "reality" film and TV genre.

Bazin's theory neglects some important questions, however, when it comes to the "rhetoric" of film. What does it mean to select something with a camera? What is does it mean to shoot something from down here as opposed to up there? What about cropping? How may an out-of-focus lens deliberately communicate something meaningful to a viewing audience? It's this type of stuff that undergirds a key understanding in filmic studies: the camera is, in many ways, the narrator because all of the choices in visual perspective have bearing on meaning. *Citizen Kane* (1941) is a veritable buffet of all the ways a camera can develop a narratological effect. The technical breakthroughs of this film, the ways in which director Orson Welles understood that the camera can tell large parts of a story without a single bit of dialogue uttered, is a big reason why this film always finds itself atop critics' Top 100 movies-of-all-time lists. Whereas choices in diegesis can best be thought of as the analog to "macro" concerns of organization in writing, think of the following techniques as the analog to the "micro" concerns of writing: the "paragraphs," the "sentences," the "words" of film.

The Mise-en-Scene

The "mise-en-scene," a term taken on loan from theatre, originally referred to choices in the arrangement of the physical space of a theater stage. Staging, in the theatrical sense, refers to the location of the actors on stage and the arrangement of those actors relative to props, lights, set pieces, and so forth. There may be some movement in these things, but generally the mise-en-scene of theatre is fixed; it doesn't change too much within a scene, at least not all of the sudden. You may think to the bareness of the primary stage space, the inclusion adjunct bleachers, and the intentional visibility of microphones on stage as choices in the mis-en-scene of the previously mentioned play, *Spring Awakening*, to illustrate this idea.

As a filmic term, the mise-en-scene refers to these things too, of course, but the possibilities of its effect on an audience are greatly expanded with the introduction of film's technological element, the camera. Cameras have the ability to move around in space on tracks and cranes, instantly traverse great distances with a telephoto lens, thus dramatically changing an audience's fixed point of view from their assigned seat in a theater to a dynamic experience that changes perspective from one scene, and even one frame, to the next.

A *moving shot* refers to any shot that travels through space whether physically or optically, thus shifting the perspective of the audience in a broad range of ways. Physical movement requires that the actual camera be moved from one point in space to another, whereas optical movement gives the *illusion* of motion through space, a feature of the technological ability of the camera's lens. Among the many techniques of moving shots, here are a few of the most common, accompanied by their usual rhetorical effect (see Table 1).

Table 1 List of Effects for Physical and Optical Camera Movement.

Physical movement	Optical movement
Crane shots use a mechanical device to move the camera through space, typically to enhance the majesty of a landscape or the size of a crowd.	*Deep focus shots* keep all the planes of the image in sharp focus from foreground to background, typically to emphasize parallel action in a single shot.
Pan shots film a scene while the camera is pivoted on a stationary base, typically to juxtapose two filmed subjects without editing cuts.	*Shallow focus shots* keep only one plane of action in sharp focus, either foreground or background, typically to privilege one object in a shot over another.
Swish pan shots film a scene where the horizontal movement of the camera is so rapid that the resultant images are blurred, typically to heighten feelings of confusion or chaos.	*Telephoto shots* portray an image like that of a magnifying glass, typically to flatten an image or crop the perspective of what's in the frame.
Track shots film a scene where the camera – typically mounted on a dolly or track – moves alongside the object it is recording, typically to emphasize the filmed subject's movement through space.	*Zoom shots* traverse the physical space of a setting through the optical power of the lens. Cameras can zoom-in to provide focus on a single subject, or zoom out to place a single subject into a larger visual context.
Hand-held shots film a scene in way that is perceptibly shaky, typically to introduce a sense of realism or unpredictability.	*Fish-eye or wide-angle shots* increase the illusion of depth in a scene by distorting the linear dimensions of the image, sometimes to include more objects in the filmed scene, sometimes to communicate a sense of disorientation.

Camera as Narrator – How the Camera Can Speak Rhetorically

In addition to altering perspective, the camera can also create a narrative voice for the film that can be "read" much like the words of a narrator who is presenting a story in literature. Cameras can "speak" in third person and first person, portray objectivity and subjectivity, let the audience see the world through a character's eyes, and even act as an external representation of a character's psychological interiority. It's easy to see how live-action films exploit these techniques, but even animated and digital films know just how dependent a film's narrative tone is to the camera. How's that? The film is shot with virtual cameras – complete with virtual camera angles and virtual camera movement – to shape our perception of the virtual actors in the virtual diegesis. In some senses, it is the movement of the camera the propels the story forward and keeps the audience interested in what's going on in the characters and events (view Andy Warhol's *Empire* (1964) if you'd like to see a film with no camera angles or movement). Table 2 contains some of the most common camera angles that filmmakers use in their cinematography accompanied by an explanation of their typical rhetorical effect.

Table 2 A Chart Detailing the Basic Types of Camera Angles and their Rhetorical Effect on the Audience.

Shot type and description	Effect of the shot
Long shots show a subject in its entirety with much of the visible surroundings.	To emphasize a relationship between the main subject and its environment or surroundings.
Medium shots show a subject from the waist-up with some of the visible surroundings in the frame.	To emphasize body language while remaining in close enough proximity to capture some finer details.
Close-up shots tightly frame an object into the borders of the photographic image.	To focus on the nuance and subtly of facial expressions, or the details of an object.
Extreme close-up shots tightly frame a small detail, leaving the overall object, and the setting cropped out of the frame.	To represent metonymy and synecdoche, a type of metaphor where as part of an object represents a much larger (often conceptual) whole.
Over-the shoulder shots include the side of a character's face and with most objects in their sight line visible on screen.	To invest the audience into a conversation or scenario without directly taking on the point of view of a particular character.
Point of view shots show the viewing audience what a character in the film's diegesis is seeing at specific moment.	To create a first-hand depiction of events as they are experienced by a film's character.

(*Continued*)

Table 2 (*Continued*)

Shot type and description	Effect of the shot
High-angle shots look down on the subject from an elevated vertical position.	To diminish or emphasize the vulnerability of the main subject.
Low-angle shots look up to the from the ground level up to just underneath the vertical axis of the main subject.	To strengthen or create a more powerful appearance of the main subject.
Dutch-angle shots or *Canted-angle shots* make the vertical and horizontal lines of the film's image appear at an angle to the vertical and horizontal lines of the film's frame.	To suggest uneasiness, discomfort, or some other abnormality within the filmed subject's interiority.

Director as Reviser – How the Director Can Arrange Rhetorically

If directors write films, then editing is the process by which the filmmaker revises their initial, unfocused draft. Editing, in filmic terms, is the process of cutting raw footage into discrete shots and joining these with other shots to create a final product for an audience. Different techniques in editing can affect an audience's spatial, temporal, or conceptual understanding of a film. Editing can be best thought of as the rhetorical equivalent of Ciceronian "arrangement," since here is where the filmmaker makes final decisions on what to include, how to present it, and in what order. These choices take place at four levels (see Figures 1 and 2).

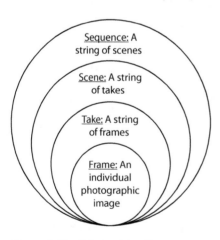

Spatial editing:
Invisible editing: A sequence of shots (often long-to-medium-to-closeup) which keeps the spatial relationships within the scene clear. *Analytic editing:* The breakup of a continuous scene for psychological or dramatic purposes.

Temporal editing:
Parallel editing: The back-and-forth cross-cutting of two or more simultaneous events. *Jump cuts:* A technique where a section of film is removed from the middle of a shot, and the film is re-edited without the gap. *Elliptical editing:* The reduction of a full chain of events to its most crucial moments.

Conceptual editing:
Match cuts: A technique where a new scene begins in the same way that a previous scene ended.

Figure 1 The Relationship of Image Sequences in Film.

Figure 2 Types of Editing Techniques and their Domain of Effect.

The process of editing as a rhetorical choice in filmmaking has a rich theoretical history. Russian film theorist Sergei Eisenstein (1898–1948) wrote several manifestos on the subject including *Film Sense* (1942) and *Film Form* (1949), now standards for any student enrolled in film studies. Eisenstein argued that the heart and soul of filmic art is "montage," a dialectical view of cinematic editing where sequential shots relate to each other in a way that generates concepts not visually present in the shots themselves. The higher meaning that results from the collision of edited images – the "tertium quid" as Eisenstein called it – is where the film's meaning really lives. True montage, for Eisenstein, is an elaborate exercise in symbolism and metaphor (the filmic analog to something like symbolist poetry – see Figure 3) that pushes the audience to make meaning not present in the images on screen while compelling them to pay extremely close attention.

Though contemporary film uses montage mostly to present a great deal of narrative information in an abbreviated period of time, montage is an extremely powerful mode of filmic expression. It is a technique unique to filmic language; text and still image

> IN A STATION OF THE METRO
>
> The apparition of these faces in the crowd; Petals on a wet, black bough.

Figure 3 Symbolist Poem "In a Station of the Metro" by Ezra Pound (1913).

are far too circumscribed by their form to present anything so dynamic. Below we'll take a look at Dziga Vertov's *Man with a Movie Camera* (1928), one of the most extreme versions of montage ever put on screen. Vertov was very much interested in the way that montage could capture a film's higher truth (a notion at the heart of its *cinema-verite* style). His film has no actors, acting, sets, or scripts; rather, Vertov wanted the juxtaposition of images in his montages to let the film speak for itself. Figure 4 illustrates a few of the most notable instances where Vertov pulls off this effect. Hopefully you can see just how "writerly" these filmic choices are.

It's often said about film that editing is where the most impressive rhetorical work takes place and this process bears a number of similarities to the process of revision in a written work. Editing shapes perception and ultimately dictates meaning. Just as a filmmaker can raise the status of a character in the audience eyes by the inclusion of a few low-angle shots and associative montage sequences, they can tear that same person down with a high-angle and a few tricks with the lighting. Editing also pares the film down to its most essential elements. As anyone who has watched a

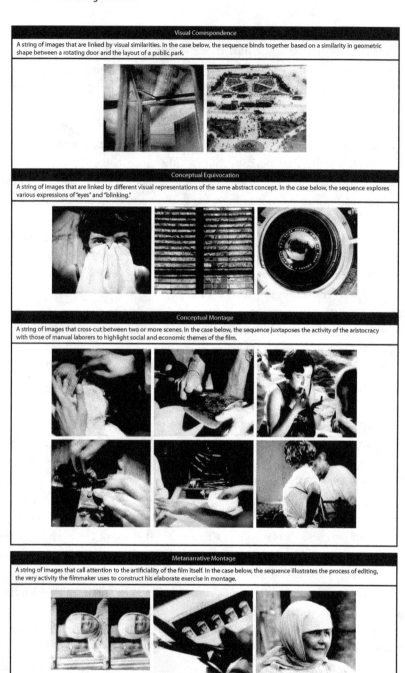

Figure 4 Various Montage Sequences in Dziga Vertov's Man with a Movie Camera (1928).

drawn-out film known, junking a couple extra minutes of needless dialogue sometimes makes all the difference in watch-ability. As Alfred Hitchcock once said, "Drama is life with all the dull parts left out."

Translating Text to Film

In Chapter 2, we stressed the degree to which a rhetorical reading must strike a balance between its concrete (tying observations to the text) and abstract (drawing inferences from these text-based observations) components. In Chapter 4, we saw how this equilibrium transfers over into the writing process in the running example of Jonathan Edwards and James Van Tholen. In text-based analytic compositions, the writer must grapple with the triad essential questions, which move from purpose-to-strategy-to-meaning in order to communicate a full picture of what's going on. Translating text to film is a useful exercise to get student writers thinking in rhetorical terms about film since it requires an understanding of the input of one language (text) output into another expressive form (film). Since most films are generally adapted from textual sources, and since any filmmaker needs to have a good working knowledge of the language of film, this form of writing and thinking requires the writer to both make and defend the narratological choices of interpretation of the original source. Translations are also active, creative enterprises – an exercise in "invention," perhaps – that, as Linda Cahir says in *Literature into Film* (2006), "exploit the source text in such a way that a self-reliant, but related aesthetic offspring is born. The translation cannot be so self-governing as to be completely independent of or antithetical to the source material." You may want to think about the questions below during the early forming stages of text-to-film translations. Hopefully you'll notice these considerations are constructed along the same lines as the concerns of a rhetorical analysis, moving from the establishing "What/How" questions to analytical "Why" questions:

> What changes from the original do you imagine – setting, time, characters, mode of dialogue? Why are these necessary?
>
> What's the focus of the textual source? How does that focus manifest itself in the filmic translation? What's important that we see about your treatment of the point of view and why?

How do you structure time? Will you have flashback sequences as the story moves along? Will you flash-forward to show what a character is considering? Will everything take place in the narrative present? Why?

What camera movements and types of shots will you choose? Why are these choices essential to your rhetorical understanding of certain parts of the text?

Let's take an example to see how this works. Consider the following passage from *The Stranger in the Photo is Me* (1991) where author Donald Murray describes the litany of memories that rush out as he looks at an old photograph of himself, just prior to his deployment in World War II. Read the passage in full, look at the filmic translation in the form of a shot decoupage, then read the analysis which explains and defends the choices in translation from text to film.

I was never one to make a big deal over snapshots; I never spent long evenings with the family photograph album. Let's get on with the living. To heck with yesterday, what are we going to do tomorrow? But with the accumulation of yesterdays and the possibility of shrinking tomorrows, I find myself returning, as I suspect many over 60s do, for a second glance and a third at family photos that snatch a moment from time.

In looking at mine, I become aware that it is so recent in the stretch of man's history that we have been able to stop time in this way and hold still for reflection.

Vermeer is one of my favorite painters because of that sense of suspended time, with both clock and calendar held so wonderfully, so terribly still.

The people in the snapshots are all strangers. My parents young, caught before I arrived or as they were when I saw them as towering grown-ups. They seemed so old then and so young now. And I am, to me, the strangest of all. There is a photograph of me on a tricycle before the duplex on Grand View Avenue in Wollaston I hardly remember; in another I am dressed in a seersucker sailor suit when I was 5 and lived in a Cincinnati hotel. I cannot remember the suit but even now, studying the snapshot, I am drunk on the memory of its peculiar odor and time is erased.

In the snapshots, I pass from chubby to skinny and, unfortunately, ended up a chub. Looking at the grown-ups in the snapshots I should have known. In other snapshots, I am cowboy, pilot, Indian chief; I loved to dress up to become what I was not, and suspect I still am a wearer of masks and costumes. It would be socially appropriate to report on this day that I contemplate all those who are gone, but the truth is that my eyes are drawn back to pictures of my stranger self.

And the picture that haunts me the most is one not in costume but in the uniform I proudly earned in World War II. I believe it was taken in England from the design of the barracks behind me. I have taken off the ugly steel-framed GI glasses, a touch of dishonesty for the girl who waited at home.

My overseas cap with its airborne insignia is tugged down over my right eye, my right shoulder in the jump jacket is lower because I have my left hand in my pocket in rakish disregard for the regulation that a soldier in that war could never, ever stick a hand in a pocket.

The pockets that are empty in the photograph will soon bulge with hand grenades, extra ammunition, food, and many of the gross of condoms we were issued before a combat jump. This GI item was more a matter of industrial merchandising than soldierly dreaming – or frontline reality.

The soldier smiles as if he knew his innocence and is both eager for its loss and nostalgic for those few years of naiveté behind him. I try once more to enter the photograph and become what I was that day when autumn sunlight dappled the barracks wall and I was so eager to experience the combat my father wanted so much for me. He had never made it to the trenches over there in his war.

When that photograph was taken, my father still had dreams of merchandising glory, of a store with an awning that read Murray & Son. I had not yet become the person who had to nod yes at MGH when my father asked if he had cancer, to make the decision against extraordinary means after his last heart attack. When this photo was taken, he had not yet grown old, his collars large, his step hesitant, his shoes unshined.

Mother was still alive, and her mother who really raised me had not died as I was to learn in a letter I received at the front. The girl who wrote every day and for whom the photo was taken had not yet become my wife, and we had not yet been the first in our families to divorce two years later. I had not yet seen my first dead soldier, had not yet felt the earth beneath me become a trampoline as the shells of a rolling barrage marched across our position.

I had no idea my life would become as wonderful or as terrible as it has been; that I would remarry, have three daughters and outlive one. I could not have imagined that I actually would be able to become a writer and eat – even overeat. I simply cannot re-create my snapshot innocence. I had not had an easy or happy childhood, I had done well at work but not at school; I was not Mr. Pollyanna, but life has been worse and far better than I could have imagined.

Over 60 we are fascinated by the mystery of our life, why roads were taken and not taken, and our children encourage this as they develop a sense of family history. A daughter discovers a letter from the soldier in the photograph in England and another written less than a year later, on V-E day. She is surprised at how much I have aged. I am not.

I would not wish for a child or grandchild of mine to undergo the blood test of war my father so hoped I would face as he had not. In photos taken not so many years later I have a streak of white hair. It is probably genetic, but I imagine it is the shadow of a bullet that barely passed me by, and I find I cannot enter the snapshot of the smiling soldier who is still stranger to me, still innocent of the heroic harm man can deliver to man.

The Translation from Text-to-Film

The following shot sequence translates the opening half of the Murray's written narrative into the language of film. This chunk of the narrative places its primary emphasis on the nature of photography, and the filmic translation has a meta, self-referential feel (watching a film about looking at picture) to show how deep reflection on a static photograph can touch off elaborate and moving recollections. The opening portion of the written narrative also deals with the transitional moments from the narrative present to the flashback-present of the photograph and, for that reason, film is a prime expressive mode to capture these transitions. Notice how the shot sequence below (Table 3) details the interpretants – both concrete and thematic – used to translate the text to film.

Table 3 Shot Decoupage for Donald Murray's "The Stranger in the Photo is Me".

Images	Spoken words	Music	Sound effects
Extreme close-up of Murray's eyes; the frame captures a furrow of his brow seeming to indicate he's looking at a photograph of a memory that's tough to confront. Grey hairs in his eyebrows and wrinkles around the eye quickly give a sense of his age. *Shot 1* *3 sec.*		Muddy Water's "Mannish Boy" is playing, diegetically, from a radio-signal stereo.	Swishing of flipping photographs
Extreme close-up of Murray's fingers handling a stack of photographs. The images are not discernible because of the speed at which he's flipping through them and the camera's focus on Murray's fingers clearly show those of an older man. *Shot 2* *3 sec.*			
Extreme close-up of Murray's eyes; the frame captures a widening of his eye sockets, alluding to a smile that cannot be seen. *Shot 3* *3 sec.*			
Extreme close-up of Murray's fingers handling more photos. More unintelligible images, but a wedding ring becomes briefly visible as it comes into frame. *Shot 4* *5 sec.*			

(Continued)

Table 3 (*Continued*)

Images	Spoken words	Music	Sound effects
Full shot, low angle of Murray putting down a stack of photos, standing from his chair and looking around his scattered and disorganized office. His back is to the camera the entire time and only a small portion of his face is visible. The scattered papers and books are arranged in such a way to focalize the audience to a framed photo of his himself, his wife, his 3 daughters on the surface of his desk. *Shot 5* *12 sec.*	"I was never one to make a big deal over snapshots; I never spent long evenings with the family photograph album. Let's get on with the living. To heck with yesterday, what are we going to do tomorrow?"		Cacophonous street noise can be faintly heard through the window. Clanging on trashcans and dumpsters are diegetically heard, but they are faint and nearly unnoticeable.
Point of view shot of framed artwork on the wall while voiceover takes place. Viewer can make out pointillism painting of Seurat, perspective shifting work of M.S. Escher, and Rafael's *School of Athens.* *Shot 6* *10 sec.*			
Full shot, low angle of Murray. The shot captures highly set window in the rear of the frame. The streams of light create a high-key effect throughout the office. *Shot 7* *8 sec.*			
Medium shot of Murray leaning both palms on his desk to inspect a stack of photos a little more closely Shot 8 2 sec.	"The people in the snapshots are all strangers."		The indiscernible street noise can now be recognized as a trash truck emptying dumpsters. It is noticeably closer and becomes louder and louder.

(*Continued*)

Table 3 (*Continued*)

Images	Spoken words	Music	Sound effects
Point of view shot of an old family photo of Murray's with a deep focus that captures the family photo from shot 5 in the middle ground and a small mirror in the background. *Shot 9* *4 sec.*	"My parents young, caught before I arrived or as they were when I saw them as towering grown-ups. They seemed so old then and so young now."		
Over the shoulder shot of Murray glancing at a photo of himself prior to his deployment in WWII. The camera focalizes over the top of the photo to a small mirror in the background. *Shot 10* *3 sec.*	"And I am, to me, the strangest of all."		
Extreme close-up of Murray's expressionless eyes in the mirror that lingers just a second too long. Once the audience's discomfort with the shot's duration sets in, there is a slow dissolve of steel-framed GI glasses that become superimposed. *Shot 11* *10 sec.*			
Point of view shot of Murray (with superimposition of eyeglass frame over camera) looks down at his hands, now wrinkle-free. Dark green GI sleeves are visible in the frame. He turns his hands over, and the wedding ring from shot 4 is gone. *Shot 12* *8 sec.*			
Close-up of Murray, in full GI garb and about 40 years younger, peers at himself in the mirror and smiles. *Shot 13* *5 sec.*			A trash truck emptying a dumpster is right outside his window now. The truck slams the dumpster on the ground, jarringly ending the music.

(*Continued*)

Table 3 (*Continued*)

Images	Spoken words	Music	Sound effects
Jump cut to medium shot of an all out firefight. There is visual chaos all over the frame. *Shot 14* *4 sec.*	*Assorted military shouting that alternate between commands and cries of terror.*	None	Diegetic dumpster slam turns to diegetic mortar explosions in the analepsis.
Over the shoulder shot of WWII soldier Murray with bullets flying towards the camera. *Shot 15* *2 sec.*			Intense firefight and explosions
Canted angle close-up of Murray ducking for cover in a trench. Several dead soldiers, at various stages of dismemberment, are strewn all over the frame. *Shot 16* *1 sec.*			
Canted angle close-up of Murray fumbling with his ammunition. *Shot 17* *1 sec.*			Noise of a launched mortar closing in on Murray's position
Canted angle of Murray's hands nervously loading his rifle. *Shot 18* *1 sec.*			
Canted angle close-up of Murray's expression that's somewhere between naiveté and terror. *Shot 19* *3 sec.*			Launched mortar explodes with deafening volume
Jump cut to narrative present. Close-up of old Murray in the mirror. A slight mist of sweat can be noticed on his brow. *Shot 20* *3 sec.*	Muddy Water's "Mannish Boy" resumes, diegetically, from the office radio.		Mortar explosion of shot 19 dissolves into sound of Soft impact of a stack of photos hitting the floor.

The Analysis of the Translation from Text-to-Film

The analysis below can best be thought of as a rationale or defense for the rhetorical choices made in the shot sequence translation. Ultimately, the translation defends two themes from the written text. First, since Murray's essay emphasizes the speaker's awareness of his lost innocence while encountering his younger persona, the translation contains jumps in time between the narrative present and a flashback sequence to fill in the gaps of identity as to who this on-screen older man is. Second, the photographs and Murray's flipping of them is also an important feature of the written narrative that's preserved in the filmic translation. Since photographs "snatch a moment in time" and hold "both clock and calendar so wonderfully, so terribly still," their continued visual presence in the filmic adaptation should remind the audience that time's passage is inevitable despite our attempts to hold it still. As you read this example analysis, note how the author naturally overlaps the structural features of the analytical essays from Chapter 4. Each part of this analysis touches on the three concerns which should be central to any analytical composition: 1) What is the author (filmmaker) trying to accomplish? 2) How does he accomplish it? and 3) What is the effect of these choices?

Donald Murray's essay *The Stranger in the Photo is Me* first appeared on August 27, 1991 in Murray's weekly "Over 60" column in *The Boston Globe*. Although appearing in a periodical, the article presents a short self-contained and self-referential narrative that focuses on photography, its role in memory, how we come to terms with our own mortality, inter-generational relationships and their role in the formation of identity, and how photographs allow us to access all of these moments in our past that could otherwise only be lost to history. To be sure, this sounds like a collection of ambitious subjects for a weekly column, but the author, a Pulitzer-Prize winning journalist and Professor of English at UNH, is a master writer who is able to pack quite a bit into a compact space. The piece gains additional poignancy since Murray, who speaks candidly about his own approaching death in the article, died in December of 2006. So, how does the filmic translation capture these ideas?

The diegesis of filmic translation stays fairly literal to the plot of the narrative. The setting, Murray's private residence, is the same as the text. The character, just Murray himself, is the only figure to appear on screen, just as he's the only character in the narrative. Since there is no camera filming the narrative, I wanted to establish some of these elements subtly through what passes into the frame. The opening sequence of the film (shots 1–4) is heavy on interpretants which foreground the interiority of the narrator.

The opening shot is an extreme close-up focusing just on Murray's eyes in order to establish that this will be a film about the inner workings of this man's mind above all else. Small clues to the narrator's identity come in and out of frame in these early shots. The grey hairs of his eye brows and the wrinkles around his eye sockets give the viewer a clue that this is an older man who's got a fair amount of experience under his belt. In the narrative, Murray explicitly tells the reader that he experiences a broad range of emotions as he's looking through the photos. Rather than have a voiceover tell the audience what Murray's emotional state is, this becomes expressed in the filmic translation through the constricting and loosening of the eye sockets ("a furrow of his brow seeming to indicate he's looking at a photograph of a memory that's tough to confront" in shot 1 and "the frame captures a widening of his eye sockets, alluding to a smile that cannot be seen" in shot 3). I chose to keep a full shot of his face hidden out of the frame in order to aptly capture the concealed tone of the narrative, and since we can't see his face completely, here is a moment that captures the line from the narrative, "I suspect I'm still a wearer of masks and costumes."

The shots that are cross-cut in with the extreme close-ups of Murray's eyes are extreme close-ups of the photographs, completing the interpretant link between the photos and Murray's interiority. In other words, it is the photographs that will take us into the mind of Murray, and this should be clear to the audience through his range of reactions to the photos expressed by his small facial mannerisms. And although the photos take up most of the frame in shots 2 and 4, there are some small clues about who Murray is through the details of his hands. They have wrinkly skin, not of someone in extreme old age, but not those of a young man either. A wedding ring becomes briefly visible in shot 4, alluding to an important portion of the narrative not covered in the shot decoupage when he says, "I had no idea my life would become as wonderful or as terrible as it has been; that I would remarry, have three daughters and outlive one."

The music, playing diegetically in the background, is a thematic interpretant. There is no music mentioned in Murray's narrative. I chose to have Muddy

Water's "Mannish Boy" playing from a radio in his office for a couple of reasons. First, the title of the song captures the dichotomy that Murray is experiencing in the narrative. The title is paradoxical, and this captures *The Stranger is the Photo is Me*'s heavy use antithetical expressions ("yesterdays/tomorrows" (p1), "wonderfully/terribly" (p2), "suspended time" (p2), "I am the strangest of all" (p3)) that work to develop the theme of the divided self during the transition from innocence to experience. Also, the paradox of the song title also matches the paradox of having two speakers who are, in fact, the same person (how can you be the greatest stranger to yourself?). Second, the actual song is based on a call and response musical structure that is befitting of his own call and response taking place in his internal conversation with his current and past self.

In shots 5–8, the editing, camera angles, lighting, setting, and sound effects all work in conjunction to develop the story. In shot 5, the viewer sees the first establishing shot in the sequence. Here, the form – that is, the type and order of the shots themselves – functions as a thematic interpretant. I chose to have the establishing shot come after the extreme close-ups as an inversion of traditional editing sequences which go from establishing shot, to medium shot, to close-up. This keeps with the motif of antithesis and inversion that is the thematic glue of *The Stranger in the Photo is Me*. Once we have the establishing shot, Murray is still partially concealed from the audience ("standing from his chair and looking around his scattered and disorganized office. His back is to the camera the entire time and only a small portion of his face is visible") in order to communicate him still as a guarded and concealed individual that the audience can't quite fully know. This is all done at a low-angle in order to put the audience on a separate plane from Murray; we can listen to his story and understand it, but this is really a story of interiority and one that keeps the audience at arm's length.

During the full perspective of shot 5 and point of view perspective in shot 6, there are a number of details in his office visible to the audience that works as thematic interpretants of the narrative's emphasis on the importance of perspective. The viewer can make out three pieces of artwork on the wall in shot 6: a pointillist painting of George Seurat, perspective shifting work of M.S. Escher's *Relativity*, and Rafael's *School of Athens*. To emphasize the narrative theme of the importance of perspective, Suerat's pointillist art symbolizes that true understanding can only be attained if the proper distance is achieved between viewer and object. If the viewer is too close, the painting will appear only as unintelligible chaos; if the viewer is too far, the details will be too murky and hazy to clearly make out; if the viewer is just right, they will be able to see exactly what Suerat is doing. This idea is similar to Murray's own understanding of the photograph in the narrative communicated through his anaphora of "I have not yet" when speaking from the voice of the photo Murray. It's the perspective of the "over 60" Murray that gives him the appropriate distance to see and understand the importance and interconnectedness of the events in his life that have all been captured in photographs. To emphasize the narrative's emphasis of probing the depths of one's past, Escher's *Relativity* is the second painting on the wall which communicates Murray experience of jump-cutting in time where normal laws of space and time do not apply. To communicate the theme of paradox and self-contradiction, Rafael's *School of Athens* can also be seen in the frame. It is a paradox; at once, it's simple but complex, orderly yet chaotic, static and dynamic, transcendent and imminent. Murray's presentation of himself in the narrative works similarly to this painting, with all of the apparent contrasts functioning to make up a complete whole.

In shot 7, the lighting and sound are used as a thematic interpretants of Murray's self-division. In the decoupage, shot 7 is described as "Full shot, low angle of Murray. The shot captures highly set window in the rear of the frame. The streams of light create a hard-light effect throughout the office." The shadows cast on the wrinkles of Murray's partially visible face, and the office as a whole is sharp-edged symbolizing the good memories along with the bad that he experiences while digging through old photos. There is also a diegetic sound effect in this scene that foreshadows what's to come in the next sequence: "cacophonous street noise can be faintly heard through the window. Clanging on trashcans and dumpsters are diegetically heard, but they are faint and nearly unnoticeable." The sound effects functions as an auditory representation of the dormant memory of Murray's war experience. This effect is brought to fruition in shot 13 and marks the fulcrum upon which the narrative present is fully transported into the analeptic episode of the shot sequence.

Shot 9 is meaningful because it is the first time in the sequence that the viewer actually sees Murray's face straight on, but as the shot sequence indicates, the audience sees Murray's face as a reflection in a mirror. The introduction of the mirror is almost like the introduction of the other principle character of the piece. The reflective effect creates two Murray's, each examining the other, as a way to express the dual speakers in the written narrative. The photograph which transports Murray into his own past is presented to the audience in shot 10. The shot is presented as point of view so the audience can not only see the picture as Murray is looking at it but also to present this from the point of view of Murray's interiority. As we vicariously look at the photo, "the camera focalizes over the top of the photo to a small mirror in the background" in order to emphasize that this viewing of the photo isn't just recalling a memory from the past, but is confrontation of a past version of himself that is now gone. As he peers into the mirror, the viewer gets their first explicit visualization of Murray's interiority as he re-enters his memory. Shot 11 is the longest shot (15 seconds) of the entire sequence. There is an eerie stillness ("Extreme close-up of Murray's expressionless eyes in the mirror that lingers just a second too long") like the peaceful calm before war. The length of the shot is intended to make the audience uneasy and confused and only "once the audience's discomfort with the shot's duration sets in, there is a slow dissolve of steel-framed GI glasses that become superimposed." He's still in the narrative present here, as the superimposed glasses are clearly an imagined object, but as he looks down at his hands in shot 12, he's fully immersing himself in the memory. This is a formal interpretant from the written narrative; there, he changes the verb tense to a conditional future tense to show that he's now speaking from the perspective of his younger self. Here, he has entered his past self visually, using the mirror and his own interiority as a portal to this other time and space.

Once the visual transformation is complete in shot 13, there's an ostensible satisfaction as he fully re-enters his former self, recalling the naiveté of the photograph from the written narrative. This contentedness, however, is offset by the mounting noise outside of this home. As the noise reaches its peak, corresponds to the jarring crash of his wartime memories ("A trash truck emptying a dumpster is right outside his window now. The truck slams the dumpster on the ground, jarringly ending the music"). The jump cut is meant to shock the viewer and abruptly transport him into the memory.

Shot 14 marks the abrupt transportation into the analeptic portion of the film. Aside from the jump cut, there is an audio dissolve of the slammed dumpster now being completed as an exploding mortar, and once the mortar has dissipated, the audience is there, right alongside Murray, in a muddied trench amid an ongoing firefight. In the written narrative, Murray never quite leaves the narrative present entirely and his concealed tone expresses the shock, horror and dismay he experienced in the war in an oblique and understated way. In the filmic adaptation, this experience is brought to the fore. In keeping with the motif of antithesis, Murray's solitary and reflective experience in his serene office is sharply juxtaposed now with the chaotic confusion of a WWII firefight, marked by both visual ("There is wartime chaos all over the frame") and auditory cacophony ("Assorted military shouting that alternate between commands and cries of terror") intended to overwhelm the viewer's senses in order to present a vicarious experience of Murray's.

The terror and confusion of Murray during his war experience is expressed through the acting, the editing, and the camera angles. The actor playing young Murray captures the juxtaposed emotions of terror and naiveté in a single expression to the point where the viewer can explicitly recognize this as a key transitional moment where the narrator is moving from innocence to experience. As the firefight continues, the viewer can notice a continual kicking up of dirt and blood onto Murray's face and uniform, a physical symbol of the taint of war that was absent from the photograph. His nervous fumbling and incompetence with his weapon suggest that he's just a kid in over his head, and he's growing up at a rate faster than he is equipped to handle. Moreover, the entire sequence (with the exception of shot 15's over the shoulder style) is canted angles. These angles, formally, are intended to portray the psychological uneasiness and tension in Murray. This effect is extended to the audience as well, for it is meant to disorient them while they are still getting their bearings from the jump cut in order to vicariously experience Murray's memory alongside him. The war sequence, too, is in contrast to the still shots of the narrative present, another interpretant of the text's antithetical motif.

The editing of this segment of the film deviates from the earlier office segments. There, all shots were mounted still shots with very little camera movement intended to convey a sense of stillness and reflection. Here, the editing happens at machine-gun speed, going from one shot to the next at a dizzying and disorienting pace. The contrast in pacing form the narrative present and the analepsis is another manifestation of the split self-motif that is sustained throughout the written narrative.

This segment of the translation, although marked by a harried chaos, does have some elements which don't entirely sever it from the opening segment, and these formal elements remind us that we are dealing with the same Murray, not an entirely separate individual. In shot 17, a distant mortar that has been launched towards Murray's position can be heard. The approaching noise should recall the approaching noise of the trash truck in the opening segment. As a structuring element, the impact of the mortar also marks the abrupt jump cut transition from the analepsis back to the narrative present, much in the same way that the slam of the dumpster sent the audience into the analepsis in shot 14.

Shot 20, the concluding shot of the decoupage, returns entirely to "over 60" Murray glancing in the mirror. The sounds of war are now gone, replaced by the original Muddy Water's track, "Mannish Boy," which now takes on greater meaning and significance in relation to his experiences in the war; he was a boy who became a man too fast through his experience in war. Beads of sweat can be noticed on his forehead leaving the viewer with the impression that this memory is equal parts intense and uneasy for Murray.

This essay should stand as a clear example of the way a rhetorical reader can translate narration from a written work into a sequence of filmic shots, as detailed and meaningful as the original. Translation – decoding of a message from language and writing it in another – is the operative word. It is an active and transformative process which involves choices that are fundamentally rhetorical and interpretive, taking the source text and refashioning it in the new language of film. The fun thing about this type of writing is the degree of variation that can happen among translations on the same exact text, since translations occur within contexts (cultural, historical, linguistic), sometimes yielding an entirely different product from the same set of raw materials. Whereas this translation intentionally focuses the viewer's attention on the constructed frame and alterations to the story's "reality," another translation may decide to present things without the notice of intrusive editing, thus giving the film an entirely different feel. A translation communicates the integral meaning and literary value of the text, and so long as a clear collaboration between written and filmic language is present, anything goes.

CHAPTER SEVEN

RHETORICAL ANALYSIS – ADDITIONAL MODELS

Throughout our discussion of analysis in the first six chapters, we've stressed the fact to no writer composes in a vacuum, that what an author says in the "present" of their writing is inextricably bound to what's been already been said about that topic in the past. It's easy to see how this logic applies to creative writers, but this is also a useful schema to think about the writing often composed by students in classroom settings. No doubt, some students learn well from prescriptive rules and approaching writing-as-process, but for students who prefer more of backwards-design model to writing instruction – seeing a finished product to reverse engineer it into its constituent parts – then this chapter is for you.

This theoretical approach is what's known as the Writing as Product model, a pedagogical method that places primary emphasis on the finished product. Long the standard in the teaching of writing, this approach expects students to use acquired skills and knowledge to examine a finished piece of writing in order to use it as a "mentor text." Employing mentor texts can be a useful heuristic to the development of your ideas and choices of form in your writing, and this is an approach that can be used to analytically write about all genres of text.

The following chapter contains four analytical essays, each tied to its own anchor text. As you read, you should think about the text in terms of rhetorical analysis: how do the concerns of Chapters 2, 3, 4, 5 and 6 figure into the process of meaning-making that you bring to the reading?

The readings run the gamut of all the commonplace genres in English classrooms: non-fiction narrative, essay, poetry, prose fiction, and even film. You'll notice some of the readings are presented singularly to spotlight a specific point that the author is making while others are paired with another text, allowing for a dialogic interaction between the two voices on a shared topic. Each text is accompanied by a brief contextualization of the authors and their work.

Following the reading is an example analytical essay. These essays, while acting as useful models to illustrate how student writers may respond rhetorically to readings of all genres, should not be understood as a final or authoritative interpretation of the work. Instead, approach them in a spirit of constructive play to see how the author has effectively analyzed and explained what's going on in the text while remembering this is but one interpretation, subject to approval, disputation, and continued dialogue. Such an approach will help to carry on the continuous conversation which swirls around every text we hold in our hands.

Non-Fiction Narrative Analysis: *Narrative of the Life of Frederick Douglass* by Frederick Douglass

Frederick Douglass is one of the first African-American abolitionists and his work, *The Narrative fo the Life of Frederick Douglass* (1845), was instrumental in the removal of slavery in the United States. The memoir traces his life, beginning in his youth and progressing all the way to his adult life as a free man. In the following passage, make note of the way that Douglass communicates the hardships of slavery to his reader through his use of diction, syntax, and other various rhetorical structures.

The home plantation of Colonel Lloyd wore the appearance of a country village. All the mechanical operations for all the farms were performed here. The shoemaking and mending, the blacksmithing, cartwrighting, coopering, weaving, and grain-grinding, were all performed by the slaves on the home plantation. The whole place wore a business-like aspect very unlike the neighboring farms. The number of houses, too, conspired to give it advantage over the neighboring farms. It was called by the slaves the GREAT HOUSE FARM. Few privileges were esteemed higher, by the slaves of the out-farms, than that of being selected to do errands at the Great House Farm. It was associated in their minds with greatness. A representative could not be prouder of his election to a seat in the American Congress, than a slave on one of the out-farms would be of his election to do errands at the Great House Farm. They regarded it as evidence of great confidence reposed in them by their overseers; and it was on this account, as well as a constant desire to be out of the field from under the driver's lash, that they esteemed it a high privilege, one worth careful living for. He was called the smartest and most trusty fellow, who had this honor conferred upon him the most frequently. The competitors for this office sought as diligently to please their overseers, as the office-seekers in the political parties seek to please and deceive the people. The same traits of character might be seen in Colonel Lloyd's slaves, as are seen in the slaves of the political parties.

The slaves selected to go to the Great House Farm, for the monthly allowance for themselves and their fellow-slaves, were peculiarly enthusiastic. While on their way, they would make the dense old woods, for miles around, reverberate with their wild songs, revealing at once the highest joy and the deepest sadness. They would compose and sing as they went along, consulting neither time nor tune. The thought that came up, came out – if not in the word, in the sound; – and as frequently in the one as in the other. They would sometimes sing the most pathetic sentiment in the most rapturous tone, and the most rapturous sentiment in the most pathetic tone. Into all of their songs they would manage to weave something of the Great House Farm. Especially would they do this, when leaving home. They would then sing most exultingly the following words: -

"I am going away to the Great House Farm! O, yea! O, yea! O!"

This they would sing, as a chorus, to words which to many would seem unmeaning jargon, but which, nevertheless, were full of meaning to themselves. I have sometimes thought that the mere hearing of those songs would do more to impress some minds with the horrible character of slavery, than the reading of whole volumes of philosophy on the subject could do.

I did not, when a slave, understand the deep meaning of those rude and apparently incoherent songs. I was myself within the circle; so that I neither saw nor heard as those without might see and hear. They told a tale of woe which was then altogether beyond my feeble comprehension; they were tones loud, long, and deep; they breathed the prayer and complaint of souls boiling over with the bitterest anguish. Every tone was a testimony against slavery, and a prayer to God for deliverance from chains. The hearing of those wild notes always depressed my spirit and filled me with ineffable sadness. I have frequently found myself in tears while hearing them. The mere recurrence to those songs, even now, afflicts me; and while I am writing these lines, an expression of feeling has already found its way down my cheek. To those songs I trace my first glimmering conception of the dehumanizing character of slavery. I can never get rid of that conception. Those songs still follow me, to deepen my hatred of slavery, and quicken my sympathies for my brethren in bonds. If any one wishes to be impressed with the soul-killing effects of slavery, let him go to Colonel Lloyd's plantation, and, on allowance-day, place himself in the deep pine woods, and there let him, in silence, analyze the sounds that shall pass through the chambers of his soul, – and if he is not thus impressed, it will only be because "there is no flesh in his obdurate heart."

I have often been utterly astonished, since I came to the north, to find persons who could speak of the singing, among slaves, as evidence of their contentment and happiness. It is impossible to conceive of a greater mistake. Slaves sing most when they are most unhappy. The songs of the slave represent the sorrows of his heart; and he is relieved by them, only as an aching heart is relieved by its tears. At least, such is my experience. I have often sung to drown my sorrow, but seldom to express my happiness. Crying for joy, and singing for joy, were alike uncommon to me while in the jaws of slavery. The singing of a man cast away upon a desolate island might be as appropriately considered as evidence of contentment and happiness, as the singing of a slave; the songs of the one and of the other are prompted by the same emotion.

Example Analysis

As any student who went through grade school knows, the Underground Railroad, the secret network which assisted escaping slaves from the American South, conducted its operations under secret codes and symbols concealing its very existence. But there's often much left out of these grade school narratives: the petty politicking to curry favor with the master, the therapeutic role of music, and (of course) the psychological effects of bondage itself. Enter Frederick Douglass. A published expose of slave life would not fly under the gaze of his masters, so Frederick Douglass composes *Narrative of the Life of Frederick Douglass* in a manner consistent with the speech patterns of slaves in the 19th century; that is, he must carefully choose his language to carry far more meaning than a surface read would initially suggest. In doing so, not only does he provide a rich demonstration of rhetorical abilities for a self-educated man, but also captures the very ethos of slave life in 19th century America, an existence where one's true thoughts and feelings must be mediated by the mantra "watch what you say."

The excerpt's lynchpin comes in the opening line's use of "appearance," a deliberate diction choice which suggests the farm's outward façade conceals an inner (and uglier) reality. An "outsiders-looking-in" perspective may well see the home plantation of Colonel Lloyd as a quaint, old-timey village – complete with "shoemaking and mending, blacksmithing, cartwrighting, coopering, weaving, and grain-grinding" – that is wholly unassuming, even charming. A reader's prior knowledge about the institution of slavery should signal that something is afoot in this apparent praise and, as the passage develops, Douglass becomes increasingly caustic about the reality which belies the appearance of Colonel Lloyd's home. The ostensible songs of happiness sung by those slaves promoted to the home are revealed as "songs of the slave [which] represent the sorrows of his heart" and the author compares these slaves to "a man cast away upon a desolate island." In light of these details, the opening line can be read as an irony. And, the very core of an ironic statement is to use language in a way that signifies the opposite of what is said.

Douglass's appearance/reality motif extends when he says, "The number of houses, too, conspired to give it advantage over the neighboring farms." In this strange but memorable image, Douglass personifies the houses of the Great House Farm as "conspiring" with one another to give off an appearance of majesty and grandeur. The verb "conspiring" – which means "to make secret plans to commit a harmful act" – is consistent with several other instances in the first paragraph which describe the Great House Farm's impressiveness accompanied by insinuations of the evil and abuse that exist just beyond its benign facade. The houses don't *complement* or *accentuate* the "beauty" of the plantation; no, they "conspire" to give "advantage" over the other farms. These connotations are shot through with themes of secrecy and exploitation, ideas that speak powerfully to the evils of the general practice of slavery while functioning as a covert message about the dangers on the farm which are not readily apparent to a passerby.

Douglass doesn't stop there. Take the way he sketches out the character traits of the slaves who get promotion to the Great House Farm in paragraph 1 ("It was associated…the political parties"). His tone ostensibly suggests that promotion to Great House Farm is something to which slaves should strive, but a close reading of what he *doesn't* say reveals an awful lot – maybe more so than what he actually does say – about his attitude towards these individuals who bootlick their way to the top. Phrases like "it was associated in their minds," "they regarded it as evidence of great confidence," "they esteemed it a high privilege" all further Douglass's wry and ironical tone. If *they* associate it with greatness, it is implied that Douglass does not. If *they* regard it as evidence of great confidence, it is implied that Douglass does not. If *they* esteem it as a high privilege, it is implied that Douglass does not. Douglass lists these traits to describe the slaves at the Great House Farm, yes, but he also uses these judgements as the scaffold for a broader criticism. He does this by shifting the very definition of the word "slave" over the course of paragraph 1. For a majority of the paragraph, Douglass uses the word "slave" to mean "a person who is the legal property of another," but in the paragraph's final phrase – "as are seen in the slaves of the political parties" – he brings an alternate meaning to the text. Here, he's referring to "slave" as a sycophantic brown-noser, an individual whose personal integrity has been taken prisoner by their ambition and cut-throat politicking. By equivocating these alternate meanings of "slave," Douglass reveals the politics involved with promotion to the Great House Farm in the characteristic doublespeak style of the passage as a whole.

Where he uses irony and equivocation to say two things at once in paragraph 1, he uses paradox to the same effect in paragraph 2. He says, "While on their way, they would make the dense old woods, for miles around, reverberate with their wild songs, revealing at once the highest joy and the deepest sadness." In this logically contradictory line, both the adjective and noun in the first pair are at odds with those from second pair: "Highest" is the opposite of "deepest," and "joy" is the inverse of "sadness." How, then, is it possible to have these emotional binaries co-existing in a single instant? Douglass seems to be gesturing at a common bittersweet (another paradoxical adjective!) experience shared by most readers – but maybe not to the degree of those in Douglass's description – where only the language of logical contradiction can capture the conflicting feelings. In doing so, Douglass stretches the use of paradox to its maximum potential by giving the reader something provocative to think about without committing himself to any one logical position.

Douglass's description of slave songs in paragraphs 3–5 extends Douglass's motif of multi-layered speech, but this time metaphor is the tool of choice.

To get Douglass's metaphor – "compose and sing...consulting neither time nor tune" – the reader needs to know a bit about musical terminology. "Time," or time signature, represents a uniform number of beats in each measure and "tune" refers to the correct musical pitch or key. Songs lacking one or both of these features will be herky-jerky, discordant, and tough on the ear. His writing, of course, cannot literally be composed in time or tune, but this metaphor suggests that his reader take a closer look at his choice in syntax to create an impression of time and tune. Where Douglass's prose style is generally eloquent, fluid, and even poetic elsewhere in this passage, his descriptions in paragraphs 3–5 are deliberately presented as cacophonous and ungrammatical to capture the sonic and emotional elements of the slave songs in a particularly powerful way. By blending the musical and the verbal, Douglass offers up a powerful cross-over of artistic mediums. He says of the songs, "The thought that came up, came out – if not in the word, in the sound; – and as frequently in the one as in the other." Read this out loud and you'll notice all sorts of grammatical and mechanical quirks which reflect a song composed with "neither time not tune." The hard stop of "came up, came out" comes off like poetic enjambment, slamming on the sentence's brakes just as it's gaining momentum. What follows is an asymmetrical pair of phrases – "if not in the word, in the sound" – which are not cleanly offset by dashes; there is a semicolon just before the second dash, giving off the effect of an extended and exaggerated silence. The final phrase "and as frequently in the one as in the other" is an ambiguous reference where it's not quite clear if "word" or "sound" is the "one" or the "other." Moreover, despite its length of 25 words, this quotation is actually just a fragment. The main subject, "thought," is followed by one long and twisting adjectival phrase with no main verb to make grammatical sense of the statement. It's in these elements of the syntax and grammar that Douglass tells us something powerful about slave life while (logically) saying nothing intelligible at all.

What sense can a reader make of a passage that's written to resist logical, linear analysis? Yes, Douglass prose twists itself into grammatical and logical knots, yet he somehow manages to express something profound and powerful about the nature of slavery in 19th century America. Perhaps through all his two-sided rhetoric, Douglass is gesturing at something larger than his own experience: the ineffable tension between the slave's day-to-day reality and the desire for emancipation and freedom, all taking place under the watchful surveillance of a ruling class who'll do anything to keep you in bondage.

Essay Analysis: "Los Angeles Notebook" by Joan Didion and "Brush Fire" by Linda Thomas

Sometimes the most interesting analyses emerge when there's multiple voices in the conversation. The two passages below, both written by contemporary Californian authors, describe the author's experiences with an annual weather event, the Santa Ana winds. "Los Angeles Notebook" is a stand-alone portion taken from a longer essay about Los Angeles in *Slouching Towards Bethlehem.* "Brush Fire" is produced in its original, uncut form. As you read, note the rhetorical strategies of each to see where the two passages purposefully intersect and diverge. You want focus on how the author's use of rhetorical strategies surrounding the subject of the Santa Ana winds to develop the essay's larger purpose. What we're doing here is a dialectical approach to reading and thinking; that is, we are holding text "A" up to text "B" to find the "C" that emerges in this clash of opposites.

"Los Angeles Notebook" – Joan Didion

There is something uneasy in the Los Angeles air this afternoon, some unnatural stillness, some tension. What it means is that tonight a Santa Ana will begin to blow, a hot wind from the northeast whining down through the Cajon and San Gorgonio Passes, blowing up sand storms out along Route 66, drying the hills and the nerves to flash point. For a few days now we will see smoke back in the canyons, and hear sirens in the night. I have neither heard nor read that a Santa Ana is due, but I know it, and almost everyone I have seen today knows it too. We know it because we feel it. The baby frets. The maid sulks. I rekindle a waning argument with the telephone company, then cut my losses and lie down, given over to whatever it is in the air. To live with the Santa Ana is to accept, consciously or unconsciously, a deeply mechanistic view of human behavior.

I recall being told, when I first moved to Los Angeles and was living on an isolated beach, that the Indians would throw themselves into the sea when the bad wind blew. I could see why. The Pacific turned ominously glossy during a Santa Ana period, and one woke in the night troubled not only by the peacocks screaming in the olive trees but by the eerie absence of surf. The heat was surreal. The sky had a yellow cast, the kind of light sometimes called "earthquake weather." My only neighbor would not come out of her house for days, and there were no lights at night, and her husband roamed the place with a machete. One day he would tell me that he had heard a trespasser, the next a rattlesnake.

"On nights like that," Raymond Chandler once wrote about the Santa Ana, "every booze party ends in a fight. Meek little wives feel the edge of the carving knife and study their husbands' necks. Anything can happen." That was the kind of wind it was. I did not know then that there was any basis for the effect it had on all of us, but it turns out to be another of those cases in which science bears out folk wisdom. The Santa Ana, which is named for one of the canyons it rushers through, is foehn wind, like the foehn of Austria and Switzerland and the hamsin of Israel. There are a number of persistent malevolent winds, perhaps the best known of which are the mistral of France and the Mediterranean sirocco, but a foehn wind has distinct characteristics: it occurs on the leeward slope of a mountain range and, although the air begins as a cold mass, it is warmed as it comes down the mountain and appears finally as a hot dry wind. Whenever and wherever foehn blows, doctors hear about headaches and nausea and allergies, about "nervousness," about "depression." In Los Angeles some teachers do not attempt to conduct formal classes during a Santa Ana, because the children become unmanageable. In Switzerland the suicide rate goes up during the foehn, and in the courts of some Swiss cantons the wind is considered a mitigating circumstance for crime. Surgeons are said to watch the wind, because blood does not clot normally during a foehn. A few years ago an Israeli physicist discovered that not only during such winds, but for the ten or twelve hours which precede them, the air carries an unusually high ratio of positive to negative ions. No one seems to know exactly why that should be; some talk about friction and others suggest solar disturbances. In any case the positive ions are there, and what an excess of positive ions does, in the simplest terms, is make people unhappy. One cannot get much more mechanistic than that.

Easterners commonly complain that there is no "weather" at all in Southern California, that the days and the seasons slip by relentlessly, numbingly bland. That is quite misleading. In fact the climate is characterized by infrequent but violent extremes: two periods of torrential subtropical rains which continue for weeks and wash out the hills and send subdivisions sliding toward the sea; about twenty scattered days a year of the Santa Ana, which, with its incendiary dryness, invariably means fire. At the first prediction of a Santa Ana, the Forest Service flies men and equipment from northern California into the southern forests, and the Los Angeles Fire Department cancels its ordinary non-firefighting routines. The Santa Ana caused Malibu to burn as it did in 1956, and Bel Air in 1961, and Santa Barbara in 1964. In the winter of 1966–67 eleven men were killed fighting a Santa Ana fire that spread through the San Gabriel Mountains.

Just to watch the front-page news out of Los Angeles during a Santa Ana is to get very close to what it is about the place. The longest single Santa Ana period in recent years was in 1957, and it lasted not the usual three or four days but fourteen days, from November 21 until December 4. On the first day 25,000 acres of the San Gabriel Mountains were burning, with gusts reaching 100 miles an hour. In town, the wind reached Force 12, or hurricane force, on the Beaufort Scale; oil derricks were toppled and people ordered off the downtown streets to avoid injury from flying objects. On November 22 the fire in the San Gabriels was out of control. On November 24 six people were killed in automobile accidents, and by the end of the week the Los Angeles Times was keeping a box score of traffic deaths. On November 26 a prominent Pasadena attorney, depressed about money, shot and killed his wife, their two sons and himself. On November 27 a South Gate divorcée, twenty-two, was murdered and thrown from a moving car. On November 30 the San Gabriel fire was still out of control, and the wind in town was blowing eighty miles an hour. On the first day of December four people died violently, and on the third the wind began to break.

It is hard for people who have not lived in Los Angeles to realize how radically the Santa Ana figures in the local imagination. The city burning is Los Angeles's deepest image of itself. Nathaniel West perceived that, in The Day of the Locust, and at the time of the 1965 Watts riots what struck the imagination most indelibly were the fires. For days one could drive the Harbor Freeway and see the city on fire, just as we had always known it would be in the end. Los Angeles weather is the weather of catastrophe, of apocalypse, and, just as the reliably long and bitter winters of New England determine the way life is lived there, so the violence and the unpredictability of the Santa Ana affect the entire quality of life in Los Angeles, accentuate its impermanence, its unreliability. The winds show us how close to the edge we are.

"Brush Fire" – Linda Thomas

October in southern California. I know this because this morning I awoke to air so dry that the graze of my nightgown against the down comforter created tiny orange sparks. The winds that blew all night snapped branches from the black pine in my neighbor's yard. The temperature is already seventy degrees at 6 a.m. I have a roaring sinus headache. And as I make the drive to work, I find myself beneath a smoky sky the color of fire.

This is chaparral country. "Chaparral" is a common word here in the lower third of the state, and it refers to the vast expanses of low-lying brush that naturally cover the hills and canyons. Chaparral foliage ranges from ground-level wild flowers that require a magnifying glass, to eight-foot scrub oak and sage bushes. In its most undisturbed state, chaparral is gorgeously beautiful – from the crooked red-brown wood of the manzanita, to the sturdy shaft of the yucca topped with spikes of creamy blossoms, to the brilliant orange threads of the dodder vine.

In October, chaparral burns, usually during three to five-day periods of strong dry northeast winds, known as Santa Ana winds. The burning of chaparral during these winds is natural. Some plants in the chaparral – such as the padre's staff – require the heat of a flame to crack open their seed pods and prepare for germination. Most of the plants store water in their root systems, and the roots – undamaged by fast-moving, wind-driven brush fires – send out new growth in the spring.

Fire in the chaparral is an amazing sight. The Santa Ana winds pass over desert and arrive in the foothills of southern California in hot, bone-dry, ten to forty mile-per-hour gusts that lower the relative humidity to three percent. The condition is perfect for fire that can rush up a canyon like a locomotive, roaring and exploding brush as it rages. After a particularly wet spring, chaparral shrubs such as buck brush, ceanothus, and coast lilac can grow so densely that with the heat of summer and the moisture-sapping Santa Ana winds, they are kindling for the fire that devours them in whirlwinds of flame. During such fires, chamise lives up to its common name – greasewood – by burning with an intense, waxy heat that can smolder for a day and longer.

As a native, I know that within six weeks of one of these brush fires, I can walk in the blackened path of the fire and find new shoots already pushing up from the burl of a chamise. And by the following spring, the same swath of fire-blackened land will be burnished with blue lupine and red Indian paint brush.

All of this would be no more than the stuff of natural history were it not for the land developers who have bulldozed chaparral zones in southern California to make way for homes, schools, and businesses. Right in the path of natural fires. This development is nothing new. As long ago as forty years, developed canyon areas of Riverside and Orange Counties burned in Santa Ana wind-driven brush fires that consumed homes right along with the clumps of mistletoe that hung from the upper branches of scrub oak. The fires make no distinction between natural assemblies and human construction.

But neither have the fires deterred developers from building in deep, once isolated canyons and ridges that have a history of burning down in October.

A few years ago, places like Bee Canyon and Peters Canyon in Orange County were accessible only by dirt roads or horseback. Now, elaborate toll roads and corridors border and lead right into such chaparral areas.

As a result, on days like this when the sky is dark with smoke, not only can I smell the odors of burning sagebrush, brush the ashes from my clothes, and down another sinus tablet, but I can also drive to the intersection of a local thoroughfare and watch the flames lick up a hillside.

And I am not alone. On this evening, my neighbors have arrived, too, their dogs and children in tow. Some have brought soft drinks. Most have cameras. In the backseat of a small import car, a teenage couple has lost interest in the brush fire and, instead, is lost in embrace, passionate kisses no one seems to notice. We are here to watch the orange flames color the sunset. Later, on the TV news, we will hear what has burned down. It will be more than the chaparral that has burned, but in the spring, only the chaparral will return.

Example Analysis

The Santa Ana – an annual wind native to Southern California – is unlike any other weather event. On one hand, it is an observable phenomenon that is both knowable and predictable. On the other hand, these winds seem to be driven by a mystical force animated by a conscious – and malicious – awareness. Joan Didion's "Los Angeles Notebook" and Linda Thomas's "Brush Fire" reflect this dichotomy. The focal point of both essays is the Santa Ana winds, but the two authors use their shared subject to dramatically different ends. For Didion, the winds are a window to ourselves, an event that makes us reflect on the depths of our own inner world. For Thomas, the winds make us look outside ourselves and marvel at our insignificance when set against the majesty of the natural world. Both Didion and Thomas's attention to the use of contrast – particularly antithesis and juxtaposition – reflect and shape the reader's understanding of each essay's underlying agenda.

Joan Didion's style in the opening of "Los Angeles Notebook" could be plucked from the pages of Stephen King. Her winds are presented as malicious, malevolent, and evil, but Didion's tension-generating style is subtle; her winds don't haunt around dreams or brandish a chain saw with a hockey mask. Rather, the wind terrorizes the author in a way she can't quite explain. The opening line, "There is something uneasy in the

Los Angeles air this afternoon, some unnatural stillness, some tension," establishes the tension for both the approaching Santa Ana period and the essay itself. The anaphora of the "some" tells us something is there – though we can't be quite sure what that "something" is – like someone who senses a ghostly apparition in their house for the first time. Also, the clauses of this sentences get increasingly shorter as the sentence move along, the written equivalent of the darting-eyed paranoia from a person on edge. The real fright of Didion's Santa Ana is summed, "We know it because we feel it," that conventional feeling we all have had when we know a threat is afoot but can't quite put our finger on what it is. This division of the "known" and "unknown" is further played out in Didion's pattern of antithesis, the defining rhetorical feature of the essay. Paragraph 2 illustrates her use of antithesis well: sounds and silence ("peacocks screaming" vs. "eerie absence of surf") and peace and violence (connotations of "olive tree" against the threatening "screaming") are apt locutions for an event that defies logical explanation. Each antithetical pair function as a reflection of the dual nature of the wind itself. So too in paragraph 3 does the reader see a sharp divergence in two mutually exclusive notions "science" and "folk wisdom" which further develop Didion's antithetical motif. All of these antithetical pairs contribute to the characterization of the winds as both mystical and violent. "The box scores of traffic deaths" and unexplainable murders are just a few tangible examples of the human behavior that wind accentuates. "Accentuate" is the key word of the final paragraph because it implies a prior existence; Didion's essay asserts that the winds merely "reveal" what's already inside us. And the behaviors of those in L.A. are not unique; they are metonymous for all men, all of human nature.

Linda Thomas is not so cynical. Her short essay "Brush Fire" strips the Santa Anas of Didion's supernatural undertones. Thomas instead characterizes the winds as an indiscriminate but necessary natural force. Her essay examines the interrelationship of life and death by placing the focus on the natural life cycles which accompany the annual appearance of the Santa Ana winds. Consequently, Thomas relies on antithesis in both form and content. Formal antithesis – contrast or juxtaposition in the essay's structure – can be found in the construction of paragraphs 1 and 2. Each begins with a direct reference to the fires and ends with an explicit reference to regrowth and rebirth. In essence, the flow of the paragraphs replicates the essay's main idea: as the paragraphs move from images of death to life, so too does Thomas relate her message of hopefulness delivered via the destruction of the Santa Ana winds. Antithesis in content is most prominent in Thomas's third paragraph. The destructiveness loaded into Thomas's word choice, "wind-driven brush fires," contrasts with her later characterizations of the wind as "natural" and "mak[ing] no distinctions between natural and human constructions." Thomas's winds lose the personified qualities of Didion's and are consequently less threatening. And even though the winds are capable of extreme destruction, the local response to the fire is not one of fear, but of entertainment and awe ("Some have brought soft drinks. Most have cameras"). The violence of Thomas's subject, contrasted to the relative calm of the casual spectators (who would bring kids and dogs?) work to present Thomas's winds as a necessary event in the course of natural cycles.

These two seemingly parallel essays diverge dramatically in terms of purpose. Like a pair of identical twins who share some basic functions and superficial similarities but are their "own person," the similarities of Thomas's "Brush Fire" and Didion's "Los Angeles Notebook" are only skin deep. At the most essential levels of purpose and intent, these works are cast into a binary opposition and exist as contrasting, not complementary, works which each examine the state of human affairs in this world. Each author's careful control of language makes this pairing an ideal case study for how language can dictate an essay's tone and the resulting audience response.

Poetry Analysis: "Paradoxes and Oxymorons" by John Ashbery

John Ashbery's "Paradoxes and Oxymorons" (1980) is less a poem and more of a live experiment which aims to explore how readers receive information and make meaning. The more a reader tries to figure out a static answer – if there even is one to be found – in Ashbery's poem, the more frustrated the reader will become. "Paradoxes and Oxymorons" is the fluid motion of play; it moves from the first line to the last (and back again to the first once the reader hits the last!) in a continual process of discovery, investigation and, above all, Ashbery hopes, interaction between reader and poem. As you read, note how the author uses rhetorical strategies to encourage the reader to experience the poem in spirit of play.

This poem is concerned with language on a very plain level.
Look at it talking to you. You look out a window
Or pretend to fidget. You have it but you don't have it.
You miss it, it misses you. You miss each other.

The poem is sad because it wants to be yours, and cannot.
What's a plain level? It is that and other things,
Bringing a system of them into play. Play?
Well, actually, yes, but I consider play to be

A deeper outside thing, a dreamed role-pattern,
As in the division of grace these long August days
Without proof. Open-ended. And before you know
It gets lost in the steam and chatter of typewriters.

It has been played once more. I think you exist only
To tease me into doing it, on your level, and then you aren't there
Or have adopted a different attitude. And the poem
Has set me softly down beside you. The poem is you.

Example Analysis

At first glance, "Paradoxes and Oxymorons" looks pretty sterile on the page. It seems to be dead on arrival when it hits the reader's eyes: four stanzas of exactly four lines, a title with terms drawn straight from a 101-poetry class, very few of the formal frills that characterizes modern poetry. It seems, before really engaging with it, more like a schoolbook exercise than rich, introspective poetry. But look at the title. A paradox is something that seems logically contradictory but, in fact, reveals some truth, whereas an oxymoron is an expression that assigns something a quality that it categorically cannot have, but meaning is found somewhere in this logical void. Each of these locutions, paradoxes and oxymorons, nudge readers in an intuitive, rather than logical, direction towards understanding. The poem as a whole, for Ashbery, is just that. It can't be understood through logical deconstruction; it's something that requires play, interaction, and a little bit of fun, in order to fully engage with it.

On first read, the opening line appears to be totally devoid of any kind of life. A reading of the first clause, "the poem is concerned," may suggest some roundabout personification, but the back end of this same sentence quickly drops any kind of fun or playfulness in favor of the deadening language of poetic deconstruction, "this poem is concerned with language on a very plain level." The speaker teases the reader (maybe Ashbery's engaging in a little bit of play himself here already), baiting them with a shadow personification only to bluntly dismiss it. For readers, this line's effect is a casting back to the seat of a classroom where poetry explication is a laborious and numbing task to be completed. This line is a declaration, a statement of meaning, and the reader is passively told the poem's meaning. There's no investigation, no perceptive process; the reader jump cuts simply and suddenly to the conclusion without understanding, the same way students may be force-fed the idea that Shakespeare is the greatest poet who ever lived before they have read a single word of his work. This move, however, by the poet seems to be self-consciously ironic.

The speaker continues: "Look at it talking to you." The imperative still connotes the "teacher talk" of the classroom as the opening line did, but the personification here is slightly intensified. It's not the borderline dead metaphor personification of a poem being "concerned" with something from line 1; the poem is "talking" to the reader now in a slightly more anthropomorphic way. "Talking," however, is distinct from "conversing"; there is no dialogue, no give-and-take, no interaction. It is still one-way communication in its most impersonal form and the speaker and poem, at this point, are still on separate planes. The remainder of the first stanza captures this gap between art and audience. The syntactical structure – as well as the content of the following lines – suggest a divide between poetry and reader with the paradoxical "You have it but you don't have it" (you hold the poem in your hands, but don't understand it) and the chiasmus-driven "You miss it, it misses you" that crisscrosses the subject and object from the first clause to the next, a syntactical switch-a-roo that captures the inability of poem and reader to connect. A surface reading of the final line subtly, and ironically, begins to bring the poem to life: "You miss each other." The reader likely "misses" the poem in a sense of misunderstanding, and the poem's meaning is "missed" on an obtuse reader whose inability to engage with the words prevents any meaningful discovery. But, there's a pun here and it's no mistake Ashbery transitions from the sterile stanza 1 to the playful remainder of the poem with a wordplay joke that requires a little excavation and work to get there. The reader "misses" the poem in the sense that poetry can be a great and sturdy companion that is longed for but not present. Likewise, the poetry has now become authentically personified; Ashbery's grants of an emotional dimension to the poem itself – it can somehow can feel the emotional loss that a playful interaction with a reader can provide.

The poem twitches to life in the opening line of the second stanza, "The poem is sad because it wants to be yours, and cannot." The personification here is not couched in dead metaphors or impersonal terms, as seen earlier in the poem. The poem, paradoxically, in this line is made out to be more human than the human who reads and rebuffs this obvious affection of a great friend. The poem's life-force reaches the first milestone with the line, "What's a plain level?" This is the first question of the poem, and it is where the reader can see that the poem has not only come to life, but it is now interacting, engaging, and challenging the reader. The diction of the question, particularly "plain level," is meant to send the reader's mind back up to the cold declaration of the opening line ("this poem is concerned with language on a very plain level"), This idea, now, is dialogical rather than declarative, and this marks the point in the poem where poem and reader can now begin their playful dialectic. Interestingly, through Ashbery's use of personification, the poem is every bit as much alive as the reader, and it's not clear who is asking the questions and who is responding. Is the poem speaking to the reader or the reader to the poem? Does it matter so long as the conversation is taking place? By mulling this question in the first place, we've walked into the trap that Ashbery has set. We are playing with the poem; we are dialoguing; we're interacting.

With the question, "What's a plain level?" the poem has come to life, but there is still a physical rift – the formal structure splits the initial statement and interjecting question by five lines – between poem and reader. Not so in line 7: "Bringing a system of them into play. Play?" Ashbery uses anadiplosis – that is, ending a statement and beginning the next with the same word – to deliberately enlist the formal structure of his verse to bring the dialogue between poem and reader into face-to-face terms, so to speak. Here the reader sees a sharp contrast between the unity created here to the distant echo of the statement and question concerned with the "plain level." At this point in the poem, the dispassionate language of analysis in the opening line is thrown out the window. "Plain level" is answered as here as play and the reader is begged to take this answer and return to line one. What will you find? This poem is concerned with "play."

So Ashbery plays. In stanza 3, he says, "Well, actually, yes, but I consider play to be a deeper outside thing, a dreamed role-pattern as in the division of grace these long August days without proof." It's tough to discern exactly what this image means, but maybe it's the beauty of the language, the play, where the reader can combine the sonic beauty of the line – with its internal rhyming of the vowels – with the visual richness of the imagery – a late summer afternoon on a dream-like, long August day – and find some tacit meaning in it. We're playing rather than understanding; remember, the poem's title indicates to the reader that this poem is heading in an intuitive rather than logical direction. After this line, the poem's shortest sentence arrives, a standalone oxymoron "open-ended" that acts as a metaphor for the whole of the poetics reading experience for Ashbery. Poems are "open" in the sense that they have endless possibility for interpretation, and "ended" in the sense that all writing has to be bound to lines, words, and the borders of a page. The reader is what brings this paradoxical chaos into some understandable, or rather intuitive, structure.

What the reader thinks to be their understanding of the poem crumbles under the force of the final line, "the poem is you." The poem is me? Again, Ashbery begs the reader to go back to the first stanza to engage in another round of play where the reader to substitutes "you" for "poem." "Look at it talking to you" turns into "Look at it (the reader) talking to you (the poem);" the reader's conversation with the poem is switched on in precisely the place where the poetic divide was once it's strongest. Was "you" the poem and "it" the reader the whole time? How does that flip the meaning on its ear? Did I walk right into Ashbery's trap? By going back and seeing where the meaning becomes new, we are enacting, not just reading about, the whole point of poetry for Ashbery: to engage and converse with the poem. Whether readers know it or not, they're now doing as he hoped. Read it a second, a third, a fourth time: the poem itself is changeless but the more you read good poetry, the more you are able to grow and change through it. With "Paradoxes and Oxymorons" like all good poems, if you have a work figured out on the first reading, something has got to be wrong: either you are not reading great poetry, or you are not reading carefully enough. Just play, Ashbery urges, and the meaning will fall into place.

Novel/Film Analysis: *Meditations in Green* by Stephen Wright and *Apocalypse Now* Directed by Francis Ford Coppola

Mediations in Green (1983) is a Vietnam War novel written in Stephen Wright's signature style of surrealism and dark comedy. Set in New York City after the end of James Griffin's tour in Vietnam, the novel details the half-real, half-hallucinatory experiences of the returning soldier re-integrating to civilian life. The novel, obviously too long to produce here in full, is well worth the read and was chosen as an example text for this chapter since it is highly stylized, more akin to prose poetry than traditional contemporary novels. If you read the novel, notice Wright attention to fragmentation, a rhetorical style to always keep things just a bit out of joint for the reader. You'll see how the writer of the essay below also draws comparisons to adaptations of Griffin's experience in the well-known Vietnam War film, *Apocalypse Now* (1979). The director focuses on the disjoint and brutality of the opening scene, using all the available expressions in filmic language that the author of the paper uses to add dimension and depth to primary analysis of the Wright's novel.

Example Analysis

Marlowe's Mephistopheles, when asked by the great and ambitious Dr. Faustus, how he was able to displace himself from hell to answer his conjuring call, responds with one of the great one-liners from Elizabethan drama: "Why, this is hell, nor am I out of it." Hell, for Marlowe, has no physical boundaries; it is space-less, timeless state of mind. The individual doesn't inhabit hell. Hell inhabits the individual. It's permanent. It's ines-capable. Whether Mephistopheles is down in the pit or standing face to face with the doctor in his library, hell is always with (or should I say in?) him. I guess wherever you go, there you are.

   Meditations in Green's James Griffin may not have made a Faustian bar-gain, but he certainly does lose his soul, and his hell is similarly inescap-able. Throughout the novel, Griffin tries to shrink time and space down a single geometric point – a singularity of the self, so to speak – in every effort to shut out the hell that was the Vietnam War. If the *Meditations in*

Green is a battlefield of ideas, then "James" and "Griffin" are the names of the opposing armies. Consider the opening sentence of the book:

> "Up late and into the street, that was my habit then, night's reside still sifting softly through my head, I'd wander down to the corner, stand shivering in the sun, waiting for the light to change and my reconnaissance to begin" (6).

Take stock of just how much tension is packed into this opening line. The opposing directions laid down by the introductory phrase's prepositions of "up" and "into"; the euphonic alliteration of the "s" sounds in "still sifting softly" and "stand shivering in the sun" counterbalanced by the harsh "t" alliterative pattern (maybe to recalling the sounds of machine gun fire) of "late into the street" and "waiting for the light to change"; the absurdity of "the sun" producing the effect of "shivering," a kind of "cold fire" oxymoron. There are many other sentences in the opening pages that read like this in order to indicate to the reader pretty early on that this novel will be a clash of opposites, and James Griffin's mind is the arena where the conflicting ideas are to fight it out. But if we ask the question, "What is this novel about?" we will get a misleading answer, because the question is wrongly formulated. This novel's meaning – if can even be definitively arrived at all since postmodernist works resist the very idea of absolute meaning – is sourced precisely in its incoherence. The correct question to ask of this novel from the outset is, "Where is James Griffin going in this story?" The novel is movement. Stephen Wright hasn't sat down to give us a story called, "My Life and Times from Vietnam," but rather, he is thinking in front of us through the proxy of James Griffin. He has not been down this path before; and we haven't either. We, the readers, are in the privileged position of being able to watch his mind at, however scarred, terrible, and frightening it may be.

Try though James Griffin may, there is no geographical solution to his deep spiritual crisis, and everything in his novel is a refraction of his internal tensions; he's a discrete battlefield unto himself where past and present, integration and isolation, sacred and profane, are all at war. Take his name, "Griffin." What is a griffin, if not the blending to two separate natures, a half lion and half eagle? One is airborne; the other terrestrial. One has feathers; the other fur. One attacks with its feet; the other with its mouth. Not only does the allusion to the mythological creature suggest that James Griffin is an uneasy blend of soldier and civilian, but also that Griffin's military duties are sketched along these lines as well: he's an image interpreter of aerial reconnaissance (airborne) photography whose duty in Vietnam is to read out film and find enemy positions and supply routes (terrestrial), a position intimately familiar with long stretches of wartime boredom punctuated by moments of sheer terror. There's division within Griffin, but this binary works outwards and informs the entirety of the novel.

The novel is structured along the lines of alternating locales – Vietnam and New York City after his enlistment has concluded – and even though the novel may come across as fragmentary in a chronological sense, there is an astonishing coherence to the novel if you are to think of it in the terms laid down by Marlowe's Mephistopheles; that is, the omnipresence of hell. Everything about the novel suggests the blurring of borders and the collapse of order.

Apocalypse Now's opening scene captures well what Wright is trying to do in his story. The dislocation of the individual – very similar to the unsticking in time of Billy Pilgrim's experience in *Slaughterhouse Five* – is a familiar trope of most literature born out of the Vietnam War. In the clip, Martin Sheen is physically in a hotel room, but mentally somewhere else. The shadow cast by the ceiling fan recalls helicopter blades when he was in-country; the dim rays of light foreshadow to his face-to-face with Colonel Kurtz; even his own blood is shed as an effort to re-enter the hell from which he can never escape. The entire scene is shot in off-balance canted angles, and as one reads many of the New York apartment scenes in *Meditations in Green*, one can't help but envisioning James Griffin in the context of this film's diegesis.

The chapters dealing with Griffin's life in America alternate with those that are set in Vietnam and, I'd argue, these chapters lend themselves to a typological, not linear, understanding. In other words, the Vietnam episodes are not made complete until the reader sees the consequential fallout in the civilian experience in America, and the degenerative progression of Griffin's deviant behavior in his post-war life is better understood with the Vietnam antecedent. The physical structure of the novel comments on the heart of its content; that is, the broken and meandering style of narration in the novel functions as an analogy of the state of mind for Griffin, the Vietnam vet.

And then there's the "meditations" themselves. The eponymous poems are the threads that stitch together the disparate locations of Vietnam and

New York, and all linked by the color green. Green is the defining color of his time spent in both locales; it captures both the ubiquity of the jungles in Vietnam and the color of the heroin powder back stateside in New York City. The meditations also, curiously, are all concerned with vegetation and many of them personify plants and sound as if they are the words of Griffin himself. For example, Mediation 10 (205) expresses the suicidal desire of a living plant that wishes to turn into a plastic shadow of itself. By placing his own suicidal thoughts into the mouth of a plant, Griffin is relegating himself to the punishment of having an unnatural, immobile body. This move speaks to the fundamental illogic and falsity of the entirely of the Vietnam experience. Human beings are creatures created to move about and sense the world around them, but Wright has incarcerated the thoughts of his protagonist into a plant. The rational soul united with a vegetative being – without the animal being to make sense of the union – is another powerful expression of the illogic and absurdity of the James Griffin's post-Vietnam existence. Meditation 14 sees a similar perversion of life. Here, the speaker outlines the steps required to bring a crop of poppy plants to life, but this is a life aimed at death; when the plants reach maturity, they will be processed and turned into heroin, a substance that Griffin will use to deaden himself to the outside world.

For many readers of literature about the Vietnam War, *Meditations in Green* is considered to be the gold standard, striking the right balance between absurdity and artistic, comic and tragic. In an interview conducted a few years after the book's release, Wright said, "I'm really very, very fortunate that I did not have to spend the rest of my life being a Vietnam veteran, because there are way too many people doing that. That's their life." Wright medicates through fiction. By creating James Griffin to bear the weight of his own Vietnam experience, he's able to step outside the inescapable hell. As Earnest Hemmingway once quipped, "My typewriter is my psychiatrist."

UNIT 2

ARGUMENT

CHAPTER EIGHT

A BRIEF HISTORY OF ARGUMENTATION

Arguments are a simple fact of life. Whether we are aware of it or not, we informally engage in the argument process every day. Sometimes, our arguments are trivial: "I think you should wear the blue t-shirt instead of the orange one," "I like the weather better today than I did yesterday." Others are more somber: "free internet access ought to a public right," "unionized labor supports the public good." Whether lighthearted or more serious, all these arguments make a claim, direct that claim to an audience, and will presumably support that claim with further reasons and evidence. A good argument, one that can alter attitudes and shape minds, is deeply connected to a writer's rhetorical knowledge, and this unit will be the natural scaffold from the first. Think of the relationship between rhetoric and argument to that of a metaphor and a simile: not all metaphors are similes, but all similes are metaphors. Not all rhetoric is argumentative, but all argument is rhetorical. And just like rhetoric, a good arguer must know what the persuasive strategies are so as to argue well and not be taken in by speech of others. Consider the following two arguments and see if you can identify the difference:

"Joe is a bachelor because he is an unmarried man."

"Go to bed because it is past your bed time."

These arguments do share a set of surface similarities. Each is ten words. Each essentially contains the same grammatical structure: an assertion linked to evidence by subordinating conjunction "because." But, if your gut is telling you that there is something which makes the arguments different, you're right. The first is what's known as an "enthymeme," a type of shorthand version of the classical syllogism, a form of deductive logic which we'll discuss throughout this chapter. Part of what makes this argument so good is that it's logically bulletproof; if a bachelor is an unmarried man, and if Joe is unmarried, he is indeed a bachelor. In syllogisms, the claim is the necessary conclusion derived from two premises: the definition of a bachelor and Joe's marital status. Its negated form is just as logically solid: "Joe is *not* a bachelor because he is a *married* man." Enthymemes operate on deductive logic and it is this pattern of thought carries argumentation through the first two-thousand years of its history.

Though it's easy to recognize the logical merit of an enthymeme, day-to-day situations rarely present themselves in ways that can be settled in deductive proofs. The world is messier than that. "Go to your room because it is past your bed time" is not categorically true like our enthymeme, but is it a good argument? Well, there is a claim ("go to bed"), supported by reasons ("it is past your bed time"), but the assent of the audience – whether or not they will accept the conclusion – is much more uncertain since the underlying assumption of the argument is subject to interpretation. Perhaps the audience understands that "a good night sleep is of the utmost importance." Perhaps the audience disagrees that bucking bedtime is "a violation of a direct order is an intolerable act of insubordination." Perhaps the audience feels that the parents "ought not to be irritated after a certain hour in the night." Assessing the validity of these assumptions – "warrants" as they are known in modern argument theory – makes all the difference in an audience's acceptance of an argument's validity. Everyday argumentation is forced to play off a number of variables that formal logic does not have to contend with: inference, probability, circumstances, politics, social norms, cultural values, personal feelings, and so on. Here is where rhetoric, the ability to use language to achieve a particular purpose or goal, can be spliced into a study of argument's everyday use. And with that, let's turn to Ancient Greece to see how argument and rhetoric have been together from the start.

Argumentation in the Classical Period

Protagoras (490-420 BC), best known for teaching that there are "two sides to every question," is a good starting point for a historical overview of argument. He was a Sophist, a member of the group of itinerant teachers who traveled the Mediterranean basin that taught the skills of persuasion to anyone who had a little extra cash on hand. If you remember from Chapter 1, instruction in argumentation sprung out of a very practical need: once the tyrannical regime of Thrasybulus of Syracuse was toppled, the redistribution of seized possessions to the citizens was brought to the courts. In those days, there were no lawyers to argue on behalf of clients. Citizens represented themselves in courts of law, but to make a good case for a claim on a piece of property, they had to know how to change the minds (and hearts) of the judge with their words alone. Protagoras, and his fellow Sophists, seized on this burgeoning market and the world's first professional teachers made their appearance in the historical record. And they were, for all intents and purposes, teachers of argument.

Protagoras's philosophy towards argument was ultimately pragmatic in nature; that is, a good argument is the argument that works (not the argument that is logical, honest, or even necessarily true). Protagoras was what's known as a relativist. Relativism believes "truth" to be absolutely relative to the knowing subject, a belief aptly summed in Protagoras's most famous one-liner, "Man is the measure of all things: of the things that are, that they are, of the things that are not, that they are not." What's true for you, is true for you. What's true for me, is true for me. Even today, we see themes of Protagorean relativism seeping back into public argumentation on all sorts of popular issues: abortion, drug legalization, capital punishment, and so forth. History has funny ways of repeating itself.

Protagoras's partner in crime was the "father of Sophistry," Gorgias (485-380 B.C.). Known for his powerful attention to language use and his dramatic delivery, Gorgias was among the most pre-eminent teachers of argument in his day. One of his most enduring legacy to argument studies was his use of ornamentation and style in both speaking and writing, often drawing off techniques from theatre and live performance. Gorgias, who knew how different verbal and physical gestures would cue corresponding reactions, was characterized as the great rival of Socrates who rigorously pursued objective truth. And he could argue nearly anything. To prove it, two of his published works, *An Encomium on Helen* and *On the Non-Existent*, took the most common-sense propositions in Ancient Greek culture and argued the opposite. Only the most careful of speakers could deliver an encomium – a speech of praise – on Helen of Troy, the face that launched a thousand ships and touched off the Trojan War, a period of great turmoil in Greek history. The real irony of this project is that it was not search after truth or because he even believed in Helen's innocence; Gorgias did it as a language game simply to show it can be done. In *On the Non-Existent*, Gorgias argued that the whole world is just an illusion; nothing is real. To do this, he advanced three propositions: first, that nothing exists; second, that if anything does exist, it is not knowable; third, that if anything exists and is knowable, then it can't be communicated. The argument is logically sound and quite persuasive, and Gorgias has been labeled a nihilist for good reason. For a nihilist, abstract truths and moral principles do not exist at all, taking things far beyond the relativism of Protagoras. Gorgias did not argue in terms of good or bad, right or wrong, true or false; he didn't have to, because he didn't believe they exist in the first place. Combine this philosophical stance with the argumentative skill of Gorgias and you have a volatile combination. Argument is a means to simply get what one wants and "winning at all costs" becomes an end in itself. If Gorgias' stance towards argumentation is the dark side of this discipline, then consider him to be Darth Vader. The scary thing about him is that he widely taught this skill to youth of Athens, thus corrupting an entire generation of young people in the process.

Isocrates (436-338 B.C.), the last of three great Sophists, was best known for emphasizing the role of probability in argumentation. He noted that most arguments take place in spontaneous contexts and adherence to hard principles in a program of argumentation, Isocrates thought, was not always useful in everyday situations. In his teaching of argument, he stressed *praxis* (the action or practice; the doing) over the *lexis* (the thought or language; the thinking) and was the great champion of *kairos* (Chapter 2). Isocrates saw the need for speakers to adapt themselves to shifting circumstances in argument contexts, telling his students to change tone, delivery, even their general claim if the situation called for it. In this regard, he is much like Gorgias, stressing neither the rightness or wrongness of what's argued, but judging its success on whether or not its convincing. Isocrates was great at what he did, too. Not only did he found the world's first school devoted to the instruction of rhetoric, but according to Pliny the Elder's Book 7 of *Natural History* (79 A.D.), Isocrates could command a fee of twenty "talents" for a single speech. To put this in perspective, a "talent" is a silver piece equivalent to 26,000 US dollars, so a single speech from Isocrates would rake in the equivalent of nearly half a million dollars.

Protagoras, Gorgias, and Isocrates had a few common threads in their teaching of argument which captures the essence of persuasion in the pre-Socratic period: argumentation is a tool (*techne*), adaptable to a given set of circumstances (*kairos*), whose main goal was to win the debate at all costs. Such a set of beliefs stood at direct odds with the rival pre-eminent thinker of the time, Plato (428-438 B.C.). Plato is among the most logical thinkers in all of history, and his program of philosophical investigation was ultimately linked to the pursuit of Truth and the Good. For Plato, a good argument is the true argument, one that searches after a form of knowledge that's immutable, fixed, and crystalline. Mathematics was the great paradigm of knowledge for Plato and much of his argumentation is better thought as adhering to the structures of mathematics – with its definite right and wrong propositions – than the dynamic and flexible language of the Sophists. Plato devoted much of this argumentative energy to his philosophical projects arguing for the immortality of the soul, and essential definitions of beauty, justice, goodness, etc. The motto of Plato's academy, engraved over the main entrance, should come as no surprise: "Let no one ignorant of geometry enter."

At this point in history, argument studies had splintered into a binary: the pragmatism of the Sophists and the philosophical investigations of Plato. Aristotle (384 B.C. – 322 B.C.) came along and took as his intellectual project nothing less than the synthesis of these two competing traditions, fusing the academic rigor of Plato with the everyday use of the Sophists. Whereas mathematics was the paradigm of knowledge for Plato, Aristotle saw all of knowledge – argument included – as an offshoot of Biology, able to be systematically studied and classified while still subject to growth and change. Aristotle was famous for criticizing Protagoras for "making the weaker argument the stronger," but he also conceded the value of winning an argument, insofar as one's methods were logically sound. At the core of Aristotle's logical project in argumentation was the classical syllogism, the central subject of Book II in *The Art of Rhetoric* (4th Century B.C.). Syllogisms are categorical propositions that follow the principles of deductive logic. The standard-form syllogism, according to Aristotle, must adhere to five rules in order to be valid:

1. It must contain exactly three terms, each of which is used in the same sense throughout the argument.
2. The middle term must be distributed in at least one premise.
3. No standard-form syllogism is valid if it has two negative premises.
4. If either premise is negative, the conclusion must also be negative.

5. No standard-forms syllogism has two universal premises and a particular conclusion.

Any syllogism that breaks one of these rules is rendered invalid. In Aristotelean syllogisms, there are four types of categorical propositions which can be used to advance an argumentative position: "all," "none," "some are," "some are not."

Symbol	Form of the proposition	Example
A	All *S* is *P*.	All cheese pizza is delicious.
E	No *S* is *P*.	No dogs are scaly creatures.
I	Some *S* is *P*.	Some men have brown hair.
O	Some *S* is not *P*.	Some women are not left-handed.

Think of all the potential combinations that can arise from these four categories in the formulation of an argument. Consider the following:

Stage of syllogism	Linguistic proposition	Symbol
Major premise	All mammals have hair.	A
Minor premise	Some mammals are cats.	I
Conclusion	All cats have hair.	A

Or we could slightly rearrange the argument, syllogistically:

Stage of syllogism	Linguistic proposition	Symbol
Major premise	No mammals have scales.	E
Minor premise	Some mammals are cats.	I
Conclusion	All cats do not have scales.	E

Syllogisms present its user with many practical problems. Try a few syllogisms out for yourself and you'll find that they are tough intellectual work, not to mention that they don't translate very well to on-the-spot, back-and-forth argumentation. Aristotle understood this and offered a condensed form of syllogistic reasoning, the enthymeme (discussed on the first page of this chapter) to meet the demands of everyday argumentation without abandoning the logical core of the syllogism. Enthymemes are handy locutions in persuasive speech and writing, and they have remained in use since their inception nearly two and half millennia ago.

Syllogisms factor into Aristotle's discussions of argumentation, but his real gift to argument studies comes in the Classical Model of Argumentation, a central piece of *The Art of Rhetoric*. The primary concern of this model is arrangement, or how to organize the parts of an argument to cohere together into a persuasive whole. The five parts of the Classical argument are:

1. *Exordium* – A section designed to identify the topic and position the audience to be receptive to it for the upcoming argument
2. *Narratio* – A section that explains the most key facts relevant to the discussion about a given topic
3. *Confirmatio* – A section that puts forth a claim about the topic and supports that claim logically-connected evidence
4. *Refutatio* – A section that addresses and rebuts an opposing argument(s) on the topic
5. *Peroratio* – A section that finishes off the argument on the topic

Even in its outline form, it's easy to see the Classical Model of Argumentation as the crossover point of argument and rhetoric. Cold, logical proofs often won't do much to touch the hearts of an audience; an audience needs to be emotionally invested and entertained in an argument as much as they need the hard proof. Chapter 9 – Classical Models of Argumentation – will deal in the specifics of how this model can be deployed, but what we can say here is that the one of the greatest virtues of Aristotle's system is just how pedagogical it is. That is, it can be easily taught and easily learned, even to those with little to no formal education in rhetoric or argumentation.

The five-paragraph essay – with its easy to remember thesis-topic sentences-support structure – has become the gold standard in middle and high school writing instruction partly because it is so easy to teach and to learn. Have you ever wondered where this mode of writing came from? It's ultimately traceable back to the Aristotle's system of argument, which you may notice also divides into five parts, though the five-paragraph essay dominance in writing instruction is mainly attributable to a single piece of legislation passed in 1944, the G.I. Bill. Among its many provisions for returning veterans from World War II, the bill offered free college tuition. American universities, once available only to those with a privileged education, now had an influx of new students with largely uneducated backgrounds. Professors scrambled. "How can we get these students to produce logic-driven writing at the college level?" they asked. The Classical Model of Argumentation answered the call and the First-Year Composition course was born. Aristotle's most useful model gradually degraded into the write-by-numbers five paragraph essay we have today, but it's worth noting just how useful Aristotle's original method has been in getting even everyday folks to argue logically and persuasively.

If Aristotle gave us the maps of arguments, then Cicero (106 B.C. – 46 B.C.) gave us the compass. Among his many contributions to rhetoric and oration, a sometimes-overlooked influence in argument studies has to do with his work on claims in *On Invention* (85 B.C.). Cicero explained that once a speaker identifies which aspects of the topic are agreed upon by all the participants and which issues are not (the point of *stasis*, which we'll discuss in Chapter 9), he then can match the nature of the claim to best fit the nature of the controversy. Cicero believed the claim determines everything in an argument, from how you'll get started to how you'll wrap things up. In *On Invention*, he identified four principle type of claims, noting "every subject which contains in itself a controversy to be resolved by speech and debate involves a question about a fact, or about a definition, or about the nature of an act, or about … the processes of deciding it." Let's take one issue, hate speech, and see how an author can present this topic along the lines of Cicero's four claim categories:

> Claim of fact – A fact is always theoretically knowable and verifiable. A speaker uses fact claims to argue that certain events occurred in the way they are described.
>
> *Example*: Hate speech regularly occurs on our campus.
>
> The arguer will go on to cite instances of hate speech to persuade the audience that it does, in fact, "regularly occur" on campus.
>
> Claim of definition – A definition is the meaning of a term. A speaker uses definitional claims to characterize the key topic favorably, but not dishonestly, to the position they hold.
>
> *Example*: Hate speech attacks a person or group on the basis of something the victim cannot control.
>
> The arguer will go on to show that most hate speech is defined on the basis of race, gender, sexual orientation, or disability – all things beyond the victim's control.

Claim of value – A value is qualitative judgments about the facts in a particular situation. A speaker uses value claims to argue the rightness/wrongness of a topic or whether something ought to be done about a situation.

> *Example*: Colleges should restrict any expression of hate speech in a public space.

The arguer will go on to outline why colleges have a moral obligation to shield its paying students from offensive material.

Claim of competence – Competence is the ability to do something responsibly. A speaker uses a competence claims to argue that a course of action is ultimately the responsibility of a specific person or group.

> *Example*: The college president ought to regulate the use of hate speech among students in both public and private spaces on campus.

The speaker will go on to say that it is the responsibility of those who set policy on campus to deal with this issue.

The elegance of Cicero's categories lies in their simplicity, a kind-of "Occam's razor" principle of persuasion. Think about how all the big issues of our own day – capital punishment, abortion, legalizing recreational drugs use, healthcare – can (and indeed have) been argued along grids which Cicero has mapped for us.

We've so far discussed argument's historical development in terms of technique, but our final Classical figure treats argument in a slightly separate way. Quintilian (35 A.D. – c. 100 A.D.), a Roman senator who lived on the outskirts of the Empire in modern day Spain, published one of the most comprehensive reference books ever written on oratory, the *Institutio Oratoria* (85 A.D.). In this book, he reworks the theories of Aristotle's Classical appeals (ethos, logos, pathos) and Cicero's five canons of rhetoric (invention, arrangement, style, memory, delivery) to produce one of the all-time greats on the subject of rhetoric and argumentation. As a preface to the twelfth and final book, Quintilian says it is the duty of his "essay to form my orator's character and to teach him his duties. Thus, I have no predecessor to guide my steps and must press far, far on, as my theme may demand." In other words, Quintilian adds to the study of argument the idea that a good arguer must be above all a *vir bonus*, a good man.

By throwing morals into the mix of argument history, Quintilian urged speakers to guard against the tempting "desire to win applause [or] to neglect the interest of the actual case." This "good man theory" of argument, as it has come to be known, represents a final knock-out punch to the outcome-oriented, Sophistic persuasion of Protagoras, Gorgias, and Isocrates.

Argumentation from the Medieval Period to the Scientific Revolution

Boethius (480–524 A.D.) is the great bridge figure in the development of argumentation, carrying the discipline from the Classical world into the Medieval period. Though history remembers him best for his philosophical tour-de-force *The Consolation of Philosophy* (524), his stealth contribution to the development of Western culture comes in his translations of the works of Aristotle (*The Art of Rhetoric*, among them) from Greek to Latin. His translations were the long-accepted authority in all academic fields and were, in fact, the only extant translations of Aristotle's writings that existed for about six hundred years (6th to 12th century) in the Latin speaking world. Boethius took specific interest in two strands of Aristotelian argumentation – topics (as we mentioned in Chapter 2) and the syllogism (mentioned earlier in this chapter) – and he published his reimagining of these concepts in *De Topicis Differentiis* (c. 523). Boethius reinforced Aristotle's need for a deductive logical foundation in argument and asserted that any logically sound argument must be built from a universal principle ('a maximal proposition', he calls it) and subsequently supported with the structures of syllogistic logic. Many of the great argumentative breakthroughs of the Middle Ages and the Renaissance – St. Anselm, Thomas Aquinas, Rene Descartes – owe a great debt to Boethius's work. Boethius's writings go well beyond treatises on argumentation. He is a major figure in writings on mathematics, philosophy, and biblical commentaries as well.

In the 16th and 17th centuries, stances towards argumentation broke into a sharp divide, represented by the schools of thought propagated by Petrus Ramus (1515–1572) and Henry Peacham (1578–1644). Ramus drove a wedge between rhetoric and logic, a division that broke with the traditions handed down from Cicero and Aristotle that always characterized logic and rhetoric as working in tandem during argumentation.

Ramus considered rhetoric as peripheral to logical projects, branding it as mere verbal ornamentation and flowery words that hold little argumentative value. In other words, Ramus applied the rigors of mathematical reasoning to the field of argumentation and his strict adherence to formal logic is more fanatical than that even of Plato. Ramus redefined argumentation, too, by breaking logic into two branches, natural and artificial logic, the former as the informal logic of everyday communication (which is often fragmentary and implied) and the latter as the systematic logic of philosophical inquiry (which is comprehensive and explicit). Both rhetoric and logic have their place in Ramus's work, but they no longer overlap for him as they had in earlier traditions.

A poet and writer, Henry Peacham viewed argumentation with a writer's sensibility. Rather than divorcing rhetoric from logic as Ramus had, he fused them (if not even privileging rhetoric over logic) in his rhetorical style guide *The Garden of Eloquence* (1577). (This is the abbreviated title used in most references to it. The full title of the work should give you some sense of Peacham's flare for the rhetorical: *The Garden of Eloquence, Conteyning the Figures of Grammer and Rhetorick, from Whence Maye Bee Gathered All Manner of Flowers, Coulors, Ornaments, Exornations, Formes and Fashions of Speech, Very Profitable for All Those That Be Studious of Eloquence ... and Also Helpeth Much for the Better Understanding of the Holy Scriptures*.) The book is divided into two categories – tropes and schemes – with each category broken out into a comprehensive glossary of all the rhetorical moves a writer can perform in just about any situation imaginable. No rhetorical stone is left unturned in this work, identifying, for example, no less than fourteen conventional uses for standard metaphors in writing. *The Garden of Eloquence*, in some ways, seems to be the natural evolution of Cicero's canon of memory. As a historical accident, this work came along in the era of the printing press, where printed texts became both faster and cheaper to produce. Peacham's storehouse of rhetorical maneuvers makes accessible, in reference book form, those things which Classical rhetoricians were once forced to commit to memory. What's more, Peacham's wrote his style guide in the vernacular English, thus granting increased access to this reservoir of rhetorical moves for anyone who spoke the native tongue, not just those with special education in Greek and Latin.

The 17th and 18th century witnessed the rise of modern natural science and nothing was immune to fallout of the Scientific Revolution, including argument. Until this time period, most academic discourse was produced in deductive terms, beginning with the general principles that worked their way down to the specifics of a topic. The scientific method flips this ordering on its ear, not forming knowledge by moving from the general-to-specific, but now from the specific-to-general. The process, known as induction, is the intellectual glue that binds the methods of science together. Induction as the basis for certain forms of argumentation was popularized by Francis Bacon (1561–1626) in *The Great Instauration* (1620) in his famous rejection of Aristotelean logic: "[I] reject demonstration by syllogism. In dealing with the nature of things I use induction throughout ... For I consider induction to be that form of demonstration which upholds the sense, and closes with nature, and comes to the very brink of operation, if it does not actually deal with it." Philosopher John Locke (1632–1704) took these inductive principles into his theory of human knowledge. When we are born, he says our mind is a *tabula rasa* – "white paper, void of all characters" – that gets the truths of experience gradually written upon it. Think about the theological implications of this flip in the logical model of reality. Human purpose no longer descends *down* from heaven; it is built *up* from sense experience, a by-product of our free choice.

In *Tractatus Logico-Philosophicus* (1953), Ludwig Wittgenstein (1889–1951) carried Bacon's scientific methods of induction into everyday language use. Rather than formulating knowledge in deductive every/only structures (Platonic definitions from Chapter 2), Wittgenstein advocated for "ostensive definition" where we define terms by recognizing that certain objects share a set of properties from which we can induce general truths about the world around us (e.g. the definition of *round* is derived from observing round things – balls, soap bubbles, planets, etc.). By changing the way we form knowledge and make meaning, these men also changed the way we argue about it. No surprise that his teacher, logician Bertrand Russell, described Wittgenstein as "the most perfect example I have ever known of genius as traditionally conceived; passionate, profound, intense, and dominating."

Inductive argumentation has both benefits and its drawbacks. First, induction deals in specifics to draw its conclusions, and people are often convinced with what they can see with their own eyes. Countering the methods of Plato and Boethius, inductive models of argumentation pattern themselves upon experimental natural science, where you accumulate sensible data in order to generalize a final conclusion. Induction downplays what cannot be experienced by the senses – the abstract principles of syllogisms as "nothing but sophistry and illusion," an observation made by David Hume (1711–1776) in *An Enquiry Concerning Human Understanding* (1748). Induction is not without its risks. Chief among its challenges is the uncertainty that accompanies the probability and inference central to the inductive process. An inductive argument must, at some point, jump from specific instances to a generalized conclusion based off a series of observable phenomena. It's impossible for any arguer to have complete knowledge of every observable instance, but how much data is enough to draw a reliable conclusion? John Stuart Mill (1806–1873) recognized this limitation of induction in *System of Logic* (1843): "Why is a single instance, in some cases, sufficient for a complete induction, while in others myriads of concurring instances, without a single exception known or presumed, go such a little way towards establishing a universal proposition?" This question has yet to be satisfactorily answered to this day.

Argumentation in the Modern Period

Kenneth Burke (1897–1993), the pre-eminent rhetorician of the 20th century, took Wittgenstein's epistemological theory and expanded its application into contexts of the rhetorical situation (the speaker-subject-audience triad from Chapter 2). In *Rhetoric of Motives* (1950), Burke argued that identification – as a psychological action – is central to any persuasive argument. In Burke's usage, identification occurs when the audience assimilates an aspect, property, or attribute of the speaker or his message and is transformed by this process. Burke argued in "The Rhetoric of Hitler's 'Battle'" from *The Philosophy of Literary Form* (1941) that Hitler's real battle was not a militaristic enterprise, but an argumentative one which launched a full-frontal assault on the German public where words were the most lethal weapons of all. Burke cites Hitler's virtuosic ability to give "one voice to the whole people, this to be the 'inner voice' of Hitler, made uniform throughout the German boundaries, as leader and people were completely identified with each other." And by "strongly insist[ing] upon the total identification between leader and people," Burke argues that Hitler pushed argument into some of its most nefarious uses in human history. Kenneth's Burke argumentative analysis on Adolf Hitler's speechmaking remains an active area of scholarship. This focus on the structures of demagogic rhetoric – particularly the trope of "common enemies" and a "unified voice" – revolutionized the study of argument's relationship to power, an idea carried on in the second half of the twentieth century by the French thinker Michel Foucault in *Discipline and Punish* (1975) and *The History of Sexuality* (1981).

Towards the end of the twentieth century, argumentation saw a final synthesis between deductive and inductive reasoning into a single, unified theory of persuasion. Steven Toulmin (1922–2009) in *The Uses of Argument* (1958) and *Introduction to Reasoning* (1979) offered a model of argumentation that made equal use of both induction and deduction. A disciple of Wittgenstein, Toulmin conceded the benefits of deductive logic in the analysis of philosophical abstractions and highly technical arguments but also observed that inductive logic was much more suited for the types of arguments we regularly engage in. We'll discuss the Toulmin Model of Argumentation in detail during Chapter 10, but the system involves three primary features:

Claim: The main argument of a speech or essay.

Joe should be fired from the store.

Grounds: The data or evidence used to support the claim.

He stole twenty dollars out of the cash register.

Warrant: The assumption – either explicit in the argument or implied – which hold the claim and grounds together.

Those who steal are not trustworthy employees.

Take note of a few things in this example. First, notice how the claim is derived *inductively* from observable evidence. The speaker likely would not want to fire Joe had he not seen him steal from the register. An argument in Toulmin's terms doesn't begin with a thesis and work its way down into supporting evidence; it begins with the observable world and works its up way to a generalized thesis – an inductive process. Second, notice how warrant is derived *deductively* as the necessary outcome of the relationship between the claim and the grounds. In this sense, the tri-partite structure resembles the major premise/minor premise/conclusion arrangement of Aristotle's syllogism, the foundational logical structure in deductive argumentation. Firing Joe because he stole from the register seems like a no-brainer. It only seems like this, however, because the underlying assumption "those who steal are not trustworthy employees" is a such a commonly held view. Like a conclusion of a well-formed syllogism, the warrant should speak for itself if the other parts of the argument are in place. Toulmin's system can both aid in the construction of arguments or facilitate the deconstruction of the arguments of others. The logical structures of Toulmin's methods make it a versatile tool for any arguer. No wonder his methods are diffuse through academia, influencing not just rhetoric and composition but logic, ethics, computer science, and even emerging fields of artificial intelligence.

The following several chapters on argumentation encourage a reaching back to the past in order to look ahead to the future. To argue well, we are not throwing out what we have done with our study of rhetoric and beginning fresh. Quite the opposite actually; the rhetorical skills that any good writer has are absolutely essential to arguing appropriately and honestly. Nor are we privileging the most contemporary methods of argumentation over classical ones; different methods of argumentation are called for at different times. Whereas the deductive methods of Aristotle may be useful for a definitional argument on fairness in the workplace, we may look to Toulmin to levy an argument of competence as to why the CEO should resign for discrimination in the office (all while speaking in the language of Ciceronian claims!) One system of argument doesn't trump another; they all come together into a complicated braid and you are in the privileged position of having several millennia of these great minds at your disposal.

CHAPTER NINE

CLASSICAL MODELS OF ARGUMENTATION

For the first of our models of argumentation, we'll return to the Classical world. The patterns of persuasion in oratory's early days are a good starting point for writers coming to formal argumentation for the first time since its guidelines are especially concrete and accessible. The methods described in this chapter will be a whirlpool of Classical methods, arranged in a way to give a contemporary writer a clear and relevant understanding of the techniques which undergird a solid persuasive essay. Aristotle's *The Art of Rhetoric*, Cicero's *On Invention*, Quintilian's *Institutio Oratoria*, and the anonymously written *Rhetorica ad Herennium* (often attributed to Cicero) form the chapter's main theoretical foundation, but we'll pull from the Plato, the Sophists, Boethius, and others as needed. At the beginning of each subheading is a specific citation to the work of these authors should you want to consider what these great minds have to say in their own words (a great debt to Brigham Young's University *Silva Rhetoricae* is owed here). But for now, here's a look at the *dispositio* – the organization of the argument – that we'll be using in this chapter in outline form:

Exordium – The introduction to an argument which familiarizes the audience with the topic at hand while positioning them to be receptive to the upcoming stance.

Narratio – The exposition, or description, which informs the audience about the key information on the topic to situate them into the discourse of the controversy.

Partitio – The claim, or statement of argument, about the topic which succinctly presents the arguable position the speaker will take.

Confirmatio – The support for the claim that is intended to convince the audience, beyond a reasonable doubt, of the merits stated in the paper's stance towards the main topic.

Refutatio – The acknowledgement of counter-positions to either concede their legitimacy or to refute their claims in favor of the one taken in the paper.

Peroratio – The conclusion of the argument that finishes things off in an engaging way to leave a favorable impression on the audience.

This chapter is organized along three of Cicero's five canons of rhetoric - "invention," "arrangement," and "style" – and the illustrative examples draw from a broad range of authors and genres to illustrate the versatility of this approach to argument. At the end of each subheading, you'll see excerpt from the prepared transcript of Barack Obama's 2009 Inaugural Address to show the principles of Classical argumentation in contemporary action. Keep in mind that the outlines and examples should work to remind you of the basic strategies for developing a sound argument. However, they are not delivered truth, and you'll see that the best writers take these basics strategies and creatively adapt them.

"Invention" in Argument – Stasis

In the Classical tradition, *stasis* is center of invention. Translated as "point of rest," the *stasis* of an argument is the exact point of disagreement between two sides – where the two sides no longer see eye-to-eye – and where argumentation begins. Knowing how to identify the *stasis* of a situation will help you find an argument's point of focus, understand why your opponents may push back at you, and recognize how not to talk past the essential points of what's really at stake. Quintilian's *Institutio Oratoria* (Book III) outlines an easy-to-follow process for finding an argument's point of *stasis*, and this procedure is still very much applicable to contemporary argumentation, both formal and informal, spoken or written. In his words:

> Let students learn, therefore, before all, that there are four modes of proceeding in every cause and that he ought to make it his first business to consider which four modes he who is going to plead. Beginning first of all with the defendant, by far the strongest mode of defense is if the charge which is made can be denied; the next, if an act of the kind charged against the accused can be said not to have been done; the third, and most honorable, if what is done is proved to have been justly done. If we cannot command these methods, the last and only mode of defense is that of eluding an accusation, which can neither be denied nor combated, by the aid of some point of law, so as make it appear that the action has not been brought in due legal form.

Here are Quintilian's ideas broken down into chart form (see Table 1):

Table 1 Quintilian's Breakdown of Stasis.

Name	Central question to focus the argument
Stasis in conjecture	Did it happen?
Stasis in definition	What do we call it?
Stasis in quality	It is justifiable?
Stasis in forum	Is this the appropriate place to have the argument?

To illustrate how this works, let's use an everyday example. Say, for instance, you are asked by your teacher to stay after class. Once your peers file out of the room, your teacher slaps your most recent exam down on the desk. "F." He looks you in the eyes and says, "You cheated on this test." How do you respond? There are four ways the argument can go depending on the point of *stasis* you identify.

Scenario 1: You could start conjecturally and dispute that the event even happened: "I didn't cheat. You must have misinterpreted the situation." At this first level of *stasis*, your accuser says you cheated and you've denied it, so the point of focus in the debate will be whether or not the cheating occurred. Your conjectural argument, then, may go on to dispute the facts themselves or at attempt least to cast a reasonable doubt on the facts as they have been presented against you. In a situation like this, there are a number of things you may call into question:

> "What did you see that made you think I cheated?"
> "Could you see me well enough from where you were sitting to know I was cheating?"
> "Did someone tell you I was cheating? Is this person a reliable source of information?"

Scenario 2: You may decide to reply not with a question of whether or not the cheating happened, but with a definitional *stasis* that focuses the upcoming argument on what you should call the action. An argument under these conditions will put the label of "cheating" up for debate in hopes of re-characterizing this action into something a little less incriminating. You may respond to your teacher by saying something like, "I didn't cheat. I collaborated with a friend to arrive at the right answer." By deflecting the accusation into the realm of definition, your argument will proceed along a different line of concerns from the first scenario:

> "What is the nature of the cheating?"
> "Can we assign this action to the larger classification of collaboration?"
> "Where did you get your definition of cheating? Is that definition accurate?"

Scenario 3: You may know that you cheated, and it's no use denying it. Along with your test, the teacher also has your friend's paper that contains the same set of answers and security camera footage that captured your theft. The evidence isn't favorable, and things aren't looking too good. Where do you go from here? Well, a *stasis* of quality – where you focus the argument to a question of whether or not the act of cheating was justified – may be called for. You may respond, "I did cheat, but everyone in the class does it. Why am I the only one who's punished?" The argument now will force the teacher to question whether or not a single act of cheating is punishable when an entire class was guilty of the same transgression, thereby deflecting the debate into larger discussions of justice and fairness. As the argument goes, some new questions will need to be addressed:

"Is cheating really as bad you say it is?"

"What would happen if we let this instance of cheating slide just this once?"

"Who says that cheating is a serious infraction? What is the source of this?"

Scenario 4: You've cheated. You know what cheating is. You know that cheating is wrong. What do you do now? A last-ditch effort may be to argue that an empty classroom with nobody else present is not the appropriate place to have this discussion, thus deeming the argument as possessing a *stasis* of forum. You may say, "Yes, I cheated, but I'd rather have this conversation with my parents and the principal present." What you've done here is refocus the argument one more time to address a new set of underlying concerns:

"Who should be involved in determining the consequences for my cheating?"

"How should my cheating be dealt with in terms of consequence?"

"Who should dictate my punishment? Where do they get their authority?"

Based on this example, there are a few things to consider when it comes how you'll determine the *stasis* of an argument. First off, you must choose a *stasis* that can be sustained throughout a complete argument. If your teacher has unmistakable evidence of your cheating – two identical papers and security camera footage which shows you leaning in to see several answers – there is no point in trying to argue conjecturally. Trying to work with a *stasis* that's simply not there is not just a misstep in the argument; it can be devastating to any chance of winning. By denying that you've cheated (when you clearly have), not only leads to you losing this particular argument, but your character and credibility will be shot when it comes to subsequent arguments since anyone who's seen you lie about this issue would have no reason to think you won't lie again.

Second, you must acknowledge that *stasis* is progressive; that is, whatever *stasis* point you think the argument calls for, know that you are implicitly conceding all the points of *stasis* that precede it (see Figure 1). For example, if you go with scenario 4 (*stasis* of forum) from the above example,

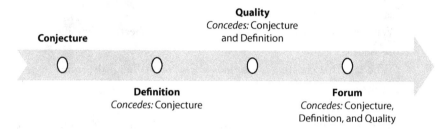

Figure 1 Progressive Concession in Points of Stasis.

you are conceding that the cheating occurred (*stasis* of conjecture), that it can accurately be described as cheating (*stasis* of definition), and that the cheating was not justifiable (*stasis* of quality).

Choosing a point of *stasis*, and sustaining this focus throughout the argument, also makes or breaks the reliability of an argument. Don't waffle when it comes to choosing a *stasis* point; it's never a good idea to jump from one point of *stasis* to another while the argument is underway since it will communicate both desperation and lack of confidence in your position. Consider how believable the student in our hypothetical scenario would be if the conversation went this way:

<u>Teacher:</u> "You cheated on this test."
<u>Student:</u> "No I didn't." (*conjecture*)
<u>Teacher:</u> "I have the test from the student you copied from and there is security camera footage clearly showing you looking on your peer's test."
<u>Student:</u> "Well, ok. But, what do you mean by cheating?" (*definition*)
<u>Teacher:</u> "I mean you stole answers from another student and passed it off as your own."
<u>Student:</u> "Ok, but isn't cheating not that big of a deal?" (*quality*)
<u>Teacher:</u> "It is a big deal and you are in big trouble."
<u>Student:</u> "I don't think this is the right place to talk about this." (*forum*)

It's easy to see how *stasis* works with a live give-and-take between opposing sides, but how can a writer of an argument determine the *stasis*? You must rely on reading, observation, and experience – the virtual voices in the dialogue surrounding any controversial issue – to decide what the point of focus in the argument should be. By choosing the *stasis* point with a little bit of foresight to the eventual argument, you can easily pre-empt or exclude certain aspects of the topic from ever finding their way into the discussion you plan to develop. Say, for example, you are writing an argument to do with the topic of the ever-increasing length of the American work week, and you settle on a *stasis* of definition since you've concluded from your research that the debate centers on a few key questions: What is "work"? Is "work" an activity confined to a physical location? How has communication technology changed the meaning of "work"? What you're doing here is setting up an argument of definition with an eye to potential objections. Opponents who argue that the increase of the work week negatively impacts family life and mental and physical health may have a point, but these arguments are irrelevant within the boundaries you've established with your choice in *stasis*. Arguments are always a bit easier when you have home-field advantage. And knowing how to use *stasis* properly will always keep you on your own turf.

"Arrangement and "Style" in Argument

The saying, "You never get a second chance to make a first impression" is a popular truism worth invoking as we begin a discussion of how to create an introduction that will be equally memorable and functional. To use an analogy for a minute, think of the writer as a young professional on his first job interview and the reader as the skeptical employer who is about to scrutinize the young man in front of him for about the next 20–30 minutes. A paper's introduction is the written equivalent of that first-hand shake, those first couple of moments when the prospective employee wants to seem interesting, reliable, and trustworthy, all at the same time. But the employer is not easily charmed. He is skeptical, scanning for weaknesses and all-the-while wondering, "Should I buy into what this guy is saying?" The stakes are high at this point, and this is no different in your writing. There is a lot you need to do, and do well, in a small amount of space.

Introductions aren't easy. In fact, they are often the toughest paragraphs to write because they contain the most thinking-per-square-inch of any paragraph in an entire composition. Introductions reflect the entirety of the writing process in a single space. A good introduction should bring the reader easily along, allow them to have a clear sense of what the author is trying to prove, and present some recognizable plan for how he will do that. A good introduction establishes direct eye contact and a firm grip with the reader; it serves to get your listeners on board with your motives and establishes a willingness within them to listen to what you have to say. Conversely, writers who blow-off the introduction come to their interview in a tattered suit, reeking of body odor. They have put the employer off and even if they have good things to say during the interview, their chances of convincing anyone that they are the right person for the job are slim to none.

Whether you're a writer who composes from beginning to end, or one who jumps into the paper's middle to feel their way around, a tight introduction is a must for any worthwhile argument. It provides coherence and focus, and good writers know that the time spent on introductions is not wasted. It helps you focus on what is essential (and what is not), all while letting you establish and polish the written voice. The Classical theorists – Aristotle, Cicero, and Quintilian – all had a great deal to say about how a writer can, and must, attend to these most important opening moments in a work of persuasion. A good introduction in the Classical tradition has three parts: the *exordium*, the *narratio*, and the *partitio*. Let's look at each in detail.

The Lead-In – The Exordium

Aristotle's *The Art of Rhetoric* (section 3.14)
RhetoricaAd Herennium (sections 1.4.6–1.7.11)
Cicero's *On Invention* (sections 1.15–18)
Quintilian's *Institutio Oratoria* (section 4.1)

In Greek, *exordium* means "beginning a web," and this is an instructive metaphor for just how complicated and elegant the opening lines of an argument should be. This first component of a Classical introduction goes by many modern-day names: "hook," "attention grabber," "lure," "lead." Whatever name your classroom teacher has assigned to it, this portion functions to announce the subject and purpose of the discourse in a meaningful and interesting way. Often in academic writing, this component is downplayed as mere ornamentation, the lard outside the meat of the essay.

But think of any time in your life you have been moved to action by an argument. The proof was there, of course, but there is another presence, beyond the logical, in effective arguments that stirs both body and soul. Good arguments engage. They entertain while they persuade. They win you over. You should get into the habit of initially engaging the audience no matter the argumentative context – formal or informal, public or private – since, as Aristotle says in Chapter 18 of *The Art of Rhetoric*, "the single person is as much your 'judge' as if he were one of many; we may say, without qualification, that anyone is your judge whom you have to persuade." Aristotle, Cicero, and Quintilian all acknowledged the importance of the *exordium* as the jumping-off point to moving an argument in a productive, and persuasive, direction. Below are six strategies, complete with explanations and examples, to try out in the construction of your own argument's *exordium*.

Inquisitive – This lead-in strategy characterizes the topic, or at least the way the writer wants his audience to see the topic. as worthy of discussion. Writers using this approach may highlight an interesting aspect of topic, one of its unusual features, an important bit of information, or something which is just plain strange or attention grabbing. Consider the example below from Annie Dillard's *Living Like Weasels* (1982).

"A weasel is wild. Who knows what he thinks? He sleeps in his underground den, his tail draped over his nose. Sometimes he lives in his den for two days without leaving. Outside, he stalks rabbits, mice, muskrats, and birds, killing more bodies than he can eat warm … obedient to instinct."

How the Inquisitive Strategy Works:
The subject of the first, four-word sentence connotes the characteristics of the people who will be the subject of the following essay: sneaky, underhanded, greedy, and maybe even a little bit reclusive. The second sentence supplements the initial implications found in the first by cataloging a series of specific actions that allude to the action of the weasel's human counterpart who is reclusive ("lives in his den for two days"), wasteful ("killing more than he can eat warm"), and impulsive ("obedient to instinct"). Dillard's essay focuses on human behavior and uses the weasel as a negative point of reference. The opening analogy easily, and humorously, shows the reader what she's going to be up against in the argument that follows.

Antithetical – An antithetical strategy for an introduction sets up one idea about a topic to contrast it with another. Often, a writer will choose an initial aspect of the topic to focus on that somehow counters the paper's main argument. Similar to dramatic irony in literature, it's in the turn from one point of view to the other where the author can seize the attention of the audience. Consider the example we had looked at earlier in Chapter 2 from George W. Bush's "Address to the Nation on the Night of 9/11" (2001).

> "Today, our fellow citizens, our way of life, our very freedom came under attack in a series of deliberate and deadly terrorist acts. The victims were in airplanes or in their offices: secretaries, business men and women, military and federal workers, moms and dads, friends and neighbors. Thousands of lives were suddenly ended by evil, despicable acts of terror. The pictures of airplanes flying into buildings, fires burning, huge – huge structures collapsing have filled us with disbelief, terrible sadness, and a quiet, unyielding anger. These acts of mass murder were intended to frighten our nation into chaos and retreat. But they have failed. Our country is strong."

> ***How the Antithetical Strategy Works:***
> In a formal address to the nation, every second counts and not a word can be out of place. Clocking in at just over four minutes, Bush's first paragraph is as busy as they come. In the first sentence, Bush's tricolon repetition of "our" in the opening three phrases ("our fellow citizens, our way of life, our very freedom") works to align himself with the American audience he's addressing, thus establishing a sense of shared plight and tragedy in the face of violence and aggression. This initial antithesis forecasts a string of antitheticals between the American citizens and the terrorist attackers which form the speech's main thematic dichotomies: victim vs. aggressor, good vs. evil, us vs. them. The antithetical strategy also operates in Bush's descriptions of "the attack's wide-reaching effects." Not only has this attack had a personal effect on individual "citizens," but Bush also describes the attack as an affront to American culture ("our way of life") and Western democratic political ideology ("our very freedom"), thus establishing another powerful contrast between the individual and the collective.

Corrective – Corrective strategies intend to show that an aspect of a topic has been ignored, misunderstood, or otherwise not paid attention to in the right way. This strategy then goes on to correct this misinterpretation, thus establishing the key definitions and terms of the argument.

Consider the example below from John Donne's "Meditation XVII" ("No Man is an Island") (1624).

"Perchance he for whom this bell tolls may be so ill as that he knows not it tolls for him; and perchance I may think myself so much better than I am, as that they who are about me and see my state may have caused it to toll for me, and I know not that."

How the Corrective Strategy Works:

In the clause that precedes the semicolon ("Perchance he for whom this bell tolls may be so ill as that he knows not it tolls for him"), the author paints a somber image of a man who is so sick that he's not even aware the ceremonial death bells are ringing as a signal his own imminent death. The ambiguous "he" switches to the personal "I" after the pause, and it's here that a reader can see Donne's corrective switch. The ignorant man of the sentence's first half is revealed to be the author himself, ignorant of his failing health ("perchance I may think myself so much better than I am") and oblivious that those surrounding him are there to pay their final respects ("as that they who are about me and see my state may have caused it to toll for me, and I know not that"). This correction is Donne's launching pad into his primary meditation on the famous idea of "no man is an island." As a side note, the famous phrase "for whom the bell tolls" is an original saying that can be attributed to this essay by John Donne. From Ernest Hemmingway to Metallica, this famous one-liner has been adapted as the title for novels, songs, and other various artistic productions.

Preparatory – It's never a good idea to surprise your reader deep in the essay. Preparing readers at the outset for what's to come is one of the most tried-and-true ways of keeping an audience on your side while seeding the argument's most relevant and important ideas. Writers can do this through an overt statement of what's to come, but they can also help the reader anticipate the central idea through the seeding of subtle hints. The latter not only demonstrates a strong command in the writing, but it also is effective way to establish the terms and limits of what the argument will focus on (and what it won't). Consider the example below from Samuel Johnson's "Obstructions of Learning" (1760).

"It is common to find young men ardent and diligent in the pursuit of knowledge; but the progress of life very often produces laxity and indifference; and not only those who are at liberty to choose their business and amusements, but those likewise whose professions engage them in literary inquiries, pass the latter part of their time without improvement, and spend the day rather in any other entertainment than that which they might find among their books."

How the Preparatory Strategy Works:

If you closely read the lead-off line, you'll see that Johnson prepares his audience for what's to come while pulling off a subtle joke. Since the essay discusses those things which inhibit learning, Johnson's style foreshadows this idea by replicating the experience of distraction through the twists and turns of the paragraph's complicated syntax. Did you notice that the entire first paragraph is a single 77-word sentence, and a bafflingly complicated one at that? The opening 15 words ("It is common to find young men ardent and diligent in the pursuit of knowledge") present a straightforward declarative idea to the reader: young men often have good intentions when it comes to learning. The remaining 62 words of his opener outline the litany of distractions which obstruct this good intention: "laxity and indifference,""business and amusements,""other entertainments." Johnson's style, in effect, buries the sentence's initial clause under a heap of subordinate clauses, all of which are the distractions that commonly pull young men away from their studies.

Anecdotal – This lead-off strategy puts a short personal account of an incident or event front and center. Readers are usually more willing to listen when some personal interests are involved. If you can illustrate emotion or personal investment in your topic, there is a greater chance that the reader may eventually share these feelings. At the very least, the reader is placed at the epicenter of the conflict and is forced to take a side or, perhaps, consider where they may fall. Consider the example below from Sven Birkerts's *Into the Electronic Millennium* (1991).

"Some years ago, a friend and I co-managed a used and rare book shop in Ann Arbor, Michigan. We were often asked to appraise and purchase libraries–by retiring academics, widows, and disgruntled graduate students. One day we took a call from a professor of English at one of the community colleges outside Detroit. When he answered the buzzer I did a double-take–he looked to be only a year or two older than we were. "I'm selling everything," he said, leading the way through a large apartment.

The professor took our first offer. As we boxed up the books, we chatted. My partner asked the man if he were moving. "No," he said, "I'm getting out." We looked up. "Out of the teaching business, I mean. Out of books." He then said that he wanted to show us something. And indeed, as soon as the books were packed and loaded, he led us back through the apartment and down a set of stairs. When we reached the basement, he flicked on a light. There, on a long table, displayed like an exhibit in the Space Museum, was a computer. I didn't know what it was then, nor could I tell you now, fifteen years later.

The scene has stuck with me. It is a kind of marker in my mental life. For that afternoon, I got my first serious inkling that all was not well in the world of print and letters. All sorts of corroborations followed. Our professor was by no means an isolated case. Over a period of several years we met with quite a few others like him. New men and new women who had glimpsed the future and had decided to get while the getting was good. The selling off of books was sometimes done for financial reasons, but the other thing was usually there as well: the need to burn bridges. It was as if heading to the future also required the destruction of tokens from the past.

A change is upon us—nothing could be clearer. The printed word is part of a vestigial order that we are moving away from—by choice and by societal compulsion."

How the Anecdotal Strategy Works:

Paragraphs 1–3 establish a few things which help to inform and foreshadow the direction of the subsequent essay. The persona of the speaker is established – a status-quo loving, used/rare bookstore owner – who is not himself a member of academia; he simply loves everything to do with printed books. This inclination should nudge the reader in the side, letting them know the argumentative position Birkerts will eventually take. The speaker stands in sharp contrast to the professor, who challenges about every expectation we could possibly have regarding an 18th and 19th century literature teacher. The two characters represent the polar opposite perspectives of the essential question at the heart of the issue in the essay: Can literature still exist as it once had in a new digital age? The author draws on many of the tools of narration – descriptive passages, characterization, pacing, dialogue – in a short amount of space, giving the reader an almost complete story arc in four short paragraphs. Paragraph 4, the final sentences, draw the camera back, allowing for a more perspective-based comments (that the professor is more of the norm than an anomaly) which funnel down into the author's claim in the final line.

Explicit – Sometimes the best strategies are the ones which seem not be strategies at all. When a speaker is explicit about some aspect of their argument right off the bat – the point of *stasis*, their motives, why they are so interested in the topic – it diffuses suspicion, thereby building a little bit of trust from the get-go. Consider the example below from Michel de Montaigne's "To the Reader" (1580).

"READER, thou hast here an honest book; it doth at the outset forewarn thee that, in contriving the same, I have proposed to myself no other than a domestic and private end: I have had no consideration at all either to thy service or to my glory. My powers are not capable of any such design.

How the Explicit Strategy Works:
From the outset, Montaigne explicitly communicates his intentions to the reader, and he does so with a touch of his characteristic irony. On one hand, the author outlines the purpose of the introspective essay (a form to which Montaigne is generally credited with inventing) as a type of writing that allows a reader to see the inner workings of a mind in motion. On the other hand, this private introspection is made public through the act of writing suggested by his direct address to the generic "Reader" (not Mom, or Dad, or Joe my best friend) in the essay's first word. Given these tonal and stylistic tensions, Montaigne explicitly brings the thematic core of his writing into focus: the personal essay as an ironic form in which the author speaks publicly about his private self.

Bear in mind that these argumentative moves are not the only effects that are available to writers. An author can hook the reader in a whole host of ways. Use some of the options from the preceding pages or create something that better fits your argumentative occasion. In any case, never forget to draw the reader into your piece.

Case Study in Classical Argumentation: Barack Obama's 2009 Inaugural Address

The Exordium

My Fellow Citizens:
I stand here today humbled by the task before us, grateful for the trust you have bestowed, mindful of the sacrifices borne by our ancestors. I thank President Bush

for his service to our nation, as well as the generosity and cooperation he has shown throughout this transition. Forty-four Americans have now taken the presidential oath. The words have been spoken during rising tides of prosperity and the still waters of peace. Yet, every so often, the oath is taken amidst gathering clouds and raging storms. At these moments, America has carried on not simply because of the skill or vision of those in high office, but because We the People have remained faithful to the ideals of our forebearers, and true to our founding documents. So it has been. So it must be with this generation of Americans.

Obama's opener is built on an antithetical strategy; he leads with gestures of humility and reverence for the past that contrast with the grim picture of the America he finds himself inheriting. The parallelism of "humbled … grateful … mindful" (a *tricolon* in Classical rhetorical terminology) sets a tone of modesty while simultaneously establishing a sense of purpose in the presidential office. The following line – "I thank President Bush for his service to our nation" – continues these expressions of gratitude, this time directed at the existing president as a demonstration of the abstract qualities from the first line (in expressing his gratitude, he is demonstrating how "humbled," "grateful," and "mindful" he is upon entering office). The fulcrum of the *exordium* is "yet," a conjunction that recasts the speech into a figurative location of "gathering clouds and raging storms" from "rising tides of prosperity and the still waters of peace." This conjunction also sends us from the present-day into the past, reminding the audience that difficult periods in history were solved by the "skill and vision of those in high office" and the fortitude and patriotism of everyday folks who "have remained faithful to the ideals of our forebearers, and true to our founding documents." No doubt, "We the People" – the opening three words of the U.S. Constitution – anticipates the final lines "So it has been. So it must be" which establishes the speech-wide motif of looking back to the past to move ahead to the future.

The Background and Context – The Narratio

Rhetorica Ad Herennium (sections 1.8.11–1.9.16)
Cicero's *On Invention* (sections 1.19–21)
Cicero's *Topics* (sections 25.97)
Quintilian's *Institutio Oratoria* (sections 4.2)

To get the reader's attention is not enough. To move an argument forward, you must provide an exposition of the relevant facts and essential information on your topic in order to sketch out the major contours of the debate for your reader. The second component of the Classical introduction, the *narratio*, does just this. It's the intelligence briefing, the virtual dossier, of your paper which preps the listener on the basics – what has happened in the past, what people are saying about it now, what context makes the argument intelligible – to sketch out the broader relevance of your topic's implications. How do you do that? Think like a journalist and give your readers the 5W's and 1 H of the situation: Who? What? Where? When? Why? How? Quintilian stressed the skill of summary as essential to narration since a listener must be able to situate themselves in the larger story of your topic. As an exercise to build proficiency, Quintilian would give his students a story to read and make them retell it front-to-back, back-to-front, middle-to-end, and middle-to-beginning. This thought exercise was crucial, Quintilian thought, in the training of how to piece together the parts of a narrative with clarity and focus.

In *A Grammar of Motives* (1945), Kenneth Burke offered an updated formulation of Quintilian's Classical *narratio*. Like Quintilian, Burke understood that argument is a fundamentally rhetorical enterprise. To effectively situate a reader into the context of an argument, Burke puts forth his theory of the *pentad* to help writers articulate exactly what is at stake and why it should matter to a reader. His theoretical framework centers on five key questions: *what* was done? ("act"), *when* or *where* it was done? ("scene"), *who* did it? ("agent"), *why* was it done? ("purpose"), and *how* did he do it? ("agency"). Though Burke describes this theory in *A Grammar of Motives* as an applied method for analyzing human relationships, its basic assumption of life-as-drama is a useful schema to help argument writers humanize a *narratio* while still outlining essential information.

Whether you follow Quintilian or Burke, you're only halfway there. Just how much narration you need depends on the circumstances, and here is where questions of *decorum* – a style that matches the rhetorical situation – come rushing in. Some types of writing call for extensive narration (a master's thesis or dissertation), but typically it's best to be clear, brief, and maybe even a little bit predictable when sketching out the facts. A focused attempt to delineate the basics, to rundown what's relevant to the immediate argument, should probably leave out more than it includes. The *narratio* must also be mindful of *how* the information is conveyed within the accepted conventions of different modes of academic discourse. In this sense, the *narratio* must conform to stylistic and methodological conventions which belong to different academic (and non-academic) fields. In Table 2, consider how each discipline calls for a different presentation of the information:

Table 2 Stylistic Conventions of Narration by Discipline.

Domain	Argument	What's needed in narratio
Science	The advantages of a new course of treatment for lymphoma	A detailed explanation of the methods used in clinical trials and an overview of competing treatments currently on the market
English	Shakespeare's troubled marriage to Anne Hathaway underwrites the depiction of Macbeth and Lady Macbeth's precarious marriage dynamics in *Macbeth*	A review of relevant literary criticism which situates this new view of the play into the larger discourse of Shakespearean scholarship on *Macbeth*
History	The dropping of the atomic bomb on Hiroshima and Nagasaki was not morally justifiable	A citing of relevant facts and events from the events which led up to the dropping of the bomb from both American and Japanese perspectives
Politics	A tax increase to fund new public-school initiatives	A reference to past precedent when taxes have been increased paired with narrational anecdotes about children who've succeeded as a result of similar initiatives

Ultimately, the writer must know the audience for the *narratio* to work. As you make choices about your own context, consider some of the following questions:

> Is there anything my audience wants to know about my topic? Is there anything they need to know?
>
> Do my readers have any experience with my topic? Can I appeal to positive aspects of that experience?
>
> What do my readers already know about my topic? How can I leverage this concisely?
>
> Are there any well-known current events that coincide with my topic? Would a narrative account of this strengthen their awareness of the issue?
>
> Are there things to which my audience may be sensitive? Should I word things differently to acknowledge these things while meeting the needs of my audience?

After all, the purpose of an argument is to convince the undecided; you will do very little to persuade those who already agree with you or to those who are steadfastly opposed. A crucial step in getting this change to occur is in the explanation of *what* your position is and *why* this position should matter.

Case study in Classical Argumentation: Barack Obama's 2009 Inaugural Address

The Narratio

That we are in the midst of crisis is now well understood. Our nation is at war, against a far-reaching network of violence and hatred. Our economy is badly weakened, a consequence of greed and irresponsibility on the part of some, but also our collective failure to make hard choices and prepare the nation for a new age. Homes have been lost; jobs shed; businesses shuttered. Our health care is too costly; our schools fail too many; and each day brings further evidence that the ways we use energy strengthen our adversaries and threaten our planet. These are the indicators of crisis, subject to data and statistics. Less measurable but no less profound is a sapping of confidence across our land – a nagging fear that America's decline is inevitable, and that the next generation must lower its sights.

Today I say to you that the challenges we face are real. They are serious and they are many. They will not be met easily or in a short span of time. But know this, America: They will be met. On this day, we gather because we have chosen hope over fear, unity of purpose over conflict and discord. On this day, we come to proclaim an end to the petty grievances and false promises, the recriminations and worn-out dogmas, that for far too long have strangled our politics.

The subject of the first sentence, "we," calls back to both his greeting ("My *fellow* citizens") and his invocation of the Constitution ("*We* the People") to extend his we-are-in-this-together tone to the next movement of the argument, the *narratio*. Obama leads with cultural commonplace ("That we are in the midst of crisis is now well understood") that implicitly concedes a number of weakness facing the country at the dawn of the speaker's presidency: housing markets, unemployment, health care, education, and the environment. Obama quickly outlines the issues without lingering too long on any particular one, coming off as a candid speaker who acknowledges the issues as a true, if not unflattering, portrait of the United States. The lead-off, "today," in paragraph 2 recontextualizes these problems of the recent past to the present moment (think of his attention to *Kairos* here). In parallel fashion to the preceding paragraph, Obama reimagines these problems from a perspective of hope (an allusion to the one-word slogan of his first presidential campaign).

The Claim – The Partitio

Rhetorica Ad Herennium (section 1.10.17)
Cicero's *On Invention* (sections 1.22–23)
Quintilian's *Institutio Oratoria* (section 4.5)

If *stasis* identifies the heart of the controversy, then then the *partitio* is where the speaker does something about it. The *partitio* is a statement that an audience is asked to accept and for which the speaker will provide evidence. This component quite literally "partitions" the introductory information (*exordium* and *narratio*) from the body of the argument. Claims should work hand-in-hand with *stasis*, and the settled upon argument of the paper should line up directly with the point of identified controversy. According to Classical theory, there are four basic types of claim.

A claim of cause focuses on how things happened, or whether they happened at all. Often these claims will argue for the relationship between events which can be independently corroborated through written records, eyewitness testimony, or other various research methods. Arguers may claim that a number of causes converged in a single effect, that a single cause led to multiple effects, or that there is a cause and effect chain (whose start and stop must be strategically decided by the writer). Claims of cause directly correlate to a *stasis* of conjecture.

Stasis of Conjecture

- Asks, "Did it happen?"

Claim of Cause

- Answers, "How did it happen?" or "Why didn't it happen?"

A claim of definition focuses on how an audience should understand the meaning of a word, person, or idea. Claims of definition argue for meaning in relation to a point of view: a moral perspective, a political perspective, a scientific perspective, a pragmatic perspective, so forth. Arguments of definition don't merely describe the topic; they assign an identity to it. In this sense, claims of definition attempt to define reality, and with even a slight alteration to the claim, the reality that the claim purports to communicate will also shift and change. Claims of definition directly correlate to a *stasis* of definition.

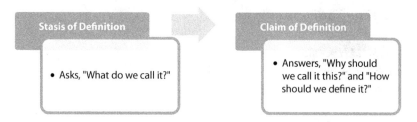

A claim of value looks at particular issue through a filter – values, ethics, politics, so forth – and argues whether or not this view is justifiable. Claims of value must explicitly identify the frame of reference used in the appraisal since complicated issues can always be understood through several perspectives, each with its own set of emphases. Value claims must also establish boundaries; the goal is not to be comprehensive, but to clearly communicate a judgement on some aspect of the chosen issue. Claims of value directly correlate to a *stasis* of quality.

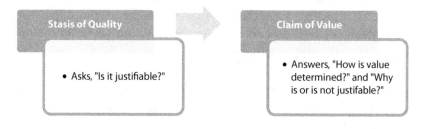

A claim of policy focuses on what should be done about an issue. Although there are any number of decisions a person could make in the face of a controversy, claims of policy tend to focus on problem-solution scenarios. Sometimes a solution is to maintain the status quo to see the challenging times through; other solutions may include a complete tear down of the old ways. Sometimes referred to as the "is/ought" distinction, claims of policy make arguments about what should be done in a given situation, even if that "something" is nothing at all. Claims of policy directly correlate to a *stasis* of forum.

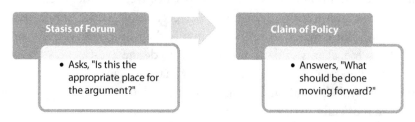

The highest virtue of a claim is clarity. The thesis is the rational element in the argument, and it governs the entire paper. As Marie Secor says in *Composition and Argument* (1997), "writers need to make their main point clear to the reader. This does not mean that you have to write five paragraph themes with the thesis statement at the end of the first paragraph, but it does mean that by the time the reader finishes the introduction, they should have a clear sense of what they are getting at. Again, the main point may be complex and nuanced, but it should not be mysterious."

Case Study in Classical Argumentation: Barack Obama's 2009 Inaugural Address

The Partitio

We remain the most prosperous, powerful nation on Earth. Our workers are no less productive than when this crisis began. Our minds are no less inventive, our goods and services no less needed than they were last week or last month or last year. Our capacity remains undiminished. But our time of standing pat, of protecting narrow interests and putting off unpleasant decisions – that time has surely passed. Starting today, we must pick ourselves up, dust ourselves off, and begin again the work of remaking America.

Judging from the available evidence in the *exordium* and *narratio*, it seems that Obama has identified the speech's stasis point as one of *quality*, which examines the relevance of foundational American values in the contemporary world. Accordingly, Obama's claim, coming at the end of the sixth paragraph, is a rightly calibrated claim of value, anticipated by the parallel phrasing of "no less" in the lines that precede it. We've been dealt a bad hand since "this crisis began," yes, but we must put our timeless American values at the center of our experience in order to "pick ourselves up, dust ourselves off, and begin again the work of remaking America." And here is Obama's call to arms, a defense or justification of why the wisdom of the past will carry our nation through the toughest of times.

Appeals and Evidence – The Confirmatio

Cicero's *On Invention* (sections 1.24–41)
Quintilian's *Institutio Oratoria* (sections 5.1–12)

The *confirmatio*, or confirmation, is where the speaker trots out the evidence to verify the claim made in the *partitio*. There are many rooms in the house of argumentative evidence: an outline of the advantages and disadvantages, corroborating examples, statistical data, citing authoritative texts and testimony, reasonably connected claims, and everything in between. These categories are certainly not exhaustive, nor do they account for the types of evidence required in specialized argumentation. They are arbitrary to some degree, but not randomly chosen. Logos – the rhetorical appeal that enlists the brains of its audience – is the primordial element of an argument's proof. And since argument is inextricably bound up with rhetoric, authors are continually finding new ways of presenting claims and supporting them. Even student writers creatively think and argue in ways that the professionals overlook. It happens all the time. Think of the advice in this section as the opposite of prescription; it will not lay out the only options for proof but nudge you in a productive direction to let you determine, as Aristotle said, the "best available means of persuasion" for a given case.

Before you put readers in direct contact with the specifics, you must first decide on which logical structure – induction or deduction – will be its delivery system. Induction and deduction have a long and complicated relationship throughout intellectual history (Chapter 8), but for the purposes of clarity, let's consider these in the following way:

Induction: This pattern of reasoning draws conclusions after the specific pieces of evidence have been presented. Sometimes induction is used for stylistic reasons. As periodic syntax can build purposeful tension in a sentence, induction can be put to the same effect in an argument at large. An author will present evidence, piece by piece, so when the conclusion makes its appearance, it feels like that natural and obvious inference. Many teachers of argument would affirm this principle, preferring that an argument pose a line of inquiry which gradually works its way *up* to the thesis through the effective marshalling of specific evidence. The thesis is written with conviction, but this conviction has been earned over the course of the argument.

A tightly rigged relationship between ideas is a must for an inductive argument to work, but if you can pull it off, all the better for persuasion since "the audience takes pleasure in themselves for anticipating the point," an idea we mentioned in our discussion of logos in Chapter 2. Induction is the go-to method of doctors and detectives, who piece together a smattering of random clues to draw logical conclusions based off the purposeful arrangement of evidence. Sometimes induction can give the effect not of order and control, but of spontaneity and shared inquiry. The writer becomes co-investigator with the audience (although the absence of apparent structure *is*, ironically, a structure). Such a pattern replicates, in text form, the process by which we make sense of the world around us.

Deduction: Derived from the formal logic of Aristotle (Chapter 8), deduction is an attractive pattern of organization since its logical substructure is airtight. Rather than work your *up* to the thesis, the evidence descends *down* from it. Deductive arguments place central importance on the claim since it dictates all that follows. A good deductive argument will make the paragraphs reflect the division of the subject and here is where topic sentences, tied to your thesis, can be helpful. Every paragraph is a coherent, logically developed whole within the broader whole of your essay, and each paragraph should have good reason for appearing where it does.

Deduction, like induction, must earn its claims. Even though the presentation is ultimately hierarchical and ordered, it does not mean that you should adopt a take-no-prisoners tone that asserts a claim and buries the reader under an avalanche of reasons as to why you're right. Your thesis may come at the beginning of your paper, but it had better come towards the end of your thinking and searching and organizing and even writing your paper. The argument plays out the meaning of the thesis, but it should do so with full appreciation of alternative points of view while recognizing the uncertainty of most situations.

Once you settle on the overall logical pattern, you now must deal in specifics. It's impossible to produce an exhaustive list of all the specific forms of evidence here, but what we can do is look at three criteria which are the general hallmarks of a solid proof. "Proofs," Aristotle said, "must be demonstrative in a way that brings the demonstration to bear on the subject of the controversy." In other words, the claim picks the fight, but the evidence is the right uppercut.

Evidence must first be relevant to the claim. Readers like clear, crisp examples which are plainly accessible. Evidence cannot distance itself too far from the claim; when it does, problems of ambiguity begin to take effect. To shore up problems of relevance, use your good judgement to know whether the evidence has a reasonable connection to what is discussed in the argument. Related to issues of relevance are questions of how up-to-date the information is. Of course, evidence must be appropriately recent, but this piece of advice is entirely dependent on the topic. Whereas the research and development in computer technology turns over a few times a year, certain mathematical concepts have not changed since the days of Ancient Egypt. Like questions of relevance, you'll have to use your good sense (your *phronesis*, as it were) to make these calls.

Evidence must also be exact. One way to ensure the precision of the evidence is to pay attention to the level of abstraction in your word choice. We live in an age of intellectual sloppiness. Good writing always involves conscious decisions about diction, and in an age like ours, this means deciding what kind of language not to use. This is a matter of both tact and respect. It is difficult to be prescriptive, but you need to be at least suspicious of language that comes from advertising, pop culture, pressure groups, and government. Here are some words and phrases to avoid:

access or impact (as verbs)	judgmental
arguably	learning experience
caring	lifestyle
bottom line	lover (when you mean "paramour")
disinterested (when you mean "uninterested")	needs (when you mean "desire")
empower	personalize
feedback	privilege (as a verb)
feel (when you mean "think")	process (as in "learning process")
hopefully	socialize
input	totally
interface	true emotion
"-ize" words in general	unique (it means "one and only"; not unusual)

If you are aware of the words you use – as any self-conscious, rhetorical writer should be – you will find yourself naturally led to productive argumentative places. The writer who attends to the specific and concrete is usually also the writer who notices the intricate details of what he is discussing, who notices which points in his argument need to come first, who knows how to seize the reader's attention, who clears away trash, and who develops his thesis explicitly.

Case Study in Classical Argumentation: Barack Obama's 2009 Inaugural Address

The Confirmatio

For everywhere we look, there is work to be done. The state of the economy calls for action, bold and swift, and we will act – not only to create new jobs, but to lay a new foundation for growth. We will build the roads and bridges, the electric grids and digital lines that feed our commerce and bind us together. We will restore science to its rightful place, and wield technology's wonders to raise health care's quality and lower its cost. We will harness the sun and the winds and the soil to fuel our cars and run our factories. And we will transform our schools and colleges and universities to meet the demands of a new age. All this we can do. And all this we will do.

Recall that earlier generations faced down fascism and communism not just with missiles and tanks, but with sturdy alliances and enduring convictions. They understood that our power alone cannot protect us, nor does it entitle us to do as we please. Instead, they knew that our power grows through its prudent use; our security emanates from the justness of our cause, the force of our example, the tempering qualities of humility and restraint.

For we know that our patchwork heritage is a strength, not a weakness. We are a nation of Christians and Muslims, Jews and Hindus – and nonbelievers. We are shaped by every language and culture, drawn from every end of this Earth; and because we have tasted the bitter swill of civil war and segregation, and emerged from that dark chapter stronger and more united, we cannot help but believe that the old hatreds shall someday pass; that the lines of tribe shall soon dissolve; that as the world grows smaller, our common humanity shall reveal itself; and that America must play its role in ushering in a new era of peace.

To the Muslim world, we seek a new way forward, based on mutual interest and mutual respect. To those leaders around the globe who seek to sow conflict, or blame their society's ills on the West: Know that your people will judge you on what you can build, not what you destroy. To those who cling to power through corruption and deceit and the silencing of dissent, know that you are on the wrong side of history; but that we will extend a hand if you are willing to unclench your fist.

Notice how Obama organizes his evidence in this excerpt: first by temporality, second by deduction. Everything is initially located in the present moment of the speech; it is no mistake that the lead-off sentence is the only one in the present tense. Obama remains stationary in time, yet looks from this perspective into the future, promising the restoration of infrastructure ("We will build the roads and bridges, the electric grids and digital lines"), science ("We will restore science to its rightful place, and wield technology's wonders"), responsible energy consumption ("We will harness the sun and the winds and the soil"), and education ("we will transform our schools and colleges and universities"). Obama then goes on to situate these future accomplishments in the steadfastness of our ancestors by invoking the national resolve needed to surmount major crises in our collective past particularly World War II and the Cold War ("Recall that earlier generations faced down fascism and communism ...").

Obama links the following three paragraphs deductively. He begins with broad claims about our nation's patchwork identity ("We are a nation of Christians and Muslims, Jews and Hindus – and nonbelievers") and moves into a specific address directed at several of these subgroups in the following paragraphs. Within these sections – clear subsets of the generalized idea from the paragraph above – Obama presents his ideas with both spatial and causal relationships. Spatially, Obama starts with American citizens of foreign heritage (all couched in a unified "we") which moves to countries abroad (now in the dichotomy of "we" and "you"). In the address to the Muslim world, Obama works causally, bringing the reader along with an elegant string a series of "if/then" clauses ("we will extend a hand if you are willing to unclench your fist") to emphasize the peacefulness of US foreign policy in the face of hostility abroad.

Refutation – The Refutatio

Cicero's *On Invention* (sections 1.42–51)
Quintilian's *Institutio Oratoria* (sections 2.4.18–19, 5.13)

Carl von Clausewitz, a German military theorist, captured the spirit of a good refutation in his famous military one-liner, "The best offense is a good defense." In similar metaphors of battle and combat, Aristotle describes refutations as "demolishing the opponent's case; thus, having put up a fight against either all of the greatest or easily refuted points of the opponent, one should move onto one's own persuasive points."

In argumentative writing, the refutation acknowledges counterarguments to your position, analyzes their disadvantages, and ultimately identifies their weak points to rebut them and bolster your case. This portion of the argumentative process is not easy; in fact, it's probably one of the hardest moments of critical thinking involved in persuasive writing. Since writers tend to argue what they believe in, open acknowledgement of alternative viewpoints is sometimes a tough pill to swallow. It's easy to argue with selective evidence, cherry-picking the best bits of data and support while ignoring the rest. It's much harder to argue with full transparency and disclosure, confronting sometimes very valid counterpoints face-to-face.

Some writers worry that providing full disclosure of opposing views may give off an impression of weakness, a green light for an assault from the other side. Since so much argumentation takes place outside of controlled academic settings, refutations are typically when the gloves come off. Effective refutations are intellectually demanding, but they are powerful precisely because of this demand. Engaging with all sides of an issue in a fair and balanced way serves to demonstrate deep sophistication as a writer. By incorporating those voices from the other side of the conversation, what may have been an argument dominated by one-sided evidence gives way to an academic process that works to arrive at a solution. It takes off the blinders and openly acknowledges the other voices even if they may seem to initially weaken your position. Refutations are crucial in creating discourse. You cannot enter into legitimate argumentation or engage in honest dialogue unless you have the guts to be challenged and possibly be sent back to the drawing board.

To refute the views of others, you first have to know what the others are saying. Refutations require you to do your homework on a topic. A weak refutation is not just detrimental to the argument; it also calls into question the ethics and integrity of an arguer who would levy such a flimsy case at his opponent. For writers who are relatively new to composing refutations, there might be some initial blockage to getting ideas down on paper since it's tough to know exactly where you should put your oar into the conversation. Below are some ideas you can use to help get started.

Knowing how to find and dismantle your opponent's argument is a skill that has long been taught. In *Institutio Oratoria*, Quintilian trained his students to write refutations by engaging in an exercise known as *progymnasmata*. Quintilian would give his students a myth or legend – which are murky and mushy in their logic – as an object of refutation. Students could discredit the poet in order to undermine the story's legitimacy, attack it as being impossible, unrealistic, illogical, or simply as a waste of time. Peter Elbow, in *Reflections on Academic Discourse* (1991), updates some of Quintilian's methods into what he calls a "believing/doubting" game, a generative process for developing specifics by stating the opposite case. His model of doubting and believing is a process he believes to take place within the mind of the writer. This method casts the writer and his opponents as participants in an imagined dialogue, and the transcript of what's "said" form the writer's "inner voice" as they begin to write about this clash of ideas. Elbow's method, Kay Halasek says in *A Pedagogy of Possibility* (1999), "constructs an author who relies on personal experiences, observations, and evaluations as the means by which he determines truth and reality." Once you've identified what points should be focused on, you'll then need to settle on an approach to take them down. Refutations follow three general forms: concession, rejection, or denial.

A concession occurs when you admit that something about your opponent's argument is true or valid, even if you've initially resisted or denied it. Long standing arguments – Can God's existence be proven? Was the dropping of the A-bomb justified? Is globalization a force for good? – remain vigorously debated due in large part to the fact that each side has legitimate things to say. Rather than try to blow your opponent to bits, concessions give credit where credit is due. This may seem counterintuitive. If I'm arguing for proposition A, why would I then highlight the merits of proposition B? Instead of ignoring what everyone knows to be at least partially true, it's better to concede the legitimacy of aspects of the argument, creating a little goodwill and respect from those who disagree in the process. Consider the following example of the concession strategy from Charles Darwin's *The Origin of Species* (1859):

"That many and serious objections may be advanced against the theory of descent with modification through variation and natural selection, I do not deny. I have endeavoured to give to them their full force. Nothing at first can appear more difficult to believe than that the more complex organs and instincts have been perfected, not by means superior to, though analogous with, human reason, but by the accumulation of innumerable slight variations, each good for the individual possessor. Nevertheless, this difficulty, though appearing to our imagination insuperably great, cannot be considered real if we admit the following propositions, namely, that all parts of the organisation and instincts offer, at least, individual differences – that there is a struggle for existence leading to the preservation of profitable deviations of structure or instinct – and, lastly, that gradations in the state of perfection of each organ may have existed, each good of its kind. The truth of these propositions cannot, I think, be disputed."

How the Concession Strategy Works:
Darwin's opening line acknowledges the existence of many objections to the "theory of descent with modification through variation and natural selection," something he concedes that he "do[es] not deny." The lines that follow detail the legitimacy of these objections and stress some of their most salient points (i.e. the idea of complex organs developing through "innumerable slight variations"). Darwin establishes some goodwill with the audience by not trivializing these objections, and when he makes his argumentative turn ("nevertheless …") he is able to leverage these counter-positions into a development of his own argument. Note how he does not flatly deny the counterargument of the development of a complex organ. Instead, he acknowledges this a probability, though he is keen to qualify this view with his own conditions: "gradations in the state of perfection of each organ may have existed, each good of its kind." He ends the concession paragraph on tones of assertiveness and confidence – "The truth of these propositions cannot, I think, be disputed"– a good example of how concessions can still maintain a cutting edge in the argument.

A rejection occurs when you dismiss the legitimacy of a counterargument. Like concessions, rejections acknowledge that a particular counterargument exists. Unlike concessions, rejections do not acknowledge the merit of this viewpoint and systematically dismantle it (sometimes referred as *reductio ad absurdum*, a 'reduction to absurdity'). Randomly choosing points of rejection is probably not a good idea since it may come off nit-picky or petty; the point of rejection ought to have some correspondence to a point you have made elsewhere in the argument, so the reader can see this subtopic presented in both its affirmative and negated forms. Rejections are often integrated quickly and naturally through the use of transitional words intended to signal the central contradiction or qualification: on the contrary, nonetheless, but, however, nevertheless, despite, in contrast, yet, on one hand, on the other hand, rather, conversely, while this may be true. Rejections sometimes also couch the counterclaim in the form of a rhetorical question: Why does X contend that this is justice? How long should Y condone this suffering? Consider the following example of the rejection strategy from Pope Leo XII's *Rerum Novarum* (1891):

"The contention, then, that the civil government should at its option intrude into and exercise intimate control over the family and the household is a great and pernicious error. True, if a family finds itself in exceeding distress, utterly deprived of the counsel of friends, and without any prospect of extricating itself, it is right that extreme necessity be met by public aid, since each family is a part of the commonwealth. In like manner, if within the precincts of the household there occur grave disturbance of mutual rights, public authority should intervene to force each party to yield to the other its proper due; for this is not to deprive citizens of their rights, but justly and properly to safeguard and strengthen them.

But the rulers of the commonwealth must go no further; here, nature bids them stop. Paternal authority can be neither abolished nor absorbed by the State; for it has the same source as human life itself. "The child belongs to the father," and is, as it were, the continuation of the father's personality; and speaking strictly, the child takes its place in civil society, not of its own right, but in its quality as member of the family in which it is born. And for the very reason that "the child belongs to the father" it is, as St. Thomas Aquinas says, "before it attains the use of free will, under the power and the charge of its parents." The socialists, therefore, in setting aside the parent and setting up a State supervision, act against natural justice, and destroy the structure of the home.

How the Rejection Strategy Works:
Pope Leo XIII initially acknowledges the counterargument of his opponents in plain sight, namely that "civil government should at its option intrude into and exercise intimate control over the family and the household is a great and pernicious error." He goes on to argue that the State, which has been growing ever stronger in the modern era, ought to have rightful limitations, chief among them is a restriction on state meddling with the concerns of nature. Pope Leo XIII defines the family as a *natural* institution, and thus sees the State's hand in matters of the family as an immoral overreach of power. He cites authoritative testimony, the free-will arguments of St. Thomas Aquinas, to bolster his position. In the end, he ultimately concludes State interference in matters of the family to be an "act against natural justice," an assertive rejection.

A denial occurs when the writer does not merely reject a point of view; they refuse to acknowledge that the counter-position exists at all.

Whereas rejections will tangle with a diametrically opposed perspective, denials won't start the fight because there is nothing to fight about. Denials are a high-risk, high-reward strategy. If they can be pulled off, nothing stands in the way of persuading your audience towards your side, but this approach can come off as dogmatic, belligerent, and close-minded if not handled with care. If you're going to go here, you best be sure you have a rock-solid case. Consider the following example of the denial strategy from Blaise Pascal's *Pensées* (1669):

"Since everything then is cause and effect, dependent and supporting, mediate and immediate, and all is held together by a natural though imperceptible chain, which binds together things most distant and most different, I hold it equally impossible to know the parts without knowing the whole, and to know the whole without knowing the parts in detail. And what completes our incapability of knowing things, is the fact that they are simple, and that we are composed of two opposite natures, different in kind, soul and body. For it is impossible that our rational part should be other than spiritual; and if any one maintains that we are simply corporeal, this would far more exclude us from the knowledge of things, there being nothing so inconceivable as to say that matter knows itself. It is impossible to imagine how it should know itself. So, if we are simply material, we can know nothing at all."

How the Denial Strategy Works:
In his refutation, Pascal outlines a denial of the philosophical stance of materialism, a doctrine that understands reality to be nothing more than matter. Pascal's denial is delivered through a systematic dissembling of this view, the argumentative equivalent of tearing an opponent limb from limb. Since materialism sees reality as an understandable mechanical process, Pascal leads-off with a broad denial of this model of reality: "I hold it equally impossible to know the parts without knowing the whole, and to know the whole without knowing the parts in detail." He goes onto claim that "we are composed of two opposite natures, different in kind, soul and body," a dichotomy in which his materialist detractors emphasize the latter at the expense of the former. From here, Pascal points to that fact that rationality is not a material phenomenon – it's spiritual – and since matter alone can necessarily have no rational properties, how could a materialist possible claim to understand anything about reality itself? The final line delivers the most definitive and devastating blow to his opponent's position: "So, if we are simply material, we can know nothing at all."

Whatever strategy you decide on for the refutation, it's important to emphasize the process of criticizing, attacking, or responding to an argument as a crucial stage in the production of innovative ideas and the construction of an argumentative case.

Case Study in Classical Argumentation: Barack Obama's 2009 Inaugural Address

The Refutatio

Now, there are some who question the scale of our ambitions – who suggest that our system cannot tolerate too many big plans. Their memories are short. For they have forgotten what this country has already done; what free men and women can achieve when imagination is joined to common purpose, and necessity to courage. What the cynics fail to understand is that the ground has shifted beneath them – that the stale political arguments that have consumed us for so long no longer apply. The question we ask today is not whether our government is too big or too small, but whether it works – whether it helps families find jobs at a decent wage, care they can afford, a retirement that is dignified. Where the answer is yes, we intend to move forward. Where the answer is no, programs will end. And those of us who manage the public's dollars will be held to account – to spend wisely, reform bad habits, and do our business in the light of day – because only then can we restore the vital trust between a people and their government.

Nor is the question before us whether the market is a force for good or ill. Its power to generate wealth and expand freedom is unmatched, but this crisis has reminded us that without a watchful eye, the market can spin out of control – and that a nation cannot prosper long when it favors only the prosperous. The success of our economy has always depended not just on the size of our gross domestic product, but on the reach of our prosperity; on our ability to extend opportunity to every willing heart – not out of charity, but because it is the surest route to our common good.

As for our common defense, we reject as false the choice between our safety and our ideals. Our Founding Fathers, faced with perils we can scarcely imagine, drafted a charter to assure the rule of law and the rights of man, a charter expanded by the blood of generations. Those ideals still light the world, and we will not give them up for expedience's sake. And so to all other peoples and governments who are watching today, from the grandest capitals to the small village where my father was born: Know that America is a friend of each nation and every man, woman and child who seeks a future of peace and dignity, and that we are ready to lead once more.

Obama's refutation strategy can roughly be classified as a rejection. He takes on three topics: skeptics of his agenda ("some who question the scale of our ambitions"), the good of the free market ("Nor is the question before us whether the market is a force for good or ill"), the false choice between liberty and security ("we reject as false the choice between our safety and our ideals") and dismantles them one at time. In a gesture of confidence, he addresses each counter-claim in plainly stated topic sentences, a direct confrontation to ideas he opposes. Each of the three paragraphs are parallel in style, patterned along an identical structure: an identification of a counter-claim followed by a reasoned deconstruction of that view.

Conclusion – The Peroratio

Cicero's *On Invention* (sections 1.52–56)
Cicero's *Topics* (sections 25.98–99)

The *peroratio*, or peroration, ties up the loose ends of an argument's strands, all while stirring the emotions of the audience one last time. Conclusions can provoke, reassure, chide, flatter, summarize, or do something else entirely. Whatever the emotional bent you land on, an argument must have a conclusion; it should not quit like a highway abandoned in a cornfield. Like introductions, these paragraphs can be a bit tricky, and many student writers fall into the trap of simply reworking their introduction to tell the reader, one more time, things that have already been said elsewhere in the paper. But no good writers do this, and no readers enjoy reading this. Recapping the major points can be part of an effective conclusion, but you must be sure that these points lead to an interesting climax which sears a final image of your topic onto the brain of your audience. Below are four strategies, complete with explanations and examples, for use in an argument's *peroratio*.

Pose a question to the reader – If you have spent your time arguing on ethical grounds, your conclusion may be a nice place to test the reader's reaction by posing a question which makes them examine their own views in light of the evidence provided in the argument. Speak directly to the reader and place him in the context of your situation, providing a sort of embedded ethics test to close things out. The audience may find that their perspective on the issue has changed and a direct recognition of that change, which forces the reader to confront it in the posed question, can be a powerful weapon for changing minds. Questions don't always seek direct answers. A string of rhetorical questions can be a powerful tactic to close things out. It drives home key points, while remaining in the pretense of an inquisitive and open-minded stance. Consider the example below from Ralph Waldo Emerson's "Heroism" (1841).

"In the gloom of our ignorance of what shall be, in the hour when we are deaf to the higher voices, who does not envy them who have seen safely to an end their manful endeavor? Who that sees the meanness of our politics, but inly congratulates Washington that he is long already wrapped in his shroud, and forever safe; that he was laid sweet in his grave, the hope of humanity not yet subjugated in him? Who does not sometimes envy the good and brave, who are no more to suffer from the tumults of the natural world, and await with curious complacency the speedy term of his own conversation with finite nature? And yet the love that will be annihilated sooner than treacherous has already made death impossible, and affirms itself no mortal, but a native of the deeps of absolute and inextinguishable being."

How the Pose-a-Question-to-the-Reader Strategy Works:

Emerson's closing paragraph revisits several of the essay's central themes but does so in a manner where the reader must now directly consider the author's points in light of their own experiences. "I *have* been deaf to the higher voices. I *do* see the meanness of politics. I often *envy* the good and brave," one may think as they work through Emerson's line of questioning. These questions are rhetorical; they promote reflection in a way that doesn't search after a direct answer while putting the scaffolding in place for the conclusion's final insight. Through shared consideration of these questions, the reader can finally share Emerson's ultimate visions; that is, love makes death impossible because through love, all mortal beings can actively participate in the immaterial, eternal world.

Sum up what you have done in order to deliver a knockout – Your conclusion may well suggest that you have proven even more than your thesis promised. You may go beyond the evidence from the paper to indicate how wide-reaching your final points may be. Or, you may adopt the language of simplicity and logically demonstrate how your claims made in the argument are, in fact, true. In either style, the conclusion offers summative statements to tie all the loose strings together. Consider the example below from David Karoly's *Climate Science Change Misinformation* (2010).

> "In summary, let me emphasize that the pattern and magnitude of observed global-scale temperature changes since the mid-20th century cannot be explained by natural climate variability, are consistent with the response to increasing greenhouse gases, and are not consistent with the responses to other factors. Hence, it is very likely that increasing greenhouse gases are the main cause of the recent observed global-scale warming."

> **How the Summing-Up-What-You've-Done Strategy Works:**
> The opening phrase ("in summary") clearly and directly signals the coming of summative information. This lead sentence notes the key pieces of information from the argument's body ("temperature changes … cannot be explained by natural climate variability, are consistent with the response to increasing greenhouse gases") while not forgetting to emphasize a commonly held counterargument, which the author has spent some time debunking earlier in the essay. The second sentence reiterates the essay's overall claim and its lead word, "hence," is a correlative transition to demonstrate the logical and causal relationship between the two statements.

 <u>Suggest that, after all, a very different argument might be made, under different conditions</u> – Recognize that your argument is valid within the scenario you have illustrated but may have to be adjusted under changed conditions. This will bring a tinge of honesty and humility to the closing few lines, while characterizing your stance as flexible, not rigid. It also acknowledges that we live a dynamic world and that your mind is open enough to bend with the flux. Consider the example below from Henry David Thoreau's "Resistance to Civil Government, or Civil Disobedience" (1866):

> "I please myself with imagining a State at last which can afford to be just to all men, and to treat the individual with respect as a neighbor; which even would not think it inconsistent with its own repose if a few were to lie aloof from it, not meddling with it, nor embraced by it, who fulfilled all the duties of neighbors

and fellow men. A State which bore this kind of fruit, and suffered it to drop off as fast as it ripened, would prepare the way for a still more perfect and glorious State, which I have also imagined, but not yet anywhere seen."

How the Different-Argument-Under-Different-Conditions Strategy Works:
For most of the essay, Thoreau discusses government in a skeptical light by noting the litany of injustices it often imposes upon the sovereign individual. In the final paragraph, Thoreau back-peddles from this stance and reimagines his arguments under a new set of conditions. *If* government treats its citizens the same as a trusted neighbor ("I please myself with imagining a State at last which can afford to be just to all men, and to treat the individual with respect as a neighbor"), then the State would be a welcome institution. He ends on a note of subtle cynicism ("a still more perfect and glorious State, which I have also imagined, but not yet anywhere seen."), suggesting that it is unlikely the State could ever undergo such as radical transformation.

<u>Try to make the last sentence memorable</u> – This piece of advice is sometimes easier said than done. After all, in the creative process, there is no one piece of advice that can instantly add style and flare to a closing paragraph just like magic. It can sometimes be an arduous process which takes writing and rewriting, tweaking and tinkering until the diction and syntax has gained the appropriate rhetorical force. A useful way to put on the finishing touches is to vary the word order and length of sentences. You have probably been taught to always place the subject first and to write sentences that are between eight and fifteen words long. Anything longer, you have been told, is the dreaded "run-on." But you can have a run-on sentence of ten words, if the connections between your words and clauses are weak or missing, and you can have a tightly-rigged sentence of a hundred words, if all the parts of the sentence are clearly related to one another. If, after a long but well-formed sentence full of parallelisms and emphatic repetitions, a sentence in which you seize the reader's attention, muster your evidence like soldiers on parade, and build to a climax, you then finish with a short staccato statement to sum it all up, what will be the effect on the reader? It will strike like a gavel on a bench. Try it. Consider the example below from Karl Marx and Friedrich Engels's *The Communist Manifesto* (1888):

"The Communists disdain to conceal their views and aims. They openly declare that their ends can be attained only by the forcible overthrow of all existing social conditions. Let the ruling classes tremble at a Communistic revolution. The proletarians have nothing to lose but their chains. They have a world to win. WORKING MEN OF ALL COUNTRIES, UNITE!"

How the Memorable Last Sentence Strategy Works:

Even a mildly perceptive reader can't help but be moved by this conclusion's strategy and what Marx and Engels have done is all the more impressive once the concluding strategy is analyzed piece by piece. The lead-off sentence calls back to the manifesto's broad theme of oppression, though the tone of this line suggests an utter refusal for further oppression. This resistance gives way to an overt call for revolution, a violent revolution, where the "ruling class will tremble" at the "overthrow of all existing social conditions." The final sentences paint an idealized picture of the outcome ("The proletarians have nothing to lose but their chains. They have a world to win.") consistent with the utopian after-effects of communism's establishment argued elsewhere in the manifesto. The final line, a ringing call to action, can rightfully be understood, then, as this revolution's first battle cry. In other words, "WORKING MEN OF ALL COUNTRIES, UNITE!" commissions the reader to take these ideas, bring them to the wider world, and demand change.

And let's look one final time at Obama's address to see how he closes things out.

Case Study in Classical Argumentation:
Barack Obama's 2009 Inaugural Address

The Peroratio

So let us mark this day with remembrance, of who we are and how far we have traveled. In the year of America's birth, in the coldest of months, a small band of patriots huddled by dying campfires on the shores of an icy river. The capital was abandoned. The enemy was advancing. The snow was stained with blood. At a moment when the outcome of our revolution was most in doubt, the father of our nation ordered these words be read to the people:

"Let it be told to the future world ... that in the depth of winter, when nothing but hope and virtue could survive ... that the city and the country, alarmed at one common danger, came forth to meet [it]."

America. In the face of our common dangers, in this winter of our hardship, let us remember these timeless words. With hope and virtue, let us brave once more the icy currents, and endure what storms may come. Let it be said by our children's children that when we were tested, we refused to let this journey end, that we did not turn back, nor did we falter; and with eyes fixed on the horizon and God's grace upon us, we carried forth that great gift of freedom and delivered it safely to future generations.

Obama's rhetoric, as we've seen across this chapter, is often seeded with rhetorical maneuvers drawn from the Classical tradition and the opening word to the final paragraph, "America," marks Obama's transition into the closing peroration. Perorations are like an argument's fireworks finale where the speaker fires off the remaining pyrotechnics to dazzle, impress, or leave a lasting impression on the speaker's mind. Throughout the address, Obama repeatedly calls upon Americans to draw on the past as they are mindful of the future, so it makes sense as a rhetorical strategy to close his final words with a direct address that demands a call-to-action as we move forward.

Obama's peroration is also a notable example of the mesh point of argument and rhetoric. For example, each of the two sentences describing Valley Forge ("The capital was abandoned. The enemy was advancing.") are simple article-subject-verb constructions, but this bare syntax also doubles as an analogy for the content of the anecdote it's relaying: just as the sentences are devoid of any language beyond basic parts of speech, so too are the soldiers from the story living in a grim and bleak state. This sentence pair is one of those instances where the form gives some clues about the content. In other words, the way the sentence is written tells the reader something about what the sentence is saying. Moreover, the speech's motif – the linkage between past and future – is writ small into the peroration, opening with a reference to the past ("let us mark this day with remembrance") and ending with a hopeful look into the future ("with eyes fixed on the horizon and God's grace upon us, we carried forth that great gift of freedom and delivered it safely to future generations").

Whether you imitate Obama or pull something from the strategies of Aristotle and Cicero, you'll want to be sure to close things out in a memorable way. You may find these strategies may work in combination or that none of them quite fit your rhetorical occasions. That's okay. There are seldom cure-all prescriptions in writing. Use what works best for you but be sure to provide some sort of insightful closure.

CHAPTER TEN

CONTEMPORARY MODELS OF ARGUMENTATION

The previous chapter showcased the many upsides of Classical models of argumentation. It is a concrete, writer-friendly framework that establishes a basic vocabulary for the persuasive writer, and its pre-established templates and straightforward methods of generating material are great starting points for argumentation, both in and out of school. But since Cicero, Quintilian and *Rhetorica ad Herrenium* all worked within an Aristotelean matrix, the logical substructure of each Classical method is ultimately reducible to deductive and formal models of reasoning. Dissatisfied with the limitations of the formal logic in the context of everyday argumentation, Stephen Toulmin in *An Introduction to Reasoning* (1979) argued for an alternative. He theorized that formal logic is an inappropriate paradigm for argumentation and developed a model of argument as an alternative to the syllogism that has come to be known as The Toulmin Model of Argumentation. Toulmin doesn't entirely break with the Classical world – you'll notice the inclusion of much terminology from Chapters 2, 8 and 9 – but his system expands the application of argument into all fields of human knowledge, from art to algebra, philosophy to physics, robotics to rhetoric. In fact, Toulmin's model is so all-encompassing that nearly any instance of language use can be understood in Toulmin's term. To illustrate some of the central concepts of his theory, we'll take a look at a running example of two "Letters to the Editor" in response to a *New York Times* feature article "How Google Conquered the American Classroom" (May 13, 2017).

We'll also look at a much lesser-known theory of argumentation derived from Barry Kroll's *Arguing Differently* (2005). Kroll doesn't break with Toulmin but extends several of his central precepts into the focused context of the college composition classroom. His argument, based on a semester long case study of his writing class, suggests that ancient theories characterize argumentation as something inherently adversarial, and contemporary popular culture heavily propagates this argument-as-battle image. Kroll's project is to "argue differently – differently, that is, from the ways argument is represented in the media, displayed in public venues, and taught in previous courses." His modes of argumentation privilege actionable outcomes, often as a result of dialogue and compromise, over the goal of simply winning the argument. His three methods – Conciliatory arguments, Integrative arguments, and Deliberative arguments – attempt to replicate the dynamics of this productive dialogue in written form while incorporating Toulmin's general resistance to the deductive structures of thought and organization from Classical theories. This chapter will largely paraphrase the methods and illustrative examples outlined in *Arguing Differently* for the purposes of clarity.

The Toulmin Model of Argumentation

Strange though it may sound, Toulmin's approach to argumentation isn't really about teaching students *how* to argue. Most students, by the time they reach high school, already know how to argue with friends and family and will rarely defer to learned strategies in the heat of the moment. Toulmin's seems to know this and instead of foisting an argument framework upon students, he leverages this existing expertise into a method of analyzing the (often unstated) relationship of ideas that are common to all arguments. Once you can analyze how an argument works, he thinks, you can turn around and build arguments that have both logical strength and everyday practicality. Most arguers place the emphasis on what's said out-loud, the claim and evidence which supports that position. Of course, it's important to do this well, but Toulmin stresses that the unstated link between the claim and evidence – the "warrant" as he calls it – is really where we make subconscious decisions about whether or not we find an argument convincing. By articulating what's often left implied, Toulmin believes we are in a better position to build sounder arguments and have a powerful tool to critique the arguments of others. In this sense, Toulmin lets us think about *what* argument we hold, but also *why* we hold that view in the first place. When we can get the silent parts of argument to suddenly speak, the real power of Toulmin's system begins to take effect.

It makes sense why the ideas professed by Toulmin didn't come along until the second half of the twentieth century since he owes a great debt to the methods of psychoanalysis. Freud's theory of the "talking cure," a term coined in a 1909 lecture at Clark University in Worcester, MA, argues that by talking about features of our subconscious, we become aware of the root causes of our actions and can subsequently direct our behavior once these unstated motivations have been exposed. Toulmin adapts this general method into the fields of logic and argumentation; that is, once we can identify an unstated assumption of an argument, we are in a position to examine it and have a plain conversation about its merits and deficiencies. For Toulmin, this is as much an exercise in ethics as it is in argumentation, and it should be no surprise that his work is taught just as regularly in Philosophy departments as it is in English classrooms. Toulmin's system is more abstract than Aristotle's, and students sometimes have a little more trouble wrapping their brains around it at first but give it time. You'll find Toulmin's lessons, if taken to heart, can be an enormously beneficial tool in your rhetorical toolbox. This argumentative model consists of three principle components with a few others tacked on to provide specificity (see Figure 1):

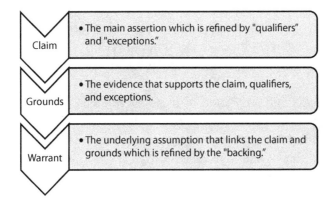

Figure 1 Components of Toulmin Argument.

The Claim – Qualifiers and Exceptions

In *An Introduction to Reasoning*, Toulmin says, claims are "assertions put forward publicly for general acceptance. They contain implications for underlying 'reasons' that could show them to be well founded and therefore entitled to be generally accepted." Like Classical argumentation, Toulmin's system relies heavily on its claim, but unlike the Classical system, whose claims exists in an isomorphic relationship with the situation's *stasis*, Toulmin's claims are generated by an analysis of the dialogic interchange between the writer, the reader, and the subject at hand. It's best, perhaps, to visualize the dynamics of this along the lines of the rhetorical triangle (Chapter 2). Consider the following line of questioning, adapted from Lesley Rex, Ebony Thomas, and Steven Engle's "Applying Toulmin: Teaching Logical Reasoning and Argumentative Writing" (2010).

Speaker: *How do I see and understand what I'm looking at?*
- What in my experience makes me care about the issue, idea, circumstance, or condition?
- How does this way of caring influence me towards thinking about it?
- How does my relationship with my readers and my current situation influence where I stand?

Subject: *What should be known about this subject?*
- What is important for a reader to understand about this issue, idea, circumstance, or condition for this situation at this moment?

Audience: *What should readers understand about this subject?*
- What would or should readers think is important?
- How would or should they feel about my claim?
- How would or should they act on my claim?

The asking and answering of these questions implicitly acknowledge a central idea in Toulmin's system: arguments are full of complications and contradictions, and these must be treated by the writer with humility, open-mindedness, and care. This is why Toulmin urges that claims be paired with "qualifiers," statements that indicate the strength of the claim. Qualifiers account for the fact that most claims may be valid in *some* circumstances but not necessarily in others, thus reflecting the many variables that present themselves in everyday situations. Claims become much clearer when they are paired with qualifying words and phrases. As Toulmin says himself in *An Introduction to Reasoning*, "Every argument has a certain kind of strength. The strengths and limitations of the initial claims are indicated by the addition of qualifiers." These can help to make a tough audience more willing to listen because you are honestly accounting for those certain scenarios and conditions where your claim may hold up and showing that you've done your homework on the issue. When attached to a claim, your argument becomes clearer, sharper, and easier to defend (see Figure 2). Take a look at the initial claim below, without any qualifiers, and then see how increasingly sharp the thesis becomes with the incremental addition of these most useful words and phrases.

it is possible
routinely
under these conditions
it may be
sometimes
for the most part
rarely
more or less
often
if it were so
it seems
many
perhaps
one might argue
possibly
in the situation
usually

Figure 2 Common Qualifying Words and Phrases.

Unqualified Claim:
People are too dependent on computers.

Claim with 1 qualifier:
In America, people are too dependent on computers.

Claim with 2 qualifiers:
In America, people *who trade stocks* are too dependent on computers.

Claim with 3 qualifiers:
In America, *most* people *who trade stocks* are too dependent on computers.

As you can see, the qualified claims are more effective because the listener knows exactly what the arguer will be defending and developing. These conditions have been accounted for with qualifiers in the form of the prepositional phrase, "In America," the adjective clause, "who trade stocks" and the adjective, "most." This arguer could easily go on to further qualify his statement to the stock trading of a particular city, of a particular company, or even a particular person. Whatever the case, to properly qualify your claim will take time; limiting your argument to certain specific conditions requires some forethought. *Never assume that readers will understand the limits you have in mind.*

Qualifiers are useful, but they are not the only way to establish boundaries with the claim. The "exception", as Toulmin calls it, is also a critical component of the claim. Exceptions, Toulmin says, "qualify the statement of our argument in a way that indicates its incomplete strength because these are extraordinary circumstances that might undermine the force of the supporting argument." Think of the exception as a special type of qualifier, one that acknowledges an instance or scenario where your claim does *not* apply, or when the claim you are making is *not* valid. There a very few arguments in the real world that are true in every possible scenario (as Obi-Wan Kenobi told his Padawan learner, Anakin Skywalker, moments before he turns to the dark side, from 2005's *Star Wars: Episode III – Revenge of the Sith*: "only a Sith deals in absolutes"). As we talked about in our discussion of the Classical refutation move of concession, most arguments have many counterarguments that are, sometimes, just as legitimate and reasonable as the case you are attempting to prove. In Toulmin's system, he urges you to confront these other voices in the crowd by heading these objections off right from the start. Let's take a look at a new example and see how exceptions can contribute to the depth of claim.

> Unqualified Claim:
> A Porsche is a good car to own.
>
> Claim with 1 qualifier and 1 exception:
> *For those with a lot of disposable income*, a Porsche is a good car to own, *unless you need the room of a backseat*.
>
> Claim with 2 qualifiers and 1 exception:
> *Except for its limited trunk space*, a Porsche *Turbo Carrera* is a good car to own *for those who live in a sunny climate suited for convertibles*.

As you can see in this example, a qualified claim that is linked to an exception(s) can be defended more honestly. But just like the inclusion of qualifiers, tacking on an exception is not a thoughtless endeavor. To do so properly, you need to investigate and think about your claim. Ask yourself, "where is my claim weak? In what instances or scenarios may my claim not apply?" Accounting for these will boost credibility by acknowledging, in the opening moments of the argument, that there are valid counterarguments to your stance. By addressing, and dismissing these reasonable objections from the beginning, you allow for more time in the paper's body to discuss *your* argument. It is true that some listeners will be opposed to what you say no matter how specific things get (this is an issue of the "warrant" which we will talk about later in this chapter) but utilizing effective exceptions will demonstrate that you have given some consideration to alternative points of view and not merely making the issue fit your agenda.

Case Study in Contemporary Argument: Letters to the Editor from *The New York Times* Article "How Google Conquered the American Classroom" (May 13, 2017)

The Claim

To the Editor:

Sadly, American public education lurches from one fad to another. Remember "schools without walls" or the "new math"? Chromebooks are simply the latest fad. There is little evidence that computers in classrooms produce student outcomes superior to traditional teaching methods, at least when the latter are implemented properly.

Elite private schools have computers, but they are far less central to the educational process. Instead, smaller class sizes and better teachers are emphasized. However, these are a lot more expensive than Chromebooks.

SCOTT OCHILTREE, WASHINGTON

To the Editor:

Good for Google. It figured out how to level the playing field across different types of schools and districts to help close the digital divide. And it has helped spawn a new generation of digital citizens who are learning how to use technology in a social, positive manner geared toward learning. Schools can be left scrambling to find ways to give each student full access to a good education. At low cost and with easy-to-use tools, Google has skinned the cat.

Yes, Google also has almost unfettered access to a new generation of consumers. That's a price worth paying given the high returns to students in the form of contemporary, relevant learning.

MATT LEVINSON, SEATTLE

Ochiltree's claim, "Chromebooks are simply the latest fad," dismisses Chromebooks as the current flavor-of-the-week in a long history of flashy, yet ineffective educational fads. He characterizes Chromebooks as the latest heir to a string of pedagogical duds, from the 1970's open classroom ("schools without walls") to the 2000's Common Core's brief but dramatic change in math instruction ("new math"). Folks in their mid-life (or even current teenage students) would each have their own analogous version of Chromebooks, thus presenting this claim well to a broad readership. Levinson's claim, "At low cost and with easy-to-use tools, Google has skinned the cat" (a play on the expression, "there's more than one way to skin a cat"), presents the broad adoption of low-priced Chromebooks as win for schools looking to level the playing field between those which have access to technology and those who've been traditionally priced out of this advantage. His claim is quite different than Ochiltree's, but rather than an appeal to tradition, Levinson goes for the wallet. And Levinson knows that *this* is often what really motivates big decisions.

Using the Toulmin Model to Compose

When setting up my *claim*, ask:	✓ What is the subject under examination?
	✓ What is my stance? Pro? Con? Both?
	✓ What position do I want my audience to adopt as the outcome of my claim?
When setting up my *qualifier*(s), ask:	✓ What specific conditions do I have in mind regarding my claim?
	✓ Can my claim be argued in absolute terms?
When setting up my *exception*(s), ask:	✓ What are the circumstances where my claim may not apply?
	✓ What conditions may inhibit the audience's confidence towards my claim?

The Grounds

The evidence, or grounds, is the foundation upon which the claim stands. Toulmin describes the grounds as "statements specifying particular facts about a situation. These facts are already accepted as true and can therefore be relied on to clarify and make good on the previous claim or – in the best case – establish its truth, correctness, and soundness." Like the Classical model says, good evidence should be relevant, precise, and up-to-date, and a lot of what Toulmin says about persuasive evidence has its antecedents in the Classical tradition (Chapter 9), particularly in regard to the Classical rhetorical appeals we discussed in Chapter 2. Below is a short-hand reminder of how you can meet the diverse needs of an audience's appetite for trust, emotion, and logic in an argument.

Ethos Appeal to character	*Pathos* Appeal to emotion	*Logos* Appeal to logic
O Establishing credentials	O Figurative language	O Measurable data (surveys, polls, censuses, etc.)
O Building bridge to audience	O Concrete diction	
O High moral character	O Highly connotative diction	O Self-evident facts
O Using appropriate language		O Scientific observations
O Showing awareness of the importance/complexity of the situation	O Personal anecdotes/ narratives	O Authority and expert testimony
	O Sentimentality	O Cause and effect
O Conceding the legitimacy of counterarguments	O Compassion and sympathy	O Induction and deduction
		O Precedent or past events

But since Toulmin's claims are dialogically generated – whereas Classical claims tend to flow from deductive processes – he stresses the collaborative dynamic between writer and audience when making final choices of what to include. Again, consider the following line of questioning, adapted from Lesley Rex, Ebony Thomas, and Steven Engle's "Applying Toulmin: Teaching Logical Reasoning and Argumentative Writing" (2010).

Credibility

– Does the evidence correspond to your reader's experience? Is there another piece (or category) of evidence that may be more identifiable to my audience?
– What does my audience consider authoritative? Should I adjust my evidence to speak in terms of a perceived authority my audience sees as trustworthy?

Sufficiency

– Does my audience have enough information to understand the argument? Is more background information required to fill in the gaps?
– How diverse is my audience? Have I developed the argument in such a way that a varied readership could understand what's going on?

Accuracy

- Are my facts verifiable? Would my audience be able to verify these facts for themselves?
- Do my quotations and statistics clearly support the claim? Would a casual reader, who is not an expert in the field, be able to see the link between the claim and grounds?
- What are my methods of gathering information? Have I disclosed these methods to my audience to ensure transparency in the argument?

Notice how each decision is filtered through needs of the audience. This is the pragmatic element of Toulmin – "what's good is what works" – that breaks with the logical abstractions of the Classical traditions. Good evidence is neither definite or fixed; each time there is a slight shift in the general makeup of the audience, the speaker must go back to the drawing board and adjust the evidence to be sure it's clear and intelligible to the audience.

Case Study in Contemporary Argument: Letters to the Editor from *The New York Times* Article "How Google Conquered the American Classroom" (May 13, 2017)

The Grounds

To the Editor:

Sadly, American public education lurches from one fad to another. Remember "schools without walls" or the "new math"? Chromebooks are simply the latest fad. There is little evidence that computers in classrooms produce student outcomes superior to traditional teaching methods, at least when the latter are implemented properly.

To the Editor:

Good for Google. It figured out how to level the playing field across different types of schools and districts to help close the digital divide. And it has helped spawn a new generation of digital citizens who are learning how to use technology in a social, positive manner geared toward learning. Schools can be left scrambling to find ways to give each student full access to a good education. At low cost and with easy-to-use tools, Google has skinned the cat.

Elite private schools have computers, but they are far less central to the educational process. Instead, smaller class sizes and better teachers are emphasized. However, these are a lot more expensive than Chromebooks.

SCOTT OCHILTREE, WASHINGTON

Yes, Google also has almost unfettered access to a new generation of consumers. That's a price worth paying given the high returns to students in the form of contemporary, relevant learning.

MATT LEVINSON, SEATTLE

Why should we be cautious of the Chromebook "fad"? According to Ochiltree, there is scant research to prove its educational worth ("There is little evidence that computers in classrooms produce student outcomes superior to traditional teaching methods"), not to mention the fact that cash-flush schools opt *not* to load their kids up with technology, but choose to invest in things that improve the in-person experience of education ("smaller class sizes and better teachers are emphasized"). Levinson supports his claim by emphasizing how Chromebooks tackle questions of access and equity ("It figured out how to level the playing field across different types of schools and districts to help close the digital divide"), a point which would resonate strongly to those whose educational experience is restricted by limited funding. Levinson also supports Google's proliferation in schools by noting how regular usage of technology in a controlled environment can instill a strong sense of digital civics, a much-needed lesson for students living in an increasingly virtual world ("And it has helped spawn a new generation of digital citizens who are learning how to use technology in a social, positive manner geared toward learning").

Using the Toulmin Model to compose

When setting up my *grounds*, ask:	✓ What information am I going on?
	✓ What additional research is needed to ensure the support is legitimate?
	✓ How is the evidence personally meaningful to the audience?
	✓ Is it possible that the audience can take the steps I propose?

The Warrant and Backing

Once the claim has been paired with its grounds, you must next identify the logical connection between them, or identify *why* the evidence supports your claim. This "statement indicating how the facts which we agree on are connected to the claim now being offered" is what Toulmin refers to as the argument's "warrant." Warrants are sometimes tough to identify due in large part to the fact that everyday argumentation rarely includes a direct discussion of them. Consider the following breakdown of the statement, "Joe should be fired because he stole money from the cash register" (see Figure 3):

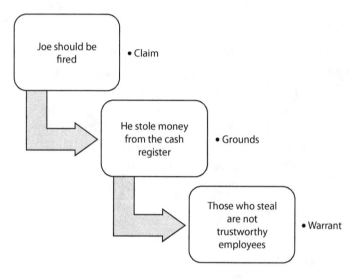

Figure 3 Link Between Claim, Grounds, and Warrant.

It's clear, probably even to Joe, that he should be fired. And the reason that this claim is convincing to its audience – those with a general sense of general decency, at least – is because "those who steal are not trustworthy employees" is a widely accepted cultural commonplace. The underlying assumption, then, makes the connection between the claim and the grounds seem reasonable, resulting in a persuasive argument. When it's written like this, the connection is obvious, but many first-time users of Toulmin find the warrant to be the most difficult stage because it requires you to make visible the thinking that is often invisible. One method to test the validity of a warrant is to rewrite the claim/grounds/warrant into an "if/then/because" clause and see if it holds up. The above example could go something like, "*If* he stole money from the cash register, *then* he should be fired *because* those who steal are not trust-worthy employees." Were you to expand this into a full-scale argument, your next task would then be to flesh out the links between the claim and evidence to make the case as to why are "those who steal are not trust-worthy employees."

Here is where writers must square themselves with exactly why they hold the view they do. When the stakes are high or the issue at hand is more contentious, explicitly stating the warrant may serve to clarify your stance of big issues – abortion, capital punishment, religion, poli-tics, etc. – that have many possible viewpoints. Warrants can come in a few varieties, which loosely coincide with the three categories of rhetorical appeals: ethos, logos, and pathos. Here are some examples which demon-strate Joe's situation.

Warrant based on Ethos
These warrants reinforce the grounds of your argument on the basis of values, ethics, morality, or other codes of conduct. If you wish to demonstrate that stealing is an immoral act, your warrant could be that "employers have an ethical obligation to fire employees who demonstrate immoral behavior." Or, you could appeal to a sense of fairness by having a warrant which asserts that "dishonest employ-ees should be replaced by honest ones."

Warrant based on Logos
These warrants reinforce the trustworthiness of the measurable and quantifiable grounds you have used in your argument. If you show that the business has lost $500 dollars per month because of Joe's criminal activity, your warrant could be that "employees who cause an operating loss to a company should be fired." Using this approach, you are not arguing theft from a moral standpoint but from a financial or economic one.

Warrant based on Pathos
These warrants reinforce the emotional content of your argument. If you demonstrate the consumer outrage from Joe's behavior and sup-plement that claim with consumer testimony, your warrant could be that "consumer outrage is a legitimate criterion for employee termination."

Just like most things involving everyday language use, there is a danger in labeling and categorizing. It is somewhat of an arbitrary process to split warrants into three categories because you will often find that when you are analyzing arguments in Toulmin's terms (and when you are composing your own), warrants will be composed by pairing two together, or by combining all three. Nonetheless, warrants are really what differentiate the "yes/no" sides of an argument.

If the warrant is not sufficient on its own, Toulmin suggests buttressing the warrant with what he calls a "backing." The backing, he says, "establish[es] the trustworthiness of the ways of arguing applied in any particular case." In other words, the backing can be thought of as the support system to the warrant that fine tunes the generalized assumption. Similar to the warrant, the backing can be directly stated or implied. And just like the warrant, backings are based upon the three categories of rhetorical appeals. Consider the following:

Backing based on Ethos
You may say, "Companies should demonstrate moral behavior and continued employment of unethical workers is a negative behavioral example for the community." This backing makes the moral/ethical reasons for firing Joe more specific because it demonstrates the wider reaching effects of immoral employee behavior.

Backing based on Logos
You may say, "Companies that operate at a loss are detrimental to local economies by hurting tax revenue and weakening competition." This backing makes the economic ramifications of the warrant more specific by showing that companies which operate at a loss affect tax-funded revenues and throw off healthy competitive balance in the market.

Backing based on Pathos
You may say "An angry client can weaken an entire customer base by polluting consumer trust with suspicion and skepticism towards the company." This backing centers on the emotional content of the consumer outrage and makes the warrant more specific because it deepens the notion that an emotionally disgruntled clientele can dismantle a whole business from the inside out.

The above examples illustrate an essential point: arguments that are in support of the same claim can have entirely different approaches depending on the nature of the warrant and the backing. As you can see, pathos-based warrant/backing combinations are no less effective than the logos or ethos-based ones. It all depends on how you, the arguer, wish to construct your approach and to what ends. Thinking of argumentation in these terms can be both exciting and empowering because it allows for an enormous amount of latitude in how you approach persuasive occasions.

Case Study in Contemporary Argument: Letters to the Editor from *The New York Times* Article "How Google Conquered the American Classroom" (May 13, 2017)

The Warrant

To the Editor:

Sadly, American public education lurches from one fad to another. Remember "schools without walls" or the "new math"? Chromebooks are simply the latest fad. There is little evidence that computers in classrooms produce student outcomes superior to traditional teaching methods, at least when the latter are implemented properly.

Elite private schools have computers, but they are far less central to the educational process. Instead, smaller class sizes and better teachers are emphasized. However, these are a lot more expensive than Chromebooks.

SCOTT OCHILTREE, WASHINGTON

To the Editor:

Good for Google. It figured out how to level the playing field across different types of schools and districts to help close the digital divide. And it has helped spawn a new generation of digital citizens who are learning how to use technology in a social, positive manner geared toward learning. Schools can be left scrambling to find ways to give each student full access to a good education. At low cost and with easy-to-use tools, Google has skinned the cat.

Yes, Google also has almost unfettered access to a new generation of consumers. That's a price worth paying given the high returns to students in the form of contemporary, relevant learning.

MATT LEVINSON, SEATTLE

Both Ochiltree and Levinson make good cases. Each has a claim that's linked to evidence, and each is well-presented in its delivery. So, who wins? Well, that depends on which warrant you find yourself most drawn to. Ochiltree's underlying assumption – "educational fads should be treated with tremendous caution" – appeals to those who've been in education for a long-time that have seen these (sometimes high-cost) initiatives die out as quickly as they came in. In-person education, a small group setting with a highly-qualified teacher, is where the real learning occurs. Levinson's argument appeals to a slightly different set. His warrant – "equal opportunity should be a school's highest priority" – has tones of social justice and egalitarianism at its core. Those who see schools as vital social institutions which reflect and celebrate these American values should be able to readily identify with this warrant.

Using the Toulmin Model to Compose

When setting up my *warrant*(s), ask:	✓ How do I justify the movement from the grounds to the claim?
	✓ Is this assumption common knowledge, or does it need to be explicitly stated in the writing?
When setting up my *backing*(s), ask:	✓ Does the warrant take the reader from the grounds to the claim successfully?
	✓ What other general information is needed to back up the audience's trust in my warrant?

Like the Classical Model, Toulmin's system is useful for arranging the overall structure of an argument. The pattern of connections between the claim and the grounds, the warrant and the backing, the exceptions and qualifiers, exist in all argumentative paragraphs regardless of their topic or scope. Though not as prescriptive as the Classical Model, Toulmin's system of argument appraisal can easily form the substructure of an entire, multi-paragraph composition. Consider Figure 4, a graphic visualization of how all the parts of a Toulmin argument hang together.

What may this argumentative grid look like when put into full operation? Outlines are useful, but examples are often the best teachers. The following semi-narrative example which discusses the implications of the Vietnam war, drawn from Toulmin's *An Introduction to Reasoning* (1979), should clearly demonstrate how Toulmin's ideas can function in everyday argumentation. As you read Toulmin's argument, consult the graphical representation in the corresponding figures to see how Toulmin charts translate to written argumentation.

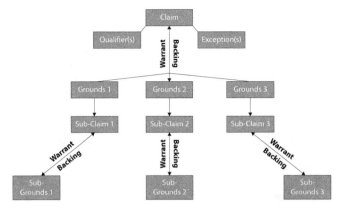

Figure 4 Multi-Paragraph Argument Built from Toulmin's System.

Suppose, for instance, that we find ourselves involved in a discussion about the Vietnam War. One part to the discussion claims that the United States ought never to have intervened in a conflict in the first place (see Figure 5). When that claim is challenged, he replies by producing three statements as his grounds:

Let's face it. The war was a civil war in the first place; its outcome had little bearing on our national interests overseas, and America's involvement only caused inflation and civil disorder at home (see Figure 6).

How are we to deal with such a response? Two kinds of critical examinations are called for. In the first place, we can examine the implied connection between the three statements he is now making – "It was a civil war," "It had little bearing on our national interest," and "It caused inflation and disorder at home" – and the original claim that American should have kept out.

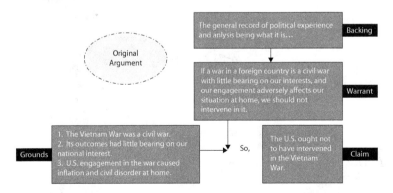

Figure 5 Original Argument – Example from *An Introduction to Reasoning* (1979).

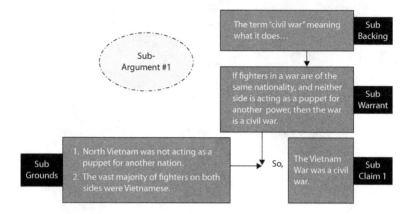

Figure 6 Sub Argument #1 – Example from *An Introduction to Reasoning* (1979).

Even if we accept those statements without further examination, the first question is "Will they settle the matter?" The first question raises the issues about warrants and backing which we discussed earlier (see Figure 7).

In the second place, however, we may wish to call in question the further statements that he produces as the grounds for his claim. Was it, after all, just a civil war? Were our interests as a nation so little involved, and so on? That is to say, we can go behind the original argument and treat each of the grounds presented as representing, in turn, a further claim whose foundation can also be scrutinized. In this way, each of the constituent statements in the original argument will become the starting point for a further argument (see Figure 8).

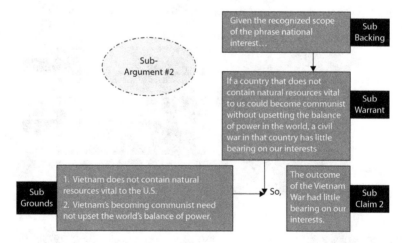

Figure 7 Sub Argument #2 – Example from *An Introduction to Reasoning* (1979).

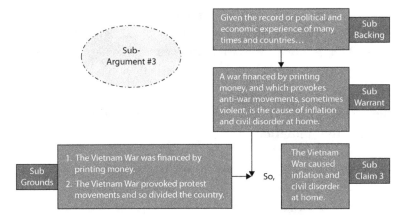

Figure 8 Sub Argument #3 – Example from *An Introduction to Reasoning* (1979).

As a result, we can analyze the content of this argument, and the assumptions on which it rests, in a way that shows how all its different elements connect together. In addition to the original argument, we shall then obtain three sub-arguments each of which is linked to the original argument by way of one or another of the three "grounds" in the argument. We can set this whole pattern of connections out in the form of a series of diagrams. The point here is not whether we agree or disagree with the conclusion of the argument or whether we accept the truth of the statements offered in support of the conclusion. The point is that we can effectively explain *in what respects and for what reasons* we agree or disagree, only if we take the trouble to examine all the assumptions and connections implicit in the argument and face the questions honestly of whether or not all the facts are stated and whether or not they really have the implications the speaker claims.

Just like the human body, the discrete components of Toulmin's system work alone and in combination, performing their individual tasks while working jointly with one another to keep the host in working order. The importance of the grounds in sub-claim 2 is every bit as important as the warrant of sub-claim 3 or the qualifier of the initial claim. If one appendage is diseased, the whole organism will be infected. Here is an appropriate time to remind you that Toulmin's system is not simply a template for creation. It also serves as a handy framework for argumentative deconstruction; that is, when you are dissecting an argument and assessing its effectiveness, make use of Toulmin's teachings and hold your analysis to his standards of scrutiny: qualified claims, clear connections between claim and grounds, warrants to show the connection between claims and grounds, backings to make those warrants more specific, and so forth. If you find these connections are well-constructed and tightly rigged – if they pass Toulmin's gauntlet – you will have a sound argument in front of you, one that has been assessed both logically and ethically.

Arguing Differently – Conciliatory, Integrative, and Deliberative Models of Argumentation

Published in *Pedagogy: Critical Approaches to Teaching Literature, Language, Composition, and Culture*, "Arguing Differently" (2005) details author Barry Kroll's experiences during a semester-long, experimental writing course. The focus of his course was to, as the title suggests, get students arguing differently, beyond the well-established cultural metaphors that character-ize argument as something combative and confrontational. Argument, in contemporary American culture, is often construed as an oppositional and adversarial enterprise where the primary goal is to defeat your opponent and win disputes; look no further than any talk show, courtroom drama, presidential campaign, or reality TV program. Kroll understands that met-aphors are not benign figures of speech that merely add poetic flare; they are powerful locutions which structure our perceptions and understanding of reality since the essence of a metaphor is to understand one thing in terms of another. In *Metaphors We Live By* (1980) authors George Lakoff and Mark Johnson describe the common metaphor of argument-as-war which has proliferated argument studies from its very beginning:

It is important to see that we don't just talk about arguments in terms of war. We can actually win or lose arguments. We see the person we are arguing with as an opponent. We attack his positions and we defend our own. We gain and lose ground. We plan and use strategies. If we find a position indefensible, we can aban-don it and take a new line of attack. Many of the things we do in arguing are par-tially structured by the concept of war. Though there is no physical battle, there is a verbal battle, and the structure of an argument – attack, defense, counter-attack, etc. reflects this … The metaphors are not merely in the words we use – it is in our very concept of an argument. The language of argument is not poetic, fanciful, or rhetorical; it is literal. We talk about arguments that way because we conceive of them that way – and we act according to the way we conceive of things.

Even in contemporary America, this argument-as-war metaphor is inescapable. Donald Trump's 2016 bid for the White House was saturated in these themes, but his bellicose style is just a symptom of a much larger disease in contemporary argumentation. His insistence on being right at any expense – decorum, civility, truth itself – reflects the cultural understanding of argument as the forum to insist upon your own correctness while smashing any detracting voice to smithereens. The way argument tends to be taught in schools reflects, and even celebrates, this conception. Kroll acknowledges that typical argumentation instruction is fraught with problems: 1) It encourages a defensive stance 2) It is damaging to maintaining relationships and facilitating productive dialogue and 3) It circumscribes the writer into a prescribed, and limited, set of options when it comes to writing. So, it is here where he sets out to explore alternative methods of argumentation, ones which privilege productive dialogue and collaboration over conquering your opposition. He describes three approaches: Conciliatory, Integrative, and Deliberative arguments, which we will now look at in detail.

Conciliatory Arguments

A "conciliatory argument" sounds like an oxymoron, but sometimes a listener is much more willing to listen if they feel that the speaker "gets" where they are coming from. Conciliatory arguments are built on a principle of emotional trust between speaker and audience. With especially volatile topics that tend to polarize, this approach attempts to get people who disagree with you to *listen* rather than to respond defensively. The hope is that you can leverage this "fairness" into the audience's consideration of an idea that would otherwise remain unconsidered. Conciliatory arguments pattern themselves on a different framework than thesis-driven argument models by leading with an initial section where writer empathizes with the opposition's concerns (think concession). Doing so demonstrates that the writer understands the specifics of an opposing point of view and can see how, in some cases, those points of view are understandable, if not completely justifiable. This is followed with a second section where the writer asserts his view, not as a collision of opposites, but in a parallel style to the concerns from the argument's lead, showing that an unfamiliar perspective on the issue can lead to equally justifiable interpretations.

The most visible difference between thesis-driven arguments and conciliatory arguments is that the latter withholds the thesis until later in the essay, whereas the former puts the thesis front and center. Leading off with a thesis, Kroll believes, often will subconsciously put the audience into a defensive position, thereby damaging the lines of communication before the specifics of your case get underway. Instead of placing the emphasis on the thesis, Conciliatory arguments focus primarily on constructing a friendly ethos of the author in its early-goings. This "I-see-where-you're-coming-from" tone treats the opposition with dignity and respect and can be quite an effective strategy for penetrating initial resistance from a hostile audience. Kroll cites Renee Askins' *Releasing Wolves from Symbolism* (1995) as a prime example of Conciliatory strategies in operation. In her argument, she advocates for the recovery of the wild wolf population in the American West, a region which saw this species hunted down to nearly nothing in the second half of the 20th century. Although her argument will go on to disagree with the unfounded reasoning of her rancher and farmer opponents (who see the wolf as a threat to their livelihood), she begins her argument by identifying with the concerns of these folks:

> If I were a rancher I probably would not want wolves returned to the West. If I faced the conditions that ranchers face in the West – falling stock prices, rising taxes, prolonged drought, and a nation that is eating less beef and wearing more synthetics – I would not want to add to my woes. If I were a rancher in Montana, Idaho, or Wyoming in 1995, watching my neighbors give up and my way of life fade away, I would be afraid and I would be angry. I would want to blame something, to fight something, even kill something.

The "if/then" logic of the opening hypotheticals articulate the breadth of concerns surrounding the reintroduction of the wild wolf. She earnestly acknowledges the fear of a fading way of life while empathizing with the fact that these folks are already behind the eight ball – "falling stock prices, rising taxes, prolonged drought, and a nation that is eating less beef and wearing more synthetics." Askins nicely walks a fine line between concession and patronizing; she does not belittle or downplay the legitimate concerns of Western ranchers and realizes the plain fact that the industry doesn't need an added stress to its already weakened condition.

Askins successfully leverages the good will of her audience in the introduction. While this move is essential to Conciliatory arguments, Kroll
cautions that writers must handle their argumentative "turn" in the essay
with great care. Whatever leverage has been built can be quickly under-
mined with too swift of a transition into the development of the argument,
leaving your opponent feeling duped, deceived, or worse. Kroll notes the
Askins does this very misstep in her argument, flipping the switch from
empathy to argument a little too quickly:

> However, it is my job, as a scientist and an advocate, to distinguish fact from
> fiction and purpose from perception. Ranchers claim that wolves will devastate
> the livestock industry in the West. Yet all the science, the studies, the experts,
> and the facts show that…

What is she implying here? Well, if her position relies on "all the
science, the studies, the experts, and the facts," her opponents (implicitly) base their view on superstition, conjecture, unreliable testimony, and
falsehoods. This "turn" is more than a misstep; it completely alienates
those whom she had spent time building trust with, and her credibility is
shot. So how could Askins have done things more carefully? Kroll cites
two strategies. The first is to focus on context, talking about how a change
of conditions can bring about a change in perspective. By noting that
traditional ways of thinking change over time, it's possible to, at least,
entertain the idea that the traditional resistance to the wild wolf population may now – under the current circumstance – be an outmoded way
of thinking. The second is to shift the focus to a larger issue by recast-
ing the question of whether or not the wolf should be reintroduced into
the wild into broader contexts: concerns of natural ecosystems (of which
the wolf plays a vital role) or upon warrants of animal rights. Doing so
still does not undermine the initial concessions from the introduction
but rather asserts that those perspectives only capture a sliver of a much
greater issue.

Conciliatory arguments should end as they began, stressing the collaborative role that all stakeholders play in complicated issues. If there is
something for all parties to gain, the conclusion is the place to trot these
out and, as Kroll says, "this kind of conclusion appeals to the audience's

self-interest, and can transform the writer's position from a threat to a promise." Askins wraps things up nicely in her essay,

> The real issue is one of making room, and there is still a little room in the West – room for hunters, for environmentalists, for ranchers, and for wolves.

The art of her conclusion exists in its ability to convey four voices – hunters, environmentalists, ranchers, wolves – all at the same time. This is not a knockout punch to opponents, but a place where all the concerns of the competing parties mesh together into a space of mutual gain. No one gets everything, but everyone can get something.

Integrative Arguments

To integrate is "to combine one thing with another so that they become a unified whole." Integrative arguments, then, use competing points of view as the virtual puzzle pieces that make up a complete picture of a controversy. The theory behind an Integrative argument is that even when people disagree, a writer can still weave together competing perspectives into actionable outcomes where all parties stand to at least partially benefit. Integrative arguments, like Conciliatory ones, are useful for topics that must balance many competing interests, values, and points of view. Since most day-to-day argumentation takes place with those whom you already have a pre-existing conflict with, Integrative arguments specifically stress strategies that strengthen the adherence of the audience to your position, if only just a fraction of that position.

A full-frontal assault will do little to change anyone's mind and introductory strategies in the Integrative arguments are particularly sensitive to this fact. Whereas Conciliatory introductions focus on the relationship of speaker to audience, Integrative arguments stress the dynamic between speaker and subject. It's often useful in the opening moments of Integrative arguments to shift attention away from the immediate controversy to a larger or more significant problem, or to move from the "is" of a situation (what's currently happening) to the "ought" (what should happen in the future). Doing so establishes common ground – ignoring the pros and cons for the moment – and gets people to at least agree to the fact that something has to be done. Kroll cites the opening of Roger Rosenblatt's "How to End the Abortion War" (1992) as an exemplar "shift":

> The veins in his forehead bulged so prominently they might have been blue worms that had worked their way under the surface of his skin ... Like his, her face was taut with fury, her lips pressed together so tightly they folded under and vanished ... For nearly 20 years these two have been at each other with all the hatred they can unearth.

See what Rosenblatt has done here. Though he eventually asserts a pro-life position later in the essay, he does not initially force a focus on abortion's moral implications. Doing so would elicit an immediate breakdown in communication. Instead, he pulls the camera angle back, so to speak, to focus on the heated stalemate that has developed over the last twenty years, thereby identifying the conflict between pro-life and pro-choice *as* the problem. By "agreeing to disagree," both sides to the debate are at least now at the same table, speaking the same language. Good integrative arguers must be good selectors at the beginning of the argument; that is, you must settle on a precise point of agreement within the conflict so that clear and demarcated relationships can come into view as the argument moves along.

With topics like abortion, the two sides will never fully agree and it's naïve to think a well-formed claim could change someone's mind on the spot. The next best alternative is what Kroll suggests to do when it comes time to assert an Integrative claim. The two parties will continue to disagree about certain issues, yes, but it may be possible to get them to cooperate on something both sides see as important. Integrative claims, then, are less an assertion of position and more a sketching out a plan of compromise. As Kroll says, "in working toward mutual gain, the writer must detail a course of action that allows both parties to achieve something – different things for each party – that matters to them." Back to Rosenblatt.

> ...people must have room in the social and political environment for making life and death decisions ... the basic moral affirmations that are, in practice if not always in theory, widely shared in our broader moral community by persons who would consider themselves to be on either the pro-life [or] the pro-choice side of the abortion question. What is shared, specifically, is a belief that life is a

primary good of life, from which it follows that pregnancy is a good and desirable condition. At the center of pregnancy is a developing form of human life, which all agree should be regarded as good and therefore, ordinarily, deserving of protection … And if at least some abortions are permissible, then abortions should be avoided and certainly not promoted, but … there are occasions when electing abortion as a response to unwanted pregnancy is both responsible and morally justified.

Right in the middle of this excerpt, Rosenblatt explicitly identifies a shared view held by both pro-life and pro-choice advocates: "What is shared, specifically, is a belief that life is a primary good of life, from which it follows that pregnancy is a good and desirable condition." He never abandons his core commitment to the pro-life position, but he's not bullheadedly stubborn about it either. Yes, abortion does involve ending human life and, yes, there should moral consequences for such an action. In spite of this, he does recognize that not all pregnancies are wanted or even consensual. If life is "deserving of protection" – and there is no protection to be had with the circumstances of the birth – Rosenblatt concedes there are occasions when electing abortion as a response to unwanted pregnancy is both responsible and morally justified. Here is where, Kroll says, Rosenblatt "invent[s] 'options' that gives each side something it wants, without asking anyone to abandon core commitments."

Conclusions in this model tend to reaffirm the integrative basis – urging the merger of disparate points of view into a unified whole – that supports the overall argument. It's not a bad idea to repeat the notion that *both* sides are actually on the *same* side when it comes to certain aspects of the issue. By reaffirming the generative energy of this cooperative goodwill, both sides can walk away feeling unified rather than bitterly separated. Rosenblatt concludes:

If one combines that sense of social responsibility with the advocacy of individual rights, the permit but-discourage formula could work. By "discourage," I mean the implementation of social programs that help to create an atmosphere of discouragement. I do not mean ideas like parental consent or notification, already the law in some states, which, however well-intentioned, only whittle away at individual freedoms. The "discourage" part is the easier to find agreement on, of course, but when one places the "permit" question in the realm of respect for private values, even that may become more palatable.

Rosenblatt is careful to couch his final recommendations in speculative "if/then" clauses, not as a sign of ambivalence, but as a gesture of respect and tolerance towards his audience. Nothing is forced on them. No moral judgement is made upon them. A thoughtful compromise of "permit but-discourage" is offered, but this solution asks *both* sides to meet in the middle. Each party gets a small win in Rosenblatt's conclusion, leaving neither alienated or feeling shortchanged. Moreover, he closes out on tones of respect, tolerance, and dignity which are three essential elements for productive dialogue about any controversial issue.

Deliberative Arguments

Of Kroll's three models, Deliberative arguments stress the dialogic dynamics of argumentation the most (the word deliberative itself means "intended for consideration of discussion"). Kroll describes this form in his essay as an "attempt to replicate, in textual form, the dynamics of thoughtful discussion, where participants express their views, question others, and refine their opinions in the interactive process of arriving at a decision." If you've ever found yourself in a big group argument (say, the dinner table) on a controversial topic – politics, religion – you know the difficulties involved in trying to keep things productive while making sure everyone gets a chance to talk. Deliberative arguments are not, says Kroll, "so simple as imagining oneself as a participant at the discussion table, because that way of understanding deliberation would lead a writer to produce a 'contribution' to the discussion, one that would surely look very much like a traditional claim-plus-reasons argument." So, we know what they aren't. Then, what are they?

Openings to Deliberative arguments draw on aspects of both Conciliatory and Integrative introductions in two ways. First, they often postpone the writer's assertion on the topic, instead preferring to highlight that the central controversy can be understood in the context of a greater or more significant problem. Like Integrative arguments, the idea behind withholding any argument about the topic is to establish a common space among the argument's participants, getting each side to acknowledge that the problem itself is significant and requires attention. In doing so, the writer takes on a tone of disinterest – not being influenced by personal involvement in something – and can consequently be seen by the reader as a trustworthy steward through the details of the argument. To keep the problem, not the potential solutions, initially in focus, Kroll suggests that "deliberative arguments begin with a description of a social problem that almost everyone will agree is significant, as in the following leads, all from newspaper editorials" (below). Such a lead-off strategy withholds any one argument on the issue and rather foregrounds the fact that there is a genuine problem afoot:

> *On low military enlistment:* For nearly 30 years, since the United States began relying on volunteers to fill the ranks of the armed forces, the military recruiter's job has been a tough one. Now that uphill battle is becoming a losing battle as the force struggles to recruit enough people – and comes up short. And the problem is only getting worse.

> *On dwindling numbers of rural doctors:* There are nearly 12,000 primary care physicians in Pennsylvania and only 13 percent of them practice in rural areas. Those who live beyond the city or the suburbs not only have to drive farther to see a doctor, they have to look harder to find one.

> *On increasing home foreclosures:* Bankruptcies are booming. More than 1.3 million households took their debts into a bankruptcy filing last year, and most of them wiped the slate clean instead of working out a plan for paying at least some of the debts.

   In all three of these lead-ins, the author's stance is at once plainly accessible and wholly hidden. On a surface read, we are getting genuine fact – military enlistment *is* low, rural doctors *are* dwindling, foreclosures *are* on the rise – with no insertion of the author's voice. On a closer read, we are being subtly lead to where the author wants to take us. By keeping a focused problem in view for all readers, it's easy to see that this problem does indeed exist, and there ought to be a dialogue about its potential solutions. It's at this point where you can now transition into the body of the Deliberative argument.

   Kroll acknowledges that developing Deliberative arguments is rife with challenges. Since the heart of the argument simulates a virtual discussion on competing proposals to a problem, there is a considerable risk of alienating those audience members whose proposals you ultimately will critique and reject. No easy task, for sure, but there will be times when the writer finds that one of the proposed solutions to a problem is superior to other options, and the argument must then take the shape of providing reasons to reject weaker proposals. How does a writer avoid the adversarial edge when arguing against some people's proposals? Consider the way it's done in Eileen Sharp's *Rural Pennsylvania Must Grow Its Own Crop of New Physicians* (1999).

> There are no canned answers to this crisis and quick-fix solutions are no more than Band-Aids on a gunshot wounds. If there is no quick solution – and I'd argue there isn't – what we can do is combine the merits of the aforementioned proposals, ease off on their pace, and use their core ideas as the first stages towards a slow, but steady, regimen of much needed medicine for America's ailing rural populations.

In staying true to the group-ethic of the Deliberative style, Sharp challenges opposing opinions without alienating them while still advocating for her overall position: an increase in the number of qualified doctors in rural areas. But rather than asserting her claim as king, she opts for another strategy. She concedes that this complicated problem resists easy answers, in essence saying that no one proposal is adequate to solve the problem on its own. Instead, she takes bits and pieces from *all* the proposals – giving each author a voice in the developing solution – and positions *this* as the actionable solution (all within the stylish metaphor of a medicinal "regimen").

If the body of the paper lays out the ways to think productively about the controversy, then the conclusion is where the writer proposes to do something about it. Deliberative conclusions often suggest action; the writer gives his audience a "greatest hits" reel of the available proposals, picking and choosing the most plausible elements of the paper's body. This can be tricky, however, since there is a temptation to claim that the action-plan unilaterally solves the controversy. It's unlikely any argument, in the span of four to five pages, could definitively solve any multi-layered, real world problem. As Kroll says, go ahead and offer an action plan but be sure to "still send a clear signal about remaining open to further input with a 'convinced but tentative' tone." A second concluding plan could suggest that the stated proposals have done little to solve the problem but have successfully opened up new ways to approach it, allowing the author to exit the argument on a thoughtfully unresolved tone. By acknowledging all the competing points of view, this strategy suggests a new argument can be made about the controversy now that new conditions (laid out in the proposals) have come to light. Doing so, keeps all the voices actively involved and demonstrates a degree of nuance and sophistication in the way the writer resolved the unresolvable. Here's how Sharp wraps things up:

'Traditional market forces have not been very effective in making health care both available and affordable to rural residents,' said The Pennsylvania Rural Health Association in 1997. That remains the case today. So, rural Pennsylvania must grow its own health care professionals. Future physicians are out there beyond the skyscrapers, the cul de sacs and the malls. The challenge is to find and encourage them.

Nothing is definitively solved in these closing lines, and the last sentence of her essay explicitly acknowledges there is more work to be done. She's not resolved, though she's not ambivalent either. She places the ailing population of rural doctors into the complicated context of the real world, noting that social problems rarely tie themselves up with a neat bow. Further deliberation is called for, but if done in the productive spirit of her essay, the audience should remain hopeful that some closure can eventually be achieved.

Seeing Toulmin and Kroll in tandem provides a fairly complete picture of contemporary scene in argument scholarship. These self-reflective, abstract systems are a welcome counterweight to the logic-driven styles of the Classical world and, when intertwined, will give you a substantial foundation upon which you can begin to produce your own argumentation, both oral and written. These great thinkers have shown us what to do; in the next chapter, we'll look at all of the things *not* to do in argument.

CHAPTER ELEVEN

ERRORS IN REASONING – LOGICAL FALLACIES

P lato's main gripe with the Sophists – and rhetoric in general – is their preoccupation with winning an argument by any means necessary. The Sophist tells you what they think will convince you, not what's logical or true, and they seize on the ambiguities of language to, as Plato said in the *Apology* (399 B.C.), "make the weaker argument the stronger." In the last few chapters we've discussed the role that sound logic plays in argumentation, but a big question still remains: how is it that bad arguments still persuade people to do things? In the Platonic dialogues, the Sophists always *appear* to know what they're talking about, but when you look closely at what they say, you'll see nothing but a logical void. Consider the exchange between Dionysodorous and Ctesippus from Plato's *Euthydemus* (384 B.C.):

Dionysodorous: Just tell me, do you have a dog?

Ctesippus: Yes, and a very bad one.

Dionysodorous: Does it have puppies?

Ctesippus: Very much so, as bad as it is.

Dionysodorous: Then the dog is their father?

Ctesippus: I have seen it myself.

Dionysodorous: Very well, isn't the dog yours?

Ctesippus: Certainly.

Dionysodorous: Then being a father and it being yours, the dog is your father and you the puppy's brother. One more little question. Do you beat this dog?
Ctesippus: No mistake, I do, for I can't beat you!

The Sophists substitute verbal trickery for truth, and it's easy to see in this exchange that there's plenty of word games going on. In this caricature of bad logic run amok, Dionysodorous apparently argues that Ctesippus' dog, who has puppies of his own and is a father, must "necessarily" be the father of his human owner. But what exactly is the logical problem with the argument in this scene? The answer is not easy. He reasons that if you are a father, you can't not be a father, so you must be the father of everything (since you can't be that which is not). What's he done is use the fallacy of "equivocation" where a word changes meaning over the course of the argument. In this case, he plays on the two uses of the verb "is." "Is" can assign identity (He *is* a dog) or attribute a quality (The dog *is* black), but it can never do both at the same time, and Dionysodorous collapses these distinctions over the course of his short argument. Recast his argument into a logical form – the syllogism – and it is obviously ridiculous: The dog is a father, the dog is yours, therefore, the dog is your father. The scary thing about this scene in *Euthydemus* is not how bad the argument is but the fact that a crowd of onlookers roars in applause for Dionysodorous's apparent argumentative "skill."

According to both classical and contemporary scholarship, the answer of "What makes a good argument?" lies in its logical strength. Dionysodorous was not the first person to use a fallacious argument, and he certainly was not the last. Logical fallacies – errors in the reasoning process – have the appearance of truth but are laden with any number of logical errors. Some of these mental missteps are so common that they creep into our everyday lives and conversation, often passing as legitimate forms of persuasion. It is our duty here to put the spotlight on these erroneous ways of thinking and expose them for what they are. Writers fall into fallacies for a whole host of reasons: as a shortcut around deep thinking, when they can't honestly argue their position or when evidence is hard to come by. If you have ever felt frustration because you know something is wrong with an argument, either your own or someone else's, but you can't quite say what it is, a study of logical fallacies will suit you well. Given that arguments deal with complex human situations, we cannot identify every type of false thinking there is. Nonetheless, we will work to identify some of the biggest mines in the minefield by splitting our discussion into three broad categories: errors of relevance, errors of vacuity/presumption, and errors of induction.

Errors of Relevance: Ad Hominem Arguments

Latin for "against the man," an *ad hominem* argument occurs when the arguer criticizes the person holding a point of view rather than addressing the point of view that person holds. As we've said throughout this book, a speaker's ethos is often the largest mitigating factor in persuasion. *Ad hominems* are often an attempt to slash at the credibility of opponent, the idea being that if the opposition can be personally discredited, so too will the ideas they hold. *Ad hominems*, when undetected, can be devastating since they take the trust an audience has with the opposition and blow it to bits. In their pure form, *Ad hominems* are easy to spot since they make an irrelevant jump from the subject under discussion to a personal attack (maybe to distract from the weakness in their own position). Here is an example:

> *Alice*: "We should remove the S.A.T.'s as a college entry requirement because it is not an indicator of success in a collegiate setting."
>
> *Bob*: "You don't like the S.A.T.'s because you home-schooled your kids and they won't do well."

See how Bob's response is directed at the person, not the argument? In his reply, Bob shifts the argument away from the topic at hand – the merits of the S.A.T. as an indicator for college success – to a personal attack against Alice. Bob implies that Alice's argument against the S.A.T.'s is selfishly motivated: perhaps Alice will be embarrassed that her children will not do well on the test or perhaps failure on the exam would reveal the choice to homeschool as the wrong one. And since Alice's motivation is rife with bias, her anti-S.A.T. argument should not be taken too seriously. What Bob doesn't do is counter Alice's argument with any number of legitimate rebuttals against standardized testing as the final word on a student's college readiness: the inequality among school districts, whether the tests measure privilege over aptitude, the quality of professional development, or how parental involvement figures into student performance.

These are all topics that could be explored at length in logical dialogue, but Bob doesn't even give them a passing glance. *Ad hominems* can be tricky though. Just because a personal attack is leveled at an opponent that doesn't necessarily mean that a fallacy has been committed. If, for example, Bob pointed out that Alice wanted to dismantle the S.A.T. because she was financially invested in the rival A.C.T., this attack would be relevant to the argument.

Ad hominems are integral to the way that conspiracy theories operate. Let's take the most well-known one in recent years, the 9/11 conspiracy theory, as an example. If you're not familiar with the theory, here it is in shorthand: The collapse of the Twin Towers and World Trade Center 7 resulted not from the impact of a jet liner but a controlled demolition. The Pentagon, too, was not hit by a jet liner as the official reports describe; it was hit by a U.S. launched ballistic missile. The United States government either deliberately ignored advance knowledge of the attacks or directly assisted the attackers in the terrorist plot. The logical arguments to support the conspiracy are dicey, a point proven by Popular Mechanics' *Debunking the 9/11 Myths: Special Report* (2005) and National Institute of Standards and Technology *Final Report* (2005). Instead, conspiracy theorists fall back on a number of logical fallacies, *ad hominem* arguments chief among them.

Films which propagate this theory – *Zeitgeist* (2007), *Loose Change: An American Coup* (2009), among several others – all use the same basic strategy to advance their argument: undermine every form of authority which supports the official 9/11 narrative to make the conspiracy look like the only "logical" explanation. Here's a glimpse inside the *ad hominem* part of the 9/11 conspiracy theorist's brain, paraphrased from Jarrod Atchison's *The Art of Debate* (2017):

–   Can we trust the news coverage of the 9/11 attacks which confirm the official narrative of the events? No. The news media made so much money from the events that they were willing to cover any version of the story, so long as millions of viewers propped up the Nielsen ratings. Journalistic review and integrity don't matter in the face of greed.
–   Does the *9/11 Commission Report* (2004) confirm the official narrative of 9/11 upon three years of investigation and scholarly review? No. The report was directed by government officials, who were themselves part of the conspiracy, so it makes perfect sense why the "official" report stays in lockstep with media accounts of that day.

– What about the eyewitnesses, some even interviewed minutes after impact, who say they saw a jet liner hit the Twin Towers and the Pentagon? No. We can't take what they say seriously either. They're either hired disaster actors who are delivering scripted lines orchestrated by the government, or they were simply too panicked in the moment to accurately describe what they saw.

Notice in each of these examples that the conspiracy theorist doesn't directly engage with an argument but goes after the person (or organization) who holds an opposing argument to take out its credibility. Since hard evidence to support the actual theory is scant, conspiracy theorists build their argument by destroying others with *ad hominem* attacks, so their narrative is the only one left. The "fake news" phenomenon – largely attributable to the Trump presidential campaign of 2016 – is the *ad hominem* writ large, exacerbated by 24-hour news cycles and social media. Both during and after the campaign, Trump often derided unflattering news stories, polls, comments, and journalistic questions as "fake news" in an effort to discredit his detractors. Consider how *ad hominems* underwrite each of the following comments made by Donald Trump:

The *ad hominem* attack – and its ability to undo any authoritative source of information – is a powerful weapon of argumentation when it goes unchecked. As Barack Obama said in a 2017 interview with *The New Yorker*, a public discourse plagued by *ad hominems* inevitably leads to a world where "everything is true and nothing is true." At the heart of "alternative facts," "ideological framing," and "post-truth" reality is the *ad hominem* argument.

Errors of Relevance: Non-Sequitur Arguments

Latin for "it does not follow," a *non-sequitur* argument occurs when a speaker draws a conclusion that does not logically follow from the provided explanation. This fallacy is sometimes referred to as a figure of irrelevance, a catch-all term for any instance where a speaker introduces an irrelevant element (either in the evidence or conclusion) into the argument. *Non-sequiturs* can take many shapes, ranging from a malformed sentence to an unstated assumption that binds an entire chain of claims and evidence together. At the sentence level, *non-sequiturs* often occur as a result of faulty rigging between clauses, coupled with the absence of much needed information. Consider the following:

> *Chris*: "I didn't get hit by a car on my way to work because I wore my lucky socks."

This is a complex sentence, a subordinate clause ("because I wore my lucky socks") which depends on the main clause ("I didn't get hit by a car on my way to work") for its meaning, but the logical relationship between the two is iffy at best. If you remember back to chapter 8, enthymemes express logically coherent statements in ways you'd see in everyday conversation. The example above is written in the same form as our enthymeme from Chapter 8 – "Joe is a bachelor because he is an unmarried man" – so what's the difference, logically speaking? Let's break them down into syllogistic form to see what's missing.

Enthymeme	"Joe is a bachelor because he is an unmarried man"	"I didn't get hit by a car on my way to work because I wore my lucky socks"
Major Premise	All bachelors are unmarried men	Lucky socks prevent accidents
Minor Premise	Joe is a bachelor	I'm wearing lucky socks
Conclusion	Joe is an unmarried man	My lucky socks prevented an accident today

When broken out this way, it's easy to see where the irrelevant evidence – "Lucky socks prevent accidents" – enters into the mix, thus derailing the validity of the argument. Instead of attributing his safety to what he decided to put on this feet that morning, Chris omits a step in the logical chain of reasoning. He could have pointed to a number of things to make his argument more reasonable: patterns in local accident reports, traffic laws to ensure pedestrian safety, the median age of drivers in the area, or the availability of pedestrian spaces on his commute. Here is where you can hopefully see how identifying a logical fallacy can lead to the reconstruction of an argument on a sounder logical foundation.

Non-sequiturs like this are easy to spot, but this fallacy can also have a stealth presence, acting as the faulty basis for an entire argument. In other words, just as *non-sequiturs* can introduce irrelevant evidence, they can also appear as an illegitimate warrant for an argument. Take Mitt Romney's 2012 bid for the White House as an example. The then-Republican presidential candidate centered his entire campaign around the *non-sequitur* assertion that a strong business background is essential to a strong presidency. In "What I Learned at Bain Capital" (2012), a press release by Romney published in *The Wall Street Journal*, he argued that his acumen in the private sector could effect large-scale change in the Unites States, implying that the first step toward running the country more like a business is to elect a businessman to the Oval Office. This argument relies on several *non-sequitur* assumptions. Being a good president requires much more than a savvy business background; in fact, the similarities between businessman and president are only skin deep. Consider the following distinctions, adapted from Doyle McManus's *Are Businessmen Better Presidents?* (2012) which identify several *non-sequiturs* in the president-as-business man warrant:

Business context	Political context
Businessmen have clear, measurable goals (mainly increasing profits)	Political leaders' aims are less precise but much more multi-dimensional.
Businessmen can constantly revamp their companies to adjust to the changing environment	Political leaders are stuck running government institutions that resist structural change
Businessmen work in a competitive marketplace where all stakeholders share the same goal, the health of the company	Political leaders have to negotiate budget deals with an opposition that's constantly trying to discredit whatever they do

To these distinctions, we could add more, but the point here is the fundamental assumption of Romney's campaign relies on *non-sequitur* logic; "it does not follow" that a successful president must have a strong background in business. Perhaps this is why Obama's campaign spent much of the summer of 2012 attacking Romney's business background, showing why the priorities of the private sector are at odds with the civic duties of commander-in-chief.

The *post hoc, ergo propter hoc* ("after this, therefore because of this") fallacy is a special kind of *non-sequitur* that conflates correlation and causation. *Post hoc* fallacies operate on the idea that because two events occur close to each other in time that they must have a causal relationship.

The anti-vaccination movement – particularly the argument that vaccinations lead to serious health complications (even death) in children – is a high-profile example of the *post hoc* fallacy in popular culture. Yes, children get vaccinated and, yes, some children have health complications whose first signs manifest themselves in early childhood. Despite the numerous scholarly studies which have debunked this myth, anti-vaxxers still contend that those countries with lowest infant mortality rates are those which vaccinate their children differently than those in the U.S. Although it could be possible that a foreign vaccination schedule contributes to the health of their infants, these arguments disregard the fact that there are numerous other factors – national health care models, access to medical treatment, and poverty rates – that contribute to the infant mortality rates, not only vaccinations. In this argument, the temporal sequence is the evidence of causality without considering the other variables which could also affect the result.

Errors of Relevance: Strawman Arguments

A strawman argument occurs when a speaker misrepresents, distorts, or doesn't fully acknowledge an opponent's argument in order to make their position, by contrast, look more attractive or persuasive. The metaphor of the fallacy's title says it all: straw dummies used for military or boxing training are much easier to beat up on than an actual opponent who can fight back and defend themselves. Consider:

Donna: "Those who want to leave the war in Iraq hate America."

Populist arguments like this one are fond of the strawman fallacy because it lumps all the competing views into a false category that becomes difficult to justify. If you accept the strawman, and still want to leave the war in Iraq, Donna has branded you as a traitor to your country. In fact, leaving the war in Iraq may have everything to do with love of country: you realize its economic impact, you don't want to put troops in harm's way, or you realize the war in Iraq is only further destabilizing the political picture in the Middle East. These arguments are tougher to engage with and require some research to refute. Donna prefers the easy road of the strawman.

Take the final presidential debate between Donald Trump and Hillary Clinton from UNLV's Thomas and Mack Arena on October 19, 2016. About half way through the event, moderator Chris Wallace posed a question to Clinton regarding her remarks on the issue of "open borders," citing a leaked transcript of a speech she made to a Brazilian bank in 2013. Wallace quoted a transcript of the speech:

> My dream is a hemispheric common market, with open trade and open borders, sometime in the future with energy that is as green and sustainable as we can get it, powering growth and opportunity for every person in the hemisphere.

Clinton was quick to offer clarification, remarking that the "open borders" she was referring to in that speech focused not on people but on the free movement of goods, capital, and energy across borders. Her response to Wallace continually highlighted the fact that "open borders" can mean different things, citing how "we trade more energy with our neighbors than we trade with the rest of the world combined." She concluded her allotted response time with a transparent admission, "I do want us to have an electric grid, an energy system that crosses borders. I think that will be great benefit to us." But once the topic of "open borders" was breached, so to speak, Trump pounced and went on the offensive. Rather than acknowledging the nuance and distinctions just made by Clinton with her definition of "open borders," Trump asserted:

> Under her plan, you have open borders. You would have a disaster on trade and you will have a disaster with your open borders…She wants open borders. People are going to pour into our country.

The logic behind Trump's strawman isn't easy to catch. Yes, she *does* want open borders and, yes, she *is* on record saying so. Is he wrong to make this assertion? Well, yes. Here's how. Before Wallace could even jump in, Trump seized on the vagueness in Clinton's language (the fact that "open borders" means multiple things, not just one) and broke down these distinctions to use it fallaciously to his advantage. On top of Clinton's ambiguous definition, add her generally liberal stance on immigration, and it became quite easy for Trump to misrepresent Clinton's view on immigration into something false but not entirely unbelievable either. Such is the danger of strawman arguments, especially in the context mass spectatorial politics. By saying that "open borders" encompasses the free movement of energy, capital, *and* people, Trump's simple message, no doubt, stuck in the brains of the 70 million viewers much more than Clinton's long and winding explanation. Given the fact that this debate, the final one before the November election, dealt such a devastating blow to Clinton's campaign on the defining issue of the election, it's interesting to consider how an unchecked fallacy may well have made the difference of who ended up in the Oval Office.

Errors of Relevance: Red Herring Fallacies

A herring is a small, silvery fish found in the waters of the North Atlantic Ocean. When herrings are smoked and salted, they turn dark red and emit a very strong smell. This fallacy's name derives from British folk-lore of escaping criminals who used these fish as a way to throw pursuing police dogs off their trail by diverting the dog's attention onto another path. Writers don't used smoked fish when committing this fallacy, but they do draw attention away from the issue at hand and send their listeners down another, irrelevant trail. A red herring fallacy, then, attempts to use misleading or irrelevant evidence to support a conclusion. Consider:

> *Ed*: "I would like to hear your ideas regarding student fundraising in order to curtail costs of prom tickets and graduation."
> *Fred*: "Student fundraising is great for class camaraderie. After all, isn't that what most of us remember from high school anyways? It's not the classes we took, or what we learned from homework, but rather the life-long relationships we made. All my groomsmen at my wedding were my high school pals, and I wouldn't trade their friendship for anything in the world."

When asked about his ideas for student fundraising, Fred shifts the discussion from the main topic (student fundraising) onto an explanation of a different issue (the lasting nature of high-school friendships). Maybe Fred is a sentimental guy; maybe Fred doesn't have a plan in place for fundraising and has been put on the spot. Whatever the case, his answer is irrelevant to the argument at hand.

Politicians not only regularly use this tactic but are actually coached on how to pull it off in the context of political debates. Brett O'Donnell, former debate coach to George W. Bush, John McCain, and Mitt Romney, calls this move "the pivot," a professionally coached Red Herring fallacy. O'Donnell describes the pivot as "a way of taking a question that might be on a specific subject, and moving to answer it on your own terms," a tactic he claims is used "better than 60 or 70 percent of the time." In *How Politicians Get Away Without Answering the Question* (2012), author Alix Spiegel describes an episode from a debate between presidential candidates George W. Bush and John Kerry. Bush was asked by the moderator what he would say to someone who has just lost their job. He began his answer by noting how he would "continue to grow our economy" and then meandered his way over other successful initiatives from his first term in office, such as his passing of the No Child Left Behind Act, an example of how he "went to Washington to solve problems." This is by no means a Republican phenomenon. During a town hall debate on December 2, 2011, a citizen asked President Obama, "What has your administration done to limit the availability of assault weapons?" In his response, he pivoted away from any talk about legislation, instead meandering into a talk of how we can "provide young people with opportunity" and "make sure our schools are working" to "catch issues before they get out of control." He ended with an exhortation that urged the increased role of "faith groups" in local communities. A Red Herring, indeed.

Not all the best examples of fallacious logic come from shoddy news reporting or political side-stepping. Sometimes, fallacies can be deliberately used as the source of humor, and John Landis's *Animal House* (1978) contains one of the best examples of a Red Herring fallacy used for comedic purposes. Towards the end of the film, Delta House, the film's eponymous fraternity, is put in front of the school's disciplinary board to receive punishment for their many infractions over the course of the film. Before the punishment is handed down, frat-boy Eric "Otter" Stratton speaks in Delta House's defense:

The issue here is not whether we broke a few rules or took a few liberties with our female party guests; we did. But you can't hold a whole fraternity responsible for the behavior of a few sick, perverted individuals. For if you do, then shouldn't we blame the whole fraternity system? And if the whole fraternity system is guilty, then isn't this an indictment of our educational institutions in general? I put it to you, Greg! Isn't this an indictment of our entire American society? Well, you can do what you want to us, but we're not going to sit here and listen to you bad-mouth the United States of America!

Follow his argument. He begins with an acknowledgment of the real reason he and his fraternity brothers are called in front of the board ("The issue here is not whether we broke a few rules or took a few liberties with our female party guests; we did") but quickly pivots into a litany of other irrelevant connections. He begins by accusing the disciplinary board of malfeasance, punishing Delta House and the whole fraternity system for the unruly behavior of a few individuals ("But you can't hold a whole fraternity responsible for the behavior of a few sick, perverted individuals. For if you do, then shouldn't we blame the whole fraternity system?"). Here, he turns the accusation back on the board, alleging they have mistaken a part for the whole (known as the fallacy of composition). From here, he digresses, widening the scope of the argument to include the educational system and all of American society ("if the whole fraternity system is guilty, then isn't this an indictment of our educational institutions in general? I put it to you, Greg! Isn't this an indictment of our entire American society?"). Otter builds up to the rhetorical climax ("Well, you can do what you want to us, but we're not going to sit here and listen to you bad-mouth the United States of America!") and the scene ends with the members of Delta House filing out of the courtroom, humming the national anthem, morally indignant that the disciplinary board would ever question the integrity of the United States.

Errors of Relevance: Faulty Analogies

An analogy is a comparison between two things, and this can be a very useful tactic to advance an argument in one of two ways. First, an analogy can render something complex in simpler terms, say, the way a factory runs in terms of a school. If your audience is not familiar with the way factories run but can draw from their firsthand experiences in schools, you will be able to make a difficult idea more accessible to an average audience without resorting to extended, technical discussions. Second, analogies can explain an abstract idea in concrete terms, say, the Trinitarian god in terms of water. Water, like God, can independently exist in three states – gas, liquid and solid – yet all of these are simply different manifestations of the same thing. Water, like God, is "three-yet-one" and "one-yet-three" in the same way that the Christian God is three beings who are one (Father, Son and Holy Spirit are all God) and one being who is three (Father, Son, and Holy Spirit are all separate, independent entities). The stronger the comparison, the more likely that an argument is persuasive.

The problem with analogies is that no comparison is perfect. All analogies involve analytic creativity to establish a clear linkage between the two objects of comparison. A faulty analogy occurs when a speaker distorts the terms of the analogy to falsely compare one thing to another. This comparison can be misleading, deceptive, or simply irrelevant to the larger argument. Consider:

> *Gail*: "Why should we invade that country? Let me explain it to you like this. What if you looked out the window and saw a $20 bill in the street? Wouldn't you go outside and take it?"

Gail's analogy has some surface similarities but once you dig a bit, the terms of this comparison break down pretty quickly. Invading a country is an act of aggression; finding $20 on the street is opportunistic. Invading a country will have huge cost in resources and human life; finding $20 on the street is a victimless, cash windfall. Invading a country is illegal by international law; finding $20 on the street has no legal ramifications. We could go on, but the point here is that once the distance in the comparison becomes too great for the analogy's explanatory value to offset, it will be branded as faulty and work against the integrity of the larger argument.

A popular (faulty) analogy that emerged in the wake of the September 11 attacks was the comparison of George W. Bush's presidency to the rise of Adolf Hitler. Proponents of this analogy point to the fact one month after Hitler was sworn in as the Chancellor of Germany, a domestic terror event – the burning of the Reichstag Parliament building – occurred in Berlin in February of 1933. William Shirer, author of *The Rise of Fall of the Third Reich* (2011), argues that this event was a false flag operation orchestrated by Hitler and the Nazi party to consolidate power and enact dictatorial measures. George W. Bush similarly experienced a domestic terror event only seven months into his presidency on September 11, 2001. On October 26, 2001, the controversial Patriot Act was rushed through Congress, legalizing the expansion of the President's authority while rolling back the civil liberties of private citizens. By latching onto these similarities, the analogy of George W. Bush-as-Adolf Hitler and the United States-as-Nazi Germany began to take off. But supporters of this analogy ignore some fundamental differences – differences which undermine the similarities – in this comparison. Let's see how this breaks down through another adapted example from Jarrod Atchison's *The Art of Debate* (2017).

Though historical research showed that Hitler had a direct role in the burning of the Reichstag, there is not one shred of hard evidence that George W. Bush had anything to do with the planning or execution of September 11. Just because another figure in history (Hitler) used a false flag even to consolidate power, that does not mean that every domestic terror event early on in a leader's term is part of a conspiracy to seize dictatorial authority.

In 1934, Hitler declared himself "Fuhrer," thus becoming the absolute dictator of Germany, declaring that the Nazi regime would last for 1000 years. The German democracy was disassembled, and the Third Reich was underway where Hitler remained its leader until his death on April 30, 1945. Despite some increase in the authority of his office, George W. Bush did not declare himself to be dictator, nor did he disassemble the institutions of democracy, the House of Representative or the Senate. Three years after the September 11 attacks, he freely submitted himself to a democratic election and only won by a slim margin (286 electoral votes to 251) over John Kerry. Bush also graciously stepped down after his second term, ceding the authority to Barack Obama, a member of the rival political party.

It's interesting to note that both Barack Obama and Donald Trump were themselves the focus of Hitler analogies during their presidencies. And it's worth noting that each of these three men were in office during the heyday of unrestricted public conversation on the Internet. The president-as-Hitler analogies that emerged largely from internet discourse are good test cases for Godwin's Law. Coined by American attorney and author Mike Godwin in 1990, the law states that "as an online discussion grows longer, the probability of a comparison involving Hitler approaches." That is, the longer an argument goes on, the greater the likelihood that someone will draw a comparison to Hitler and Nazi Germany. And, as the saying goes, when you bring up Hitler, you've lost the argument.

Errors of Relevance: Sentimental Appeals

In Chapters 2 and 9, we talked about the power that emotion (pathos) can play in arguments. Emotional arguments can be both persuasive and appropriate, but you can always have too much of good thing. Sentimental appeal fallacies target the heart of the audience in the hopes that they will forget to use their brains when appraising an argument. This fallacy distracts from the main issue at hand by introducing tangential or irrelevant emotional appeals as a diversionary tactic. Consider:

> *Henry*: "I understand that this tract of forest needs to be cleared for increased housing, but I can't approve this measure in good conscience, knowing that we will displace hundreds of chipmunks from their homes. How would you like it if a bulldozer showed up at your front door tomorrow morning?"

It's tough to know Henry's motives here. Perhaps he wants to divert the manpower used to clear forest into urban development (which would require further investigation on the part of the writer), but he is arguing for the stoppage of woodland clearing on emotional terms. So, in this case, he decides to use a sentimental appeal, hoping the mass displacement local chipmunk populations will be enough to stir up public support in favor of his position. But, sentimental appeals are not valid arguments, and listeners should be skeptical when they recognize one at use. They are often used when real facts and evidence are contentious or hard to come by.

In her first bid for the White House, Hillary Clinton returned to her alma mater, the all-female Wellesley College in Wellesley, MA, on one of her campaign stops in November of 2007. Knowing her audience, Clinton characterized her mission to be the first female president on emotional grounds:

In so many ways, this all-women's college prepared me to compete in the all-boys club of presidential politics…When I came to Wellesley, I never in a million years could have imagined I would one day return as a candidate for the presidency of the United States. If we don't stand for women's rights, we will never stand for our best values.

Though Clinton had many legitimate credentials, she's here attempting to gain support on emotional grounds. Her argument is not built on political viewpoints or proposed policy changes, but rather on a sympathetic image of herself as the lone underdog in a political world overflowing with men that finally needs a strong woman in office.

Scare tactics are a specific type of sentimental appeal that rely on stoking fear in the audience in order to coerce agreement to a position. Classical rhetoricians referred to this move as *argumentum ad baculum* ("argument to the stick"), and its intention from the ancient world to our own has remained consistent: scare people into doing what you want. In scare tactics, the speaker often creates suggestive scenarios that prey on the fears of an audience. The most effective scare tactics match the message to the anxieties and worries of the audience, though these appeals are often excessive and overblown when looked at with a balanced, logical eye.

> *Isabella*: "Having a home with no security system is no different than leaving your family for dead. It turns everyone you love into fodder for armed robbers, rapists and murderers. You may as well put a neon welcome sign on your front lawn. Get them protected! Buy Smith Home Security right now!"

Isabella, an apparent saleswoman, has a clear agenda (to sell security systems) but the approach used is fallacious. Aside from being guilty of falsely equivocating "no security system" to "leaving your family for dead," she fear-mongers up a scenario of constant threat and slyly characterizes break-ins as something that will always result in serious physical harm by choosing armed robbery, rape, and murder as her examples (most break-ins are only property crimes). She stirs the audience's fear and then provides an outlet. Just when the emotional response of the audience reaches its fever pitch, she offers a way to rid these threats: "Buy Smith Home Security right now!"

Let's consider the anti-vaccination argument again, but this time focusing on the fear-driven nature of its message. From outspoken celebrities touting their dangers to 2016 presidential candidate Jill Stein's call for increased regulation in their production, the validity of vaccines-as-reliable-medicine has been called into question under the influence of the "anti-vaxxer" campaign. Its argument puts fear to use in two ways. First, many anti-vaxxers oppose vaccinations on the grounds that it leads to autism and other brain disorders in young children. Though no federal law exists to have children vaccinated, all 50 states require children to be vaccinated against diphtheria, tetanus, and pertussis (the "DTaP" vaccine), polio (the "IPV" vaccine), and measles, mumps, and rubella (the "MMR" vaccine) before entering public school. In a nation that has been built upon the principles of freedom and liberty, it should come as no surprise that anti-vaxxers often characterize these required vaccinations for school as a disturbing example of governmental overreach into the personal lives of its citizens. And if other children are immunized – the thinking goes – the unvaccinated children should be at no risk. What these parents fail to realize, however, is that those who are already unfortunate enough to suffer from a weakened immune system now have an even higher chance of experiencing complications if they happen to contract diseases which can be kept in check by a simple vaccination. By refusing to take a very small risk in vaccinating their children, parents are putting other children with medical issues at risk of disease and even death. It's not a matter of personal belief. It is a moral imperative.

Second, anti-vaxxers base their dire claims which link vaccines to autism on a *single* scientific study from 1998 which overstates the role of the MMR vaccine's toxic ingredients – mercury, formaldehyde, aluminum – as the primary cause of these mental disorders. This "scientific" conclusion has been devastating to parental confidence in vaccination programs, resulting in eruptions of diseases (e.g. the 2014 measles outbreak in the western United States) thought to be eradicated long ago. Though the claims of this study have been widely reported, its conclusions have been refuted outright by thousands of peer-reviewed research studies, and the fraudulent study itself was actually retracted in 2010. The doctor behind its publication was found guilty of ethical, medical, and scientific misconduct and was stripped of his license. The bogus study has been called by D.K. Flaherty in a 2011 issue of *Ann Pharmacother*, "the most damaging medical hoax of the last 100 years." Nonetheless, the anti-vaxxers still keep the frightening conclusion drawn from this single study at the center of their position, an uneasy combination of scare tactics and hasty generalizations.

Errors of Vacuity: Appeals to Ignorance

Everyone has had to make a decision in the face of the unknown; sometimes you just have to make an educated guess on the available information. We may fall back on our past experience to help us weigh our options against a field of probabilities, but there comes a point when a speaker crosses the line from educated guess into an appeal-to-ignorance argument. Whereas educated guesses leave room based on principles of probability, appeal-to-ignorance fallacies derive certain conclusions from an unknown or missing premise, essentially asserting that whatever has not been proven false must be true, or vice versa. Consider:

> *Jeff:* "No one can prove the Loch Ness Monster exists, so it must not exist."

Jeff's conclusion that the Loch Ness Monster doesn't exist is derived from the absence (or vacuity) of evidence to the contrary. It doesn't necessarily follow that the monster does not exist (perhaps he just hasn't been found yet?), though the enthymeme-like feel of this statement makes it appear as if this conclusion comes from a logically exhaustive process. Henry's argument could be easily reversed and still contain the same logical flaw: "No one can prove the Loch Ness Monster doesn't exist, so it must exist." This fallacy has become the go-to method of monster hunters, ghost chasers, and conspiracy theorists, all of whom assert their conclusions based off the lack of evidence to the contrary. Check out History Channel's *Ancient Aliens*, a show whose use of the appeal-to-ignorance is so rampant that it could easily be renamed *Appeal-To-Ignorance: The Television Series*.

Many modern scholars have taken up the appeal-to-ignorance fallacy, critiquing it as a bunk scientific method that poses as reliable science. J.A. Cover's *Philosophy of Science: The Central Issues* (1998) describes the appeal-to-ignorance as "pseudoscience" or "statements, beliefs, or practices that are claimed to be scientific and factual in the absence of evidence gathered." But in a culture where science is often regarded as the highest form of authority, arguments that masquerade with the *appearance* of this authority can be incredibly persuasive and damaging. During the

"Red Scare" of the 1950's, this fallacy could be found just by walking out your front door. This period in American history is best remembered for its "Communist Hysteria" in which thousands of U.S. citizens were accused of being Communists or Communist sympathizers with little to no evidence. Senator Joseph McCarthy became the poster boy for this type of appeal-to-ignorance justice, so much so that the term "McCarthyism" appeared in the general lexicon to describe any accusation without proper regard for evidence. In one case, when asked about a particular individual's connection to Communism, Senator McCarthy testified thus:

> I do not have much information on this except the general statement of the agency...that there is nothing in the files to disprove his Communist connections.

See how the illogic of the appeal-to-ignorance logic works here? Since he can't disprove his connections to Communism, he must be Communist. Playwright Arthur Miller picked up on the bunk logic of this period of American history in his play *The Crucible* (1953), allegorizing the appeal-to-ignorance zeitgeist of the Red Scare into the context of the Salem Witch Trials of 1692–1693, another terrible period in American history depicting evidence-free accusations. Even in contemporary culture, the appeal-to-ignorance has been used to justify all sorts of questionable decisions. In 2003, Colin Powell addressed the United Nation about the United States invasion of Iraq on the grounds that Saddam Hussein had weapons of mass destruction that once posed a threat to our country. He said:

> This [the lack of evidence for the weapons of mass destruction] is all part of a system of hiding things and moving things out of the way and making sure they have left nothing behind.
>
> If you go a little further into this message, and you see the specific instructions from headquarters: "After you have carried out what is contained in this message, destroy the message because I don't want anyone to see this message." "OK, OK." Why? Why?
>
> This message would have verified to the inspectors that they have been trying to turn over things. They were looking for things. But they don't want that message seen, because they were trying to clean up the area to leave no

evidence behind of the presence of weapons of mass destruction. And they can claim that nothing was there. And the inspectors can look all they want, and they will find nothing.

Powell bases much of this argument on the fact the Saddam Hussein *once* possessed weapons of mass destruction in 1980's and 1990's. The UN Weapons Inspectors found no evidence these weapons were still there in 2003, but Powell concludes that the lack of WMDs is only proof that Iraq, indeed, still has them and is hiding them from prying eyes. Later intelligence confirmed that Hussein had possession of no such weapons, but this single appeal-to-ignorance fallacy set into motion more than a decade and a half military involvement in the Middle East. The indefinite detainment of terror suspects in Guantanamo Bay, Cuba and other US black sites across the globe have been justified along similar lines: we can't prove that this individual isn't affiliated with terror organizations, so we'll assume that he is.

Errors of Vacuity: False Dichotomies

A dichotomy separates things into a set of binary options, and people like it when life is simple and orderly. Is this decision good or bad? Is that painting beautiful or ugly? Should I vote Republican or Democrat? A false dichotomy fallacy preys on this desire for orderliness by reducing a complex issue, which has many sides and possibilities, to just two polarized extremes. At best, false dichotomies reflect faulty or missing research which reflect a genuine belief that the problem at hand can be solved with a pair of "either/or" solutions. At worst, false dichotomies illustrate manipulation of evidence where a speaker may intentionally oversimplify an issue to get their way (when one of the intermediate possibilities may be a better solution). Consider:

> *Kyle*: "Larry, I know you're unsatisfied with how much playing time you've been getting lately. Either quit the team or shut up and stay on the bench!"

Kyle may be trying to help, but he's offering up a false dichotomy as the solution to the problem of playing time. There are, in fact, many workable solutions, not just two, to solve Larry's need for increased playing time: spend more time in the gym, study the team's playbook more closely, work harder at practice, speak to the coach privately, and so forth. Larry could end up quitting the team or shutting up and staying on the bench, but this conclusion should only be arrived when all of the possible solutions have been examined and evaluated.

False dichotomies, like we've seen with other fallacies, can be very dangerous when deployed in the wrong context to a susceptible audience. Contemporary politics brims with examples of this divisive "you're either with us or against us" rhetoric:

> *Hillary Clinton* (during an interview on *CBS Evening News with Dan Rather* – September 13, 2001): "Every nation has to either be with us, or against us. Those who harbor terrorists, or who finance them, are going to pay a price."
>
> *George W. Bush* (during a speech to a joint session of Congress – September 20, 2001): "Every nation, in every region, now has a decision to make. Either you are with us, or you are with the terrorists."
>
> *Sarah Palin* (during a speech criticizing Republicans who didn't support Donald Trump – June 24, 2016): "You're either with us or you're against us. That gang, they call themselves Never hashtag, whatever, I just call 'em Republicans Against Trump, or RAT for short."

What about neutrality? What about settlement through diplomacy? What about coming together instead of factionalism and division? Those other options are thrown into the vacuum, disappearing altogether from the conversation. False dichotomies perpetuate the ugliest elements of factional politics that separates individuals into groups. Often, these groups become essentialized – given a collective identity poised in dia-metric opposition – in the eyes of the other based on those divisions. Such hostility is fertile ground for all sorts of atrocities, and it's a shame when shoddy logic gets in the way of productive politics and sound social policy.

Errors of Vacuity: Dogmatism, Circular Reasoning, Self-Sealing Arguments

"Dogma" is a set of authoritative principles that are perceived as unquestion-ably true. A dogmatic fallacy occurs when the correctness of an argument is assumed to be beyond question, essentially fusing the claim and the evidence of an argument into one amorphous, logical blob. Dogmatic speakers reason along the lines of "I am right because I am right," which is why this fallacy is also sometimes referred to as circular reasoning. This spatial metaphor is nice visualization of how bogus this logic works: the claim *is* the evidence and the evidence *is* the claim. What's missing is any type of real proof which leads a listener *from* the evidence *to* the conclusion. Consider.

> *Mike*: "The death penalty is immoral because there is no way it can ever be morally justified."

What's the claim? The death penalty is immoral. What's the evidence? It cannot be morally justified (i.e. it's immoral). Dogmatic statements run into what logicians refer to as tautological errors or saying the same thing twice in different words. Speakers who believe so strongly in the correctness of their position will often deploy self-sealing arguments, a special type of dogmatism where the argument is worded in a way that cannot possibly be refuted no matter how you answer. Consider:

> *Nicolette*: "High schools need more law and order in the hallways to perform more effectively."

This argument cannot be refuted since it leaves no room for any method of reliable testing to show either its truth or its falsity. Its wording encompasses both outcomes. If the school performs more highly, this affirms that an increase the increase in disciplinary measures on students has done the job. If the school maintains its low performance or even drops, all the more reason to increase the law and order in the hallways until the performance rating reaches the desired outcome.

In the first few decades of the 20th century, the battle for the master narrative of human origin was on, and The Scopes Trial of 1925 became the public battlefield in which the two chief ideologies of the time – Creationism vs. Evolution – would duke it out, using dogmatic fallacies as the weapon of choice. The debate still rages today as to which ideology should lay claim to the greatest question of human existence, "Where do we come from?," and there's been little flexibility from either side. Evolutionists are fond of the (disparaging) dogmatic argument against Creationists that goes something like this: "The only reality is the material world so must necessarily come from something here in the material world." The argument is circular – reality is material, so we must also be material – and modern evolutionary theory dogmatically assumes that no divine being every played a role in creation. Creationists simply reverse this argument to suit their ideological position, saying something like the following, "Since everything in our world comes from something before it, there must necessarily be a first cause in the universe, which we can refer to as God." Like the evolution argument, the Creationist position ultimately asserts its conclusion (God exists) based on equivalent evidence (because God has to exist). Logically speaking, Creationism and Evolution are not as diametrically opposed as they think. Maybe one day this question of our ultimate origins will be settled, but in the meantime, there is lesson to be learned about dogmatism, the unquestionable "rightness" of an ideological position.

Errors of Induction: Hasty Generalizations

Induction, if you remember from earlier chapters, is the logical move from evidence to a conclusion, and an audience should be able to plainly see links between. When you "jump to conclusions," you make a generalization on the basis of an insufficient number of examples to reasonably draw the inference, and this error of induction is what's known as a hasty generalization. Just because you may have seen something in one or two instances does not mean that it is true in all cases. Prejudices, stereotypes, and superstitions are common examples of this fallacy in action that we see all around us in our day-to-day activities. Consider

> *Owen*: "When I drove through New York City last summer, I was cut off, honked at, and nearly driven off the road by two rowdy drivers. New York drivers are terrible."

Some New Yorkers may very well be bad drivers, but Owen is guilty of hasty generalizing this conclusion based off only a single instance. To accept this claim as reasonable, there needs to be a greater amount of empirical evidence than merely an isolated incident.

Speakers use this fallacy for a whole host reasons – some intentional, some unintentional – but this strategy is central to the marketing tactics of many major retailers. Let's take T.J. Maxx as an example. This clothing store is best known for selling designer clothing at generally lower prices than other major department stores (in fact, it has more than 1,000 stores, making it one of the largest clothing retailers in the United States). Sometimes consumers are surprised when they enter a store to see (often at the front entrance) a designer dress selling for $75 that normally retails at $300. Many of the items in the store go for typical retail price, but T.J. Maxx will sell the dress at a loss (what's known in marketing jargon as a "loss leader") in hopes of getting you to hastily generalize that since this dress is sold at a deep discount, all of T.J. Maxx's products must be a bargain. Clothing retailers are far from the only companies that create conditions for consumers to make errors of induction. Stores that specialize in sporting goods, electronics, home goods, groceries, nutrition supplements (really, you name it) all have their own version of a "loss leader," hoping to acquire you as a regular customer via bad logic.

Errors of Induction: Slippery Slopes

As its metaphorical title indicates, a slippery slope fallacy suggests that a minor cause or inconsequential action will touch off an irreversible chain of events that lead to dire consequences. Of course, any prediction of how a chain of events will unfold involves some guesswork, and even meticulous methods can still yield false predictions. What separates this from a slippery slope is that the fallacy tends to characterize the path from initial cause to final effect in a grossly oversimplified way (and here is where the breakdown of induction enters into the mix). Slippery slopes often ignore the many peripheral factors that could alter the chain of events they describe. Consider:

> *Paul*: "Capital punishment erodes our respect for human life. By making this the law of the land, it won't be long before murder will be legal."

The execution of criminals has been used by almost every civilization at every point in human history, but no society has ever legalized citizen-on-citizen murder on the basis of state-sanctioned capital punishment. You may well believe that capital punishment does disrespect human life – and there are a lot of solid arguments to support this – but it's a big leap to say that murder will be normalized in day-to-day affairs based on the highly-limited usage of capital punishment for society's most horrible offenders.

As we mentioned before, The Scopes Trial, or The State of Tennessee vs. Scopes, was a 1925 legal case in which a high school biology teacher, John Scopes, was accused of violating the state law which prohibited the teaching of evolution. Clarence Darrow, the defense attorney, used the following slippery slope fallacy in court as an attempt to illustrate the danger of restricting the teaching of evolution in school:

> If today you can take a thing like evolution and make it a crime to teach it in the public school, tomorrow you can make it a crime to teach it in the private schools, and the next year you can make it a crime to teach it to the hustings or in the church. At the next session, you may ban books and the newspapers. Soon you may set Catholic against Protestant and Protestant against Protestant and try to foist your own religion upon the minds of men. If you can do one, you can do the other.

Darrow argues along the lines of the following logic: if we allow A to happen, then B will happen, then C, then D, leading up to X, Y, Z. Essentially, he says that if we restrict the teaching of ideas in one location, who is to say where we draw the line? First, we'll censor the public schools, which opens the door to private schools and churches. But, why stop there? Let's censor books and newspapers that disseminate *any* new idea. And if we ban books, we can never be tolerant of competing ideas, leading to religious strife and, thus, imploding the very structure of American society. The censorship of evolution, Darrow argues, is the flashpoint of this disaster scenario. Looking at this logically, it seems unlikely that the outcome of this one trial would have ruined American society in the way Darrow describes.

Being able to recognize these fallacies will be doubly beneficial to your daily life, both in and out of school. In school, knowing how to circumvent bad logic in written and oral arguments will give you a leg up on those around you. Though things may not end up perfectly, if you can begin to write and think while remaining mindful of bad logic's corrosive effect on an argument, you're well on your way to producing thoughtful and productive argumentative discourse. Outside of school, knowledge of these fallacies will equip you with a set of powerful tools to engage head-on with the arguments of others, letting you deconstruct bad arguments with good logic, so as not to be mindlessly led to dangerous places. Knowledge of fallacious logic is essential to civic responsibility. As Thomas Jefferson said at the dawn of the Republic, "An educated citizenry is a vital requisite for our survival as a free people."

CHAPTER TWELVE

ARGUMENTATION – ADDITIONAL MODELS

I n the last few chapters, we've talked about the history of argument, the basics of argument construction in classical and contemporary contexts, and errors in reasoning to avoid at all costs. In essence, we've defined the principles of skillful writing in a variety of real-world contexts. Now, we'll take a look at these principles in operation within the focused setting of essay writing for school. And whether you draw from Aristotle or Toulmin, Cicero or Kroll, the basic parts of an argument don't really change. Every argument, in one way or another, asserts a claim and presents evidence to justify it within a selected pattern of organization.

A major difference between real-world argument and school assignments is that the point of *stasis* – the heart of the controversy – is often defined for you in the assignment's prompt. Some arguments may put you in a defensive posture, offering a proposition that you must defend, challenge, or qualify. Other arguments may require you to assess an argument in terms of degree; the prompt acknowledges a controversy exists, but you are called to say something about the extent to which you agree or disagree. You may define a term, arguing for a way a particular concept ought to be understood in wider world. You may do some combinations of these, but you must ultimately forward, counter, or qualify a claim in response to a task.

Once you've decided on the claim, you'll need to decide on a pattern of organization and here you'll have some choices from Chapters 9 and 10. You may choose the hierarchical pattern of the Classical model where each sub-topic sets up the next in order to carry the reader easily along to the conclusion. You may structure your argument around an extrapolation of a warrant, developing your paper along the lines of Toulmin's model. You may, yet, arrange your argument in more of a Kroll-like horizontal fashion, where a coordinative structure aims to find compromise, rather than victory, in the discourse of the controversy.

Finally, you'll need examples. Examples address the "How do you know?" question and it's here where the quality of your choices will determine the persuasiveness of your argument. The prompt should define what's in and out of bounds, but most of the time you'll be asked to draw upon your reading, observation, and/or experience to build your case. You need not feel that you have to use all three – shoehorning categories of evidence into an argument make it feel forced – but the best arguments contain a judicious mixture of distinct types of evidence to appeal to as many different readers as possible.

Presented in a similar Writing as Product style found in Chapter 7, the following chapter contains four argumentative essays: two standalone prompts, one prompt based on a short reading, and another prompt based on a pair of short readings. Each essay is accompanied by a string of marginal annotations which highlight the argumentative strategies the author has employed. You should hear echoes of all the preceding chapters inside these writings. They contain a clear argumentative structure, but they don't sacrifice readability and engagement for logic. They are equal parts argumentative and rhetorical, a guiding principle of this unit and one you should follow in your own work. The prompts are meant to represent a typical swath of argument tasks in academic settings and, should you ever be asked to compose an essay along these lines, these examples should serve as useful models.

The Role of Homework in Education

In her book *Doing School: How We Are Creating a Generation of Stressed-Out, Materialistic, and Miseducated Students*, author and professor Denise Clark Pope argues most students "do school" – go through the motions of daily school procedures – instead of learning and enjoying time spent in school. She cites homework as one of the largest mitigating factors in this negative experience.

Pope is an outspoken advocate for a reduction of homework that students receive. Her work has inspired "no homework" policies in both public and private schools across the United States, as well as policies which limit nightly homework to as little as 15 minutes per subject.

In a well-written essay, develop a position on the strict limiting, or elimination, of homework in high school. Use appropriate evidence from your reading, experience, or observations to support your argument.

Example Essay

Most kids hate homework: it takes away from nap schedules and Netflix watching, from time with friends and family. It's a safe bet to say that most teens would like homework to disappear altogether, but homework is, in many ways, the cornerstone of the learning process. No doubt, some teachers drown their students in vocabulary lists, chapter reviews, and mindless worksheets, but when homework is a well-designed and purposeful extension of what's going on in the classroom – an independent performance task that engages a student's higher order thinking – it is useful on a personal and academic level. The elimination of homework should be off the table for all schools; even to limit it to an arbitrary number like 15 minutes per subject is unnecessarily damaging to both the student and to the learning process.

> The author opens by acknowledging a commonplace (homework occupies a large chunk of out-of-school time) but is quick to qualify the definition that the essay will use when referring to this term.

> The author develops his thesis over a series of sentences in the opening paragraph. The attention to detail provides clarity and focus to the essay's main assertion: homework's positive effects of "on personal and academic levels."

Homework does more than merely help a student grasp class work more completely; it can teach skills that are directly transferable to life beyond school walls. Whether they know it or not, students gain several simple skills each time they sit down to do work at home – among them responsibility, time management, and perseverance. Students learn responsibility from homework because it is their duty to get their homework done in order to maintain a strong academic record. Since most homework is factored into a course's overall grade,

> The author opens his discussion with an implied refutation of the cliché question about school work: "when am I ever going to need this?" The author argues homework teaches life skills transferable beyond school.

students learn accountability for their choices should they choose *Call of Duty* over Calculus. Related to this are time management and perseverance. Homework teaches students to organize their time, prioritize tasks, and make a plan to accomplish all that's asked of them. The stick-to-itiveness that homework demands builds an unmistakable grit

> The author's leading body paragraph sets up the deductive pattern of organization. The author has described the broad benefits of homework first to then show how these transfer directly into academic settings.

that can be applied to academic and personal pursuits: getting a cover letter just right, finishing an expense report for tomorrow's presentation, writing a respectful eulogy. Like chemistry or rhetoric, many of these tasks aren't necessarily "fun," but all of them are purpose-driven, if unglamorous, tasks that require the iron willpower and attention to detail that years of meaningful homework can build.

Some school districts have tried to put strict, and arbitrary, time limits on the amount of homework per night, but purposeful work and their associated academic gains cannot simply be packaged and parceled out in 15-minute units. Research argues that in order to make one year's gains in reading, stu-

> The author relies on several logical appeals, citing research which describes yearly academic gains and how the elimination of homework outside of school will limit these annual gains.

dents need to read for at least 40 minutes a day. What happens to those gains if schools eliminate or limit homework? (And mind you, those are only the "normal" or expected gains of an academic year, the ones that ensure students don't fall completely behind. If students are not engaging meaningfully with work outside of school – whether it's reading, science, or math – they will certainly never be able to perform *above* grade level.)

How can anyone ever become engaged in literature if they only read fifteen minutes a day? Imagine

> The author gets increasingly specific, now confining his argument of homework to a specific subject.

a reluctant reader's 15 minutes with *Hamlet*: Will Claudius confess to King Hamlet's murder and come clean to the court of Denmark? He's going into the confessional booth. Here it comes, "I stand in pause where I shall first begin and…" Time's up. Maybe we'll find out tomorrow. But wait, it's the weekend. And we drop on Monday. Next Tuesday we'll find out for sure. Tuesday's here. Wait, what is he confessing to again? I'm confused. The disjuncture in the learning process caused by homework's absence is not just confined to reading. Imagine

> The author switches style on the fly, moving from a traditional argumentative voice to internal monologue. The interior thoughts of a student illustrate just how frustrating school can be without the continuity provided by homework.

trying to become fluent in Italian, or grasp the principles of velocity, or parse the nuances of slavery from the Lincoln-Douglass debates. Without the independent practice that homework demands, it simply can't be done.

Pope and her anti-homework proponents make valid points: for many high-achieving students, time spent on excessive homework leads to stress, physical health problems, a lack of balance, and alienation from the teenage social scene. Most of those symptoms can be

> The author concedes the legitimacy of some anti-homework concerns but remains steadfast in his pro-homework position.

avoided with good time management and organization, yet critics of homework still assert that there are better ways for students to spend their after-school hours than completing worksheets – perhaps learning to play an instrument or participating in clubs and sports. This argument is misguided on two counts. First, authentic homework ought to be a purposeful

> The author builds their refutation by disassembling common counterarguments. The author does so by identifying a strawman fallacy (the false characterization of all homework as mindless worksheets) and arguing that busyness caused by homework can actually be a healthy stress.

extension of learning, not merely worksheets to be mindlessly completed. Second, why should activities come at the expense of homework? Plenty of students can get both done successfully and are better for it. Busy schedules are not a terrible thing. As I once learned during a session of science homework, "bodies in motion stay in motion, while bodies are rest stay at rest." A well-managed homework plan will keep students in "constructive motion" and continue to inculcate the discipline and time-management skills discussed earlier in this essay.

> The author closes on the same commonplace note upon which the essay opened. He concludes with a reassertion of his thesis that even if you don't find value in the subject of homework, there is lasting value in the work skills used to complete it.

None of the arguments against homework outweigh its overall benefits to the student. Doing homework goes hand in hand with being a good student, but also helps to cultivate responsible individuals and productive workers. There will always be nights where students will curse their math homework, but once the cursing has settled, that homework has taught them much more than just math.

Online Over-Exposure and Its Civic Implications

In Steven Johnson's 2009 article, "In Praise of Oversharing," he discusses the virtues of living our lives publicly in online spaces and how "oversharing, in a strange way, turns out to be a civic good." In a well-written essay, develop a position on Johnson's claim that sharing our personal lives online can serve a valuable purpose in our society. Use appropriate evidence from your reading, observation, and experience.

Example Essay

Ever since social networks hit the scene in the early 2000s, the world has embraced them with open arms. Twitter, Tumblr, Facebook, and Snapchat are just a few high-profile spaces where individuals interact virtually. For better or worse,

> The author opens with a brief historical contextualization of the argument's central topic into some well-known contemporary examples.

many people rely on these websites to stay connected with those close (or not so close) to them. But, is this type of public exposure a good idea? Well, it depends. It's easy to deride social media for its promotion of "me" culture, but such a position is uncharitable to the good that social media can foster among its community of users. Sharing one's personal information online can perform a public service – inspire creative collaboration, offer support, and even save lives – so long as each sharer knows what's at stake each time they hit post.

All sharing is not created equal, and it must be examined along the lines of intention, content, and forums that people use to "overshare." This draws a distinction between the types of oversharing that perform a public service and the types that are unhelpful at best and pernicious at worst. Intention matters. There is nothing wrong with those who want to reveal their authentic selves online. This well-intentioned emotional openness can reveal people's vulnerabilities, fostering a culture of honesty and sincerity that meaningful conversation requires. The line between what's appropriate and what's not is nebulous, but "mindful" or "intentional" oversharing can lead to an establishment of trust and faith in fellow human beings. Facebook CEO Mark Zuckerberg predicted that each year, online users will share twice as much information as we did the year before. As a result, people will be more comfortable and more likely to trust one another – if their oversharing is presented in a spirit of authentic openness.

> The author's argument is driven by the tri-partite division of the thesis ("inspire creative collaboration, offer support, and even save lives") while remaining considerate of the claim's central qualifier ("so long as each sharer knows what's at stake each time they hit 'post'").

> This essay goes beyond general commentary and provides a compelling discussion of the topic. For example, the author's evidence largely deals in specifics. References to Mark Zuckerberg, YouTube's co-founder Chad Hurley, Reddit, Tumblr, and Twitter are among the author's specific details used to corroborate the thesis.

This type of oversharing can create a safe environment for people to grow and flourish among like-minded individuals. Look no further than the front page of the internet, Reddit. Users can join any number of established Sub-Reddit communities according to their interests, where they can post content, read the posts of others, and interact with users from all over the globe. Users can even form Sub-Reddits of their own, creating a virtual space for like-minded users to come together on just about any topic a user can dream up. These self-selecting forums promote a helpful level of "oversharing" that allows users to create genuine communities. Reddit's administrators have devoted a substantial amount of resources to moderate and limit the site's most toxic users, including banning Sub-Reddits deemed "hateful." Site developers have also instituted "karma" points for activity on the site (which can subsequently be used to upgrade to Reddit Gold accounts) to encourage positive and productive collaborations among its users. This philosophy of positive personal sharing promoted by Reddit has caught on. It is the #11 most-visited site in the world, registering half-a-billion visits per month.

To some, sharing personal information on the internet is vital to a sense of self and personal identity. The internet – organized into various communities, forums and chat rooms – can be a wonderful place to go for those seeking empathy when they need it the most.

> This paragraph endorses some of the benefits of sharing but is very careful to qualify all of these statements by with condition of "the content you share matters."

The content you share matters. Consider the loneliness and dread that must accompany a diagnosis of terminal lymphoma. It's tough to picture anything more existentially jarring, but then imagine happening upon a blog that details the writer's inner struggles with this very same disease. The fear and loneliness are suspended for a moment as the reader connects with someone who understands, in ways that family and friends cannot, what this diagnosis means.

In this case, sharing what many would consider to be the most private of moments has very positive consequences on the community created among its online readership. Readers, in turn, can share valuable advice, form ad-hoc support groups and even catalogue archives which could help future patients who stumble upon the blog at

> The author, in deductive fashion, specifies the broader comments from the previous paragraph. He now focuses on the effect positive sharing can have within specific social groups and sub-cultures.

a future point in time. The internet can be a wonderful place to find solace among those who struggle with the same hardships. In some cases, posting this kind of content is a matter of life and death. Think about the vulnerable/minority groups who find solace in virtual communities when there is nowhere else to turn. In a world where LGBT+ kids commit suicide at four times the rate of non-queer youths (and Questioning kids commit suicide at twice the rate), sharing personal info and building a real community can be a literal lifeline. Johnson's argument of oversharing as performing a much-needed civic duty is best illustrated here; that is, there will always people out there willing to give advice and show support, so long as you share your own story on the internet.

However, it would be irresponsible to detail the "good" of public sharing without addressing its potential dangers. First, there is the misstep of making public what should remain private. Hurt feelings from being grounded after coming home an hour past curfew is no reason to tell your 900 Facebook friends and 650 Twitter followers about how "stupid" your parents are. Odds are, many of these 900 friends are no friends at all: you've met them once or twice, some are probably friends of a friend, or even a family member of a friend. Whatever the relationship, these folks probably don't need access to your every thought and certainly don't need real time updates on every detail of your life. Privacy, where one's personal information is protected from public scrutiny, is a right afforded to citizens by the US Constitution, though users are increasingly forfeiting this right by publishing their inner life for the world to see. We would do well to remember that privacy is a constitutionally protected right for a reason. A teenager venting about her parents to 900 people might want to consider that it's not just her own right to privacy she is forfeiting – it is her parent's right to privacy, too. In a world where advocacy and human rights groups spend months and millions in court in the name of the Fourth Amendment, it is folly to give it up so quickly for the brief glow of online attention.

> The author, in this paragraph in the next, addresses a competing point of view. He doesn't set this up as a traditional refutation, but instead describes these viewpoints in a way that makes a reader consider nuances of the topic.

> The author draws on the authority of a foundational US document as a justification for the argument of this paragraph.

This "brief glow" can be pernicious. Consider the uptick in self-centered behaviors since the explosion of social media. Social media is sometimes derided as facilitator of "selfie culture," a zeitgeist captured best by YouTube co-founder Chad Hurley, "Everyone, in the back of his mind, wants to be a star." In a pre-web world, fame was once reserved for those who demonstrated nobility and virtue beyond the bounds of normal men: a Marcus Aurelius, a William Shakespeare, a Sigmund Freud. In our contemporary world saturated by outlets

> The author uses a wide-swatch of evidence in this paragraph: references to historical, contemporary, and pop-culture figures; quotations from authoritative sources; causal reasoning.

for public exposure, fame is often reduced to its lowest common denominator: being noticed. Laughing in a Chewbacca mask, lip-syncing in a car, or landing a flipped water bottle is sometimes all it takes to vault oneself into public conversation and internet superstardom. Such fame typically breeds more attempts to be noticed, often one-upping the vulgarity and shallowness of what came before.

Of course, part of oversharing responsibly has to do with common sense, particularly about the decision to keep aspects of one's interior world private while making others available for public consumption. Negativity is inevitable among large groups of people, but there are a few criteria to observe that will minimize unwanted ridicule when posting. Users can edit out certain bits and highlight others – not from a position of dishonesty, but with a mindset of maintaining control over what other users see or don't see. Posting with the axiom of presenting oneself with "qualities you'd like to be recognized for" should help oversharers link up the right kind of audience for their posted content. Online privacy (a phrase that's only partially oxymoronic) can still be upheld by transferring basic elements of face-to-face interaction into cyber-communities: tact, decorum, and mutual respect.

It has never been easier to make new friends than it is today. Anyone with an internet connected laptop can link themselves up with a community of like-minded individuals, letting them find research partners, new friends, or even husbands and wives. Though headlines often focus on the negative usage of online tools, there is much to be said for its productive and positive uses. If users share positive information or ideas, they may inspire others half a world away from just a push of a button. And when the whole world is watching, each user must put his or her best foot forward each day.

> The author offers a brief conclusion which sums up the essay's main idea: the internet is a great source of purposeful communication, but like any powerful technology it has its share of both promise and peril.

Are Kids Too Coddled?

In Frank Bruni's essay "Are Kids Too Coddled?," the author argues that children and teens alike are overprotected in ways that ultimately may harm their ability to feel and be successful. In a well-written essay, defend, qualify, or refute Bruni's assertion that youth are too coddled – and that this coddling has a negative impact on them.

Example Argument

In his article "Are Kids Too Coddled?," Frank Bruni articulates a growing national frustration against coddled children, those who are overprotected and indulged at home and at school. Just about everyone has their own personal horror story with this topic: bloated honor rolls, rotating sports captains, participation trophies, just to name a few. This type of protection against any perceived setback or disappointment comes from a good place – parents and school leaders *do* sincerely want the best for these kids – but its effect displaces its intentions by decreasing natural motivation and even debilitating children whose learned helplessness makes it difficult to meet life's challenges. Such a practice will inhibit a child's ability to ultimately be a successful, autonomous, and self-reliant individual.

> The author argues for a position in relation to Bruni's claim while outlining several limits to his own claim, thus effectively demonstrating the use of both qualifiers and exceptions.

Coddling – overprotection of a child – particularly inhibits adolescents from experiencing the formative nature of figuring-it-out-on-your-own, something necessary for one's personal and moral development. Failure is increasingly seen as intolerable, something which children must be guarded against by any means necessary. Consequently, effort – just trying – is often conflated with accomplishment and expectation of unearned accomplishment leads to entitlement. In my school, I see students increasingly expect that teachers will diagnose the situation, swoop in, and offer safety and supports at the first sign of a stumble. Such an expectation outsources personal responsibility onto the teacher and limits the development of skills in self-advocacy. Higher education, that great transitional period from childhood

> The author identifies a false equivalency in a common counterargument to his position that forwards his own point of view.

> The author expands their central thesis into other contexts, thus expanding the scope of his argument while adding new dimensions to the original topic.

to adulthood, is sadly not immune to this either. In a study conducted at the University of Miami, nearly half of incoming freshmen expected that their professor should reach out to them if they are having trouble in the course, and approximately one quarter believed their professor should keep track of how well they are keeping up with assignments and following the syllabus. A staggering 96% of students believed their grades will be as good or higher than high school. Numbers this high suggest that the vast majority of students have never had to struggle to achieve good grades or success of any kind. Is not failure an acceptable byproduct of reaching higher and digging deeper?

Children learn more when they are pushed outside their comfort zone. By adults assisting students through this discomfort – rather than coddling them to avoid it in the first place – they will develop collateral skills of stress and time management, perseverance, and a greater sense of independence. Advanced Placement classes at my school are a good example of this. A few years ago, AP courses changed from a highly selective program for the grade's top few in a given discipline to a democratized credential grab for students, many of whom barely had even marginal interest in the subject matter. Not only did the curriculum's rigor and pace need to be downshifted, but many students expected that they would receive a good grade in the course because they were now "AP students." What's more, at the first sign of a grade slipping beneath the satisfactory level, I'd often hear grumbling among the teachers about how their inbox would light up with one parental complaint after another, laying the blame at the foot of the instructor (not the student who blew off the rigorous responsibilities of the college-level workload). As a student who works hard – and doesn't always receive top marks for that work – I became frustrated when "just showing up" became tantamount to "hard work." Hard work builds character as well as success; if you coast rather than struggle, you'll never achieve half of what you're capable of. This principle is transferrable to just about every context, from art to sports to school. Ultimately, it's up to the student to work

> The author uses anecdotal evidence of his own experiences with Advanced Placement courses but only after it has been properly contextualized by the previous paragraph.

> The author works deductively in this paragraph, starting from the specific anecdote and then generalizing a broader point in the final few sentences.

hard, learn from mistakes, and practice, practice, practice. After all, it's "practice (not parents) that makes perfect."

Those who coddle probably wouldn't term it as such, but they no doubt presume that protecting children from feelings of inadequacy will result in increased confidence and success down the road. This is the "chicken-or-the-egg"
question for young adult development.

> The author bridges his argument from real-world contexts into a discussion of imaginative literature. The author provides just enough plot details to make the point relevant and closes out the discussion with a return to the essay's main thesis.

Self-esteem and confidence are necessary for successful individuals – no one disagrees with that – but do these traits appear spontaneously or emerge through resolve in the face of setbacks? By not preparing children for the challenges of college and beyond, excessive nurturing comes at a sizable price. Biff Loman, from Arthur Miller's 1949 play *Death of a Salesman*, is the archetypal image of an overprotected, parentally-puffed up teen. His father, Willy Loman, spends most of the play's flashback sequences doting on his oldest son, never teaching him to work hard or learn from his own failures. Instead, Willy assures Biff he'll be simply *be* successful. Biff doesn't work hard or learn from mistakes; he's been fed on the idea that being "well-liked" and having the "appearance" of success is all you need to get on in life. In the narrative present of the play, Biff is 34, lives at home, and can't hold a steady job (perhaps Miller's wry commentary of the adverse effects of parental coddling). This is fiction, yes, but how many Biff Loman's do you see walking around the halls of your school? I see plenty.

The relationship between coddling and success is pretty clear. Children must periodically struggle in order to develop the traits of an independent and successful person. If children are not challenged and pushed because of the well-intentioned intervention of adults, it's no

> The author concludes his argument with a memorable final sentence which paraphrases, and repurposes, a quotation from the source text.

wonder that these skills will never come to be. Children today are sometimes referred to as the "Generation Snowflake," an age group too emotionally vulnerable to cope with views that disrupt their own worldview or sense of expectation. I assume this term is thrown around with some degree of hyperbole. But these days, you never know.

Print vs. Digital Textbooks

Since the opening of America's first public school in 1634, students have relied on printed text as the primary source of information in the classroom. For centuries, students have flipped the pages of Shakespeare, handled stacks of scientific research, or thumbed the pages of a Calculus textbook in the pursuit of a well-rounded education. Since the digital revolution of the early 2000's, however, the primacy of the print text in American classrooms has been increasingly threatened by the digital textbook.

Digital textbooks, electronic texts that must accessed through an electronic device, have gained increased visibility in 21st century classrooms. Supporters of this emerging technology laud increased interactivity, ability to customize content, and its easily modifiable displays to accommodate students with learning needs. Opponents of digital textbooks point to an overwhelming preference for printed text by students, question the cost of making a completely digital transition, and the contest the cognitive benefits – learning, attention spans, and information retention – of digital texts. The question remains, then, as to which media – printed or digital – should be at the center of 21st century student's educational experience.

Write an essay in which you evaluate the most important factors a school should consider when deciding to replace printed texts with digital texts.

Example Argument:

I will never forget the day when my new iPad arrived in the mail. I had spent the entire summer doing countless chores around the house in order to bank enough money to buy myself Apple's 128 GB gizmo, and I'll never forget the thrill when I finally heard the thud that brown shipping box finally land on my front door step. In all but thirty seconds, I had run up to my bedroom, ripped open the box, plugged in the charger, and saw the soft glow of my very own digital Apple for the first time. The next several hours flew by. I was entranced, even

> The author opens the essay with an attention-grabbing narration that personalizes the issue of textbooks vs. e-books. In doing so, the author shows – not merely tells – the main assumptions which will eventually inform the essay's position.

transfixed, by pretty much every pre-loaded application on the iPad, but one particular program that especially piqued my interest was iBooks. I was an avid reader back then, and this app allowed me to buy and download any book I wanted – via the online bookstore – in a matter of seconds! Not only that, I found that reading and flipping pages on the beautiful high definition display made the process of reading more enjoyable and interactive than ever before. Simply put, it was not long before the thought entered my mind that iPads and other e-readers should replace the books at school and in the library; students would no longer have to lug around heavy text-books on their backs, and reading would become a much more popular activity. And recently, I discovered that I was not alone when I had this idea.

For some time now, I have been wondering why the United States has not yet made a complete transition from textbooks to tablets; what could be holding us back from fully revolutionizing our entire education system in this technologically advanced era? But once the glitz and flash of the tablet is removed, it seems that tablets are not the perfect learning tools that their marketers purport them to be. In fact, they pose a number of serious problems to the economy, the environment, and the way our students learn (early research suggests a range of detrimental effects that e-books have student reading and thinking, but

---

The author outlines a number of reasons why digital textbooks are attractive. Though the essay eventually takes a stance which opposes the adoption of e-books, these opening lines suggest that the author has a pragmatic, real-world perspective on the issue. It also suggests that the author is not so dogmatic on his position that his is unwilling to concede upsides of the counter position.

The author transitions back into the "I" voice. This move maintains the essay's tone – halfway between formal and colloquial – and keeps the author's argument (couched here in a personal anecdote) front and center.

The author now lays out the thesis. This thesis is complete with qualifiers ("until the full effect of e-books has been born out") and a clear three, point construction which corresponds to the essay's body paragraphs. The positioning of the thesis, at the end of the essay's second paragraph, demonstrates confidence and control in the writer's style since they choose to assert the thesis in an unorthodox (but no less effective) position in the essay.

at best, the body of research is too inconclusive and immature to make a head-first switch). Until the full effects of e-books has been born out, schools should hold off on the educational reform of replacing textbooks with tablets for a few reasons: digital textbooks are more expensive than textbooks, they have a more destructive impact on the environment than textbooks, and they actually amplify deficiencies in students' research skills.

The first reason to hesitate is a financial one. Digital textbooks are significantly more expensive than printed textbooks. Lee Wilson, the president and CEO of PCI Education in San Antonio, responded to Apple's iPad textbook initiative by writing a report in early 2012 called "Apple's iPad Textbooks Cost 5x More Than Print," in which he estimated that "it will cost a school 552% more to implement iPad textbooks than it does to deploy books" (Wilson). In other words, one textbook would cost a school $14.26 per year, while an iText would cost $71.55 each year (Wilson). He divides the cost of a textbook and the cost of an iText into the five sub-categories of content, management, device, network, and training and found that e-books are significantly more expensive than regular books in all aspects except management. Digital books require costly devices, such as iPads and Kindles, and wireless networks, which textbooks do not need. We must also keep in mind that, although textbooks are expensive, schools reuse them for several years, and so the annual costs for printed books is much smaller than it may seem (Wilson). Simply put, tablets are not a financially feasible option for textbook replacement in an economy where many municipalities are struggling to stay afloat as it is. Bring-your-own-device solutions are problematic too; one

> The author expands on the argument from the source by providing three original examples of the start-up costs of e-books in different context: the town-level, in the home, and in higher education. These points, too, also function as a sort of refutation against those who may advocate these positions as counterclaims to the arguments of the Wilson source.

> The author provides both direct quotes and paraphrase from a source in support of the body paragraph's main point. The direct quotes help to keep the author's argument grounded in the specifics the source material's argument, while the paraphrase demonstrates the author's ability to read, internalize, and ultimately provide an overhaul (in words and presentation) of the source material.

doesn't have to look past the headlines of our current political discourse to see that unemployment is painfully high and many families – who already worry about money problems – would be shouldered with the additional burden of paying for their children's tablets. For college-bound students, textbooks are a major component of the expenses they pay for tuition and switching from printed books to tablets and digital books would not guarantee lower costs either. With all things equal, tablets-over-textbooks may seem wonderful, but as Wilson says, "That ain't happening in this economy" (Wilson).

> The author underscores his string of original points with a quote from the Wilson source that succinctly summarizes the overall position of the paragraph. Such a move synthesizes the source material with the author's point of view, while also concluding the paragraph in an attention-grabbing style.

Second, tablets should not replace textbooks because they have a number of often hidden costs to the environment that traditional textbooks do not. In April of 2010, *The New York Times* published an article called, "How Green is My iPad?" in which the authors, Daniel Goleman and Gregory Norris evaluate and compare printed books and e-readers based on the environmental consequences brought about by the manufacture and use of each reading device. They assess the products' effects on the environment at each of the five stages of their life cycles: materials, manufacture, transportation, reading, and disposal. In this study, they reveal that the manufacture of an e-reader releases 66 pounds

> A clear transitional word ("Second") leads the reader into the next major movement of the argument with precision and clarity.

> The author isn't entirely dismissive of the e-book manufacturing altogether; he seems to suggest that he'd be willing to the amend his environmentalist position should changes in the manufacturing process take place that lessen the level of waste. The author also directly asserts the warrant – the moral grounds – upon which this part of the argument rests.

of carbon dioxide, while making a book releases "100 times fewer greenhouse gases" (Goleman and Norris). At the end of the analysis, Goleman and Gregory conclude that, "With respect to fossil fuels, water use and mineral consumption, the impact of one e-reader payback equals roughly 40 to 50 books. When it comes to global warming, though, it's 100 books; with human health consequences, it's somewhere in between" (Goleman and Norris). Until the manufacturing effect of tablets on the environment can be kept in check, it would be morally wrong to introduce a transition from books to tablets when the environment already hangs in a delicate balance. Instead of conserving natural resources, the manufacture of e-readers like iPads and Kindles requires the consumption of excessive amounts of water and minerals found in the earth and replacing textbooks with tablets would cause us to build even more e-readers at the cost of our increasingly limited natural resources. This is also to say nothing of the CO_2 emission resulting from tablet production. The replacement of textbooks with tablets must wait until the manufacture and use of tablets has become significantly less harmful to the environment.

> The author blends direct quotation and his own words to support the paragraph's main idea. Alternating freely between the source's words and those of the author showcase a high-degree of control in the writing.

Finally, schools should focus on some of the existing gaps and deficiencies in students' reading and retention skills before a switch over from text to e-books is seriously considered. The economy and the environment are important factors, sure, but we must focus on the one priority that rises above all other matters in the textbook vs. tablet debate: how effectively and thoroughly each option accomplishes the task of teaching students the skills they will need to become conscientious consumers of information and lifelong learners. Teachers have a right to be concerned. The internet, which has already caused their students to depend too much on search engines like Google, has created a generation of students who largely struggle to assess the quality and reliability of online sources and "borrow" the work of other people much too

> The author delays his most important point until the end. The body of the essay organizes the evidence well and does so according to a recognizable plan (ascending weightiness of points, in this case). The author's ultimate point is most focused on the context of education and the placement of this point at the end acts as an argumentative knock-out punch.

easily. Without careful instruction on the ethics of the research process, tablets can unleash all the internet has to offer onto students, a scenario of information overload of the highest order. A transition from books to tablets could severely delay the learning of these skills, which are a vital part of a student's education. Tradition persists for a reason.

I do not hate tablets; in fact, I love them. I think they are fun, fascinating, and exciting, and they most certainly have the potential to offer so much to the enhancement of America's education system and our students' learning process. iPads, Kindles, Nooks, Galaxy Tabs, and the many other tablets and e-readers that are being built today could give schools and teachers the ability and means to enrich their curriculums with videos, animations, links, interactive documents, and much more. But I must be realistic and say that there are significant economic, environmental, and educational problems that must be resolved before we begin to introduce the use of tablets in schools on a greater scale. There is no doubt in my mind that an inexorable digital revolution has already left the station, but our education system should wait until the necessary preparations have been made to get on board. We just aren't quite ready yet.

The author is careful to qualify his claims – some of the tonally strongest moments of the essay – as he starts to wind things down. Notice the inclusion of words like "if", "without", and "could" which help to establish the limits and conditions of the paragraph's argument. Though the author does adopt a strong point of view, his passion is tempered by these qualifying words and phrases which don't brand the opposition as obviously wrong or misinformed.

The author returns to the opening strategy from the introduction; that is, he is willing to concede the upside of e-book technology, but maintains his overall position that both he, and schools pondering the decision to make the switch, should he both hesitant and cautious. The final line of the essay suggests a tone of open-mindedness, not ambivalence, and leaves a trustworthy and credible impression on the reader as the argument draws to a close.

Works Cited

Goleman, Daniel, and Gregory Norris. "How Green in My iPad?". *The New York Times*, The New York Times, 4 Apr. 2010, archive.nytimes.com/www.nytimes.com/interactive/2010/04/04/opinion/04opchart.html.

Wilson, Lee. "Apple's iPad Textbooks Cost 5x More Than Print." *The Education Business Blog*, Headway Strategies, 1 Nov. 2017, www.educationbusinessblog.com/2012/02/apples_ipad_textbooks_cost_5x.html.

UNIT 3

SYNTHESIS

CHAPTER THIRTEEN

A BRIEF HISTORY OF SOURCE-BASED WRITING

Even though the university has been around since the high Middle Ages, its most recognizable feature – the research paper – is a relatively recent acquisition in the history of academia. As we mentioned in Chapter 1, medieval universities primarily focused their attention on the great minds of the past – Plato, Aristotle, Cicero, Quintilian – and used the Trivium (grammar, rhetoric, logic) as the primary means of communication for the exchange of ideas. For about seven hundred years, things changed very little in higher education: there was a single teacher for any given discipline, enrollment was comprised of a wealthy few, and instruction leaned heavily on the promulgation of the ideas of Classical thinkers. Believe it or not, students in classically structured universities wrote significantly less than students do today. This was because oratory and public debate occupied a much more central role in the original university model (after all, "professor" comes from the Latin *profiteri*, "to declare, to claim"), This pedagogy had largely fallen out of fashion. A typical experience for a 19th century university student may look a bit strange to us now. Take the following description from an 1827 article from *The Harvard Register* detailing student life: "the scholars had regular declamations on Fridays, public disputations every week [and] for three weeks during the month of June, the graduates attended the recitation room on Mondays and Tuesdays, subject to the examination of all who chose to visit them ... These were called the Sitting of the Solstices, or the Weeks of Visitation." Comprehensive oral exams, a feature of the modern

Ph.D. experience, are perhaps the last surviving relic from this by-gone era. Given that universities were largely responsible for training society's public figures – lawyers, politicians, teachers, clergymen – it makes sense why spoken rhetoric occupied such a principal position in the preparatory training for the wider world. But by the middle of the 19th century, things began to change.

In 1859, Charles Darwin published *The Origin of Species*, and once this work found its way into academic discourse, the university system could never go back. The influence of Darwin's ideas went well beyond biology and evolutionary theory. It touched off the rise modern natural science, a paradigm shift whose effects reached every branch of academia. As science began to form the prevailing model of reality, induction became king, and testable empirical methods supplanted the deductive abstractions and maximal propositions of the ancient world. And because of Darwin's emphasis on observation and research, it wasn't long before *every* discipline in the university became organized for research. All this began in Germany during the late 19th century but spread quickly around the globe in a matter of decades. Here's how.

In both Europe and the United States, Darwin's intellectual contributions coincided with a rising middle class who sought the university as a necessary credential for participation in economic life (not unlike the way some students treat college degrees today). Enrollments began to spike around the turn of the 20th century, and this influx of non-traditional university students forced a number of wholesale changes. Instruction in abstract classical ideas dropped off. Tradition fell into disuse. The number of specialized disciplines grew, spurred on by the demand for training in emerging middle-class professions, which lead to the hiring of more faculty with an increasingly niche expertise. This change in hiring practices had several unintended consequences. Professors increasingly found themselves overrun by larger and larger class sizes (resulting in the increased instructional role of graduate students and part-time instructors) or discovered themselves teaching a course for which they had little formal training. Knowledge became increasingly fragmented, and the three parts of the Trivium were eventually absorbed into specialized disciplines: rhetoric retreated to English departments, grammar became the domain of Philology and Linguistics, and logic migrated to Philosophy. Once disaggregated, the Trivium no longer was the engine of academic discourse it once was. Of the three, rhetoric underwent the most drastic changes in its use.

Declamations, disputations, Weeks of Visitation, Sitting of the Solstices – all the old expressions of rhetoric in higher education were rendered all but obsolete by the onslaught of the changes faced by the early modern university at the turn of the 20th century. More and more, professors turned to quantitative measurements of student performance, giving rise to the distant ancestor of the modern "A-F" grading system. In order to effectively enact a quantifiable measurement of student performance, professors gradually deemphasized the role of oratory and debate in place of "current-traditional rhetoric," a reductive approach to composition that emphasized prescriptive rules and technical correctness. Described by R. Gerald Nelms in "A Brief History of American Composition Studies" (1993) as the "almost perfect doctrine of writing instruction for an education system that desires easy evaluation," current-traditional rhetoric was a double-edged sword. On one hand, written discourse experienced a newfound importance and became placed at the center of nearly all student work done in the humanities. On the other hand, current-traditional rhetoric tended to present writing as an immutable set of rules-to-be-followed, thus downplaying the expressive and generative elements of writing that composition instructors today hold so dear. Add this widespread proliferation of writing to the increased specialization among university faculty, and it wasn't long before professors found themselves in hybridized roles of researcher and teacher. This emphasis on subject-specific research eventually trickled down to the taught curriculum, and it wasn't long before students themselves began participating in these research activities. No surprise, then, that almost every college and university today require its students to compose a research paper as the final word on what they've learned.

In 1930, the term "research paper" appeared in for the first time in the *English Journal*, and this mode of writing has remained an invariable ordeal for both teachers and students ever since. On the face of things, the research paper is problematic in almost every way imaginable. Just the phrase itself strikes fear into student's hearts and rightfully so. It is often a massive event, sometimes spanning several months, where students are asked to generate a topic, find relevant research to support it, and then develop a written response of ten, fifteen or even twenty plus pages. The extensive accountability routines – note cards, sentence outlines, paper conferences, and rough drafts – do little to alleviate mounting fears, and students often feel as if they are lost for months at sea. Students in advanced composition classes are routinely asked to do these things, yet instructors are often frustrated when the exercise rarely yields the desired success. Why?

Much of the advanced discourse that takes place in high school and college requires research, and this is among the most difficult of academic moves. Since research takes you beyond personal reactions to an issue and puts you into dialogue with other (sometimes clashing) viewpoints, knowing how to work with source texts is a fundamental academic skill, though its often undertaught in composition classrooms. Producing a discourse that is shaped by the "other voices in the room" rests on your ability to digest information from almost any type of source – novels, images, essays, film, lectures, paintings, scientific findings, and so forth – and be able to speak clearly and sensibly about it. In source-based writing, you must identify relationships among and between the sources. But without a strong program of training, problems happen.

"It's very clear that [students] don't how to analyze their sources," says Rebecca Moore Howard, a professor of writing and rhetoric at Syracuse University; "they don't understand it and don't know how to do anything but grab a few sentences and go." This observation, detailed by Dan Berrett's "Freshman Composition Is Not Teaching Key Skills in Analysis, Researchers Argue" in *The Chronicle of Higher Education* (2012), examined source-based writing from student papers at 16 institutions in the 2011–2012 school year, from community colleges to the Ivy League, and the results were disheartening to say the least. Howard reported that students rarely look past the first few pages of the source they cite and often stitch together a patchwork of text with little evidence that they've absorbed the deeper levels of a source's argument. Citing a student's paper with 10 sources on the subject of eating disorders, Moore argues that even students who are earnest in their attempts "just fell flat when dealing with the sources." This may be due in part to way we graze texts online – scanning and skimming along the surface – but Howard insists that "the trouble is [students] are not learning how to read deeply," let alone knowing how to blend these voices into a coherent, unified whole. A more recent study from 2017 conducted across several sections of Expository Writing at Framingham State University in Framingham, MA found comparable results in the mid-to-lower range papers. Researched arguments tended to be "rooted entirely in summary or adapting of sources [with] too much reporting, not enough critical thinking" leaving "readers to connect the dots, hiding behind source authority." Here is our charge for the final unit of this book.

Make no mistake about it, source-based argumentation is intellectually challenging and demanding of your time, patience, and attention. But, if you've kept the skills contained in this book close to your heart, the proper scaffolding is in place. In our work with rhetorical analysis, you have learned to read with a writer's eye, to break source material down into its constituent parts in order to say something about it. In our work with argumentation, you have learned how to build purpose-driven persuasive prose, to argue with an ethical responsibility while remaining attuned to the pitfalls of shoddy logic and mental shortcuts. Throughout, you have learned to cultivate style and arrange according to purpose. You have, effectively, set the stage for what's to come. *You are ready.*

Research writing *can* be an arduous process, but it *can* also be a deeply critical and intellectual exercise that is highly rewarding. And (insofar as writing for school can be fun) research writing can and should be approached in a spirit of play. Kay Halasek notes this in *A Pedagogy of Possibility* (1999): "What compositionists have not examined in any concentrated and programmatic fashion is the generative effects of having students 'play' with subject," and the research paper should be just this: an opportunity to explore something interesting and to make connections across disciplines. Source-based papers are unique among routine writing assignments from school in the sense that they often take students outside of borders of their English classrooms and textbooks in order to enter into real-world discourse on controversial issues. When deeply involved in this type of exploration, writers often see the world in a new way, viewing everything in day-to-day life with a critical lens because everything can be a potential topic or, at least, direct you towards one. What's more, effective research writing – synthesizing your own views with the surrounding world – is writing and thinking of the highest order that puts Bakhtin's theory of heteroglossia from Chapter 1 into motion. As he puts it in *The Dialogic Imagination* (1981), your ideas are always "half someone else's" and only "become one's own when the speaker populates it with his own intention, his own accent, when he appropriates the word." In other words, research writing isn't merely a rundown of other people's ideas. It is a constructive process that promotes a writer's discovery, inquiry, and the formation of knowledge. To get here, researchers must know how to consider sources critically and discuss them knowledgeably to write dialectically where one's conclusions are derived from the consideration of opposing views. Easier said than done.

Most scholars would agree that successful research writing consists of knowing how to weave multiple perspectives into one. As Anthony Petrosky said in "From Story to Essay: Reading and Writing" (1982), you must discover, analyze, and argue with source material to put "together impressions of the text with our personal cultural, and contextual models of reality. When we write, we compose by making meaning from available information, our our personal knowledge, and the cultural and contextual frames we happen to find ourselves in." In higher education, multi-source research arguments are commonplace and having blind spots in this skill set puts you at a sizable disadvantage. Let me illustrate by example. In my first week of college, I was given the following assignment:

> "Compare the creation stories of the Enuma Elish and the Book of Genesis using sources that feature contrasting ideas and synthesize a conclusion based on these results."

I didn't really know where to go with this at the time. I had little clue on how to read a source thoughtfully, identify claims and details, or how to integrate these observations with my own. I put down a thesis and, refusing to deviate from my set path, went for it. When I got the paper back the following week, I'll never forget my teacher's comment: "Your thesis may come at the beginning of your paper, but it had better come towards the end of your thinking and searching and organizing and even writing your paper." Although I was a little upset at the time, the comment reflected my paper's refusal to budge from its dogmatic thesis (and the evidence that was shoehorned to fit with it). In this unit, we'll aim to pre-empt situations like mine. If you have some experience here, then you already have some experience with the synthesis essay. If not, the lessons of this unit will acquaint you with the principal elements of source-based argumentation. It is here that we can state the theoretical core of the book's final unit:

1. Effective writers evaluate rhetorical situations to make decisions throughout the writing process.
2. Reading and writing are dialogically related and are used for inquiry, learning, thinking, and communicating.
3. Writing is a recursive and collaborative process and that effective writing often requires multiple drafts.

4. Effective writing follows conventions determined by the situation and will apply academic conventions as needed.

Part cognitivist, part social-constructionist, this book's approach to the research process will hopefully illustrate how this intellectually demanding work can serve a number of productive ends. It teaches independent learning. It teaches conscientious consumption of information. It teaches how to go beyond surface generalizations. It teaches how to situate oneself into long-standing dialogue and debates. It's important to say this because it's only when students and teachers interpret academic writing tasks in the same way that things start heading in a productive direction.

CHAPTER FOURTEEN

GENERATING IDEAS FOR RESEARCH

"Invention, it must be humbly admitted, does not consist in creating out of void, but out of chaos; the materials must, in the first place, be afforded: it can give form to dark, shapeless substances, but cannot bring into being the substance itself. Invention consists in the capacity of seizing on the capabilities of a subject, and in the power of moulding and fashioning ideas suggested to it."

–Introduction to *Frankenstein*, Mary Shelley, 1831

Mary Shelley–the author of literature's greatest creator, Dr. Frankenstein– acknowledges the centrality of invention in bringing order to chaos. In the context of composition, coming up with something worth writing about is not easy, and giving "form to [the] dark, shapeless substance" of experience is often the toughest stage of any research project. How do you negotiate this problem of invention? As Sharon Crowley says in "Teaching Invention" (2002), "Invention may occur haphazardly (people sometimes have flashes of invention in the middle of the night, or while they are doing something that is unrelated to composing)." But for those who don't have fortune of spontaneous inspiration, Crowley goes on to note that invention can also be generated through a number of teachable systems. Some approaches are grounded in rhetorical theory (looking at the *stasis* of a topic from Classical argumentation), some take-on a deductive approach (generating "significant statements"), some are reading-based (dialectical journals and imagined dialoging with a text), while others are more free-from and associative (connection charts and questions-from-answers diagrams). We'll treat all of these approaches in this chapter, not to be prescriptive, but to lay out options so you can choose the most generative style for your topic and approach to writing.

Classical Theory-Based Invention: Looking at Stasis

In Chapter 9, we discussed *stasis* as a crucial stage in Classical systems of argumentation, and it can be just as useful of an inventional strategy in research writing. *Stasis* ("the point of rest") is the heart of a controversy as you see it and is organized according to a progressive, four-tier system of concerns: conjecture, definition, quality, and forum. As we mentioned earlier in the book, explicitly identifying *stasis* will give focus and clarity to what exactly you plan to argue, what type of counter-arguments could be generated against you, and how to focus your early research on the essential points of what's really at stake. Here's a reminder of the central concerns of each stage of *stasis*:

Name	Central question to focus the argument
Stasis in conjecture	Did it happen?
Stasis in definition	What do we call it?
Stasis in quality	It is justifiable?
Stasis in forum	Is this the appropriate place to have the argument?

Let's take an example topic – capital punishment – to see how an examining *stasis* can provide some initial focus to point you in the right direction for research (Figure 1).

By looking at capital punishment within the four points of *stasis*, we find two promising leads and two dead ends. For conjecture, there is nothing to argue about since capital punishment's usage is a plain fact. For forum, the scope of the problem could not possibly be resolved in a short research paper, thus discounting it as a legitimate forum for resolution. Arguments of definition and quality, however, both have promise since there are arguable points to both sides. From here, you can begin to work your way into some relevant source material.

Point of stasis	Central question	Inventional response
Stasis in conjecture	Does capital punishment happen?	No one is arguing whether or not this practice occurs. It's easily verifiable to see that many states – Alabama, Arizona, Arkansas, California, Florida, Kentucky, South Carolina, Utah, Tennessee, Virginia and Washington – use it. As a result, there is no arguable controversy here.
Stasis in definition	What should we call capital punishment?	Here is a controversy. Proponents of capital punishment describe it as the legally authorized killing of someone as punishment for a crime. Opponents tend to frame this practice as state-sponsored murder. Where do I stand of this topic and how could I argue for an interpretation of the term?
Stasis in quality	It capital punishment justifiable?	Here is another controversy. Supporters of capital punishment will often point to moral arguments, citing it as form of justice or reparations for heinous crimes. Detractors often point to social arguments, citing its disproportionate application to minority groups and low economic groups. Which of these contexts seems to be most essential to the heart of the controversy?
Stasis in forum	Is a research paper the appropriate place to have the argument about capital punishment?	A research paper may be a place to have this argument, but any real resolution is going to come from legal contexts whose scope goes well beyond the a five to seven-page paper. Like the stasis of conjecture, a short research paper is not the proper forum for this discussion.

Figure 1 How Stasis Can Promote Invention.

Deduction: Generating "A Significant Statement"

In Act III, iii of *Hamlet*, Claudius – overrun by his conflicting feelings of guilt and ambition – says, "I stand in pause where I shall first begin and both neglect" and you may feel similarly overwhelmed as you put pen to paper in this first step of the research process. If this is this case, it may be worthwhile to consider writing "a significant statement" about your topic to get things off the ground. Because this step is interested in getting initial impressions down on paper – and no answer is wrong here – it's important to note that "not paying attention to your personal reactions may lead you to feel disconnected from the communication going on – as though some other people were arguing about something that you had no interest in," a point made by Charles Bazerman in *The Informed Writer* (1994). To make explicit what you think about your topic *is* to involve yourself in the ongoing dialogue surrounding the issue. If you can first find out where you are coming from, you will eventually find where you will go.

This method is most useful with research projects in the humanities that require you to dig into one, or several, primary texts as the object of the research. As in any good reverse engineering or "backwards design" process, you can start by explicitly identifying your key insights into a text by writing a "significant statement," an idea that follows designs from David Bartholomae and Anthony Petrosky's *Facts, Artifacts, and Counterfacts* (1986). Significant statements are not merely a one-line precis or summary. Rather, this is an exercise that gets you thinking in rhetorical terms about your subject by considering how the main elements of written discourse – the author, the audience, the text itself – affect the way a reader may interpret the text (see Figure 2). Advanced students often make these insights intuitively, but if you're struggling to come up with a worthwhile topic, some focused scaffolding may be in order. Working with an organizer like Figure 2 may work, or perhaps poking around online to browse some paratextual information will help you to read with more focus and

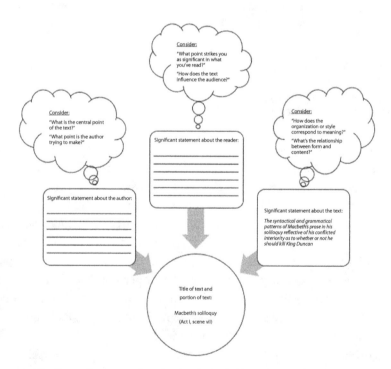

Figure 2 Significant Statement Exercise for Macbeth (Act I, scene vii).

purpose. Find that Shakespeare's troubled marriage to Anne Hathaway underwrites the dynamic between the Macbeths? Start there. Wonder how Shakespeare's primary audience would understand this scene in live performance differently than a 21st century, mediated presentation? Start there. See that Lady Macbeth buries her intentions under thick layers of metaphor and analogy? Start there. No reader can find everything in a text, but every reader can find one thing, and sometimes that's all it takes to get things going in the right direction. Significant statements provide focus to analysis, but more importantly they give space for you to ground your analysis in what you have found intriguing or unusual. You may need to search around a bit, but once you connect with the text via your interests, the insights will unravel right along. Since most well-executed writing can address several of these concerns at once, do not feel pressure to find the "right" direction in this initial stage. By responding in this way, as Bartholomae and Petrosky say, "passages that were silent now suddenly speak and each line of questioning allows a reader's wavering attention to be renamed and given priority as an act of attention."

Reading-Based Invention: Imagined Dialogue Exercise

Adapted from Paul Heilker's *The Essay: Theory and Pedagogy for an Active Form* (1996), this inventional method asks you to write an imagined dialogue with a text on a topic you provisionally plan to research. This exercise promotes *reading* about a topic, and Heilker claims that this assignment, which he uses when students are researching a topic, creates for each student "a script that documents how his or her thinking developed over time in dialogic interaction and integration with…other voices." Here's how it works:

1. Browse in the library or online for a reading related to your provisional topic. The article can be from popular sources, academic journals, newspapers – really anything that gets you thinking about subject through text.
2. As you read, stop when you come to the first bit of information that, as Heilker says, you find "shocking, surprising, intriguing, important, interesting, remarkable, or stimulating."
3. Write the author's last name followed by a colon in your notebook. Following the author's name, record the bit of text that caught your attention by quoting or paraphrasing it.

4. Underneath the quote, write your own name followed by a colon. Respond to what the text has said as if you were having a conversation with the author.
5. Return to the reading and follow this same procedure so that you have a transcript of your conversation with the author that includes four to five exchanges where you "talk back to what the author says in the reading."

Here is Heilker's dialogue in action, based on a reading of Chapter 1 of David Bartholomae and Anthony Petrosky's *Facts, Artifacts, and Counterfacts* (1986).

> <u>Bartholomae & Petrosky</u>: "We don't have students shuttling information from text to teachers and back again but shutting themselves between languages – theirs and ours – between their understanding of what they have read and the understanding of what they must say to us about what they read..." (4).
>
> <u>Me</u>: David, I've heard this line of reasoning before. This sounds like a point you made in "Inventing the University" (1986). And while I agree with the heart of what you say, I'm not so sure that I can get on board with the false dichotomy that you set up here. It reads as if you are setting teachers and students into an "us" and "them" scenario, suggesting that no student is capable of participating in academic discourse free from serious intervention. This doesn't give the credit that some students deserve and lumps all kids together into the same majority.
>
> <u>Bartholomae & Petrosky</u>: "For our hypothetical student to have something to say, she must replace Margaret Mead's words with her own. This is a bold and difficult act. She is, as she knows, in a 'remedial course', a course for poor readers and writers. And Margaret Mead is not only a writer, some represented to her in a published text, she is a writer who has been assigned in a course where the student is a student" (6).
>
> <u>Me</u>: Here, I agree with you completely and I think you've articulated this unspoken feeling that many students have very well. Just by reading published texts, many students ascribe an unquestioning authority to that text, making them unwilling or unable to engage with the ideas in any type of critical way. In other words, they think to themselves, "How could I dispute what this person has said? I'm only 18 years old. What do I know?" You also accurately capture what many teachers do in response to this feeling of disenfranchisement, which is to give an "authorized translation" (7) of the text which students often become overly reliant on, allowing many to flip on the auto-pilot switch when it comes

to analysis. "The teacher has told me what this means," they may think, "so whatever I thought about the text must be wrong."

Bartholomae & Petrosky: "They [students] leave their books blank to so a rereading stands only as the act of going back to an empty text – to read it again; this time, they hope, to get it right" (18).

Me: I completely agree that annotating is crucial for students to have any hope of "getting" the text, as you say. I like the way that you characterize annotating as a low-stakes, informal process. Yes, students should begin to get into the habit of recording their notes, observations and questions of a text – really, anything that may strike them as important in some way, even if you are not quite sure of why it's important at that particular point. Readers can find all sorts of writing intriguing even if they are not quite sure why, as I once found Dante's *Divine Comedy* before I really had much of a clue about what it meant.

Bartholomae & Petrosky: "Our students obsessive concern over the fact that they don't remember everything they read, their concern to dig out the right answers, their despair over the passages that seem difficult or ambiguous are symptoms of a misunderstanding of the nature of texts and the nature of reading that must be overcome if students are to begin to take charge of the role they might play in the classroom" (19).

Me: I'm really of two minds with what you've said here. There are some classrooms, sure, that emphasize factual recall above all else, but the cure for this is not if the student can just alter their philosophy of reading. Many of these factual recall obsessions are sourced in the fact that this skill is linked to grades. In a high school context, it seems that you may want to address this comment not just to the teacher, but also to the policy makers – principals, superintendents, school committees, etc. – who can effect change across the board. An individual teacher deviating from the accepted practices to empower students with a new philosophy of language and readings sounds great, but this is a much tougher thing to enact in day-to-day practice.

Bartholomae & Petrosky: "These interpretive schemes [from page 34], as predictable as they may be, have incredible heuristic power for a class fascinated with the slopes and valleys of their own lives and drawn to the power of the theory or the generalization" (35).

Me: This was a fascinating observation about teenage interpretive schemes that I had never really thought much about before, but it is right on the money. Students do tend to deal in absolutes when speaking about issues of identity and transition, and a lot of the most effective assignments I do brush up against one of these binaries that you listed out on page 34. To get students interested in the process of abstraction, you say, it's worth it to tap the energy of our experience and then slowly transition this into an academic vocabulary. It's certainly useful, I think, to start with our vocabulary before sliding us into that of the academic institution. Excellent observation here.

As you can see, this imagined dialogue works as a jumping off point to research since it gets you reading in a way that helps generate ideas that can be used in subsequent stages of research and writing. This method's highest virtue is that it lets you figure out what's internally persuasive, rather than having the text take over and tell you what to think about the topic. This liberating process is what Bakhtin calls "ideological becoming" – positioning yourself in response to a text – which resists the trap of just letting the reading dictate what your stance should be. By *responding to* the text, you begin to make up of your mind about it and begin the process of "coming to know." And by actively engaging with a text, you are participating in your own ideological becoming.

Reading-Based Invention: Dialectical Journal

A dialectical journal (sometimes known as a double-entry journal) is a variation on Heilker's imagined dialogue exercise that grounds the generation of ideas firmly into the process of reading. You'll first need a text related to your topic; if you have a few provisional texts, all the better. In this form of invention, you are asked to divide your paper vertically. The left-hand side of the page is reserved for textual evidence – important quotes, ideas, themes, etc. – that should be tracked with page numbers for easy reference later. You may want to think of the quotes you select as part of a process where you are, as Joseph Harris says in *Rewriting* (2006), "recirculating the author's writing, highlighting parts of the texts for the consideration of others" to put a personal stamp on the ideas presented in the text. You may want to also read the passage several times, each time selecting quotations with a different purpose in mind to generate different potential paths for further research. If you struggle to read with distinct purposes in mind, consider the method below (Figure 3), adapted from Block and Duffy's *Comprehension Instruction* (2011).

Strategy	Question(s) to pose to the text as you read
Predict	Were there any places in the reading where you thought the author was trying to foreshadow something? Did this come true? If it did, what tipped you off? If it didn't, why do you think the author made these suggestions of purpose?
Monitor	Were there places in the reading that were more difficult to understand than others? Why may the author have written that portion in a dense or tough to understand style?
Image	Were there any passages that were rich in imagery? What were the images that came to your mind? Can you connect these images to other places in the text?
Infer	Were there places in the reading that you understood because of your prior knowledge on the topic? Was it an allusion? A reference to a fact or anecdote? Do you think the author assumes the reader will know it?
Evaluate	Were there places in the reading that you made a judgement about? Do you think the author wants the reader to take a moral stance? Are they suggesting something here about the larger takeaways for the reader?
Synthesize	Were there places in the reading that you connected to things outside of the reading? How did this connection add depth and dimension to your understanding of the passage?

Figure 3 Different Strategies for Quote Selection in Dialectical Journal.

Once you've selected quotes, it's time to reflect on them. The very format of the dialectical journal promotes reflection: the left-hand column is for quotation and summary, the right-hand column is for analysis, inquiry, and connection. This type of writing is a powerful metacognitive tool that requires you consider the nuances of your own thinking process for the purposes of generating substantial ideas for further inquiry. Consider the following example dialectical journal based on Chapter 4 ("Language") of Ralph Waldo Emerson's essay "Nature" (1836).

"Language is a third use which Nature subseries to man. Nature is the vehicle, and threefold degree. 1. Words are signs of natural facts. 2. Particular natural facts are symbols of particular spiritual facts. 3. Nature is the symbol of spirit." (paragraph 1)	Emerson builds a methodical construction of his definition of language through its uses, progressing from the most empirical/observable to the most spiritual/mystical. He takes each one at a time and builds from his previous conclusions to his final point.
"Words are signs of natural facts." (paragraph 2)	He believes that words are reflections of natural things. It's easy to see what physical objects are all about

here (rock, tree, desk, etc.). Abstractions, however, Emerson asserts, are traced back to the natural world. He catalogs a series of examples, "Every word which is used to express a moral or intellectual fact, if traced to its root, is found to be borrowed from some material appearance. *Right* means *straight*; *wrong* means *twisted*. *Spirit* primarily means *wind*; *transgression*, the crossing of a *line*; *supercilious*, the *raising of the eyebrow*. We say the *heart* to express emotion, the *head* to denote thought; and *thought* and *emotion* are words borrowed from sensible things, and now appropriated to spiritual nature."

"The same tendency may be daily observed in children" (paragraph 2)

He returns to his praise for children (or innocence represented/imaged by children). This image takes on additional resonance at this point, connecting to his explanation of Beauty in the previous chapter. Only those with an unaffected mind can see the world for what it is.

"Particular natural facts are symbols of particular spiritual facts." (paragraph 3)

In the first degree of his definition of language, he says that words – representing both physical and abstract objects – are reflections of nature. Now he is saying that nature is a reflection of the spiritual. In a sense, he is saying that the natural world is a language to convey the spiritual:

Words (represent) ➔ Nature (represent) ➔ Spiritual

"Man is conscious of a universal soul within or behind his individual life, wherein, as in a firmament, the natures of Justice, Truth, Love, Freedom, arise and shine. This universal soul, he calls Reason: it is not mine, or thine, or his, but we are its; we are its property and men." (paragraph 4)

These virtues lie within nature that can only be experienced through the individual. Ideas of community, congregation, etc. are incompatible with this. It is a religion of one, a contemplative experience that can only be done alone. Justice, Truth, Love and Freedom lie within each individual since each is part of a greater whole, the universal oversoul through which we experience when we transcend our mortal selves.

"As we go back in history, language becomes more picturesque, until its infancy, when it is all poetry; or all spiritual facts are represented by natural symbols. The same symbols are found to make the original elements of all languages." (paragraph 5)

The theory of the origins of language given in this and subsequent paragraphs was common during the Romantic period. Emerson will use it to claim that poets possess a revolutionary power insofar as they can use language to reshape the values of society, a claim that is also made by Percy Bysshe Shelly in "A Defense of Poetry" (1821).

"The corruption of man is followed by the corruption of language. When simplicity of character and the sovereignty of ideas is broken up by the prevalence of secondary desires, the desire of riches, of pleasure, of power, and of praise, – and duplicity and falsehood take place of simplicity and truth, the power over nature as an interpreter of the will, is in a degree lost; new imagery ceases to be created, and old words are perverted to stand for things which are not; a paper currency is employed,

Here is a condemnation of a series of things that characterize the society (and all societies, really) in which Emerson lives. Money, hedonistic pleasures, power, and flattery are all things that sidetrack language as an expression of Truth. If, as he said earlier, language reflects the natural world and the natural world reflects the spiritual, we can observe the corruption of the way in which humans are oriented through the degeneration of language he speaks of here.

when there is no bullion in the vaults." (paragraph 6)

"Old words are perverted to stand for things which are not; a paper currency is employed, when there is no bullion in the vaults." (paragraph 6)

He likens new language that does not reflect the spirit (its real value) to money with no gold backing (its real value). Money is simply an image of the bullion it represents in the same way that language that does not reflect spirituality or truth in a word anchored to nothing. It ceases to function as it should, according to Emerson.

The poet, the orator, bred in the woods, whose senses have been nourished by their fair and appeasing changes, year after year, without design and without heed, – shall not lose their lesson altogether, in the roar of cities or the broil of politics… And with these forms, the spells of persuasion, the keys of power are put into his hands. (paragraph 9)

He returns here to the governing idea of the 2nd degree of the definition of language; that is, how the poet has the power to shape and govern society. The poet, in his definition, is one who can see nature and experience the transcendence found in nature. Cities do not strip the poet of this ability to see, rather the poet must use his experience to shape the experiences of others. It is the poet's duty.

"Whilst we use this grand cipher (language) to expedite the affairs of our pot and kettle, we feel that we have not yet put it to its use, neither are able. We are like travelers using the cinders of a volcano to roast their eggs."

This recalls earlier ideas of how language is majestic but is often used for trite purposes. His closing simile above reflects this mismatch: volcano (grand/majestic) is used to roast eggs (commonplace/pedestrian).

Free-Form and Associative Invention: Connection Charts

If you are researching an everyday issue, jotting down ideas onto a connection chart could be a suitable place to start. This chart is aptly named, and its idea is simple: think about issues surrounding your topic and find real-life connections to news stories you have seen, your personal family history, fiction and non-fiction film, visual art, and so forth. These ideas should web inwards toward the central topic. Let's say you wanted to research and argue some aspect of "dishonest business practices." You don't really know what yet, and you're not quite sure how to begin. Consider:

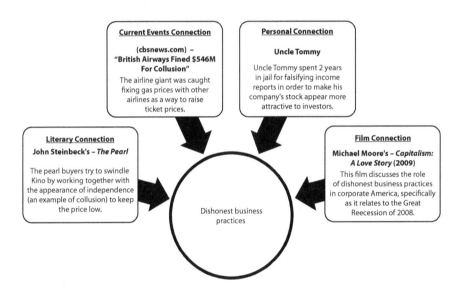

A chart like this will help you to expand the breadth of the topic at hand, connecting it to many diverse areas, not just one. Bear in mind that the ideas you get down do not have to make it past the cutting room floor. You are simply generating ideas, looking for commonalities, and searching for possible paths down which you may take your research. There is, however, an inherent danger in this brainstorming method: the writer must have a number of related experiences to the topic at hand to leverage into a successful connection chart. If your prior knowledge on a subject is limited, the following methodology, where you embrace and utilize the questions you have at this pre-writing stage, may be a more suitable and productive alternative.

Free-Form and Associative Invention: "Questions from Answers" Chart

Using this method, you first identify what you know already about your topic, and then jot questions that spring from those bits of information. This may be an effective way to establish angles of investigation – a way of building "essential questions" – that have one foot in your prior knowledge and one foot in the unknown. Notice below that this writer has a few facts, let's call them "answers," about the issue of "dishonest business practices." The "questions" that spring from this starting point help to establish possible subtopics or ideas which may lead to more focused and specific research.

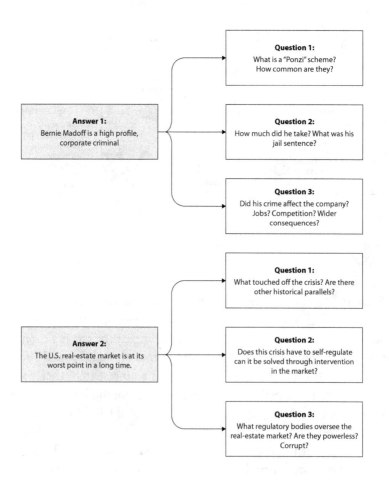

From the above chart, there may be a number of angles you would settle on to dictate the direction of your research: particular criminals who have had wide reaching effects, causes of the housing market collapse, investigation of the real power of regulatory bodies. The focus that these questions provide will help dictate the direction the subsequent research will take. Be mindful, though, that there is a great deal of back-and-forth when conducting research, and even though you may have some bright ideas at this stage, they very well may change as you think through and research your topic more closely.

Like so much with composition, you are going to have to find what works best for you. Use some of the above ideas, combine them, or use something that has worked in the past. As any author will tell you, the best pieces of writing are often preceded by some variation of the exercises above, but it's important to remember that all of those processes are, as Anne Berthoff said in *Forming, Writing, Thinking* (1989), "'forming activities' in which students should discard the faulty notion that when you compose you 'figure out what you want to say before you write', and accept instead this more helpful slogan: 'You can't know what you mean until you hear what you say.'" And you can't begin to "authentically" speak until you've figured what you're going to talk about through the process of invention.

CHAPTER FIFTEEN

FINDING AND ANALYZING SOURCES

I t's important to say at the outset that the inventional processes detailed in Chapter 14 will only yield a provisional topic – not a thesis – and this initial line of inquiry can (and often does) change over the course of your research project. Don't be concerned with getting the thesis "right" at this stage; just concentrate on refining a central idea that, at this early stage of development, you plan to explore in the final paper. You should never feel that you must articulate a thesis until you have done a significant amount of research, evaluated the sources, and made a final determination about what direction your paper will go. Your thesis may come at the beginning of your paper, but it should come at the *end* of thinking, researching, and organizing process. It is the transformation of a topic into a thesis worth arguing about where the real challenge of research happens, and this change requires that you have solid source material and have given a quality reading of it. In this chapter, we'll detail the ways to both find and analyze sources to support your research project.

There are a great many places you can go to track down information for your project. So many, in fact, that it can be overwhelming – maybe even a little intimidating to someone who is coming to source-based writing, especially for the first time. Add to this the complication that different contexts call for different forms of researched evidence, and it's sometimes difficult to know where to begin. As Jarrod Atchison says in *The Art of Debate* (2017), "There is no such thing as ideal evidence in the abstract. Context is key... Knowing the types of evidence you can use in a debate is critical but figuring out which type is appropriate for the argument you are trying to make is the more important skill." Where you look for information ultimately is dictated by what you plan to research, but the best general starting point for just about any research project is the library.

Finding Digital and Print Sources

Nearly all high school and university libraries have made the move to digitization which means that print catalogs and electronic databases are universally accessible through keyword searches. The problem with these digital databases is almost never a question of not-enough-information; it's more often an issue of getting the student researcher to effectively filter through the avalanche of potential sources that come along with every new keystroke. The enormous quantity of information and its wide range of focus makes the task of choosing sources rife with difficulties.

Keyword searching is the most flexible way to navigate digitized databases since this process can return results that match exactly what you're looking for. Having apt keywords is, well, key, and you'll want to first brainstorm a number of keywords related to your topic. Thinking of synonyms for your central idea is helpful and helps you refocus your search each time a new one is used, creating more chances for a successful hit on the database. There is no one "right" keyword search, and it's likely that you'll have to try a number of combinations of keywords to get a collection of useful sources. As your topic begins to take on focus, you'll need to be increasingly specific with your search terms. Here is where a "Boolean" keyword search may help.

The logician George Boole (1815–1864), from whom "Boolean" takes its name, invented a system of linguistic logic to define the relationship between objects (much in the same vein as a Venn diagram). A Boolean search is a type of database query that allows users to combine keywords with terms such as "and," "or," and "not" to produce more relevant results, and many research catalogs have adopted Boolean syntax as way of defining results for a database search. Let's say, for example, that you wanted to perform a general search on the topic of the way women are portrayed in popular media. Searching the keywords – "women," "image," "media" – in isolation will produce results that are frustrating, to say the least. The top three results for a general search of "women," at the time this book was written, returned the following: "Female Nursery Worker Stabbed by Three Women in London," "Women-Only Showings of *Wonder-Woman* Receive Cheers – And a Few Gripes," "The Sexist Way We Pile on Hilary Clinton and Stifle Women in Democracy." A Boolean search of "women AND image AND media" yielded much more useful and focused results: "The Media's Effect of Women's Body Image," "The Body Image of Women: Depression, Eating Disorders, Self-Esteem," and "Men and Women Self-Image: The Negative Side of The Media." Swapping keywords – "body image" instead of "image" – will focus the results even more. See Table 1 for an outline Boolean search terms and their effects.

Table 1 List of Common Boolean Search Terms.

Guide to Boolean keyword searches		
Boolean search term	Example search string	Effect on search
AND	Women AND images AND media	Results will contain all search terms
OR	Media OR images	Results will contain multiple keywords that appear in combination or on their own
NOT	Media NOT images	Results will exclude certain selected keywords
*	Wom*	Results will retrieve all forms of a word (i.e. "wom*" will return results for "woman," "women," "woman's" "women's") to broaden results from a single query
Complex search that combines multiple Boolean terms	Women AND (media OR images)	Results will be focused, but very narrow

In addition to keyword searching, many online databases allow for what's known as "subject searching," a form of source discovery distinct from keyword searching. It is less flexible than keyword searching, as it works off a pre-existing list of subject headings automatically generated by the database (see Figure 1). Sometimes, entering a general search term into a database ("women") and then refining your search based on "subject searching" is a generative way to accumulate information. The upside of subject searching is that you are guaranteed to find relevant results since the filter terms have been back-engineered from existing titles already logged within the database.

Library catalogs that inventory print sources will often have an interface which allows you to search by keyword, subject, title, author, etc. Figure 2 below details a semi-narrative account of a search process conducted on the electronic catalog of a library's print sources:

Figure 1 Illustration of Subject Searching.

If you are researching in the library of a high school or college, it is likely that your school has subscriptions to online databases and journal storage websites. You should find these sites to be of great use to you when you are gathering information for your topic. Most of the search results on these services are accompanied by abstracts, which are short summaries, to help the researcher locate useful research more quickly. Many of the results are full-text articles that are print-ready in PDF and HTML format. For a few of the best databases, check out Table 2.

General internet searches can also produce useful results but proceed with caution. A good way to determine the provisional credibility of an online source is to locate some key pieces of the following information: a title, a known author, date of publication, and a URL address. If any of these are missing, the source should probably not be considered. Since the internet is so vast, it's tough to know where to begin. See Figure 3 for a categorized list to help you out.

The type of sources that you'll be drawn to are, in some ways, topic dependent, and you'll need to assess the degree of "scholarliness" that your topic demands of the source material. For example, a paper that explores themes from Roman architecture will be heavy on academic sources while an argument about supporting recent legislation on sports concussions will more likely draw from periodicals and sports publications. Other papers, say one that discusses the detrimental effects of sensationalist journalism on

Library Catalog Research – Step 1:

Type the general topic category into the search engine bar and filter it by "Keyword" (circled). Here, the search term "corporate corruption." It is broad and will yield a wide range of results.

Library Catalog Research – Step 2:

Take a look at the search results. You will find you may have to do a lot of filtering. The second result looks interesting. You can locate this text by its call number which indicates its location in the library's stacks. Based on these results, I may want to find similar titles by the author, Ralph Nader. Return to the main search page.

Library Catalog Research – Step 3:

Return to the main page. Now I want to see if there are any book results from Ralph Nader. Type "Ralph Nader" into the search bar and filter results by "Author."

Library Catalog Research – Step 4:

Scan the results. By looking at these, I may decide to begin an investigation of "dishonest business practices" from an environmental viewpoint if I use results #2 and #5. I can consider these titles, or I can further refine my research by returning to the main page and, through Boolean searching, combine "dishonest business practices" with "environment."

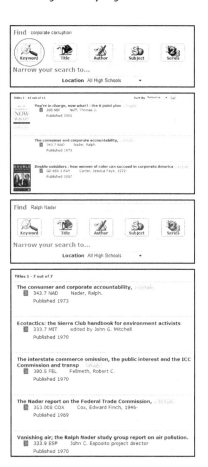

Figure 2 Walkthrough of Recirculating Search Terms.

democracy, may look at both popular sources and academic ones. Choosing sources with the appropriate degree of scholarship is central to a well-balanced research paper. You must consider a source's level of expertise, its intended audience, the publication's purpose, among other things, to evaluate its usefulness in a research project. Table 3, adapted from Robert Harris's *Using Sources Effectively* (2002), provides a nice visualization of the competing characteristics for the most common categories of sources.

Evaluating Digital and Print Sources

Though a source may fit the category you're looking for, that doesn't automatically mean that you've found a gem. You must next evaluate a source

Table 2 Descriptions of Most Common Research Databases.

Site name and link	Description
www.jstor.com	J-Stor is short for "Journal Storage". This site is a fully searchable database of over 1,079 journal titles in eighteen collections representing fifty-one disciplines, and 262,042 individual journal issues, totaling over 33.7 million pages of text. This site requires a subscription, but most high schools and colleges have one.
http://search.ebscohost.com	EBSCO Host is a wide-ranging data base that offers full-text journals, magazines, books, monographs, reports, and various other publication types. Depending on your topic, EBSCO Host has over 300 constituent search engines that are content specific, allowing you to search in your specific area. This site also requires a subscription.
Modern Language Association **MLA** www.mla.org	This site is a subject index for books, magazines, and websites. The titles that are indexed date back to 1925; the database includes over two million citations from more than 4,400 periodicals and 1,000 book publishers. This site also requires a subscription.

for its quality. Thinking back to our discussion of what makes good evidence in the context of Classical argumentation from Chapter 9 is a good place to begin. Though sources will differ from one another in their content and style, there are some constants when it comes to evaluating the source for its credibility and reliability. If you remember from Chapter 9, sources should be screened along the lines of three broad questions:

Is the Information Relevant?

To be relevant, the evidence needs to have some sensible or logical connection to something you plan to discuss in the argument. If a person were to make the argument for the value of raising chickens in the city but then cites testimony of farmers who raise only their chickens in the countryside, this source would be guilty of using evidence that is not relevant.

Is the Information Appropriately Precise?

To be precise, the evidence needs to be appropriately exact and accurate. Take, for example, a popular source that makes an argument about the

Using the Internet for Research

Periodicals:

American Prospect: http://www.prospect.org/
Associated Press: http://www.ap.org/
BBC News: http://news.bbc.co.uk/
The Boston Globe: http://www.boston.com/news/globe/
CBS MarketWatch: http://www.marketwatch.com/
Chicago Sun-Times: http://www.suntimes.com/index.html
Chicago Tribune: http://www.chicagotribune.com/
Christian Science Monitor: http://www.csmonitor.com/
CNET News: http://www.news.com/
CNN: http://www.cnn.com/
Daily Telegraph (London): http://www.telegraph.co.uk/
The Economist: http://www.economist.com/
Financial Times: http://www.ft.com/home/us
Forward: http://www.forward.com/
Guardian: http://www.guardian.co.uk/
Ha'aretz: http://www.haaretz.com/
Iraq.net: http://www.iraq.net/
Independent: http://www.independent.co.uk/
International Herald Tribune: http://www.iht.com/
Inter Press Service: http://www.ips.org/
Jerusalem Post: http://www.jpost.com/
Jewish Week: http://www.thejewishweek.com/
Los Angeles Times: http://www.latimes.com/
Nation: http://www.thenation.com/
Newsweek: http://www.msnbc/site/newsweek/
New York Review of Books: http://www.nybooks.com/
New York Sun: http://www.nysun.com/
New York Times: http://www.nytimes.com/
Observer: http://www.observer.com/
Reuters: http://www.reuters.com/
Times (London):http://www.timesonline.co.uk/tol/global/
Time: http://www.time.com/time/
SA Today: http://www.usatoday.com/
U.S. News and World Report: http://www.usnews.com/
Wall Street Journal: http://online.wsj.com/public/us
Washington Monthly: http://www.washingtonmonthly.com/
Washington Post: http://www.washingtonpost.com/
Washington Times: http://www.washingtontimes.com/

Other Libraries

American Library Association: http://www.ala.org/
Massachusetts Library Association: http://www.masslib.org/
Boston Public Library: www.bpl.org
Internet Archives: www.archive.org
Internet Public Library: http://www.ipl.org/
Smithsonian Institution Libraries: http://www.sil.si.edu/
The Library of Congress: http://www.loc.gov/index.html

Government:

The White House: http://www.whitehouse.gov/
The Supreme Court: http://www.supremecourtus.gov/
House of Representatives: http://www.house.gov/
Department of Justice: http://www.usdoj.gov/
Department of Agriculture: http://www.usda.gov/
Department of the Treasury: http://www.ustreas.gov/
Environmental Protection Agency: http://epa.gov/
Customs and Border Patrol: http://cbp.gov/
Federal Bureau of Investigation: http://www.fbi.gov/
Central Intelligence Agency: https://www.cia.gov/
Internal Revenue Service: http://www.irs.gov/
NASA: http://www.nasa.gov/
U.S. Post Office: http://www.usps.com/
U.S. Mint: http://www.usmint.gov/
U.S. Department of Defense: http://www.defenselink.mil/
Army: http://www.army.mil/
Navy: http://www.navy.mil/
Marines: http://www.usmc.mil/
Air Force: http://www.af.mil/
Coast Guard: http://www.uscg.mil/
National Guard: http://www.ngb.army.mil/default.aspx
U.S. Marshals: http://www.usmarshals.gov/

International:

United Nations: http://www.un.org/
World Trade Organization: http://www.wto.org/
International Currency Converter: http://www.xe.com/

Figure 3 List of Online Websites for Research.

danger of rising sea levels and the threat it poses to humans that says, "If the temperature rises just a little bit, the sea level will slightly increase, and many cities will be in danger." There are several fuzzy phrases that make this statement imprecise, and consequently, less effective. When the stakes are high, and the small numbers matter, be sure to address these issues with the sharpest language available. Rather than "a little bit" say "just 2.5 degrees Fahrenheit." Rather than "slightly increase," say "rise by 4 inches." Rather than "many cities," say "major world cities that exist at or under sea level such as London, Amsterdam, Venice, and Miami."

Is the Information Current?

To be current, the source must contain the most up-to-date information to support your argument effectively. It is misleading to use out-of-date evidence when more up-to-date information is available. If a writer were

Table 3 Differences in "Scholarliness" for Common Source Types.

Variety of scholarliness in research sources				
	Academic publication	**Journalistic publications**	**Popular publications**	**Sensational publications**
Author	Written by academics, scientists, or experts in the field	Written by staff writer or expert in the subject	Written by staff writer or freelancer	Written by staff writer or freelancer
Audience	Other academics or those trained in the field	Well-informed and educated public	General reader without much prior knowledge	Less-educated reader
Purpose	To share findings, propose theories, or disseminate studies	To inform on a general topic	To inform and entertain on a general topic	To entertain
Style	Highly specific and sophisticated	More general; complex topics are presented are broken down into understandable terms	General and simplified; many specific details are omitted	Sensationalized and simplistic; presentations often distort the facts for entertainment purposes
Citations	Includes details bibliography of cited sources	May include a partial list of cited sources	Sources are often not cited	Sources are not cited, if even used at all
Editorial Process	Article has been peer-reviewed or refereed by other experts in the field	Article is approved by editorial board	Article is approved by editorial board or editor	Article approved by editor

to argue the value of a P.C. over a Mac but cites the specs from a 2012 Mac against a 2015 P.C., that author would be guilty of using outdated information to, deceptively in this case, build their argument.

On top of screening a source's content, you must also assess the credibility of the publication, the author, and the information itself. Consider Figure 4, an annotated example of Joel Demski's "Corporate Conflicts of Interest" published in the Spring 2003 edition of the *Journal of Economic Perspectives* in Figure 4:

Whether you have found your own sources or if they have been provided for you, you are going to have to consider each source critically to properly weave those perspectives into your own argument. In order to do this, you must first be equipped with finely tuned, analytical reading skills – many of which were the focus of this book's first two units – to make sense of exactly what it is the source authors are writing about. As you sit down to analyze your sources, it's worthwhile to think about them from both a

Journal of Economic Perspectives—Volume 17, Number 2—Spring 2003—Pages 51–72

Corporate Conflicts of Interest

Joel S. Demski

A conflict of interest arises when an executive, an officeholder or even an organization encounters a situation where official action or influence has the potential to benefit private interest. Examples include the physician who has a financial interest in a diagnostic laboratory, a congressman whose spouse is a lobbyist or corporate director, or a professor with a financial interest in a particular textbook. Empire building, nepotism and all manner of influence activities offer other illustrations. Such conflict is as old as history itself, and as an historical matter, it is important to acknowledge that conflicts of interest arise and do morph into financial fraud. Consider a few examples from the fairly rich gallery of rogues and abuses over recent decades.

The Equity Funding case is noteworthy for the large number of active participants: the head of the firm, with the assistance of other top managers and numerous employees, began falsifying insurance policies in 1965, which among other steps involved company forgery parties where fake policies, medical records and even death records were created. Of course, these fake policies brought in no revenue directly. But they supported false revenue estimates that pumped up the company stock price, allowing it to make acquisitions with stock, and the policies were often resold to other reinsurance companies. In turn, manufactured death claims for fictitious policies that had been sold in the reinsurance market were part of the scam. By the time 22 company employees were indicted in 1973, they had recorded 64,000 false policies and had issued $25 million in counterfeit bonds—and $100 million of corporate assets was missing. The company's auditors were found guilty of fraud for failing to detect the scam and served prison time (Dirks and Gross, 1974).

■ *Joel S. Demski is Frederick E. Fisher Eminent Scholar, Fisher School of Accounting, University of Florida, Gainesville, Florida. His e-mail address is 〈joel.demski@cba.ufl.edu〉.*

Determining A Source's Value

1. Is the publication credible?

Scholarly sources are central to many research projects. Words such as "Journal" or "Review" in the title means that the articles are sent out to "peers," or other members in the field, for anonymous review. If you are unsure about its "scholarliness," read up on the magazine's peer review process. In the case of this source, Journal of Economic Perspectives, the article is a scholarly, peer-reviewed publication. Sometimes the credibility can be derived from the organization that puts these out on the work. This information can usually be found in copyright statements. In this case, this journal is sponsored by the American Economic Association, a non-profit organization dedicated to the scholarly study of economics based out of Vanderbilt University.

2. Is the author credible?

Take some time to locate the author's credentials. These can help to illustrate that his/her argument is well-researched, and it can also alert you to any bias the author may have. In this case, the author's credentials are listed at the bottom of the page. He is a college professor, an expert on their subject he is writing about, at a large research university.

3. Is the information credible?

Some fields of research turn over every couple of years, while others are more or less immutable over time. For example, if you were researching the latest methods of genome mapping, you would want the most up to date information available, both in terms of the article's publication date and ther esearch that the author consults. But if you were researching historical information on, say, Shakespeare's *Hamlet*, it is likely that the date of publication would make little difference. Use your discretion here. In the case of this article, the information is fairly recent for the topic, being published in 2003.

Figure 4 Example Annotations for Source Evaluation.
The Journal of Economic Perspectives © 2003 American Economic Association.

rhetorical and argumentative standpoint. The challenge with this is that you are on your own now. Reading and annotation are no longer a matter of coming up with answers to questions about a text. It is now a constructive experience which makes you consider what type of questions need to be asked in the first place and how these findings might be expanded, intensified, or challenged in the eventual argument you construct. You can critically appraise a source in two ways:

Rhetorically: As you may remember from earlier chapters, a rhetorical analysis asks you to explicate the passage (that is, the removal of layerafter layer), exactly as if you were an anatomist examining the text's intricate organs and their workings. Your reading should progress deductively, moving from the initial identification of the author's purpose all the way down to how the specific components, diction and syntax, complement this overall meaning. It's also important to remind you at this stage that good authors have many tricks in their bag; you may not be able to find examples of every rhetorical device in every single passage. You should, however, try to exhaustively connect images, notice word play, recognize motifs, and synthesize meaning with what is front of you.

Argumentatively: In this mode, you must analyze the argument each source is making. Putting the source material up to Classical and Contemporary scrutiny is an excellent way to determine whether the argument made in the source is, indeed, worth your consideration as a legitimate voice in the conversation. Also, it will allow you to quickly dispel the notion that complex issues can be understood in a reductive "pro" or "con" fashion. Instead, by reading the argument to appraise it, you'll begin to see the author's main stance and how this point of view interacts with the larger spheres of debate related to your topic.

Most students are adept at answering questions about a text, but few are expert at asking them. This tends to be the most difficult step for students because to ask probing questions "means making public what is private – a process dependent on explication, illustration, and critical examination of perception and ideas," a proposition noted by Anthony Petrosky in "From Story to Essay: Reading and Writing" (1982). Asking good questions requires that you engage and explore how your own knowledge meshes with the purposes of the text. A key strand in the recent compositional theory of Kay Halasek's *A Pedagogy of Possibility* (1999), this "participative pedagogy" brings to the forefront the generative effects of "play" with both subject and form as a means of exploring the text you hold in your hands.

While you should certainly be encouraged to throw your own thoughts and experiences into the mix as you read, your analysis of source material should adhere to some general guidelines as you put pen to paper (or fingers to keyboard). Each time you interrogate a text, you should think about your inquiry in two parts: a "where-in-the-text-do-I-see-this" part (that ties the question to the text) and a "why-does-this-observation-matter" part (that extends the textual observation into the context of your developing argument). Other annotation methods from Chapter 3 (the marginalia approach in particular) are a useful storehouse for initial observations. If you're not quite sure how to hook into a text, consider Table 4 (reproduced here from Chapter 2):

After you have scrutinized your sources and begun to think more deeply about the many perspectives of the issue, you must now find and establish your provisional argument. It is important to remember to not

Table 4 "Where" and "Why" Questions for the Appraisal of Source Material.

The "Where" question	The "Why" question
Where does the main point of the passage show up?	Why do you think it shows up at the beginning? Why does it delay until the middle? What's gained by waiting until the end?
Where does the author/character show us that he's worth listening to? Where does he connect with you emotionally? Where does he provide hard proof?	Why are these important to your understanding of what the author/character has to say? How do these either draw you in or push you away from what's said?
Where does the author/character's proof or examples appear in the passage?	Why do you think they're in the order they are? Why may it start with a shock and work back? Why may it begin with broad claims and follow with specifics?
Where do you see the author/character making an assumption?	Why does this assumption matter to what they are saying? Why is it bias? Why does it seem honest?
Where do you see any usually long sentences? Short sentences? Fragments?	Why would the author place these sentences where it does? How do they emphasize, or de-emphasize, the point it's making?
Where do you think the author/character may not be telling us everything they know? Where do they seem genuinely confused?	Why would the author/character not be forthright? What is gained or lost by this move?
Where do you see patterns in the writing? Where does the author/character repeat things?	Why do you think these patterns are meaningful? What is the point of using the same verbs over and over again? Adjectives?

cast your issue into a dichotomous framework, the "yes/no" debates which we dealt with in detail in Chapter 11. It is vital to keep an open mind. Strong, mature research prose can only happen if the writer resists the temptation to oversimplify the issue with a trite and obvious thesis. All legitimate research writing invites critical, careful thinking, and the best arguments will be those in which the thesis and developmental plan suggest clearly that the writer has given some thought to the complexities of the assigned topic.

At this stage, you will now have to take your general topic and narrow it down appropriately to fit the scope of your assignment. Sometimes teachers impose limits on length; others tell students to take the space they need. Regardless, you will likely need to trim your topic down to something you can handle. One of the biggest missteps student writers make when it comes to research writing involves topic choice. Often, students will generate topics that are too broad and generalized, typically resulting in a paper that's a mile wide and an inch deep. Some topics are too narrow, and trouble sets in not in the act of covering too much, but rather not being able find enough, or any, information to support what the paper's main topic. Let's piggyback on the example from the previous chapter to see how a topic may be trimmed down to an appropriate size.

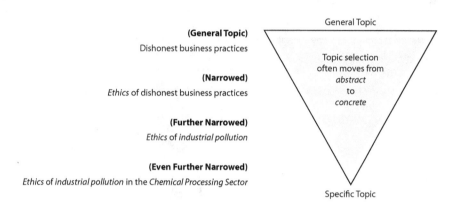

(General Topic)
Dishonest business practices

(Narrowed)
Ethics of dishonest business practices

(Further Narrowed)
Ethics of industrial pollution

(Even Further Narrowed)
Ethics of industrial pollution in the *Chemical Processing Sector*

General Topic

Topic selection often moves from *abstract* to *concrete*

Specific Topic

As you can see, streamlining your topic will help to make things a little more manageable for you. You may begin researching, thinking that you want to find information on the dishonest business practices related to 2008 financial crisis, but through your research and topic narrowing, you realize you can write a much more interesting paper on the ethical behavior of a specific branch of the private sector.

But you don't have your thesis, not yet. From here, you can *begin* to generate your thesis statement. As we have said before, the thesis must not be vague nor should it be just a topic – it cannot be a statement of case. A thesis is an argument – something to be proven by the researcher (you) that is set in dialogue with evidence from known experts and credible perspectives (the source material). A good thesis will provide focus and coherence for the entire paper. At this stage, ask yourself, "What are two or three (or more) possible positions on this issue that I *could* take?"

But why should you have multiple claims? Well, it's good to give yourself some flexibility at these pilot stages and not feel as if you are locked into a single angle of investigation. It is best not to handcuff yourself to a single thesis early on because there is likely to be a great deal of back and forth as the research progresses. New ideas may come to light, some of which may contradict your original thesis, and you may have to tinker and adjust accordingly. Always be flexible.

As your claim begins to materialize, remember the characteristics that it should possess: a balanced voice that is free of bias, clear qualifiers/

exceptions which account for certain scenarios and conditions, and, above all, a discernable argument/case to be proven. Keep Toulmin's guidance in mind here; he can be a tremendous help. Remember, to write a qualified argument, you must anticipate objections to your position and recognize and respect the many sides to your topic. A reasonable voice recognizes that there are more than two sides to an issue, more than pro and con. This indicates that you have an open mind that is willing to consider alternative perspectives.

CHAPTER SIXTEEN

INTEGRATING SOURCES AND AVOIDING PLAGIARISM

After you provisionally vet your sources and come to a working thesis, you should begin to think about the ways you may integrate your research into your developing argument. The sources you've accumulated to this point represent the "library" of materials that you will continue to think about as you write your project (though you'll mostly likely be locating and adding new materials to the preliminary bibliography as you proceed.) Synthesizing the points of view from the information you've found is not easy; it demands you identify how perspectives converge or diverge, how themes are presented, and which patterns are present. All this mental algebra is not for its own sake; it should stimulate and support what *you* want to say about your topic. It's now time to give your sources a fuller reading for two purposes: to provide an overview of your field of research on your topic to a reader of your paper and to begin to put your provisional claim in conversation with those of the source material. We'll look at several strategies in this chapter of how this can be done.

The "Parlor" Approach

One way to dialogue with sources is to "talk" directly to them and see what emerges in the middle space between your claim and theirs. Think of this strategy as an imagined deliberation, a role-played debate where the many possible sides of your issue are put on the table for consideration – not to declare a winner – but with the intention of clarifying what's at stake. Deliberative argument models, discussed in Chapter 10, are a good primer for this type of work. Source material should play a generative role in the formulation of your position, but this challenging move is easier said than done. "The insistence on 'winning' in every confrontation, or the refusal to acknowledge the other person's point of view" says Marie Secor in "Composition and Argument" (1997), "is not at all what we mean when we say we teach argument in the composition class. What we do mean is that we try to teach our students to see the discourse that they produce-such as the papers they write in our course or any other-as making and supporting a claim for an audience in response to a situation in which they participate verbally." The "new voices" from your research should help to broaden and expand your own thinking on the topic while situating you more firmly into the ongoing discourse of your topic. Imagining a dialogue with a spectrum of views simulates the larger discourse communities in which we find ourselves in day-to-day lives. It adds an element of reality to the research process: it forces us to ask tough questions; it makes us deal with legitimate counter-positions; it makes us move beyond the echo chamber to become more rigorous thinkers and writers.

Personal observation and experiences can still play a role in college-level research writing, but the real force behind a researched argument rests on the writer's ability to offer thoughtful, reasoned comments on *other* people's ideas: books, magazines, scholarly journals, and even images all will come into play. Should you engage in this imagined deliberation, you must do so in a spirit of charity. Shoehorning sources to fit your position and nitpicking opposing ones down to nothing (a *reductio ad absurdum*, rhetoricians would call this) will do very little to move your argument forward in any productive way. Kenneth Burke's famous "parlor" metaphor from *The Philosophy of Literary Form* (1941) – from which this strategy derives its title – illustrates this strategy in action:

Imagine that you enter a parlor. You come late. When you arrive, others have long preceded you, and they are engaged in a heated discussion, a discussion too heated for them to pause and tell you exactly what it is about. In fact, the discussion had already begun long before any of them got there, so that no one present is qualified to retrace for you all the steps that had gone before. You listen for a while, until you decide that you have caught the tenor of the argument; then you put in your oar. Someone answers; you answer him; another comes to your defense; another aligns himself against you, to either the embarrassment or gratification of your opponent, depending upon the quality of your ally's assistance. However, the discussion is interminable. The hour grows late, you must depart. And you do depart, with the discussion still vigorously in progress.

This metaphor illustrates what high-level writing should be after; that is, you must strive to move past an isolated analysis of each individual source in order to place your claim central among what others have to say. For example, you may think to yourself, "How is the claim from Source A opposed to Source C? Does Source B provide additional information that could have helped Source D's argument? Is source E too biased to be valid? How does source F make the generalizations of source G more concrete?" When you begin to think in this way, you will notice patterns emerge among and between source material, but since source-based writing requires your argument to be built with the input of sources, you will need to use some discretion with which sources – and what parts of those sources – you eventually plan to use.

Consider the example below to illustrate this relationship in miniature. First, read the brief overview of the topic, globalization and its relation to American interests, represented in the source material to establish a frame of reference. Then, read the central line of inquiry that holds the cluster of sources together and consider your initial reaction. Finally, read the sources themselves, after which you should take a look at the way each source contributes to the imagined dialogue. (A quick note about the readings that follow. For purposes of brevity, I have identified the key passages, excerpted from larger works, to focus on the central ideas in a way that's more wieldy and sensible for illustrative purposes. The citations are provided and, should you read the works in full, you'll see key connections/ ideas are much wider-reaching than the focused snippet provided here.)

Overview

The world is getting smaller every day. Economies, businesses, politics, and even mass entertainment are becoming increasingly international, leading some to describe the contemporary period as one of "globalization."

While international interactions have been happening in the United States since 1492, the modern period has seen a dramatic shift in the way one culture spreads to another. For a majority of human history, the proliferation of cultural influence often occurred at the point of a sword, but the modern period has adopted subtler methods. Global influence in the 21st century is acquired much more surreptitiously by economic and cultural domination. Countries are less frequently using tanks and planes to create influence abroad. Instead, they send their restaurants, businesses, languages, and popular culture to "put down their flag" elsewhere, absorbing many facets of the native culture in the process.

The United States of America is at the center of this debate. Some believe that America spreading its culture and economy far and wide hurts other societies by "Americanizing" the world under the guise of globalization. Others feel that this spread of American culture and ideas is in the best interest of places who have not yet been exposed to liberal democracy and free markets, thus seeing great benefit from an "Americanization" of the world.

Central Line of Inquiry

Develop a position on the impact of the proliferation of American influences and ideas across the globe.

Sources

Source A

Williamson, John. "Globalization: The Concept, Causes, and Consequences." Congress of the Sri Lankan Association for the Advancement of Science Colombo. Sri Lanka. 15 December 1998. Keynote Address.

The following source is an excerpt from a larger speech entitled, "Globalization: The Concept, Causes, and Consequences." The speaker is John Williamson, an American expert in economic situations outside of the United States. This speech was given while Mr. Williamson was the Chief Economist for the South Asia Region at the World Bank.

Globalization has become a familiar enough word, the meaning of which has been discussed by others before me during this conference. It is the world economy which we think of as being globalized. We mean that the whole of the world is increasingly behaving as though it were a part of a single market, with interdependent production, consuming similar goods, and responding to the same impulses. Globalization is reflected in the explosion of foreign direct investment (FDI): FDI in developing countries has increased from $2.2 billion in 1970 to $154 billion in 1997. It has resulted also in national capital markets becoming increasingly integrated, to the point where some $1.3 trillion per day crosses the foreign exchange markets of the world, of which less than 2% is directly attributable to trade transactions. An increasing share of consumption consists of goods that are available from the same companies almost anywhere in the world. The technology that is used to produce these goods is increasingly standardized and invariant to the location of production. Above all, ideas have increasingly become the common property of the whole of humanity.

Globalization certainly permits an increase in the level of global output. FDI brings the best technology, and other forms of intellectual capital, to countries that would otherwise have to make do without it, or else invest substantial resources in reinventing the wheel for themselves. It may also bring products that would otherwise be unavailable to the countries where the investment occurs, which presumably increases the quality, and therefore the value, of world output. And international capital flows can transfer savings from countries where the marginal product of capital is low to those where it is high, which again increases world output. What impact is globalization likely to have on the long-term possibilities of economic growth in developing countries? Globalization is tending to make the technologies and the knowledge for this process to occur more readily available, and therefore to enable the process to be telescoped in time. (Singapore may be a small country, but there is no previous case in history of any country that did not enjoy massive resource discoveries going from stark poverty to affluence in under 30 years.)

But it is surely also true that globalization is bringing new dangers. The virulence of the East Asian crisis was primarily a result of countries exposing themselves to the full force of the international capital market before they had built up an unquestioned reputation for being able as well as willing to service their debts come what may, which meant that when investors became concerned about their potential vulnerability as a result of the Thai crisis there were no other investors willing to step in and provide stabilizing speculation even after exchange rates and interest rates had clearly overshot.

Source B

Courtney Smith, Malorey Thelen, Nick Paul, William Carey. "How Has Globalization Impacted the United States and American Citizens?" Assessment of Globalization in U.S. 13 Sep. 2012.

The following is a section of a paper on the effects of globalization written by three university students while attending Transylvania University.

Globalization has greatly impacted the United States and American citizens. First and foremost, globalization has spread American influence throughout the world. Globalization has opened up more markets for the United States, which in effect helps American companies sell their products worldwide. There has been a rise of multinational corporations and their influence has greatly increased. Globalization also aids in the ability for American corporations to sell their products outside of the country and aids in keeping the nation "on top" or "near the top" economically. Globalization has increased the real-time communication abilities between international organizations and nations. This has allowed for a greater emphasis on international cooperation. The world has in a sense become "smaller" because the nations can in a sense communicate easily. This has impacted the United States in situations such as the 9/11 terrorist attacks as well as it has given the United States the ability to communicate with allies as well as enemies in time of peace, but also in time of conflict. Globalization also allows for cheaper products for Americans to purchase and lower prices. This is due to the cheaper labor that makes the product. These cheaper prices allow for the standard of living for Americans to increase.

Source C

Mondal, Sekh Rahim. "Interrogating Globalization and Culture in Anthropological Perspective – the Indian Experience." *Journal of Globalization Studies*. 3.1 (2012): 152–160.

The following is written by Sekh Rahim Mondal, the chair professor of Anthropology and Sociology at the Centre for Himalayan Studies and at the University of North Bengal. A significant researcher on the subject matter,

*Mondal provides his views on globalization as it impacts India, his home coun-
try. The following excerpt refers to part of Mondal's research which outlines his
view on globalization in general, not just in India.*

Globalization has become a dominant ideology as well as a virgin field of study
in contemporary social science research. From the terminological point of view,
globalization means an increasing interdependence of world societies and their
transformation into a single whole.

Contemporary globalization is an increasing flow of technology, trade,
finance, ideas, peoples and cultures brought about by sophisticated technology of communications, travels and also by the world wide-spread of neolib-
eral capitalism. Globalization is the process of local and regional adaptations
in many areas of human life under emerging global situation. Currently there
occurs significant restructuring at three basic levels, namely, changes in economic life, changes in power and politics and changes in knowledge, culture
and identity. Thus, globalization has generated a powerful force which has
affected the world wide living conditions. The term global village was coined
by Marshall McLuhan (McLuhan 1962) to describe the present form of global
connectivity. Global village establishes closer contacts between diverse groups
of unknown people, increasing interaction and friendship amongst them and
thereby initiates the emergence of the world community and world citizens.
The world citizens denote nothing but the imagined global community's members who are expected to promote global culture and global civilization.

The global culture is not an extended version of the local cultures; rather it
is the cultural interaction of the global and the local level. A local culture is the
product of face-to-face interaction of members of a distinct society, whereas
the global culture is a product of interaction among people of diverse societies
living far from each other. As regards the local-global cultural interaction, it is
necessary to see how the global cultural flows become locally appropriated,
incorporated, syncretized and hybridized.

Source D

Shimemura, Youchi. "Globalization vs. Americanization: Is the World Being
Americanized by the Dominance of American Culture." *International Society for
the Comparative Study of Civilizations*. 1.47 (2002): 80–91.

The following source is an excerpt of a journal article entitled, "Globalization vs. Americanization: Is the World Being Americanized by the Dominance of American Culture?" The author, Shimemura Youchi, provides a perspective on globalization in Japan and how America influences her country. Youchi Shimemura is a professor at the Musashino Women's University in Japan.

Japan is, in my estimation, probably the most Americanized society in the world. McDonalds has more than 30,000 franchise restaurants in 121 countries and areas around the world. Their golden arches can be found even in Tian'anmen Square in Beijing, Myong-dong in Seoul, and Red Square in Moscow. But McDonald's Japan with more than 3,000 restaurants is "the biggest McDonald's franchise outside of the United States." In fact, McDonald's Japan has been so successfully integrated into Japan that the story is told of a little Japanese child who arrives in Los Angeles, looks around, sees McDonald's Golden Arches and says, "Look, Mom, they have McDonald's in this country, too." We also have Tokyo Disneyland which is the most popular theme park in Japan, attracting nearly 18 million visitors a year, and in April 2001, Universal Studios Japan, which is a replica of Universal Studios in Los Angeles, was opened in Osaka, the third largest city in western Japan. If you walk around any major city in Japan, you'll soon realize that Japanese society is flooded with American cultural goods.

Japan looks like America on the surface: there are McDonald's, Starbucks, Kentucky Fried Chicken, Tower Records everywhere, and people wear American jeans, American tee shirts, American shoes, listen to American pop music, and watch American movies and TV dramas. Young people these days even dye their hair blonde to look like Americans. However, although everything American is extremely popular in Japan, Japan is not America. If you make a careful analysis of how Japan has absorbed and assimilated American culture and other foreign cultures in our land, you will see the inevitable process of foreign cultures being transformed to fit into our culture. Japanese society has been certainly Americanized in many ways, but at the same time American culture in the process of being assimilated into such alien soil as Japan has to be Japanized. Otherwise, it would not be successfully accepted by the Japanese. For example, as I just mentioned, Japan is surrounded by a number of American cultural products, but they are almost always transformed to adjust to the Japanese cultural environment.

As Thomas Friedman in his best-selling book The Lexus and the Olive Tree points out, "McDonald's Japan has been absorbed by Japanese culture and architecture." For example, they offer a Japanese menu to suit the tastes of the Japanese: Teriyaki McBurger, Green Tea Shake, and iced Coffee. And at McDonald's restaurants in Kyoto their Golden Arches are not yellow-colored but are a more modest brown color to fit into Kyoto's traditionally serene landscape. What has been happening to McDonald's has been happening to Japanese Sushi – globalization and localization. Sushi can now be purchased and eaten in a number of major cities around the world. Actually, it has become part of daily cuisine in many parts of the world, but in its process of globalization it has become de-Japanized. In the past, overseas sushi restaurants were mostly run by Japanese, catered to expatriate Japanese, and employed all-Japanese staff. But this is no longer true. Many are now run by non-Japanese; most often they are Korean or Chinese, and customers are now mostly non-Japanese.

Source E

Norberg-Hodge, Helena. "Consumer Monoculture: The Destruction of Tradition." *Global Dialogue*. 1.1 (1999): 70–77.

The following is an excerpt of a journal article entitled, "Consumer Mono-culture: The Destruction of Tradition." In its entirety, this source identifies and explains the impact of globalization on foreign countries, particularly smaller societies and economies. This article is from Global Dialogue, *an electronic journal site that advocates the exchange of ideas on pressing contemporary issues concerning social, political, economic, and cultural concerns. The journal is meant to have various perspectives, encouraging debate.*

For the people of the "Third World," the pressure to conform to the expectations of the spreading Western consumer monoculture is destroying traditional societies, eliminating local economies and erasing regional differences. But this monoculture is also leading to divisions, uncertainty and collapse, where previously there had been unity, security and stability.

My own experience among the people of Ladakh, or "Little Tibet," in the trans-Himalayan region of Kashmir, is a good, if painful, example of this destruction of traditional cultures by a faceless, Americanised consumer monoculture. When I first arrived in the area twenty-three years ago, the vast majority of Ladakhis were self-supporting farmers, living in small, scattered settlements in the high desert. Although natural resources were scarce and hard to obtain, the Ladakhis had a remarkably high standard of living, with beautiful art, architecture and jewelry. They worked at a gentle pace and enjoyed a degree of leisure unknown to most people in the West. Most Ladakhis only really worked for four months of the year, and poverty was an alien concept. In recent years, though, external forces have caused massive and rapid disruption in Ladakh. Contact with the modern world has debilitated and demoralized a once proud and self-sufficient people, who today are suffering from what can best be described as a cultural inferiority complex.

In traditional Ladakhi culture, all basic needs (food, clothing and shelter) were provided without money. All labour needed and given was free of charge, part of an intricate and long-established web of human relationships. Because Ladakhis had no need for money, they had little or none. So when they saw outsiders – tourists and visitors – coming in, spending what was to them vast amounts of cash on inessential luxuries, they suddenly felt poor. Not realizing that money was essential in the West – that without it, people often go homeless or even starve – they didn't realize its true value. They began to feel inadequate and backward. And as their desire to be "modern" grows, Ladakhis are turning their backs on their traditional culture. I have seen Ladakhis wearing wristwatches they cannot read and heard them apologizing for the lack of electric lighting in their homes – electric lighting which in 1975, when it first appeared, most villagers laughed at as an unnecessary idiocy. Even traditional foods are no longer a source of pride; now, when I'm a guest in a Ladakhi village, people apologize if they serve the traditional roasted barley ngamphe instead of instant noodles.

Ladakh is now being integrated into the Indian, and hence the global, economy. In political terms, each Ladakhi is now one individual in a national economy of eight hundred million, and, as part of a global economy, one of about six billion. As a result, local economies are crumbling. In Ladakh, as elsewhere, the breaking of local cultural, economic and political ties isolates people from their locality and from each other. At the same time, life speeds up and mobility increases, making even familiar relationships more superficial and brief. Competition for scarce jobs and political representation within the new centralized structures increasingly divides people. Ethnic and religious differences begin to take on a political dimension, causing bitterness and enmity on a scale hitherto unknown. With a desperate irony, the monoculture creates divisions that previously did not exist.

Source F

Cowen, Tyler. *Creative Destruction: How Globalization is Changing the World's Cultures*. New Jersey: Princeton University Press, 2002. Print.

The following source is an excerpt of Chapter 1 of the book Creative Destruction: How Globalization is Changing the World's Cultures. *In its entirety, the book describes new forms of globalization, ones without the use of military or violence. The author explains how this new "creative globalization" functions through the spread of economy and culture as a medium of exchange and interaction.*

The Canadian government discouraged the American book-superstore Borders from entering the Canadian market, out of fear that it would not carry enough Canadian literature. Canadians subsidize their domestic cinema and mandate domestic musical content for a percentage of radio time, which leads to extra airplay for successful Canadian pop stars like Celine Dion and Barenaked Ladies.

The French spend approximately $3 billion a year on cultural matters, and employ twelve thousand cultural bureaucrats, trying to nourish and preserve their vision of a uniquely French culture. They have led a world movement to insist that culture is exempt from free trade agreements. Along these lines, Spain, South Korea, and Brazil place binding domestic content requirements on their cinemas; France and Spain do the same for television. Until recently India did not allow the import of Coca-Cola.

Benjamin Barber claimed that the modern world is caught between Jihad, a "bloody politics of identity," and McWorld, "a bloodless economics of profit," represented by the spread of McDonald's and American popular culture. John Gray, an English conservative, has argued that global free trade is ruining the world's polities, economies, and cultures. His book is entitled *False Dawn: The Delusions of Global Capitalism*. Jeremy Tunstall defined the "cultural imperialism thesis" as the view that "authentic, traditional and local culture in many parts of the world is being battered out of existence by the indiscriminate dumping of large quantities of slick commercial and media products, mainly from the United States." Fredric Jameson writes: "The standardization of world culture, with local popular or traditional forms driven out or dumbed down to make way for American television, American music, food, clothes and films, has been seen by many as the very heart of globalization."

The next move – and this is the most challenging move – asks the you to imagine presenting your position on the issue to each of the authors of the research sources. In role-playing the author/creator of each source, you need to create an imaginary conversation between yourself and the author/creator of the source where the merits and drawbacks of the stated position are deliberated on in a civil and productive way. The chart below details the researcher's general position of how the source material responds to the central line of inquiry: "Develop a position on the impact of the proliferation of American influences and ideas across the globe." This example set of notes should help illustrate the type of thinking which should take place during the process of discussion and discovery between the author and the sources.

Central Line of Inquiry: Develop a position on the impact of the proliferation of American influences and ideas across the globe.

How would this source respond to the central line of inquiry?	How would this source respond to the arguments from the other sources?
A This source is a "springboard" to the discussion of the impact of globalization on the world outside of America. The source is not directly positive or negative, but instead it remains neutral in that it shines light on both sides of the argument. Look no further than the final two paragraphs. On one hand, America is described as a good influence on others through the spread of American values and culture. On the other hand, the final paragraph highlights the drawbacks of globalization by focusing on its potential perils. The source's main argument is one that suggests that globalization has myriad effects that prevent it from resisting a "just positive" or "just negative" perspective. The fact that this main argument isn't directly stated highlights the grey area of how globalization affects countries outside of the "powerhouses" like the United States.	This source, in one way or another, connects to all of the other sources. Williamson's speech provides a general outline and overview of the concept of globalization which provides a nice frame of reference for the sources that follow. This source has clear links to Shimimura (Source D) and Norberg-Hodge (Source E). Shimimura outlines a number of positive effects of American globalization in Japan, whereas Norberg-Hodge counters this idea, instead showing its negative results in Ladakh, India. In short, the abstract ideas put forward by Williamson are concretized by these other sources. The fact that Japan gained new products (like McDonald's food) and economic growth are specific positive results which this source describes, whereas when Ladakh' society and economy were destroyed (losing their tight-knit community), Norberg-Hodge highlights the negatives from Source A.
B This source, written from the point of view of three university students, outlines a surprisingly positive view on the impact of globalization. The source's argument comments on the prompt by essentially advancing the thesis that American influences will be better for the rest of the world. The author begins with a straightforward declaration of this sentiment, "Globalization has greatly	Source B runs parallel to argument of Shimimura (Source D). Although Source B talks about mainly what happens inside the United States and what globalization does for the United States, while Source D talks mainly about the benefits in Japan, the two are closely linked. For instance, Source B mentions how "globalization also aids in the ability for American corporations to sell their products outside of the

(Continued)

How would this source respond to the central line of inquiry?	How would this source respond to the arguments from the other sources?
impacted the United States and American citizens. First and foremost, globalization has spread American influence throughout the world. Globalization has opened more markets for the United States, which in effect helps American . . ." The authors seem to suggest that the world will be better with these American ideals and influences in place. They already work out great for America, the source says. Why would it be different anywhere else?	country and aids in keeping the nation on top or near the top economically." Source D recontextualizes this notion in Japan: "Japan looks like America on the surface: there are McDonald's, Starbucks, Kentucky Fried Chicken, and Tower Records everywhere, and people wear American jeans, American tee shirts, American shoes, listen to American pop music, and watch American movies and TV dramas." Source F (Cowen) counters the thesis of Source B by presenting an interpretation that American markets and influence have gone overboard.
C This journal article provides a perspective on globalization through the eyes of an anthropologist. The source largely deals with the topic of contemporary globalization by drawing distinctions between different levels of what the process can do. The text concludes with an interesting picture of how globalization and local cultures interact: "The global culture is not an extended version of the local cultures; rather it is the cultural interaction of the global and the local level. A local culture is the product of face-to-face interaction of members of a distinct society, whereas the global culture is a product of interaction among people of diverse societies living far from each other." The source provides a reconciling view on the central line of inquiry. It does not necessarily criticize globalization, but instead describes how globalization fits into the local cultures. In this sense, this source justifies the inevitable globalization of the world, and the author finds that the globalization of American culture will work to the benefit of other societies if they are willing to understand it in a spirit of charity.	This source contrasts sharply to the ideas presented in Source F (Cowen) which describes how globalization is more destructive of the societies it infiltrates and absorbs, whereas this source describes it as the, "modern world [being] caught between Jihad, a 'bloody politics of identity,' and McWorld, 'a bloodless economics of profit' represented by the spread of McDonald's and American popular culture." With words like "Jihad" and "bloody politics," Cowen sees globalization as a harm to the receiving society, whereas Source C sees the upside of globalization more as a synthesis between local cultures, not simply taking them over. Additionally, Source C matches up with the ideas presented in Source D (Yimimura). Here, the author describes how the Japanese culture adopts American ideas and cultural elements by properly integrating them within their society so that the source culture remains at the forefront, while still accepting other outside influences. Source C corroborates this sentiment, suggesting that local cultures and outside influence can be reconciled and harmonized so as to promote progress.
D This journal provides a Japanese perspective on how American influences affect the author's country of origin. The author, a professor at a women's university, describes how American ideas and culture have penetrated her country and how Japan is receptive toward the changes. She explains how Japan typically tries to integrate foreign ideas with Japanese culture rather than rely only on the foreign influence as the sole dictator of the cultural trajectory. Source D provides insight on the issue posed in the central line of inquiry via inclusion of a concrete example that shows how globalization directly affects a society outside of the United States. The source stands	This source lines up well with Source C (Mondal) by more-or-less reiterating his sentiment, "As regards the local-global cultural interaction, it is necessary to see how the global cultural flows become locally appropriated, syncretized and hybridized." Source D re-imagines this "hybridization," now between American and Japanese culture, and this connection puts these two sources in tandem. For example, the author notes that despite having so many American infiltrations like McDonald's, the core culture is not consumed, ". . . and at McDonald's restaurants in Kyoto their Golden Arches are not yellow-colored but are a more modest brown color to fit into Kyoto's traditionally serene landscape." This harmonized view

(Continued)

How would this source respond to the central line of inquiry?	How would this source respond to the arguments from the other sources?
alone among the others in the sense that the author argues that the impact of American culture can be used to the benefit of the foreign country, if used appropriately and in moderation. In this sense, this source generally leans toward the stance that there is some good to the vast spread of American culture by highlighting its utility abroad, not merely dismissing it as an "unnecessary influence."	of globalization, however, contrasts with some of the other sources, primarily Source E (Norberg-Hodge). Whereas Source D provides a generally positive picture of the Americanization of Japan, Source E finds that in Ladakh, India, the people "began to feel inadequate and backward. And as their desire to be 'modern' grows, Ladakhis are turning their backs on their traditional culture." In this sense, the two sources speak in different voices, disagreeing on the effects of globalization on the receiving culture.
E This source provides a particular situation of globalization's impact on a society, this time with the "third world" society of Ladakh. Throughout the source, the author describes the complete change (and essential destruction) of a once traditional society before globalization hit. Norberg-Hodge contributes to the central inquiry by showing how globalization can be dangerous for the world as it can completely change some societies, a change that is not for the better and nearly impossible to reverse. She also hits the emotional side of this process, noting that "local economies" are dying and people are becoming isolated from who they were before. Such usage of pathos-charged scenes makes the reader feel sympathy for the society while villainizing globalization on those outside of America, despite our ethno-centric thinking that it may help make others more "modern."	This source picks up on ideas found in Source F (Cowen). Source F provides insight on how the American influence is "creatively destroying" the world by driving aggressively at the idea that our culture and the Americanization of the world can prove deadly for traditional cultures and beliefs of the receiving society. Understood in light of Cowen's arguments, the Ladakh situation demonstrates the corrosive effect of globalization on a culture's identity by economically and culturally changing it. This source sharply juxtaposes Source D (Shimimura). While Source D outlines a specific situation of how globalization may work positively, Source E illustrates the exact opposite scenario by showing the other extreme of globalization and its horrible effects on societies outside the United States.
F This source, drawn from a book entitled *Creative Destruction: How Globalization is Changing the World's Cultures*, describes how globalization often works in the modern world. Cowen views the entire process as a conflict between different nations who are trying to make their influence predominant, and in this battle, he explains how others are trying to stop America from infiltrating their nations. He argues that the current processes of globalization are "creative" in that it does not destroy or take over societies with sword and shield, but rather with economy and culture. The source's argument comments on the central line of inquiry in that it provides a perspective which sees many nations partaking in this race for dominance abroad. While the source essentially takes the position of globalization-as-negative, it does so by advancing the thesis that globalization leads to the supplanting of local cultures with the new foreign influence.	Source F directly contrasts with several sources in the cluster, notably Source B (Smith, et al.). The main argument that Cowen puts forward is that "the modern world is caught between Jihad, a 'bloody politics of identity,' and McWorld, 'a bloodless economics of profit,' represented by the spread of McDonald's and American popular culture." Whereas Cowen's stance is clearly negative, Source B supports globalization by noting how it "aids in the ability for American corporations to sell their products outside of the country and aids in keeping the nation [America] 'on top' or 'near the top' economically. Globalization has increased the real-time communication abilities between international organizations and nations. This has allowed for a greater emphasis on international cooperation." With this view of globalization as a universal good, working out in everyone's best interest, there is a sharp conflict in Source F, which essentially escribes globalization as an influence war whose losers are irrevocably changed.

You can see here the importance of a well-constructed claim. If you have a fuzzy focus, the sources will have no one to talk to and all productive conversation breaks down. The claim is the centerpiece of the sources; it determines which sources you will eventually include as well as connection you may draw among them. After you have conducted the imagined conversation, you may need to tinker with your original thesis because, at this point in the process, it may well have adjusted or even changed altogether. Nonetheless, the "parlor" approach helps to map out how your source material could potentially be integrated into the final argument.

Critically Engaging the Different Parts of a Source's Content

The virtual discussion detailed above will help to critically build your point of view, but this method has its limitations. Its chief shortcoming is that it handles the sources from a bird's eye view, paraphrasing their main stances to put them in some sort of relation with your developing thesis. The methods we'll discuss here get into the weeds of the individual sources, giving you useful tools to extract the most important perspectives while dealing in specific paragraphs, lines, and words. These exercises engage with source material in three discrete ways: critiquing assumptions, posing counter-positions, extending on ambiguities. Doing so will help you, as Mary Goldschmidt argues in *Marginalia: Teaching Texts, Teaching Readers, Teaching Writers* (2010), build a legitimate point of view that is now more situated in the discourse of the subject in addition to helping assuage common misconceptions that lurk in source-based argumentation, namely

1) seeing the text in "black and white" (where a reader either completely accepts or dismisses but can't assess merits as well as faults).
2) believing the "author is always right."
3) not being able to critique the author's views or "read against the grain."
4) understanding what single sentences "say" (or mean) but not understanding what they "do."
5) failing to see writing as an instance of language use that can be read from multiple perspectives, by different audiences, with different agendas.

To show these ideas in operation, we'll look at three sources from a hypothetical research "library" of sources on the topic of schooling and testing.

Critiquing the Warrant or Underlying Assumption of a Source

In Stephen Toulmin's *An Introduction to Reasoning* (1979), he discusses the "warrant" as the connective ligament that binds the claim and evidence. Warrants are often unstated but are powerful drivers of arguments that determine its direction and an audience's reaction to it. Knowing how to identify a warrant is essential to argument appraisal; knowing how to *use* it for the purposes of your own research is a powerful dialectical method of source integration. Consider the following quotation from Paul Goodman's "A Proposal to Abolish Grading" (1966), an essay which argues that grades are a hindrance to the educational experience and should be done away with.

> "Let half a dozen of the prestigious universities – Chicago, Stanford, the Ivy League – abolish grading, and use testing only and entirely for pedagogic purposes as teachers see fit…[since] for most students the competitive grade has become the essence."

Paul Goodman, a giant in 20th century pedagogy, is an intimidating person to critique, and student researchers without much background in educational theory may feel justifiably reticent to challenge his authority, but here is where analysis of a warrant can yield some useful insights. What is the warrant inside of Goodman's claim? Let's break it down into the stages from Chapter 10:

> Claim: Prestigious universities should abolish grades.
>
> Data: Competitive grading has become the "essence" of education.
>
> Warrant: Students and teachers from elite academic institutions would thrive in a gradeless system.

Once you've squared yourself with the assumption(s) a source makes, you now have a toe-hold in how to critique it. What is Goodman assuming about elite academic institutions that other institutions (higher education, high school, middle school, etc.) do not have or are not capable of? On one hand, you could affirm Goodman's warrant by acknowledging that removing grades would be a win-win: students who have spent their lives in hyper-competitive grading contexts would likely thrive when the pressure of grades is removed, while the study skills and academic rigor that got them where they are remain in place. On the other hand, you could counter Goodman's warrant on grounds of common-sense experience: most students who end up at these institutions do so because of the credentialing an Ivy League degree will grant them in the job market. And if the aim of higher education for these folks is to get a leg up on your competition, removing grades may have a drastic effect on student motivation, thereby sucking the academic marrow out of the institution altogether.

You could press this line of questioning further. What does Goodman assume about the types of students who attend these institutions? Do you think this is a fair assessment of them, or he is glossing over elements of them to suit the purposes of his argument? What does he assume about the professional judgement of the professors? Do public university professors, or high school teachers, not have the same fidelity to the well-being of their students? By posing some of these questions, hopefully you can see that whether you agree or disagree with this warrant is beside the point. The insights yielded by an analysis of it is where the real value of this method takes effect since your response will generate some proto-commentary on the issue that can eventually be used in writing of the paper, moving you beyond the common trap of merely recapping an argument.

Posing Counter-Arguments or "Believing and Doubting"

In *Writing Without Teachers* (1973), author Peter Elbow describes an approach to source analysis – "believing" and "doubting" games – that is designed to break bad research habits among students (and faculty). Elbow observed that academia tends to approach sources with a one-dimensional mind, often equivocating "criticism" with a "tearing down," a search-and-destroy method of reading that probes for weaknesses and contradictions in a source's argument. Elbow sees this method as a "counter-intellectual enterprise" which often leads students to seek out research that either validates their already formed opinion or ones which can be easily obliterated in strawman-laden refutation. Elbow proposes that to get the most out of your research you should "believe" the sources you initially oppose and "doubt" the sources with which you provisionally agree. By "believing," Elbow suggests that readers fully invest themselves in a source's point of view – even if that point of view is opposed to the one that will be held in the paper – to see the merits of its positions, perspectives, and evidence.

By "try[ing] to have that experience of meaning," believing encourages the construction of a thoughtful perspective on the source which is fairer, balanced, and objective. By "doubting," Elbow proposes that a researcher scrutinize every element of a source's argument, leaving no logical stone unturned. This is tough intellectual work since as Elbow notes, "The truer it seems, the harder you have to doubt it." As a result of reacting against those arguments in your selected source, you will hopefully acquire some clarity on *why* you hold the opinions and positions you do and be able to write sensibly about these insights. Consider the following from Howard Gardner's "Test for Aptitude, Not Speed" (2002). In the essay, the author argues along the following lines: if a test is test is a measurement of student knowledge, and students need time for thought and reflection to complete tests, then tests should be administered in untimed settings in order to demonstrate what they really know. Below, the author quotes from his detractors:

> "Speed [on tests] is of the essence."

Let's take this claim and cast it into a "believing" and "doubting" framework, based on reading, observation, and experience.

Believing	Doubting
If I were to *believe* this proposition, what are some of the benefits of timed testing?	If I were to *doubt* this proposition, what are some of the drawbacks of timed testing?
— Some assessments are designed for the test taker to make rapid and valid choices in limited amount of time.	— Questions of fairness and equity come into play since not all students can access complex material in time-pressure scenarios.
— In a relatively low-consequence context, timed testing prepares students for future tasks in life which require an individual to perform skilled worked under pressure.	— Untimed tests allow for more complex, multi-part questions which can measure higher levels of student performance.
— Most tests are administered with reasonable time restrictions and more time will not always end up yielding a good (or even right) answer.	— Tests should measure correctness of information, not how fast a student can respond.
— Setting a time limit could help reveal the amount of information that has been retained from a lesson.	— For tests with writing, untimed assessments allow for time to draft and revise compositions, a more accurate reflection of the writing process.
— Timed tests measure related skills of time organization and an ability to prioritize tasks.	— Untimed testing reduces the emphasis on "test taking skills" in the curriculum.
— Though timed exams may be a healthy challenge for advanced students, those with cognitive and/or language needs are often at a disadvantage.	— Untimed testing reduces student anxiety of finishing on time, thus providing more accurate and actionable data for the teacher.

By putting a source through a gauntlet of both believing and doubting, "we can," as Peter Elbow says, "get farther and farther into it, see more and more things in terms of it or 'through' it, use it as a hypothesis to climb higher and higher to a point from which more can be seen and understood".

Provide Clarification on Ambiguities and Generalities

In Chapter 2, we discussed Socrates's method of definition; that is, a true definition adheres to "every/only" categories (every triangle has three sides and only triangles have three sides). This deductive method of definition is neat and orderly, but everyday language use – as you would find in source material – can rarely be parsed along these lines. Instead of the categorical definitions of Socrates, we'll turn to a method from Socrates's great rival, Gorgias. Gorgias was best known for his use of "ostensive definition" or defining things by pointing out examples of those things in the real world. This form of thought is one of the oldest methods of disputation where arguers find ambiguities or generalities in the language of another and exploit these linguistic loopholes for their own argumentative uses. The 20th century linguist Ludwig Wittgenstein clarified this idea in *Tractatus Logico-Philosophicus* (1953) thus: "the ostensive definition explains the use – the meaning – of the word when the overall role of the word in language is clear."

"Ostensive definition" can be a powerful tool of engagement with source material. Even the most careful of writers don't compose everything they say in "every/only" terms, which means that there are always opportunities to identify ambiguities in a source reading. And if you can lock into these unresolved moments in a writer's diction, *you* can step in to provide clarification (for the purposes of forwarding your own view or argument). In process, you'll move the argument from the realm of the general and the abstract to the specific and the concrete. Consider the following statement from Diane Ravitch's *In Defense of Testing* (2000).

> "[Tests] encourage students to exert more effort"

What is the ambiguity here? It's unclear as to what Ravitch means by "more effort" and here is where you can expand this assertion with some potential examples of what "more effort" (good or bad) may look like.

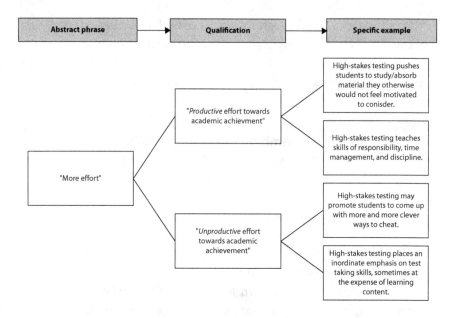

From here, you can apply your own commentary on a point made in the source. To do this effectively, you must be able to scan a text for its fruitful ambiguities. But how do you read with an eye to convert general and abstract into the specific and concrete? A few hints:

1. Check the verb. Verbs are the motors of prose. If the verbs are abstract, the writing will be abstract too, leaving the door open for further clarification. Don't let an author 'open' doors when they can be 'barged down.'
2. Check the subject. Readers want sharp, crisp images in writing, not nouns that are vague and flabby. Don't let a sentence like "a rescue was attempted" slip by without notice. Readers want to know about heroes who rescue with bravery and skill: "The S.W.A.T. team scaled the forty-foot wall."

Avoiding Plagiarism

Adapted from *The MLA Handbook for Writers of Research Papers, Seventh Edition*, (2009):

Derived from the Latin word *plagiarius* ("kidnapper"), to *plagiarize* means "to commit literary theft" and to "present as new and original an idea or product derived from an existing source." Plagiarism involves two types of wrongs: using another person's ideas, information, or expressions without acknowledging that person's work or passing off another person's ideas, information, or expressions as your own to get a better grade or gain some other advantage (52).

Read this definition again and notice how it's presented. It successfully side-steps all the common mistakes when it comes to source attribution: it identifies the source, places quotation marks around words from the source, and clearly marks the boundaries between original words and those from the source. Plagiarism is the theft of another person's word or ideas. It is an academic offense that carries along with it some very unpleasant consequences. You steal words when you lift someone else's language verbatim or with surface alterations, do not provide quotation marks to show that the expression is not your own, or do not provide the proper citation. Teachers and professors have come to resign themselves to the existence of some of the necessary evils that lurk in the dark corners of the World Wide Web. Of course, that doesn't mean you should use materials from the Web in place of your own writing and thinking, but it does mean that teachers are powerless to stop you from consulting them. That being the case, this short section will try to impress upon you the vital importance of academic integrity – that is, submitting work that is, indeed, entirely your own. Plagiarism is not only shamefully lazy, but it is a slap in the face to the academic process while cheapening the effort of students who actually do their own work.

Consider the following side-by-side of Pauline Hopkins's "borrowings" that found their way into her novel *Of One Blood* (1903):

From "The Improvvisatore" by Emma Hardinge Britten	From *Of One Blood* by Pauline Hopkins
Crossing the room, the earl, by the waning light, gazed steadfastly at the book. It was an immense family Bible, with heavy clasps grown far too stiff and rusty by disuse for the delicate fingers of his fair wife to open... There, on the open page, he perceived heavy marks in ink, underscoring the following lines from the 12th chapter of St. Luke: "For there is nothing covered that shall not be revealed, neither hid that shall not be known." On the margin, at the end of this passage, was written in a fine, female hand, the single word, "Beatrice."	Crossing the room, Aubrey gazed steadfastly at the book. It was the old family Bible, and the heavy clasps had grown stiff and rusty. It was familiar to him, and intimately associated with his life history. There on the open page were ink lines underscoring the twelfth chapter of Luke: "For there is nothing covered that shall not be revealed, neither hid that shall not be known." On the margin, at the end of this passage, was written in a fine, female hand, the single word, "Mira."

What's going on here? Although literary authors may sometimes allude to other piece of literature for effect, this seems like a pretty clear-cut case of plagiarism and, indeed, it is. Hopkins neglects to refer to her source by name, or place quote marks in her text to indicate that many words are borrowed from a source. There is no shame in giving credit where credit is due. How do you do that? Again, put quotation marks around the quote. When citing ideas, signal the beginning of someone else's thought or discovery by letting the reader know, in your own paragraph, who that someone else is. That will tell the reader where the source reference begins. The note, which may come right away or at the end of the paragraph, will tell him where the references ends. Anything outside of those "brackets" – the name of the person you are quoting on the front end and the note on the back end – must be your own, both words and ideas. In the case of *Of One Blood*, the words are stolen, and Hopkins has attempted to hide the theft.

As you begin to write the early drafts of your paper, you'll want to check your work carefully to be sure you have not inadvertently committed plagiarism, the much more common (but no less serious) scenario for most student writers. Read the following excerpt from the Translator's Postscript in Robert Fagles's translation of *The Aeneid* (2006). Then, take a look at the following examples from a hypothetical research paper which use Fagles's work as a source. Use these to help you distinguish between legitimate documentation and what is nothing of the kind.

> *Seeing is believing that all three epic poems coexist, but giving voice to that belief is another matter – enough to leave one standing "silent, upon a peak in Darien." So let me extend these questions of style to others that also affect a translator, his mood and mind, and his appreciation of his author. Whether or not such things find full expression, they may inform his approach, and perhaps a part of his work as well* (Fagles 395).

<u>Source Inclusion Attempt #1:</u> As Robert Fagles notes, seeing is believing that the *Iliad*, the *Odyssey*, and the *Aeneid* coexist, but giving voice to that belief is another matter. These concerns extend to questions style that also affect a translator, his mood and mind, and his appreciation of his author (Fagles 395).

> Some students have the idea that a parenthetical citation is all you
> need to cover your bases, the get-out-of-jail free card of academic

writing. And, notice here that the plagiarist has provided the appropriate endnote. What is the trouble, then? Well, the words belong to Fagles and not the student; the very structure of the paragraph belongs to Fagles, too. No quotation marks are used, and the student has made just a few surface alterations to the text to pass Fagles's work off as original words. They are not.

Source Inclusion Attempt #2: As Robert Fagles notes, the relationship between all three epic poems give voice to another matter – questions of style that also affect a translator, his disposition and attitude, and his indebtedness of his author. It's impossible to say whether such things will realize complete expression in a translation, but they may influence his approach, and perhaps part of the work itself (Fagles 395).

> This second attempt is also guilty of plagiarism, this time in a way that's tougher to spot. If you read the source and the student's attempt closely, you'll notice that what the student has written doesn't belong to him. It's Fagles's work. What if you use a thesaurus and change the source's language by supplying synonyms? Sorry, that still will not do. The source text has provided the writer with everything but some nouns and verbs – even those new nouns and verbs ("relationship" for "coexist," "disposition" for "mood," "attitude" for "mind, "realize" for "find," and so forth), both what they are and where they are, suggest Fagles's work.

Source Inclusion Attempt #3: It's plain to see, says Robert Fagles, "that all three epic poems coexist" (Fagles 395). Fagles is right. The fact that these poems bear such close similarities give rise to other concerns in Virgilian scholarship, concerns which deeply affect the translator, his attitude towards the text and his reverence for the author. Do these things find full expression in the translation process? It's hard to say, but what one can confidently say is that these variables shape his process, and they may even find their way into the final product.

> Plagiarism may also involve the stealing of ideas as we see with this failed attempt of source attribution. The writer has provided quotation marks and a parenthetical citation in the lead-off line. So far so good. But look at what appears in the subsequent lines.

By bracketing the quotation off with a citation, the writer is suggesting that what follows (which has no citations at all) is original, both in thought and presentation. Take a close look at these lines against the source. What follows the quote doesn't belong to the student; these ideas are Fagles's through and through. The ideas, what they are and how they hang together, are stolen from the source.

<u>Source Inclusion Attempt #4:</u> As the author says, "Seeing is believing that all three epic poems coexist, but giving voice to that belief is another matter" (Fagles 395). Here, Fagles raises a fundamental question for modern readers who are encountering the work of Virgil in translation: are we getting Virgil's direct ideas, or the ideas of Virgil pressed through the translator's sieve, a process which often reduces Classical texts into a sounding board for modern politics? It's tough to say if such constraints would "find full expression, [but] they may inform his approach, and perhaps a part of his work as well" (Fagles 395).

> This writer has done everything he needs to do. The quotations, both at the beginning and the end, let the reader know where his paragraph is dealing in words and ideas of the source text. What appears outside of the quotation is original, both in thought and presentation. See how the student has used Fagles's distinction between what's printed on the page and its implied "voice" to move into a discussion of the challenges historical distance presents to the translator and how a reader may negotiate this rift. The writer has absorbed the source text, digested its ideas, and produced something fresh and new, all while giving credit where credit is due.

Even in these examples, it's tough to know what needs to be cited and what does not. As a general rule, when you cite somebody's words, be sure you place them in quotation marks; if you are not citing the exact words, you must provide a complete overhaul of the language and the word order in the source. You must, in other words, do your own writing, even if you are not at the moment doing you own thinking. And even then, if the idea is not entirely your own, you will still need to provide an attribution to indicate where it was drawn from. Simply, if there is any question at all as to whether something needs to be documented, provide a citation.

As you begin to think about which quotes you may incorporate into your own writing, it's important to remember, as Don Bialostosky says in *Liberal Education: Writing and The Dialogic Self* (1991) that "quotation is the very act in which one voice creatively absorbs another and defines it in relation to that second voice. When we interrupt the quoted text, interrogate it, clarify its point, or expose its ambiguities, we make an opening for our own utterances and give it shape to our own roles in the conversation." You must clearly articulate to your reader the stance or attitude you have towards the quotation and this can be accomplished by setting the quotation up with a well-chosen signal phrase that indicates the use you plan to make of the source. Essentially, there are three ways a source can be put to use in your research: direct quotation, paraphrase, and summary.

Quotation of Source Material

Going back to the earliest days of rhetoric and argumentation, direct quotation is the most tried and true method of establishing an authoritative tone. Since published authors are often experts in their field, quotations provide you with a sort of "loaned credibility" to speak commandingly on the information at hand. Quotations can do a great many things in a source-based essay: it can provide expert testimony, supply corroborating evidence, frame a historical context, or present a jumping-off point for further analysis and commentary. "How you actually go about incorporating other texts into your own prose," Joseph Harris says in *Rewriting* (2006), "can also say a good deal about the stance or attitude you want to take towards them." It's true there are conventional rules of *how* quotes should be run-into your writing – and we'll discuss these in length in Chapter 19 – but, as Harris says, "quotations can't, and shouldn't, always be reduced to a simple matter of rules." Look at the last couple of lines and see how the quotation solidifies and authorizes my own commentary on quotations and their use.

There are a whole host of problems students tend to run into when introducing quotes, chief among them is neglecting to introduce quotations with signal verbs which indicate how the writer has positioned themselves in relation to the ideas found in the quoted material. Consider the following "Table of Quotation Verbs" (Table 1) – adapted from *Using Sources Effectively* (2002) – to help clarify what we mean here.

Table 1 Table of Quotation Verbs.

Signal verbs to introduce quotations		
Says	*Agrees*	*Concedes*
The verb introduces the quotation as information.	The verb indicates that the source agrees with another source or your own position.	The source agrees that a conflicting point is valid.
Adds		Acknowledges
Believes	Accepts	Admits
Comments	Agrees	Agrees
Described	Assents	Allows
Discusses	Concurs	Concedes
Emphasizes	Parallels	Grants
Explains	Supports	Recognizes
Argues in Favor	*Argues Against*	*States Erroneously*
The verb indicates that the source is being used as supporting evidence.	The verb indicates that the source is responding critically to another source or your own position.	The verb indicates the source makes a statement that you are skeptical of.
Argues	Attacks	Alleges
Asserts	Contradicts	Asserts
Contends	Denies	Assumes
Demonstrates	Differs	Charges
Holds	Disagrees	Contends
Indicates	Refutes	Claims
Maintains		Declares
Implies	*Continues*	*Concludes*
The verb indicates the source presents information tentatively or skeptically.	The verb indicates you are making repeated references to a source.	The verb indicates the source draws a point of discussion to a close.
Hints	Adds	Completes
Implies	Builds	Concludes
Indicates	Continues	Decides
Offers	Expands	Determines
Point towards	Extends	Finds
Proposes	Goes on to say	Resolves
Suggests	States further	Settles

Consider the following example of direct quotation:

Although grief is an expression of an individual's intense, deep, and profound sorrow in response to an event or situation, Judith Butler notes in *Precarious Life: The Powers of Mourning and Violence*, "many people think that grief is privatizing, that it returns us to a solitary situation and is, in that sense, depoliticizing. But I think it furnishes a sense of political community of a complex order, and it does this first bringing to the fore the relational ties that have implications" (22). Each of these poems – "Howl" and "America" by Alan Ginsberg and "Don't Let Me Be Lonely" by Claudia Rankine – are just that. On the surface, they are particular to the experience of the author (often times being prohibitive to the audience's complete understanding of the allusion), but these specifics operate in the style of an open letter, a message addressed to a particular person but actually intended for a wide readership.

The technical elements of the quotation are all there. In a typical research paper, with several secondary references, simply use page citations and then indicate somewhere which text the page numbers come from. End run-in quotations in this sequence (as this author has): quote marks, page reference in parenthesis, full stop. And put only one full stop ("period") in a sentence.

> **This**: "…silly not to" (68). **Not this**: "…silly not to." (68). **Or this**: "…silly not to. (68)"

But more than the technical elements, it's clear that the author has put this secondary source to use in a purposeful way since the quotation is included as a frame for further analysis. By using Butler's words, the author is able to contextualize the poetry of Ginsberg and Rankine and frame what follows in terms articulated by the quotation.

Paraphrasing of Source Material

Paraphrasing – the expression of a written or spoken idea using different words – is a method of source integration that stands halfway between quotation and summary. Like quotation, paraphrasing is anchored in the source text, complete with an acknowledgment of the borrowing, in order to retain its authoritative tone. Like summary, you are the filter through which the source text passes, and paraphrase should include a near-overhaul of the diction and syntax of the original to ensure it is, indeed, your own. Paraphrasing is often used by writers looking to achieve greater clarity in their argument, and it is a particularly useful move when incorporating jargon-laden material from academic sources and scholarly journals. In addition to providing clarification, paraphrasing works well when you want to reorder the ideas from a source text for emphasis, provide a simplified explanation of a complicated idea in your own words, or simply add in some stylistic variety (since quote-after-quote can get tiresome to read after a short run). Consider the following example of a paraphrase:

> Most troubling to me is the way in which the slippage between teacher expectations for students' class participation and student readiness to engage in dialogue can alienate students. In the paradigm of the dialogic classroom, "the thoughtful and deliberate student is often judged and described with the same words as the student who...refuses to engage in learning," (Schultz 6) with the result that quiet students may be stigmatized as unmotivated, slow, or resistant – labels which can follow the student from class to class and year to year. When teachers define participation solely as speaking, they also render mute non-verbal indicators of engagement such as students' enthusiasm for the subject, attention in class, and investment in their work because these qualities "do not count" as active participation. Unfortunately, the traditional participation structures of a dialogic classroom leave students little opportunity to understand silence as anything more than their failure to meet classroom expectations (Schultz 6).

See how the author has bridged the direct quotation of Schultz's theory into a paraphrase of it that provides clarification to its finer points. A reader of this paraphrase is not bogged down with pedagogical jargon or technical terms; instead, the author has (stylistically) blended his own words with Schultz's ideas for maximum force.

Summary of Source Material

One way to incorporate research into your writing is to present a summary of a source's argument. Summarization is useful move for writers who wish to reference large chunks of text – chapters, units, even whole books – without resorting to extended discussions of content that's obscured by specific detail and technical language. Summary also has use when it comes to providing a reader of your argument with context or a frame of reference through which the main topic can be understood. Summary is often used to situate an argument into larger circles of discourse, providing an overview of key theorists and ideas in a particular line of research. Should you choose to summarize, you'll want to observe many of the same conventions as you would when integrating a quotation: identify the source by author and title, overhaul the diction and syntax, put quotation marks around borrowed words, and provide the appropriate documentation when needed. Consider the following example of summarization in research writing:

> David Bartholomae's "Inventing the University" (1986) hones in on the common errors of novice writers (college freshmen) who feel that they must adopt an inauthentic academic language in order to enter into the university community. His project is stated pretty clearly about halfway through the essay, "I was looking to see what happened when a writer entered into a language to locate himself (a textual self) and his subject; and I was looking to see how, once entered, that language made the writer" (12). While his argument asserts that there is some degree of falsity in the academic voice of students, more recent research argues that students can enter academic discourse without being forced into the language of a community that is not their own.

The author has quoted from Bartholomae, but then goes on to summarize large chunks of his argument for the purposes of brevity. A reader doesn't need to know the ins-and-outs of every aspect of the arguments in "Inventing the University." Sometimes, less is more, and the few lines the of summary the author has provided is adequate to get the point across.

As a final step before the writing of the paper, you should compose all of your ideas and source material into some intelligible format. Outlining, a process which identifies, orders, and hierarchizes ideas in a piece of writing, often forms the backbone of the eventual argument that you will present in the final draft. Teachers often assign formal outlines to student writers for this reason. Outlines vary in their degree of formality, but they do force you to make crucial decisions about which ideas are the most important and how the ordering of these ideas will reflect your interpretation and intended emphases. You must also, at this stage, decide how to integrate the source material: should you use their words? paraphrase their ideas? some combination of the two? Sketching out your ideas before you write is an upfront time investment. You will spend a fair amount of time at this initial stage, but this process will undoubtedly pay off in the final draft of the paper, making it tight, coherent, and unified.

CHAPTER SEVENTEEN

WRITING THE SOURCE-BASED ARGUMENT

W e've reached the ultimate step in the research sequence, so it may seem like, in some senses, we have arrived and that the arduous work has been done: the thinking through of topics, the selection and analysis of sources, the formulation of a thesis. There should be a very justified sense of satisfaction in this, but the writing of the research paper is going to be tough. It will be intellectually challenging and creatively demanding. This stage not only asks you to think about the topic in new and interesting ways, but to do so while remaining self-conscious of the moves you make as you plan, think, and write. At this point in the research process, you should have a clear idea of the direction you plan to take in your own paper but may feel stymied on how to expand your paper past the barebones, to get your concepts out of your head (where you can often explain it to yourself in just a paragraph) and transfer them into a reader's head with some degree of explicitness and clarity. This chapter aims to address the most common errors in development that student writers encounter as they are trying to expand their argument to the expected word count.

In this chapter, we'll discuss some broad strategies to get things off the ground for you. These strategies, as you'll see, emphasize structure over style for a very important reason. You cannot write "outside of the box" until you are familiar *with* the box – the conventions, the structure, the order of ideas – of source-based writing. Style and voice will come, but you cannot flex these stylistic muscles until you have skeleton to attach them to. Feel free to riff on these structures as you see fit, and remember, as we've said elsewhere in this book, that the outlines and examples serve to remind you only of the basic strategies for developing a sound argument. Yes, skillful writing is an expression of a writer's inner voice and vision, but that voice can be heard only insofar as its expressed to a reader through some intelligible form and structure.

To illustrate these basic ideas, we'll briefly discuss the components of introductions, body paragraphs, and conclusions, though much of what we'll say here echoes information from Chapters 9 and 10, the two chapters devoted to argument models. Consult those chapters for more detailed information and examples as needed. We'll look at an example to show these principles in operation. We'll also look at a non-example – an illustration of research writing that violates the criteria of good source-based writing – to pre-empt some of the most common missteps found in research writing.

The Introduction

In source-based contexts, where topics tend to be multi-dimensional and complex, introductions must do a great many of tasks in a short space. They must discuss the major contours of the topic, establish a trustworthy tone, layout the thesis, all while maintaining a readable and engaging voice. Depending on the breadth of your topic, the introduction may span multiple paragraphs. In one way or another, your introduction should contain the following:

Attention-seizing device: One of the most crucial moments in a paper is the opening couple of lines that create a first impression. All introductions introduce a topic, but a good introduction should do so in a way that's engaging and relevant to the approach the paper will take. The opening lines, in other words, should catch the reader's interest while justifying the importance of your topic. There are a number of ways to do this, drawing from Classical and Contemporary strategies:

- Inquisitive strategy (Classical): Highlight an interesting aspect of topic, one of its unusual features, an important bit of information, or something which about it which is just plain strange or attention grabbing.

- Antithetical strategy (Classical): Set up one idea about a topic to contrast it with another. Often, a writer will choose an initial aspect of the topic to focus on that somehow opposes the paper's main argument.
- Corrective strategy (Classical): Show that an aspect of a topic has been ignored, misunderstood, or otherwise not paid attention to in the right way. This strategy then goes on to correct this misinterpretation, thus establishing the key definitions and terms of the argument to follow.
- Preparatory strategy (Classical): Begin with generalized statements about a topic that gradually funnel down into the particulars of the issue to establish the terms and limits of what the argument will focus on and what it won't focus on.
- Anecdotal strategy (Classical): Narrate a short story or sequence of events to emphasize emotion or personal investment on your topic.
- Explicit strategy (Classical): Acknowledge your motives or interest in the topic to diffuse suspicion and build trust.
- Conciliatory strategy (Contemporary): Empathize with opponents to your position to build trust and ultimately leverage it towards the position you hold.
- Integrative strategy (Contemporary): Focus on the nature of the problem to build consensus with the audience that a solution is needed, thus building common ground.
- Deliberative strategy (Contemporary): Lead with a description of the problem to emphasize the idea that action is needed.

<u>Establishment of Context</u>: You'll next need to preview what is to come by creating a context for thinking about the topic, allowing readers to enter into the ongoing discussion around the topic, issue, or problem. This important portion of the source-based argument stimulates initial thoughts and provides a frame of reference. Whether the task is narrowly focused or broader, this part of the introduction should let people know something about what people are already talking and writing about. While this segment ought to be helpful, it can be dangerous; if too extensive or provocative, it can distract readers by posing questions or raising issues that command such heavy attention that they will lead readers astray. For topics dealing with multiple sources, it may also be a good idea to establish the key theorists or sources which are central to the argument. You may want to introduce the texts and pertinent background information about the

authors or simply allude to the general topic of the source texts to reveal the general character of the topic. Whatever the case, readers need a lead up to your thesis. When determining how much information you need, consider the following (drawn from our discussion of the classical *narratio* in Chapter 9):

– Is there anything my audience wants to know about my topic? Is there anything they need to know?
– Do my readers have any experience with my topic? Can I appeal to positive aspects of that experience?
– What do my readers already know about my topic? How can I leverage this information in a way that's both clear and concise?
– Are there any well-known current events that coincide with my topic? Would a narrative account of this strengthen a reader's awareness of the issue?
– Are there things to which my audience may be sensitive? Should I word things differently to acknowledge these things while still being sensitive to the experiences of my audience?

Claim or thesis: A reader of your argument should have a clear sense of your stance on the issue. The more specific, the better (think: Toulmin's concept of qualifiers and exceptions). Claims should clearly relate to the evidence to come (think: Toulmin's warrant), though different teachers of writing will advocate for various places where the thesis should appear. Some argue it should come as the final sentence of the introduction – a kind of rhetorical climax to the paper's introductory elements – while others suggest placing it up-front for explicitness, or in the middle for style. Though it's up to you where it appears, keep "clarity" as your guiding principle. Nothing is more damaging to a paper's force than an otherwise well-done thesis that's buried inside a bunch of clutter, and it's a shame when style gets in the way of brains.

The claim is obviously topic dependent, but Classical theory roughly hews four types of claims. They are as follows:

– A claim of cause focuses on how things happened, or whether they happened at all.
– A claim of definition focuses on how an audience should understand the meaning of a word.

- A claim of value looks at particular issue through a filter – values, ethics, morals, so forth – and argues whether or not this view is justifiable.
- A claim of policy focuses on what should be done about an issue.

Here is a look at an example of a well-done introduction for a research paper arguing for the practical application and uses of imaginative literature in day-to-day human affairs.

In 1919's "Tradition and the Individual Talent," author T.S. Eliot describes the ways in which the fiction of the past is inextricably bound up with concerns of the present. This apparent paradox that Eliot gives his readers offers some insight into the role that fiction – even ancient fiction from the remote past – plays in our lives, here in the 21ˢᵗ century. The literary tradition is chock-full of imaginative literature, and this form has endured from Mesopotamia to Meso-America to Modern America. How is it that this one art form has endured from the earliest strata of human society to the modern day?	The author opens with a historical allusion which frames the topic. The author makes quick mention of the uses of fiction which have been shared cross-culturally to suggest the scope of the topic. The author asserts his argument while acknowledging there are many ways to look at the topic.

Here's one way of looking at it: fiction is not merely an intellectual exercise of old books written for its dusty readers but is rather the coherent arrangement of the great ideas of the past that shapes us into who we are.

Here is a look at an example of what not to do in an introduction for a research paper arguing that Advanced Placement courses do more harm than good to high school students.

The human body is quite similar to a volcano; if too much is endured it erupts without a warning. Advanced Placement classes are a similar source	The author introduces the topic through an analogy which is both abrupt and underdeveloped.

of stress of high schoolers. Advanced Placement classes are defined as, "A college level class where a student gets the opportunity to learn about a specific subject in more depth. If the student passes the AP exam in May with a score of 3 or higher, then that student will be able to receive college credits" (De Leon 3). Advanced Placement classes entail an immense amount of focus, energy, and hard work to remain in the class and possibly earn enough credits to be exempt from that specific course in college. The students who undergo the additive stress one endures from these college courses must have enough motivation to carry out the work the course entails. If a student is lacking motivation, one may run the risk of scoring below a college's requirement on the Advanced Placement test and therefore, wasting their time in an Advanced Placement class in high school because one's score will not be accepted as passing. An Advanced Placement class is without a doubt artificial to one's long-term benefits, running the risk of increasing amounts of stress and the failure to meet college's scoring requirements.

> The author presents some background/overview of the situation at hand, but the information comes off a bit clunky and disjointed. The author should clarify the narration and reframe its purpose to introduce competing views on typical student experiences with AP courses as part of an ongoing debate.

> This author's thesis is plagued by absolutes and ambiguities in the diction. The author should revise the thesis to remove the absolutes, clarify the ambiguity of "long term benefits," and make edits to the qualifier "running the...scoring requirements," and include both qualifiers and exceptions.

The Body Paragraphs

There is no one best method of arrangement for the body paragraphs, and each source-based writing project will call for a different configuration. You may find extended discussion, running a page or over, is needed at times in your argument where a well-timed, one sentence paragraph does the job in driving a point home in other places. Adhering to a dogmatic set of "rules" can encumber mature writers, but for most students doing college-level research for the first time, some basic structures are a much-needed support. Body paragraphs in research writing are reducible to four basic ingredients: a main idea, evidence, analysis, and a link back to larger claims. In acronym form, this M.E.A.L. plan (as its termed by Duke University's Writing Studio) will serve most writers well.

1. <u>Main idea</u>: Use topic sentences. Brilliant writers can get away without them, but even they will not try it too often. As the thesis is to the essay, so the topic sentence is to the paragraph. Somewhere in your paragraph, usually towards the beginning, you should state explicitly what point you are trying to prove now or what illustrations you are about to explain. Make your paragraphs reflect the division of your subject. A topic sentence, tied to your thesis, can be helpful here and every paragraph should be a coherent, logically developed whole within the broader context of your essay.

2. <u>Evidence</u>: Evidence and analysis, the salt and pepper of research writing, should always work in tandem and form the bulk of what you are writing in the body paragraphs. In the last two chapters, we discussed the many forms evidence can take (scholarly sources, journalistic sources, popular sources, sensational sources) and various methods of integration (direct quotation, paraphrase, summary). It's best to present a judicious mixture of these methods. Since each method has its own upsides and drawbacks, a well-rounded paper may call for authoritative quoting in some places while modes of evidence are best rendered in your own words in other places.

3. <u>Analysis</u>: Evidence doesn't speak for itself. Analysis occurs when you write out from your quotes, bridging the words of the sources to your own insights on the topic. You must signal to your reader the way you have handled the quoted material – to make visible the thinking that is often invisible – since, as Kay Halasek says in *A Pedagogy of Possibility* (1999), "the act of presenting another's words – even through accurate, direct quotation of another's exact words – is an act of representation and interpretation." Make your interpretation explicit to the reader; body paragraphs should be no place for a reader of your paper to guess what's on your mind. Mature writers organize and structure their writing intuitively, but if you need some concrete assistance, take a look back to our discussion of quotation, paraphrase, and summary from Chapter 16. These methods are powerful frameworks to articulate what's often left unsaid. Remember that your reader (and your instructor) has to deal with your document, not your good intentions.

4. <u>Link Back to the Larger Claims</u>: Most readers like to have paragraphs which end with clear resolution. It's up to you to provide this closure, to show the connection between this paragraph and the paper's main ideas. It's probably best to avoid cardboard signals like, "This idea links to my argument because…," but that doesn't mean you shouldn't show why a paragraph has been legitimately included. What does this point add? How does it relate to what's come before and what follows?

Here's an example of a well-formed body paragraph from the same exemplar as above, a research paper arguing for the practical application and uses of imaginative literature in day-to-day human affairs.

Not only does fiction play a central role in the shaping of culture-at-large, it can have an equally profound effect on the formation of individual values and world views. An entire genre of fiction, the "bildungsroman," is devoted to the exploration to how one comes of age and a reader's experience with the adolescent alienation of Holden Caulfield or the flutters of Jane Eyre's young romance offers an articulate framework that gives meaning to one of life's most turbulent and ineffable periods. But as readers grow up, so do their needs in reading fiction. Caroling Leavitt's "Judy Blume's 'In the Unlikely Event" details the 2015 release of Judy Blume's novel *In the Unlikely Event*, the author's first release after a prolonged, 17-year absence from the literary scene. Blume, best known for her work in children and young adult fiction, brings her prose into own adulthood, and in doing so, lets her fiction discuss concerns relevant to this new adult audience. Her sophisticated narrative techniques of "short chapter bursts, newspaper reports, and scripted dialogue" (Leavitt 1) is

> The author leads off the paragraph by drawing a clear connection to what's preceded and by suggesting what's to follow.

> The author uses a clear signal verb, "details," to indicate that this first quotation will be used to deliver neutral information.

> The author blends direct quotation and paraphrase of source material to suggest that Blume's style is directed at a mature audience.

> The author extends the textual evidence into analysis that chases the implications of Blume's growth in style on her readership.

not only stylishly post-modern, but it speaks "the language" of adults and offers insights far beyond the maturity of her former, pre-pubescent audience. Her style, however, retains the same "emo-tional immediacy as her books for chil-

> The author ends with a brief state-ment that links the presented evidence back to the paragraph's overarching idea.

dren, [and] makes us feel the pure shock and wonder of living, the ways we get through catastrophe" (Leavitt 1) In some ways, Blume's corpus of fiction illus-trates the many ways that imaginative literature can serve the real-world needs of its readership. Whereas "Tales of Fourth Grade Nothing" has something impor-tant to say to its elementary school audience, "In the Unlikely Event" speaks to the concerns of Blume's newfound audience: all grown-up, more mature, and (whether they like it or not) forced into a position of how to negotiate the dif-ficulties of adult life. In short, fiction has the power to shape the worldview of any audience, young or old.

And here is an example of a body paragraph that stumbles and falls. This non-example is excerpted from the same writer as the introduction above, a research paper arguing the Advanced Placement courses do more harm than good to high school students.

In understanding why Advanced Place-ment classes are too stressful for high school students, one must look at the evidence the students themselves pro-vide to argue against Advanced Place-ment courses in high school. Students that enroll in an AP course or multiple AP courses in high school are indirectly ask-ing for additional stress. AP courses add stress to every aspect of a student's life. Students who endure the added stress that Advanced Placement courses tend

> The author seems to draw from personal experience for support, but there is an awkward project-ing of their experience onto a "generic student." Sometimes the "I" voice can be an invigorating and energizing force in a paper's body, but in this case, it is the engine of the paragraph's hasty generalization fallacy.

to have, indeed have less time to enjoy their social lives due to the greater amounts of homework and studying that advanced classes entail. Teachers often times see many students in a daze and under a lot of pressure to meet multiple deadlines for various assignments. It is not uncommon anymore for a teacher to "See kids in tears," (Tucker 7) due to the inhumane amount of stress and pressure a student is under at such a young age. "With four or more hours a day of homework, even sleep is an afterthought" (Tucker 3). As a young adult, it is important for all students to vget an accurate amount of sleep each night to perform their very best in the classroom each and every day. However, with the numerous AP classes students are enrolling in nowadays, that task is next to impossible. The main reason students are taking AP courses in high school is due to the fact that their parents as well as themselves "want every opportunity to stand out on a college application" (Tucker 8).

> The author seems to be establishing common views that many students share regarding AP courses, but the writing seems to be coming off as a generalization of the author's particular experience. The author should explicitly say this or qualify this section with an acknowledgement that this is a consensus view held by the majority of students.

> The author ends the paragraph with a quotation that neither links back to the main idea or to what will be subsequently developed.

The Conclusion

All source-based arguments need some final closure. The easy way out is to recap what you've already said, but no good writers do this, and no readers enjoy reading this. Instead, conclusions should deal in specifics, discussing the implications of what you've just argued. Why is it important we act in the way you've proposed? Why does understanding a word in the way you've argued for matter in the real world? Why is your view on the topic justifiable and what bearing would this have on the life of a reader? In essence, conclusions must explicitly address the "So, what?" concern of an essay. Like introductions, there are a number of ways to do this, drawing from Classical and contemporary strategies:

– Pose a question to the reader strategy (Classical): Test the reader's stance on the issue you have just finished presenting by posing a question to the reader which makes them examine their own views before the essay is put down.

- Sum up what you have done in order to deliver a knockout strategy (Classical): Suggest that you have proven even more than your thesis has promised by going beyond the evidence from the paper to indicate how wide-reaching your final points may be.
- Suggest a different argument under different conditions strategy (Classical): Recognize that your argument is valid within the scenario you have illustrated but may have to be adjusted under changed conditions.
- Try to make the last sentence memorable strategy (Classical): Finish with a short, staccato statement to capture the argument's essence in under five words.
- Conciliatory strategy (Contemporary): Stress the collaborative role that all stakeholders play in your topic.
- Integrative strategy (Contemporary): List the mutual gain for both sides should the audience adopt the proposal or position you have put forward.
- Deliberative strategy (Contemporary): Use fragments from competing points of view to recast the issue into the context of a larger problem that all parties would agree must be solved.

Here's an example of a well-formed conclusion from our go-to example, a research paper arguing for the practical application and uses of imaginative literature in day-to-day human affairs.

Does life imitate art? Or does art imitate life? While this question can't be easily settled, what's certain is that fiction's "staying power" across human history says something about the formative role it has played. Yes, fiction perpetuates cultural ideas and transfers knowledge from one generation to the next, but its role in our lives runs much deeper than storehouse of cultural capital. It makes us who we are. As we read about the lives	The author poses a question that's central to the paper and goes on to chase the implications of that question across history.
	The author provides summarization but now in a way that clearly addresses the paper's underlying "So, what?" question.

of fictional characters, we vicariously decide on a course of action to see an outcome, all without endangering our physical selves, but while completely

investing ourselves into their plight, with full soul and spirit. The saying "You are what you eat" can be reimagined in the context of academic life as "You are what you read."	The author closes by reworking a famous phrase to match the argument that has been made throughout the paper.

Here's an example of a malformed conclusion that ends off our running example, a research paper arguing the Advanced Placement courses do more harm than good to high school students.

In life, all human beings have the right to do what they desire. AP courses are a choice, not a necessity. However, many students find AP classes to be a necessity when applying to college and desiring an acceptance from their top university. AP classes are designed for college, so is it not logical that they be taken in college? I believe that AP courses should only be allowed in colleges, for the layout of the course varies in the ways that high school teachers organize and teach the course compared to the various ways college professors organize and teach	The author leads with a generalization that's so broad it's tough to see how this clearly relates to the topic. Most of this conclusion recaps of what's already been said elsewhere in the paper, but the author needs to address the issue of why these claims matter as the paper draws to its close.

the course. Plus, Advanced Placement courses are far too stressful and time consuming for a high school student to endure, as well as risky. This is because many colleges are not accepting AP credits received in high school. Therefore, many students find themselves wasting time and energy that they could have spent on a different, valuable course. Advanced Placement classes should be strictly limited to colleges; after all, college is primarily the definition of an AP course.

The approach to research writing detailed in this chapter will no doubt come more naturally to "experienced readers [who understand] that both reading and writing are context-rich, situational, and constructive acts" as Christina Hass and Linda Flower say in "Rhetorical Reading Strategies and the Construction of Meaning" (1988). Though these more sophisticated writers already have in their mind's ear the "sounds" of thought, such a process can be both generative and constructive for writers coming to this type of work for the first time. In David Bartholomae's "The Study of Error" (1999), he notes that, "basic writers…are not performing mechanically or randomly but making choices and forming strategies as they struggle to deal with the varied demands of a task, a language, and a rhetoric. Errors, then, are stylistic features, information about *this* writer and *this* language; they are not necessarily 'noise' in the system, accidents in composing, or malfunctions in the language process." Though Bartholomae's discussion of error focuses on student missteps at the sentence level, the spirit of his comments translates to the larger interpretive issues that are at stake in this source-based writing. In other words, the words and thoughts contained in the source-based writing perform a vital function for the developing writer while giving feedback to the reader about your present understanding.

So, once you've put the last period on the last sentence, it might be worth your time to have someone else – a classmate, a friend, a parent, a tutoring center – take a look at the paper to see if it makes sense. Long writing projects lead to blind spots in the author's head, and fresh eyes will catch what you'll often miss. The best acid test of a research paper's clarity is if someone can pick it up on a cold read and follow your argument from front to back. Discussing the readings of your paper with another will invite the writing to "assimilate new ideas, to accommodate others' opinions and experiences, and to develop deeper, fuller perspectives from which to examine what they read and write," notes Hephzibah Roskelly in *Breaking (into) the Circle* (2003). The subsequent talk will help the knowledge to flow in new directions, and though there is potential for a clash of interpretations in this process, that's where the fun is. Things shouldn't devolve into "I'm-right-you're-wrong" shouting matches, but they should lead to productive conversations about conflicting interpretations and what labels apply, so you can together negotiate a more complex understanding of the purposes and functions of your research project. As Mary Goldschmidt concludes, "by sharing observations as a culminating activity that allows students to see additional similarities and differences, they can assess the conclusions of others and appreciate the mutually constructive roles of reader and text."

CHAPTER EIGHTEEN

SOURCE-BASED ARGUMENTS – ADDITIONAL MODELS

Presented in a similar Writing as Product style found in Chapters 7 and 12, the following chapter contains three source-based argument essays. For the purposes of space, each essay is trimmed down from its full-form to focus on the core elements of research writing. Each essay is preceded by a small context setting paragraph intended to give you some sense of the project's scope: historical context, general lines of inquiry, and a prompt to which the essay responds. Like Chapter 12, each essay is accompanied by a string of marginal annotations to highlight the various argumentative and rhetorical strategies the author uses over the course of the piece. These annotations should be thought of as a warehouse of successful moves to be browsed, possibly even imitated, as you begin to develop your own source-based essay. Like we said in the opening of Chapter 12, try to notice the echoes from all the book's preceding chapters inside these writings as you read. They contain a clear argumentative structure, but they don't sacrifice readability and engagement for logical soundness. They are equal parts argumentative and rhetorical while effectively integrating various, sometimes clashing, points of view represented in the source material. They state a thesis and develop an appropriate pattern of organization, but they are not reductive in the claim nor are they overridden with fallacies in the paper's body. In all, these essays represent a blend of the skill set outlined in this text. And if you can successfully bring these together in your own work, you will join the very few who can actually look closely at a topic, examine it constituent parts, and write sensibly about it.

NSA Surveillance: Violation of Civil Rights or Justifiable Security Measure?

Introduction

On June 5th, 2013, a British newspaper, *The Guardian*, published a ground-breaking story based on information provided by National Security Agency (NSA) contractor Edward Snowden about the United States government's surveillance program of its own citizens. The program, known by the code name Prism, granted the NSA direct access to data held on private citizens from Google, Facebook, Apple, and many other telecom corporations.

Once revealed, many citizens argued that the NSA violated its own citizen's civil rights by spying on them without their knowledge or consent. Many other groups argued that spying was a justifiable security measure to protect innocent civilians who live in a complicated, technological world. There has been no closure to the digital dilemma exposed by *The Guardian* in 2013, and the popular debate about ethical behavior in the cyber-world still persists.

Assignment

Take a position that defends, challenges, or qualifies the surveillance measure taken by the NSA.

Example Response

"The right of the people to be secure in their persons, houses, papers, and effects, against unreasonable searches and seizures, shall not be violated, and no Warrants shall issue, but upon probable cause, supported by Oath or affirmation, and particularly describing the place to be searched, and the persons or things to be seized" (NARA). So reads the Fourth Amendment to the American Bill of Rights; the right to personal privacy against unlawful search and seizure is a lawfully given right, set up by the government, to ensure that its power is never abused. Since the amendment's ratification in the late 18th century, questions about the balance between personal and national security have existed in the national conversation. Initiatives such as the National Security Act in 1947 – which banned intelligence operatives from working domestically – and a series of laws passed in the 1970s to prevent political spying (ACLU) were all productive steps in limiting the scope of government in the day-to-day lives of citizens. Then there was September 11, a national tragedy where four planes hijacked were crashed by the Al Qaeda terrorist group: two of them crashing into the World Trade Center, one into the Pentagon and the other into a field in Pennsylvania, killing thousands of American civilians. American paranoia soared and so began the practice of warrantless wiretapping by the NSA initiated by President George W. Bush. Though President Bush's "inherent executive authority" (ACLU) to enact spying programs on his own citizens sounds like a comprehensive response to terrorism prevention in the Digital Age, will domestic spying really solve any problems with national security? Is it morally justifiable (or even effective) to disregard the Constitution and implement widespread domestic surveillance on civilians to prevent another 9/11? Under the current situation, the NSA's

---

In an unusual move, the author begins the essay with a "cold quote" (a quote with no lead-in phrase or setup). Though most teachers of writing discourage this move, the author confidently invokes the source material to provide an immediate basis for the subsequent argument. The follow up sentence demonstrates an understanding of the Amendment's purpose while subtly suggesting the direction of the essay's argument.

In a short statement of transition, the author moves from a historical point of view to a contemporary one.

Through a pair of rhetorical questions, the author suggests the two fundamental assumptions the essay will address: the effectiveness of mass surveillance and the moral implications of mass surveillance.

The author's thesis statement responds to the rhetorical questions and offers a clear, two-part approach to the issue raised in the assignment's prompt.

abuse of power is not only morally wrong and in direct violation of the Fourth Amendment to the Constitution, but it is also ineffective and distracts from the valuable intelligence we already have.

Historically, domestic wiretapping been largely ineffective in preventing future attacks. One of the highest profile cases of overlooked information obtained from illegal surveillance relates to 9/11. In his 2013 article, "Would NSA Surveillance Have Stopped 9/11 Plot?" Peter Bergen

> The author acknowledges that anecdotal evidence is easily refutable, so he is sure to acknowledge that the 9/11 example is just one instance in a much larger pattern of behavior.

details several missed opportunities by the CIA to share information about two 9/11 hijackers in the months leading up to the attacks. The government had records of suspected terrorists and didn't follow up on it by catching them right then and there, nor did they share this information with other branches of the government. This is an oversight with major consequences, but this is not the first case of missed opportunities. For example, in 2008 U.S. authorities were given tips by family members of David Coleman Headley, who was central in planning the terrorist attacks in Mumbai that killed 166 people, of his affiliations with militant groups and these tips were never followed up (Bergen). The government has routinely missed opportunities to seize on terror tips not because of some vast conspiracy, but because the sheer volume of information in broad surveillance programs is too big to sensibly navigate. Surveillance of domestic phone calls takes the focus even further away from the vast pool of information that the government already has and makes suspicious activity a needle in a haystack of useless information. Tapping the phone records of every American does nothing more than cloud up the information that the government already has.

Proponents of warrantless wiretapping say that the NSA should intercept communications "for only one purpose – to protect the lives, the liberties, and the well-being of the citizens of the United States from those who would do us harm" (Knowlton). As patriotic as this view is, it is equally as hypocritical. Spying on American citizens is the exact opposite of protecting their liberties; it is actually in direct violation of those liberties listed in the

> The author acknowledges opposing viewpoints and does so by invoking some source material to keep things focused and specific. The remainder of the paragraph – through combination of source material and the author's own thoughts – explains why the pro-surveillance point of view from Knowlton is problematic.

U.S. Constitution (NARA). More than this, there is no proven record that the government effectively uses the information obtained in surveillance it already has to protect the lives and well-being of U.S. citizens. Even when domestic wiretapping has been in place through the Bush Administration and into the Obama administration, there have been other terrorist attacks both against and by Americans. What has domestic surveillance done to stop these attacks? Is spying on American citizens without any warrants really the solution to all problems in the war on terrorism? When we take a look at these questions it is easy to see that the government has a lot of work to do internally with the information it already has before it starts trying to get clues from bringing in bulk phone calls.

> The author demonstrates two moments of maturity in the writing as the conclusion begins. First, he is sure to acknowledge that a problem as complicated as mass surveillance resists easy answers or solutions. Second, he is able to effectively summarize some of the essay's main point by use of parallelism ("isn't the way to solve this problem") to give the recap with a reader-friendly rhythm and pace.

The war on terror cannot be solved with one motion. There is no miracle solution. Things are going to go unnoticed, and tragedies are going to happen, but tapping into domestic phone calls to prevent such attacks isn't the way to solve this problem. Violating the U.S. Constitution isn't the way to solve this problem. The various intelligence agencies we already have in place – the FBI, the CIA and the NSA – should first focus on the stream of information they get from traditional intelligence gathering, and work closely to more effectively share this information with the other branches of government. Though this may not be the only solution,

> The author again acknowledges that his assertions are merely a suggestion to address aspects of this very complicated problem. The concession the author uses when he says, "Though this may not be the only solution, or even the best solution" demonstrates that his point of view is a mature and thoughtful contribution to the ongoing discourse of this issue that is not dogmatic or close-minded.

or even the best solution, the bottom line on the issue of the mass surveillance is this: tapping into domestic phone calls without the proper procedures is illegal, whether ordered by the President or not, and is an ineffective way of trying to prevent future terrorist attacks.

Works Cited

ACLU. "NSA Spying on Americans Is Illegal." *ACLU*. American Civil Liberties Union, 10 Feb. 2014. Web. 15 Sept. 2016. https://www.aclu.org/other/nsa-spying-americans-illegal.

Bergen, Peter. "Would NSA Surveillance Have Stopped 9/11 Plot?" *CNN*. Cable News Network, 30 Dec. 2013. Web. 18 Sep 2016. https://www.cnn.com/2013/12/30/opinion/bergen-nsa-surveillance-september-11/index.html.

Knowlton, Brian. "Ex-NSA Chief Defends Monitoring Program." *New York Times*. New York Times. 23 Jan 2006. Web. 18 Sep 2016. htttps://www.nytimes.com/2006/01/23/world/americas/exnsa-chief-defends-monitoring-program.html.

National Archives and Records Administration (NARA). "Bill of Rights." Archives.gov. The Charters of Freedom. 26 Jun 2017. Web. 18 Sep 2017. https://www.archives.gov/founding-docs/bill-of-rights-transcript.

The Ethics of Driverless Cars

Introduction

A driverless car (sometimes called a "self-driving car" or "autonomous car") is a robotic vehicle designed to travel between destinations without a human operator. In recent years, driverless cars have steadily increased their presence on American and international roadways.

Supporters of driverless cars cite a number of potential benefits to their widespread adoption. Driverless cars would potentially offer a drastic reduction in human-driver error – costly in both lost lives and money – as well as increased efficiency in traffic patterns, commuting time, and general road safety. Despite these merits, critics of driverless cars question the reliability of driverless software, the startup costs of adjusting roads to meet the needs of autonomous vehicles, and the current lack of regulation regarding their use.

Neither side, however, has found easy resolution to the ethical dilemmas raised by driverless cars; that is, how should an autonomous car's software be programmed to "decide" between multiple harmful courses of action in the event of an unavoidable crash?

Assignment

Evaluate the most important factors that should be considered while determining the "ethics setting" of a driverless car.

Example Response

Automated technology, fraught with both great promise and grave peril, is the source of some of the greatest existential questions of our generation. As each year passes by, it seems that our day-to-day life has become increasingly automated, from the machines that monitor our vital signs to those which talk us through the self-checkout at Wal-Mart. One particular automated technology that has recently seized the public imagination is the driverless car. Though the thought of relinquishing control of the wheel may make some drivers uneasy, driverless cars have, so far, shown exciting potential. Unlike us (humans), driverless cars won't drive drunk. They won't speed. They won't fall asleep. They won't lose focus. They won't check a text at a busy intersection. In controlled circumstances, it may seem like the driver is superior to its human occupants, but what about the question of ethics when a crash in unavoidable? Should the occupants be saved before pedestrians? Can a car be moral? Like a human being, it's certainly possible for a driverless car to operate with a sense of ethics, so long as its "teachers" impart a utilitarian stance to maximize safety for the greatest number of individuals.

> The author balances the essay's initial generalization with two common scenarios of automation that would be common to the general reader's experience. From there, the author then transitions into the specific focus of the essay, the driverless car.

> The author uses repetition at the beginning of each sentence (anaphora) for emphasis. These short sentences – inserted between a series of much longer syntax constructions – illustrates a mature control over the essay's voice and style.

> The author asserts his claim but does so with a series of qualifying words and phrases which establish the specific limits and conditions the remainder of the essay will follow.

Here's a quick scenario to illustrate this point. Imagine that you're in your driverless car and, as always, it drives to your destination without you having to do a single thing. All of the sudden, a group of kids unexpectedly run out in front of you, and your car calculates that there is now way to avoid this accident because, if you were to swerve, you would crash into a wall. Theoretically, your car has two apparent choices: either kill the kids in front of you and preserve your life or swerve out of the way to save the children and crash into the wall where you would die on impact. This question is only a model example, an adaptation of the ethical "trolley scenario" referenced in Patrick Lin's *Wired* article, but it does raise a deep ethical question about how driverless cars should be programmed. For most readers of this scenario, it seems morally sensible to kill the driver, for the sake of preserving the lives of the many. This stance, the one with which I would also agree, is unabashedly utilitarian, a stance that judges moral action on "the principle of utility [or] the greatest happiness principle" (Mill 5).

But matters of life and death are hardly this simple. All fatal scenarios have their own unique set of circumstances, a point discussed by Patrick Lin, and they must be evaluated on a case-by-case basis. In his article "Here's a Terrible Idea: Robot Cars with Adjustable

> The author demonstrates a deep understanding of the source material by leading with a blended paraphrase of Lin's article and Schwitzgebel's Op-Ed. Such an approach illustrates that the author understands the source material and is able to present it in a way that fits with the essay's style and purpose.

> The author directly quotes John Stuart Mill's source to establish the essay's philosophical basis.

> The author acknowledges that ethical scenarios are rarely "black" and "white" and offers a thoughtful qualification to the more generalized considerations from the previous paragraph. The author returns to a discussion of Lin in more detail.

> The author quotes a key portion of Lin's argument and uses the quote to critique some of its basic assumptions (while simultaneously advancing the author's own argument on the issue).

Ethics Settings," he talks about the ability to adjust ethics settings on a driverless car and argues for the dangers of putting this power into the hands of the car manufacturer. He says, "The point is: Even with the ethics setting adjusted by you, an accident victim hit by your robot car could potentially sue the car manufacturer for (1) creating an algorithm that makes her a target and (2) allowing you the option of running that algorithm when someone like her – someone in the losing end of the algorithm – would predictably be a victim under a certain set of circumstances" (Lin). Lin asserts that, no matter what, someone will end up on the losing end and have to die. The subtext of this point is an argument against driverless automation altogether. But Lin overlooks a crucial point in this argument and that is the fact that the owner the driverless car has – through purchase of the vehicle – accepted all liability and responsibility for whatever happens, not unlike the liability associated with a fatal accident in a human operated car. Such is the risk of car ownership in the brave new world.

> The author sharply concludes his paragraph with a memorable phrase, one that showcases sophistication in writing ability and inclusion of relevant outside knowledge ("brave new world" is an allusion to the futuristic novel by Aldous Huxley which bears the same name).

> The author's topic sentence purports to explore a key idea from the previous paragraph in greater detail. The phrasing of this sentence, too, keeps the main idea of this sentence close to the task given in the assignment's prompt.

> The author alternates between paraphrase and quotation across a series of sentences, demonstrating how source material can be effectively included.

If the owner is to be held liable, it's worth considering whether or not the owner should have some agency over their car's settings. Eric Schwitzgebel forwards this point as he offers a thoughtful alternative to the all or nothing approach of pre-set ethical set-

> The author contrasts the points from Schwitzgebel from his own position on the issue. In disagreeing, he is forwarding his own position; that is, a utilitarian ethic is the best available option for a driverless car in this given set of circumstances.

tings in driverless cars. He favors adjustable settings depending upon the circumstance. If, for example, there is another passenger in the car, a driver may adjust the vehicle's setting to "safety mode" (Schwitzgebel). This mode would force the car to strictly adhere to the laws of the road, reducing any chance of fatality to a smaller percentage. Conversely, rushed drivers may opt for an "aggressive mode" that programs for "maximum allowable speed and aggressiveness" (Schwitzgebel). While there may well be situations that call for each of these modes, Schwitzgebel's strongest assertion comes with his proposal of the "ethical utilitarian mode." There is the obvious problem with predetermined "mindsets" – safe or aggressive – for the car, not the least of which is that moral and ethical considerations really don't enter into the decision-making process. Setting a "utilitarian" program would not eliminate all the unforeseen things that can happen on the road, but it would inform the vehicle's action along the lines of an ethical principle. Just like humans who decide to act in accordance with their own set of received morals and ethics, a philosophically programmable car would be nothing more than an extension of the owner's morality.

> The author concedes that the philosophical debate at the center of this essay resists an easy solution. Such a concession illustrates care and subtly in the author's treatment of this complicated issue.

No philosophical debate has ever been cleanly settled and there will always be those who find, sometimes quite legitimate, objections to a course of action. The utilitarian stance for the "ethics" of driverless cars, however, has a number of merits which cannot be easily ignored. A utilitarian "conscience" simplifies the complicated issues surrounding this new technology as much as it can be simplified: it can be dealt with lawfully, it promotes the greatest degree of safety for the most number of people, and if every car is programmed the same way, then all outcomes won't be a matter of opinion or emotion, but rather law and logic. Naysayers will no doubt point to

> The author recapitulates his main points but doesn't merely repeat what's already been said in the essay. The author also doesn't characterize opposing viewpoints as deluded, uninformed or misguided. The re-assertion of the argument's main tenets is done in a way that respects the reader, even those readers who may hold a different opinion than the one argued in the essay.

the injustice of death at the hands of automated technology, but road fatalities are simply not avoidable no matter who's behind the wheel, human being or otherwise. Unintended death is inevitable with powerful technologies like the driverless car. The utilitarian car, at least, downplays the role of human folly behind the wheel, while allowing every person to be truly equal in the eyes of the car.

Works Cited

Lin, Patrick. "Here's a Terrible Idea: Robot Cars with Adjustable Ethics Settings." *Wired.com.* Conde Nast Digital, n.d. Web. 26 Aug. 2016. https://www.wired.com/ 2014/08/heres-a-terrible-idea-robot-cars-with-adjustable-ethics-settings/.

Mill, John Stuart. "Utilitarianism." Utilitarianism by John Stuart Mill. N.p., n.d. Web. 26 Aug. 2016. www.earlymoderntexts.com/assets/pdfs/mill1863.pdf.

Schwitzgebel, Eric. "Will Your Driverless Car Kill You So Others May Live?" *LATimes.* Los Angeles Times. 4 Dec. 2015. Web. 26 Jan. 2016. http://www. latimes.com/opinion/op-ed/la-oe-1206-schwitzgebel-driverless-car-safety-algorithm-20151206-story.html.

Should Creationism be Taught in Public Schools?

Introduction

Since the Scopes Trial of 1925, a silent battle over the question of where we, human beings, ultimately come has been raging in our nation's classrooms and in this battlefield of ideologies, "Creationism" and "Evolution" are the names of the opposing armies. Creationism asserts that the universe and living organisms originate from divine creation, a point of view closely associated with teachings of Christian theology. Evolution, derived from the scientific breakthroughs of Charles Darwin in the mid-19th century, argues that living organisms develop over time from the traits of pre-existing species. In recent years, public schools in the United States have come to privilege the evolution narrative – a widely accepted scientific theory around the world – but there is a growing movement to incorporate Creationism into the curriculum alongside its scientific counterpart.

Assignment

Take a position that defends, challenges, or qualifies the claim that Creationism should be taught alongside Evolution in public schools.

Example Response

In the latter part of the 19th century, an ideological movement known as Positivism began to put absolute faith in the truth of science for the first time in human history. Partially due to the scientific breakthroughs of Darwin in the middle of that century, this new world view gained more and more traction as the governing theme of the 20th century. As the colossus of science saw its ascent, the old authority of religion was gradually dismantled and torn-down. The Scopes Trial of 1925 became the public battlefield in which the two chief ideologies of the time – Creationism vs. Evolution – would duke it out. The trial dealt a knockout blow the religious explanations of human origins, but despite this legal proclamation, many US citizens retained their belief in a God-centered explanation of the cosmos. The debate still rages today as to which ideology should lay claim to the master narrative of the greatest question of human existence, "Where do we come from?" This question resists easy answers, but despite their apparent differences, Creationism and Evolution should be taught alongside one another in public schools.

It's ironic, for sure, that Creationism and Evolution often brand the other as close-minded and obtuse, since each ideology encounters the same logical problem. Evolutionists are fond of the (disparaging) appeal-to-ignorance argument against Creationists that goes something like this: "Since we can't

> The author opens his argument by situating the central conflict into contexts of legal and intellectual history.

> The author continues his contextualization of the topic into the focused setting of schools, the main context of the paper's argument.

> The author is careful to present his thesis without dogmatic tones (which he criticizes later in the essay), while still asserting a clear position.

scientifically prove that God exists, he therefore does not exist, and our origins must necessarily derive from something here in the material world." The Institution for Creation Research corroborates this vacuous assumption made by hardcore evolutionaries, "The basic assumption of modern evolutionary theory is that no supernatural being has ever been involved in the universe…[and] science has been changed to imply naturalism" (Morris). As this quote suggests, there is an ironic dogmatism in the "rightness" of science, an accusation that is often leveled at science's Creationist opponents. What's more, those who put complete faith in the evolution narration do so in a way that undermines the basic principles of scientific inquiry; that is, one must assume God doesn't exist in order for the remainder of the Evolution hypothesis to take effect.

> The author uses source material to draw out the main idea of his analysis, the logical contradictions inherent in Creationism and Evolution. The author quotes the sources but chases the implications of these ideas with a fresh framework of logical deconstruction.

> The author makes a good case for Creationism which reads against the grain of typical mainstream views on the controversy. As a result, the author's voice is balanced, nuanced, and thoughtful.

Creationists often reverse this argument to suit their ideological position, saying something like, "Science hasn't yet disproven the existence of God, and since everything in our world comes from something else, there must necessarily be a first cause in the universe, which we can refer to as God." This is what's known as the "intelligent design" argument, an official sounding name for a logically inconsistent explanation of the world and our place in it. Like the evolution argument mentioned above, the Creationist position ultimately asserts its conclusion (God exists) based on the lack of evidence to the contrary (science hasn't proven that God doesn't exist).

> The author succinctly summarizes the preceding two paragraphs in a single, linking sentence.

> The author, in Integrative argument fashion, does not cast his proposition into "either/or" terms but rather suggests a resolution which sketches out mutual benefit for all parties involved.

John Trevor's political cartoon from the *Albuquerque Journal* captures this argument reversal well and goes on to show that maybe Creationism and Evolution are not as diametrically opposed as they think. They are cut from the same logical cloth.

> The author makes use of an image source (political cartoon) by paraphrasing its visual elements as corroboration for the paragraph's main idea.

In our world of trigger-warnings and avoidance of dissenting opinions, the question of Creationism and Evolution has never been more charged. So, what is one to do? An easy answer would be to avoid both, a retreat into nihilism which glibly asserts that nothing exists, or if it

> The author explicitly addresses the "So what?" question of the Creationism vs. Evolution debate by adopting a tone that is thoughtfully unresolved.

exists it is not knowable and cannot be communicated. While convenient, this position is a bit of a cop-out on the question of existence and prefers to throw up one's hands instead of using the God-given (or nature-given?) faculty of reason to come to terms with this vexing question. The current scene on this issue is grim, "by assuming that only ignorance could explain Creationist beliefs, scientists have unwittingly fostered resentment among the Creationists, the very people with whom they should be hoping to connect" (Laats). Rather than privileging one over the other, perhaps Creationism and Evolution can be taught side-by-side to provide students with a comprehensive picture of the competing views of existence in order to let them critically choose their own path. This approach, consistent with modern themes of tolerance and multi-culturalism, would neither silence opposing views or shield students from ideas which happen to run counter to their own. As Adam Laats argues in his essay, "To Teach Evolution, You Have to Understand Creationists," both ideologies need the other to get the full picture, in the way up needs down, male needs female, good needs evil.

> The author concludes by recasting the Creationism vs. Evolution debate into larger societal concerns of the erosion of critical thinking and free-speech. This move targets a cultural commonplace in order to favorably frame the proposed solution to the controversy at the heart of the paper's argument.

Why not let students see what's out there for themselves? A co-teaching of these competing origin narratives aligns to principles of free-speech and would reinforce critical thinking skills that seem to atrophy more and more as time moves by. The dialectic presented with Creationism and Evolution can add depth and dimension to all subjects, not just theology and science, and help the knowledge learned in school flow in new directions. If academic institutions are committed to the pursuit of truth, it stands to reason that teaching both is the best course of action.

Works Cited

Laats, Adam. "To Teach Evolution, You Have to Understand Creationists." *The Chronicle.* The Chronicle of Higher Education, 19 Nov 2012. Web. 14 Sep 2016. https://www.chronicle.com/article/To-Teach-Evolution-You-Have/135832.

Morris, John. "Should the Public Schools Teach Creation?" *Institute for Creation Research.* Institute for Creation Research. 17 Feb 2013. Web. 14 Sept. 2016. http://www.icr.org/article/should-public-schools-teach-creation/.

Trevor, John. "Creationism Vs. Evolution." Albuquerque Journal. 17 Feb 2013. Web. 14 Sep 2016. http://editorialcartoonists.com/cartoon/display.cfm/95542/.

ADDITIONAL RESOURCES

CHAPTER NINETEEN

MLA CITATION GUIDE

Any source-based argument that you have ever read, or maybe even composed yourself, depends upon the body of knowledge that preceded it. Your research may be an original and insightful contribution to a field – it happens all the time – but you need to give credit where credit is due. It is not shameful, nor is it a sign of weakness that you have drawn on other perspectives to shape your own; it is quite the opposite actually. A healthy bibliography not only is evidence of your due diligence as a thinker and writer, but it also signals to your reader that your argument is well situated into the discourse of your subject. As you probably know, source material needs to be documented in two ways by using parenthetical citations that work in conjunction with a formal works cited page. The following chapter will help you to properly account for these two requirements by utilizing the parameters set forth in the Modern Language Association (MLA) format. The information contained herein reflects the 2016 MLA updates, published in *The MLA Handbook, 8th Ed.*

Parenthetical Citations

In MLA style, referring to the works of others in your text is done by using what is known as parenthetical citation. These special acknowledgments appear in the body of the paper itself and are required whenever you incorporate another author's words, facts, ideas, or opinions into your own writing. Each type of source requires a slightly separate way of referring to it in the body of the paper; the table located at the end of the chapter will be useful to sorting out these differences in formatting conventions. For most references you'll be making, the citation immediately follows a quotation or paraphrase of a source's ideas and contains the author's name followed by the relevant page number(s). Take a look below at an example argument for the merits of internet censorship:

> Censorship of the Internet restricts freedom of information, but proponents insist on attempting to control it by "installing blocking software on computers in the public libraries" (Kaminer 19).

This in-text citation points to the fact that the second portion of this sentence was drawn from a source. Like a hyperlink, this brief acknowledgement points readers to the Works Cited page, where the reader can find more out about the source:

> Kaminer, Wendy. "Street Censors." The Boston Globe: 13 March 1997: A19. Print.

But depending on how you choose to integrate the borrowed idea, your citation may take on many different forms because citations are not meant to distract from the argument at hand. They are like the Secret Service of your paper; they are precise and accurate, but they should barely be noticed. Give only the necessary amount of information to direct the reader to the full citation at the paper's end. Here are some variations, depending on your rhetorical choices, of how citations can show up in a paper:

> *Paraphrase which introduces the author by name*:
> Smith made the case for reducing carbon emissions in 1976 in Oslo, Norway (15–19).
>
> *Paraphrase which does not introduce the author by name*:
> The case for reducing carbon emissions was made in 1976 in Oslo, Norway (Smith 15–19).

Two paraphrases in same sentence which introduces author by name:
As Smith contends, environmental devastation from automobiles can be curtailed by adopting more efficient gasoline (114) and stricter car inspections standards (123).

Two paraphrases in same sentence which do not introduces author by name:
Environmental devastation from automobiles can be curtailed by adopting more efficient gasoline (Smith 114) and stricter car inspections standards (Smith 123).

Direct quotation which introduces author by name:
I am of two minds on Smith's point that "CO_2 emissions can be linked most strongly to automobile emissions" (102–103).

Direct quotation which does not introduce the author by name:
It is disputable that "CO_2 emissions can be linked most strongly to automobile emissions" (Smith 102–103).

Two direct quotations which introduce the author by name:
As Smith contended in his 2010 commission report to the U.N., Environmental devastation from automobiles can be curtailed "by urging stations to sell cleaner-burning15% ethanol gasoline" (114) and "installing regulatory bodies to oversee new, stricter standards for yearly automobile inspections" (123).

Two direct quotations which do not introduce the author by name:
Environmental devastation from automobiles can be curtailed "by urging stations to sell cleaner-burning 15% ethanol gasoline" (Smith 114) and "installing regulatory bodies to oversee new, stricter standards for yearly automobile inspections" (Smith 123).

These choices are largely a matter of style. It is a good idea to strike a healthy balance between paraphrased information and direct quotations. A paper that is overrun with direct quotations becomes tiresome after a short run, just like a paper containing only paraphrased information does not illustrate that the author has scrutinized the source material. Whether you are paraphrasing or directly quoting, end run-in quotations in this sequence: quote marks, open parenthesis, author's last name (if there is one), page number, closed parenthesis, period. Below are some other variations on how parenthetical citations may look in your final paper depending on the type of source or how the source is being referred to:

Author's name in text:
Cunningham discusses Dante throughout Chapter 1 (12–13).

Author's name in reference:
His views on Dante changed over the years (Cunningham 45–46).

Multiple authors:
(Cunningham and Dowd 436).

Multiple pages not consecutive:
(Cunningham 32–33, 96).

Two different works cited:
(Cunningham 98; Molinari 45).

Video:
(Cunningham 2:38–3:43), includes time in video

Sometimes, it is necessary to directly quote large tracts of information. To incorporate quotations that are longer than two lines of poetry or five lines of prose, you must offset the information into what is known as a "block quotation." When breaking for the block quote, you must "enter" down to a new line, tab in, produce the quote and provide the appropriate citation. When finished, "enter" down to a new line, put the cursor flush to the left margin and continue your writing. Also, there are several formatting changes to keep in mind (see inset). Here is an example of what a block quote should look like when incorporated into your paper:

The Works Cited Page

Any paper that utilizes parenthetical citations within the paper's body needs to have a Works Cited page at the end which lets the reader know

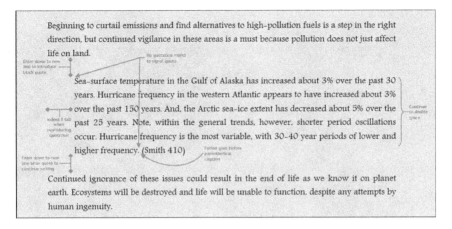

the source from the quoted or paraphrased material from the paper was drawn. Parenthetical citations are meaningless without their works-cited counterpart. Here are some of the major rules to observe when composing this most important page:

- Begin your Works Cited page on a separate page at the end of your research paper. Headers and formatting should be uniform to other pages in the paper.
- Label the page "Works Cited" (do not underline the words Works Cited or put them in quotation marks) and center the words Works Cited at the top of the page.
- Double space all citations, but do not skip spaces between entries.
- Entries should be arranged in descending alphabetical order according to the author's last name. If the author's name cannot be located, alphabetize by the work's title and run it directly into your list.
- Capitalize each word in the titles of cited works, but do not capitalize articles, short prepositions, or conjunctions unless one is the first word of the title or subtitle: *A Walk in the Woods, The Aeneid, In Through the Out-Door.*
- Use italics or underlines to signify the title of longer works (novels, dramas, anthologies, etc.) and quotation marks for titles of shorter works (articles, short stories, poems, etc.)

Here is an example of what a works cited page should look like in its final form.

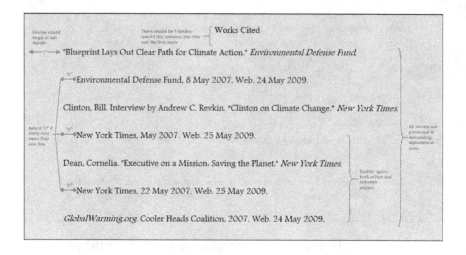

The following contains example works cited entries which reflect the wide-ranging variety of sources that are out there. Each entry contains a heading that specifies the general category of the source, followed by an example of works cited entry and what a parenthetical citation within the paper for this source would look like. When documenting your own sources, be sure to follow these guidelines closely.

Modern Language Association 8th Edition – Citations Guide for Print and Electronic Sources

Book with One Author:
Author Last Name, Author First Name. *Title*. Publisher, Date.

Example:
Brodeur, Greg. *The Joy of Teaching Freshmen*. Harvard UP, 2016.
 In-text citation: (Brodeur 23–28)

Book with Two Authors:
Author Last Name, Author First Name, and Second Author First Name Second Author Last Name. *Title*. Publisher, Date.

Example:
Brown, Carl, and Corrie Anderson. *Pedagogy & Methodology Revisited*. Penguin Books, 1976.
 In-text citation: (Brown and Anderson 45)

Book with Three or More Authors:
Author Last Name, Author First Name, et al. *Title*. Publisher, Date.

Example:
Alberini, Kristen, et al. *A Guide to Organizational Politics: Understanding the Nuances*. Petegrine Publishers, 2011.
    In-text citation: (Alberini et al. 24)

Book with Editor but no Author:
Editor Last Name, Editor First Name, editor. *Title*. Publisher, Date.

Example:
Schuster, Samuel, editor. *A Survey of English Literature, 1700–1800*. Cambridge UP, 2009.
    In-text citation: (Schuster 201)

Book with Editor and Author:
Author Last Name, Author First Name. "Article Title." *Book Title*. Edited by Editor First Name Editor Last Name. Publisher, Date. Pages.

Example:
Duggan, Christian. "How to Be a Great English Teacher." *Handbook of Teaching English Well*. Edited by Kelly Smith. The British Museum Press, 1932. pp. 90–95.
    In-text citation for portion written by author: (Duggan 55)
    In-text citation for portion written by editor: (Smith v–viii)

Book with Two Editors:
Editor Last Name, Editor First Name, and Second Editor First Name Second Editor Last Name, editors. *Title*. Publisher, Date.

Example:
Mansella, Anthony, and Keith Carr, editors. *Collaborative Planning Revisited*. Walter de Gruyter, 1989.
    In-text citation: (Mansella and Carr 107)

Classic Work:
Title. Publisher, Date.

Example:
Tanakh: The Holy Scriptures: The New JPS Translation according to the Traditional Hebrew Text. Jewish Publication Society, 1985.
    In-text citation: (*Tanakh*, Genesis 1.1), then (Genesis 1.1)

Anthology:
Author Last Name, Author First Name. "Essay Title." *Book Title*. Edited by Editor First Name Editor Last Name. Publisher, Date. Pages.

Example:
Karb, Jonathan. "For the Love of Teaching English: A Poem." *The Art of Poetry: An Anthology*. Edited by Mike Gordon. U of California P, 2013. pp. 23–33.
   In-text citation for portion written by author: (Karb 27)
   In-text citation for portion written by editor: (Gordon xii–xxv)

Online Book:
Author Last Name, Author First Name. *Title*. Publisher, Date. *Database/Source*, url.

Example:
Cunningham, Liam. *Mushroom Hunting*. Cassell, 1826. *GoogleBooks*, google.com/cunningham/mushrooms.html.
   In-text citation: (Cunningham 32)

eBook:
Author Last Name, Author First Name. *Title*. Publisher, Date. *Database/Source*.url.

Example:
Peterson, Ronald. *Student Discipline*. Harvard UP, 2011. *Destiny eBookCollection*. destiny.milfordpublicschools.com/rpeterson/studentsdis.html.
   In-text citation: (Peterson 95)
   If no pages, in-text citation for chapter or section: (Peterson, ch. 2)

Encyclopedia:
"Entry Title." Encyclopedia Title. Publisher. Edition. Date. Pages.

Example:
"School Library." The Encyclopedia of School Libraries. The Library Press. 15ᵗʰ ed. 2003. p. 34.
   In-text citation: ("School Library" 34)
If many volumes, in-text citation using volume number: ("School Library" 2: 34)

Dictionary:
Author Last Name, Author First Name. "Entry." Dictionary Title. Edited
by Editor First Name Editor Last Name. Edition. Number of Volumes.
Publisher, Date. Pages.

Example:
Cunningham, Eamon. "Rhetoric." A Dictionary of Literary Terms. Edited
by Amanda Cunningham. 2nd ed. 4 Vols. Macmillan, 1876. p. 78.
    In-text citation: ("Rhetoric") or (Dict. of Literary Terms).

Article from Newspaper:
Author Last Name, Author First Name. "Article Title." *Newspaper Title*.
Day. Month. Year: Pages.

Example:
Jones, John. *"Using Chromebooks." The Milford Daily News*. 15 Jan. 2017:
B12–33.
    If print newspaper, in-text citation: (Jones B12)
    If online newspaper, in-text citation: (Jones)

Article from a Popular Magazine:
Author Last Name, Author First Name. "Article Title." *Magazine Title*.
Month. Year: Pages.

Example:
Dowd, Tim. "The Essence of Teaching." The New Yorker. Jan. 2003: pp.
121–123.
    If print magazine, in-text citation: (Dowd 121)
    If online magazine, in-text citation: (Dowd)

Article from Journal:
Author Last Name, Author First Name. "Article Title." *Journal Title*
Volume, Number (Date): Pages.

Example:
Bronson, Sally. "The Importance of Writing Nature Journals." *Modern
English Teacher Quarterly* Vol. 33, no. 4 (2015): pp. 189–200.
    In-text citation: (Bronson 193)

Article from online Database:
Author Last Name, Author First Name. "Article Title." *Journal Title*,
Volume, No. (Date): Pages. *Database Title*. url.

Example:

Nicks, Jim. "Young at Heart." *English Teacher Review,* Vol. 33, no.4 (2003): pp. 233–234. *Gale Literature Resource Center.* www.gale.com/englishteacher/nicks.html.

In-text citation: (Nicks 233)

Webpage:

Author Last Name, Author First Name. "Article/Page Title." *Webpage.* Publisher, Date. url.

Example:

Contreaux, Sean. "The Salem Witch Museum." *FieldtripsMA.org.* Massachusetts Board of Field Trips, 2016. www.fieldtripsma.ord/ thesalemwitchmuseum.html

In-text citation: (Contreaux)

If no credited author, in-text citation using webpage title: ("The Salem Witch Museum")

CHAPTER TWENTY

TERMINOLOGY GLOSSARY

Ab ovo: (Literary) From the Latin *ab ovo* ('from the egg'), this term describes a narrative structure that proceeds in a chronological order from beginning to end. OPPOSITE of *EN MEDIAS RES*. SEE *PACING*.

> "Once upon a time and a very good time it was there was a moocow coming down along the road and this moocow that was coming down along the road met a nicens little boy named baby tuckoo.... His father told him that story: his father looked at him through a glass: he had a hairy face."

These are the opening descriptions of James Joyce's *A Portrait of the Artist as Young Man* (1916), a bildungsroman, or coming-of-age story, that tells the life of the main character, Stephen Dedalus. In an unusual move, Joyce opens the story from Stephen's earliest perceptible memory: a nursery rhyme his father told him at the age of three. The story begins, well, at the beginning of his conscious life and proceeds from this point to tell the story of Stephen's religious and intellectual awakening.

Abstract: (Grammatical) From the Latin *abstractus* ('drawn away'), this term refers to ideas, concepts, and qualities. Abstract nouns are often uncountable nouns (e.g. "liquid," "gas," "sadness," etc.), though they can still be referred to in the singular or as countable nouns (e.g. "a dinner," "a friend," "an enemy," etc.). Related to issues of *DICTION*. OPPOSITE of *CONCRETE*.

'Abstraction' is the inductive process of observing many particular things in order to identify a single, related generality shared among them. The concept of justice, for example, may be generated from seeing crime, punishment, and reparations brought on by the sentence.

Even "justice" itself can be referred to in increasingly abstract ways that be iterated indefinitely. Consider:

Degrees of abstraction in diction choices or "the ladder of abstraction"		
Abstract	**Somewhat concrete**	**Most concrete**
Justice should send you to jail.	*Breaking the law* should send you to jail	*Legal code 3F paragraph 2* should send you to jail.

Acronym: (Rhetorical) From the Greek *akros* ('point') and *onuma* ('name'), an acronym is a word formed from the initial letters or syllables of a sequence of words.

Letter acronym: "M.A.D.D." stands for Mothers Against Drunk Driving

Syllabic acronym: "Rom-Com" stands for Romantic Comedy

In each structure, the acronym is both pronounced and used as a standalone word, unlike initialed abbreviations which are pronounced as individual letters (e.g. "C.N.N." for Cable News Network).

Active Voice: (Grammatical) From the Latin *act* ('do'), active voice is a syntactical term for a sentence where the subject is the doer, not receiver, of the action. OPPOSITE of *PASSIVE VOICE.*

"Jack hit Ricardo in the mouth."

In this sentence, the main subject, Jack, is the one doing the "hitting" and the sentence is, therefore, presented in the active voice.

Adage: (Literary) SEE *APHORISM, EPIGRAM.*

Adjective: (Grammatical) From the Latin *adicio* ('to attach'), adjectives are words that modify nouns. They can appear in sentences in two ways:

Before the noun it modifies: "I am holding hot coffee."

The adjective "hot" is modifying the noun "coffee"; the adjective modifies the noun by appearing before it.

After an auxiliary verb: "The coffee is hot."

The adjective "hot" appears after the auxiliary verb "is" while still modifying the sentence's main noun, "coffee."

Adjective Clause: (Grammatical) A clause (a group of words containing a noun-verb pair) that describes a noun and functions adjectivally in a sentence. Adjective clauses are typically signaled by a relative pronoun (*who, whom, which, that, where* and *when*).

"I'm standing in the room that changed my life forever."

The adjective clause "that changed my life forever" describes the noun "room." The noun of this adjective clause is "that," the relative pronoun, and the verb is the past tense verb "changed."

An adjectival phrase/clause without a clear noun to modify is called a *dangling modifier*. Sometimes the noun or pronoun is in the sentence, but it is too far away, with a different noun intruding between. That can cause confusion. Consider:

"Fierce and sleek, we relied upon Rommel, our Doberman, for protection."

If they were so fierce and sleek, what did they need a Doberman for? The pronoun "we" has intruded between the modifier and the noun it is supposed to modify. Revise by rearranging:

"Fierce and sleek, our Doberman, Rommel, gave us all the protection we needed."

Adverb: (Grammatical) From the Latin *adverbium* ('added to a word'), an adverb is a word that modifies a verb, an adjective, another adverb, or an entire sentence.

Adverb modifying a verb: "Nina ran *quickly*."

Adverb modifying an adjective: "Nina is *pretty* fast."

Adverb modifying another adverb: "Nina ran *really* quickly."

Adverb modifying an entire sentence: "*Honestly*, Nina is the fastest runner on the team."

Allegory: (Literary) From the Greek *allegoria* ('speaking another way'), an allegory is a system of interconnected symbols that work to represent ideas or concepts not readily apparent in the primary narrative. A narrative's allegorical meaning is often didactic, moralistic, or even satirical.

> In George Orwell's *Animal Farm* (1945), the animals on the farm represent different social classes and the series of events reflect the circumstances that replicate the lead up to the Communist Revolution in 1917 in Russia. The characters function in their own right but also have symbolic value which point towards this period of history.

Alliteration: (Rhetorical) From the Latin *alliterationis* ('putting letters together'), alliteration is the repetition of consonant sounds, usually at the beginning of words. This is done to stress certain words, phrases, or lines.

> Johnny: "The cool cucumbers calmed my crazy cousin."

> The consonant "c" is the repeated sound in the above sentence. If placed central among other non-alliterative sentences, the repeated sounds would draw focus to this line in order to emphasize its content.

Allusion: (Literary) From the Latin *allusio* ('a playful reference'), an allusion is a passing reference to a familiar person, place, or thing drawn from history, the Bible, mythology, literature, etc. Allusions create a resonance in the reader or in the mood of the story by employing a subtle reference (as opposed to acknowledged quotations), and writers will often adapt the reference to suit the new context.

> "Mr. Jones's lecture was Shakespearean it was so carefully crafted."

Here, the speaker is using the well-known linguistic abilities of William Shakespeare to reference the quality of language choice in the lecture, without resorting to an extended discussion of Shakespeare's work.

Ambiguity: (Rhetorical) From the Latin *ambiguitas* ('acting both ways'), ambiguity is the use of language when multiple meanings are possible. This can be a result of one of two things:

> Insufficient attention to other denotations/connotations: Chi Chi's advertising slogan in the 1980's used to be, "Chi Chi's, when you want to feel a little Mexican." Presumably, the advertisers meant Mexican food, but the context could suggest you would go to Chi Chi's if you want to touch a small Mexican person. Though clearly not intended, these adjective and noun definitions are both acceptable in the context. The author has neglected other meanings.

> Intentional choice to bring multiple meanings to the same word: "After finishing his presentation, while battling a stomach bug, Tony was relieved." The author intentionally meant to bring both denotations of "relieved" to the table: one meaning alleviation of anxiety, the other meaning the passing of a painful sickness.

Amblysia: (Rhetorical) From the Latin *amblysia* ('blunting'), amblysia is modified language used in preparation for tragic or alarming news. SEE *EUPHEMISM.*

> "I'm afraid I have some bad news. The United States Secret Service has been infiltrated by foreign spies and matters of national security are now in the hands of our enemy."

> The speaker has briefly primed the crowd for the terrible news that is to follow. This preparatory statement is used in to soften the shock to the listener.

Anachronism: (Literary) From the Greek *anakhronismos* ('out-of-time-ness'), an anachronism is a historically inaccurate detail in a text typically used to synthesize ideas and perspectives from different times into a unified reference.

In T.H. White's *The Once and Future King*, which takes place in the Middle Ages, the character of Merlin wears bifocals, which were not invented until the 19th century.

Merlin is a visionary character in the story that is able to see events and place them in a larger perspective. This historically inaccurate detail, which focuses special attention to his eyes – a trait not emphasized in any other character – is done purposefully to draw attention this quality of his character.

Anacoluthon: (Rhetorical) From the Greek *anakolouthon* ('not in proper sequence'), anacoluthon occurs when a sentence begins in one way, pauses, and ends in another in the manner of an incomplete or broken-off thought. SEE *APOSIOPESIS*.

> "Alright kids, today we are going to learn – ahhh, let's go play dodgeball!"

The dash separates two distinct emotions in the sentence. The first half is stern and bookish, but it seems the speaker has a change of heart in the middle of the thought. The dash breaks the thought which then transitions into a lighter, more playful tone.

Anadiplosis: (Rhetorical) From the Greek *anadiplosis* ('doubling up'), anadiplosis is the repetition (or close repetition) of the final word of a clause at the beginning of the following clause for emphasis.

> "Fear is the path to the dark side. Fear leads to anger. Anger leads to hate. Hate leads to suffering."

In this quotable quote from *Star Wars*, each sentence ends with the word that starts the following sentence, and this pattern repeats over a series of lines. This syntactical order emphasizes the causal nature of the sentences; that is, one can't go from "fear" to "suffering" without first experiencing the interceding steps.

Anagram: (Rhetorical) From the Latin *anagrama* ('back letter'), an anagram is when letters of a word or phrase are rearranged to make a new word or phrase. These are most often found in titles of works to embed hidden meaning.

United Tastes of America is a program on the Cooking Channel which chronicles the history of American cuisine. The word "Tastes," which captures the essence of the show's food-oriented content, is an anagram of the word it replaces, "States."

Brian Eno's album *Before and After Science* includes a song entitled "King's Lead Hat," an anagram of "Talking Heads," a band Eno has worked with.

Analogy: (Rhetorical) From the Greek *analogie* ('double relation'), an analogy is a comparison between two things on the grounds that they share an abstract, third element. SEE *SIMILE, METAPHOR*. There are two principle uses of an analogy:

> To explain something complex more simply: A transmission line is simply a pipeline for electricity. In the case of a water pipeline, more water will flow through the pipe as water pressure increases. The same is true of a transmission line for electricity.

> To explain something abstract more concretely: God is a father, who sits on a throne, and loves his children.

> Each of the examples compare one object in terms of another (waterline to electricity, and God to a father) in order to make the qualities of the original object more understandable to the audience.

Anaphora: (Rhetorical) From the Greek *anaphora* ('carrying back'), anaphora is the repetition of the same word or phrase at the beginning of successive phrases or clauses. This is used as an emphasizing device. SEE *PARALLEL STRUCTURE*.

> Clauses: The commander rallied his troops, exclaiming, "*We will face them* at dawn! *We will face them* in the evening! *We will face them* at the gates of Hell!"

> Phrases: "I am *the best there* is, *the best there* was, *the best there* ever will be!"

> Whether an author uses a clause or phrase, each of the above statements utilizes repetition to draw the reader's attention to the main concept of the sentence.

Anastrophe: (Rhetorical) From the Greek *anastrophe* ('turning back'), anastrophe is the inversion of normal word order in a sentence.

> "Size matters not. Judge me by size, do you?"

> The normal syntactical arrangement of each sentence has been inverted. The first sentence removes part of the compound verb by eliminating "does" and places the adverb "not" following the verb it modifies, not before. The second sentence removes the possessive pronoun "my" just before the word "size" and it places the audience of the question following the main statement, not before. Typically, this technique is used purposefully to draw attention to a sentence or heighten its aphoristic feel.

Anecdote: (Rhetorical) From the Greek *anekdota* ('unpublished stories'), an anecdote is a short story or recounting of events used in either fiction or non-fiction. Anecdotes provide specific focus and personal flavor to a written piece.

> "When I entered my freshman year of high school, I was shiftless and lazy. But as the year went on, a few things taught me how to pick a goal and stick to it. In September…"

> If asked to write a paper about the value of determination, the speaker may begin with a personal anecdote like he has done above. Readers are usually more willing to listen when some personal interests are involved. If you can illustrate emotion or personal investment on your topic, there is a greater chance that the reader may eventually share these feelings.

Antagonist: (Literary) From the Greek *antagonistes* ('competitor, opponent, rival'), an antagonist is the character or force in a literary work that opposes the main character.

> In Jack London's *To Build a Fire* (1902), the main character comes into conflict with the barren wilderness. In this story, nature is the antagonist.

In William Golding's *The Lord of the Flies* (1954), the main character, Ralph, is challenged by the antagonist, Jack, who attempts to kill him in the concluding chapter.

Antecedent: (Grammatical) From the Latin *antecedere* ('to go before'), an antecedent is the word that a pronoun replaces in a sentence or series of sentences.

"Judith was a mean, old lady. One time, she bit me right in the nose."

In the second sentence, the pronoun "she" takes the place of its antecedent, "Judith," from the first sentence.

Antithesis: (Rhetorical) From the Greek *antithesis* ('setting against'), an antithesis is an opposition or contrast of ideas often expressed in balanced phrases or clauses.

"Napoleon was <u>loved</u> by his men, but history will remember his <u>brutality</u>."

This sentence balances two opposing observations about the same subject that are presented with some sense of unity or relatedness. Technically, the first phrase is the thesis ("Napoleon was loved by his men") and the second is the antithesis ("history will remember him for his brutality"). It is only in the synthesis of the two statements, however, that the speaker's theoretical meaning of Napoleon as a paradoxical historical figure appears.

Aphorism: (Rhetorical): From the Greek *aphorismos* ('a definition'), an aphorism is a concise statement that illustrates a deep truth or widely held belief.

"Simplify. Simplify."

"Early to bed and early to rise makes a man healthy, wealthy, and wise."

Fit for a bumper sticker, each of these statements illustrate a deeply held belief that has been accepted as a piece of common wisdom.

Aphoristic statements are powerful because of their content but also because of their brevity or conciseness.

Apocope: (Rhetorical) From the Greek *apocope* ('cutting off'), apocope is the deliberate removal of a letter or letters from the end of a word, usually reflecting an informal or colloquial usage. SEE *ELLIPTICAL CONSTRUCTION*.

> "I need to grab a taxi (cab) so I'm not late for bio (logy) and trig (onometry)!"

> These types of abbreviations are common to everyday habits of speech and sometimes go by undetected. An author may deliberately use this device to illustrate an awareness of a certain region/culture or to create an informal tone.

Aposiopesis: (Rhetorical) From the Greek *aposiopesis* ('becoming silent'), aposiopesis is a breaking off of speech, usually meant to indicate rising emotion or excitement. Both an ellipsis (...) or dash (–) can mark this effect in writing. SEE *ANACOLUTHON*.

> "I love to annoy you" (*touching his arm for the 5th time*)

> "If you touch me, just one more time –"

> The annoyance in the response is tangible, and sometimes emotion can be best illustrated in writing by what is *not* said; anything he would say most likely would not capture the frustration he is feeling as the dash has.

Apostrophe: (Rhetorical) From the Greek *apostrophe* ('a turning away'), apostrophe is a mode of speech where an abstract idea, dead person, thing, or place is addressed directly even though there is no way for that entity to respond. SEE *PERSONIFICATION, METAPHOR*.

> "America. In the face of our common dangers, in this winter of our hardship, let us remember these timeless words. With hope and virtue, let us brave once more the icy currents, and endure what storms may come."

This closing remark, drawn from Barack Obama's 2009 Inaugural Address, utilizes apostrophe in the first word where he collectively addresses "America," a place, as if it would be able to understand the words and advice that follows.

Appositive: (Grammatical) From the Latin *apponere* ('set near, set before'), an appositive is a modifier that is built from a noun which modifies another noun or pronoun often for the purposes of emphasis or clarification. Appositives are usually set off by commas. For example, in the sentence,

> "Mr. Smith, the teacher, stood in front of the room."

> In the above sentence, "the teacher" (a noun), provides additional clarification as to who Mr. Smith is.

Archaism: (Rhetorical) From the Greek *arkhaismos* ('something old'), an archaism is a form of speech or writing that is outdated, obsolete, or no longer current. Archaisms can purposefully allude to or evoke associations to older traditions in writing, thought, or practice. Archaisms can also be used purposelessly.

> "Him the Almighty Power/Hurled headlong flaming from th' ethereal sky/With hideous ruin and combustion down/To bottomless perdition, there to dwell/In adamantine chains and penal fire,/Who durst defy th' Omnipotent to arms."

> This quotation from John Milton's *Paradise Lost* (1667), which describes the fall of Lucifer from heaven into hell, is an example of a *purposeful* archaism. The archaism is not with the subject matter (which is old, but certainly not irrelevant to Milton's contemporary audience), but rather the syntactical arrangement of the lines. He mimics the syntax of Latin (a dead language in 17th century England) rather than his native language of English in order to tap the energy of existing Classical traditions in conjunction with biblical ones.

> "Whilst thou accompany me to purchase a cheeseburger and milkshake at McDonald's?"

This statement is an example of *purposeless* archaism. The food, beverage, and restaurant suggest that this statement is delivered in 20th or 21st century America. Since the reader can locate the time period, the expressions, "whilst" (an 18th century British term meaning "will") and "thou" (a 16th century British second person pronoun meaning "you") are archaisms with no meaningful purpose, maybe other than pretention.

Archetype: (Literary) From the Greek *archetupon* ('impression, pattern'), an archetype is recognizable theme, symbol, or character that holds a familiar place in a culture's consciousness.

Theme: "rugged individualism" in American Literature

Cultural archetypes help to establish national identity in writing and literature. The "rugged individual," for example, is an American literary archetype that often represents this American ideal that stresses an individual's self-reliance and independence. Authors such as Ralph Waldo Emerson, Henry David Thoreau, and Ayn Rand write in this style.

Symbol: "glasses" in William Golding's *Lord of the Flies* (1954)

"Glasses" are an archetypal symbol of intelligence. In Golding's novel, they are worn by Piggy, the character who is constantly questioning and investigating concerns of human nature.

Character: "the hero" in *Beowulf* (800 A.D.)

Beowulf, the main character in the poem that bears his name, is the archetypal hero of 8th century Anglo-Saxon England. He demonstrates battle prowess but also represents a number of Christian ideals; he is the representative figure for a world which was changing over from a Pagan worldview to a Christian one.

Argumentum ad: (Argumentative) From Latin phrase meaning "assertion or proof to," this term distinguishes the different objects to which an author can appeal in persuasive writing. When used in isolation, or not in conjunction with other argumentative techniques, the author may encounter logical fallacies (SEE Ch. 11: Errors in Reasoning – Logical Fallacies). The major categories are:

Argumentum ad baculum: ('to the stick') An argument which appeals to force or coercion.

Argumentum ad crumenam: ('to the wallet') An argument which appeals to material interests and concerns such as money, possessions, property, and so forth.

Argumentum ad hominem: ('to the man') An argument which attacks the person holding the counterargument rather than the issue at hand.

Argumentum ad ignorantium: ('to ignorance') An argument that relies on an audience who is ignorant, or uninformed, on the topic at hand.

Argumentum ad populum: ('to the people') An argument which is meant to stir an emotional response from the audience.

Assonance: (Rhetorical) From the Latin *assonare* ('to sound towards'), assonance is a type of internal rhyming in which identical or similar vowel sounds are repeated. Like alliteration and consonance, this is done to focus, or draw the reader's ear to certain words, phrases, or lines. SEE *CONSONANCE; ALLITERATION.*

"The table was hiding a baby with rabies."

Assonance rhyming is subtler than consonance because vowels don't have the sometimes harsh and grating effect that repeated consonants do. But like consonance, assonance is a rhetorical device meant to focus the reader's eye and ear to particular passages.

Assumption: (Rhetorical) From the Latin *assumere* ('to take up'), an assumption is a belief or principle, stated or implied, that is taken for granted.

"I always wash the lettuce before I eat it."

In this statement, the speaker assumes that unwashed produce poses a risk to his health. This statement is understood and does not, therefore, need to be stated.

Asyndeton: (Rhetorical) From the Greek *asyndetos* ('unconnected'), asyndeton occurs when coordinating conjunctions (*for, and, nor, but, or, yet, so*) that would normally connect a string of words, phrases, or clauses are omitted from a sentence. OPPOSITE of *POLYSYNDETON*.

"Sammy was brave, fearless, afraid of nothing."

The conjunction "and" that would normally connect the final phrase to the others is missing. This rhetorical move is done, sometimes, to give the effect that the words are spoken or conversational. Other times, it can suggest that the list is incomplete, and things are left unsaid.

Atmosphere: (Literary) From the Greek *atmos* ('to inspire'), atmosphere is a compound term that encompasses the tone (the author's attitude towards a subject) and mood (the audience's attitude towards a subject).

In John Steinbeck's *The Pearl* (1947), the opening chapters have an atmosphere of despair and uneasiness seen in the author's descriptions and the plot's action (tone) which are intended to evoke a similar feeling of hopelessness in the audience (mood).

Audience: (Rhetorical) From the Greek *audire* ('to hear, listen'), an audience is the intended recipient for a piece of writing or speech. One of the three participants in Aristotle's rhetorical triangle (*The Art of Rhetoric*, 4th Century B.C.), speakers and writers need to consider their audience when composing. In the most general terms, an audience can be either broad or narrow. A more detailed rundown of audience appears in Ch 2: Rhetorical Analysis – A Guided Methodology (e.g. *immediate, mediated, primary, secondary, self-deliberative, discourse community*).

Broad: The audience of a YouTube video comes from all types of backgrounds and has diverse opinions, attitudes, and educational experiences.

Narrow: The audience for *Motherboard Soldering Weekly* is made up of experts and specialists, people whose interests and educational backgrounds are quite similar.

Bombast: (Rhetorical) From the Latin *bombax* ('padding'), bombast is inflated or pretentious language that does not match the context of its use.

> "I have an affinity for that peculiarly American sandwich, known to commoners as a hamburger. I think I will ingest one, accompanied by my favorite libation."

> When speaking of the commonplace action of eating a burger and drinking a beer, the language is unnecessarily inflated, or bombastic.

Cacophony: (Rhetorical) From the Greek *kakaphonos* ('harsh sounding'), cacophony is an author's choice of words, usually alliterative, that create harsh, discordant, and grating sounds when read aloud. Cacophonic passages typically are found in scenes of violence, discomfort, or danger. SEE *CONSONANCE.*

> "And squared and stuck there squares of soft white chalk/And, with a fish-tooth, scratched a moon on each/And set up endwise certain spikes of tree/And crowned the whole with a sloth's skull a-top."

> In the excerpt from Robert Browning's poem, *Caliban Upon Setebos* (1864), the reader can see – and hear – the clashing and discordant consonant sounds of a hard "K" (squared, stuck, squares, chalk, scratched, spikes, crowned, skull) mingling with sounds of a hard "T" (stuck, soft, white, fish-tooth, set, tree, a-top") throughout the passage.

Caricature: (Literary) From the Italian *caricatura* ('to load'), a caricature occurs when an author exaggerates or distorts certain traits/characteristics of an individual for a ludicrous effect.

> If a character has large ears, the author's descriptions may focus on their abnormal size and the writing could contain repeated references to hearing and sounds.

In literature, the weak and gullible Roderigo in Shakespeare's *Othello* (1604) as well as the effeminate courtier, Osric, in *Hamlet* (1609) are examples of caricatured minor characters whose exaggerated traits provide comic relief to the main storyline.

Chiasmus: (Rhetorical) From the Greek *khiamsos* ('crisscross arrangement'), chiasmus is the reversal of grammatical structures in successive phrases or clauses. SEE *ANTITHESIS*.

"Fair is foul, and foul is fair."

These lines, spoken by the witches in the opening scene of Shakespeare's *Macbeth* (1606), demonstrate this concept in action. The quotation contains two clauses separated by a comma and coordinating conjunction. From the first clause to the second, the word order is reversed, with "fair" and "foul" swapping places.

"In the end, the true test is not the speeches a president delivers; it's whether the president delivers on the speeches."

In March 2008, presidential hopeful Hillary Clinton delivered this statement and, while the reversal of grammatical structures is apparent, the power of this statement relies on the dual usage of "deliver" in both of the clauses.

Circumlocution: (Rhetorical) From the Latin *cicumlocutio* ('talking around'), circumlocution is unnecessary wordiness, or the use of many words when a few would express an idea with greater clarity.

"The baserunner successfully avoided the tag."

If the base runner avoided the tag, does it add anything to say that he *successfully avoided* the tag? *Successfully* is redundant and therefore the instance of circumlocution in this sentence.

"William Shakespeare, a great English playwright…"

Circumlocutions can also take the form of typical clichés in academic writing. In the sentence above, almost no reader is ignorant to the fact that Shakespeare wrote plays. *A great English playwright* is this sentence's instance of circumlocution.

Claim: (Argumentative) From the Latin *clamare* ('to cry out, proclaim'), a claim is the proposition put forth in an argument. Claims can be absolute or qualified.

> Absolute: "Ants are a nuisance."
>
> Qualified: "*Carpenter* ants are a nuisance, *except when they kill smaller pests.*"
>
> Qualified claims are almost always preferred because they are most specific and account for certain scenarios and conditions of a situation which "black/white," absolute claims do not.

Clause: (Grammatical) From the Latin *clausa* ('the formula of a sentence'), a clause is a statement that contains a noun and a verb. There are two types of clauses, dependent and independent.

> Dependent clause: "Odysseus being very cunning and able to get out of any scrape."
>
> A dependent clause is one that depends upon another clause for its meaning. Subordinate or dependent clauses are usually signaled by conjunctions (*because, if, since, when, where, whether, although, whoever, after, before* and many others) and are linked to the rest of the sentence by commas. The above example may look like a complete sentence, but it lacks a verb. "Being" looks like one, but it is a particle – an adjective built from a verb. Kindly supply the real deal:
>
> Independent clause: "Odysseus was cunning and could get out of any scrape."
>
> A clause is a statement that contains meaning in itself and may stand alone as a sentence. Independent clauses can be linked to each other by a semicolon, or a comma followed by a coordinating conjunction (words that provide a loose link among items that are equal in rank, such as *and, but, or, nor, for, yet*, and a few others). The above example can stand alone as a sentence because it has a clear subject and verb.

Cliché: (Literary) From the French *cliché* ('stencil'), a cliché is an expression that has become ineffective through overuse.

"Don't put off for tomorrow what you can do today," "As easy as pie," "There's no place like home," "A chain is only as strong as its weakest link," "Many hands make light work," etc.

Although some may contain some truth, their force has become weakened through overuse in day-to-day activity. The term cliché is often used pejoratively or in derision.

Colloquialism: (Rhetorical) From the Latin *colloquialis* ('conversational'), a colloquialism is an informal expression that is conversational in nature and usually reflects the culture or an area or group; vernacular. Colloquialisms are acceptable in writing if used purposefully since they can subtly and indirectly provide characterization.

> The name an author may utilize for something as simple as a deli sandwich can reveal important details to a character's upbringing and background. A "sub" would place him in New England, a "grinder" to California, a "hoagie" to New Jersey/Pennsylvania, a "poor boy" to St. Louis, and a "po' boy" to Louisiana.

> These are all colloquial variations of the same thing, but they work to subtly reveal characteristics of particular regions without resorting to an extended discussion.

Colon: (Grammatical) From the Greek *kolon* ('a limb'), a colon (:) is a form of punctuation typically used to introduce lists in a sentence (though they can also be used to introduce speech or quoted material, to highlight a contrast, or to produce a staccato effect by replacing a conjunction). Colons should not interrupt independent clauses.

> "Today at camp, we did my favorite things: hiking, camping and storytelling."

> Here, the colon does not intrude on the independent clause "Today at camp, we did my favorite things." It follows the independent clause and introduces a list of the speaker's favorite summer camp activities. An incorrect placement of a colon in this sentence would be "My favorite things at camp are: hiking, camping and storytelling" because the colon intrudes on the completion of the independent clause.

Complex Sentence: (Grammatical) From the Latin *com* ('with') and *plectere* ('weave, braid'), a complex sentence is composed of at least one dependent clause and one independent clause joined together into a single sentence.

> "Because you dropped that fly ball, you are benched."

> This sentence combines a dependent clause in the first half to an independent clause in the second half. When joined like this, they form a complex sentence.

Compound Sentence: (Grammatical) From the Latin *com* ('with') and *ponere* ('put'), a compound sentence is composed of two or more independent clauses that are joined together into a single sentence. Independent clauses can be joined by a *SEMICOLON* or a comma and *COORDINATING CONJUCTION*.

> "Commas do not link independent clauses; semicolons do, or commas followed by conjunctions perform this function too."

> This sentence joins three independent clauses ("Commas do not link independent clauses;" "semicolons do," and "commas followed by coordinating conjunctions perform this function too"). Independent clauses 1 and 2 are joined by a semicolon, and independent clauses 2 and 3 are joined by a comma and coordinating conjunction.

Concrete: (Rhetorical) From the Latin *concretus* ('grown together'), concrete words refer to specific, particular, or material details (often grounded in empirical experience). OPPOSITE of *ABSTRACT*.

> "He grinned as he pocketed the coin."

> The description, drawn from William Strunk and E.B. White's *The Elements of Style* (1918), relies on concrete adjectives and nouns. The abstract form of this statement would be "He showed satisfaction as he took possession of the payment." In the above sentence, all of the terms are made specific and answer the crucial questions of "what?" and "how?" ("showed satisfaction" to "grinned," "took possession" to "pocketed," and "payment" to "coin").

Connotation: (Rhetorical) From the Latin *con* ('together') and *notationis* ('marking'), connotation refers to the implied of suggested meaning of a word. OPPOSITE of *DENOTATION*.

> There are many connotations of the word "fox": *slick, sneaky, attractive, seductive*, etc.

Consonance: (Rhetorical) From the Latin *consonantem* ('correspondence of sounds'), consonance is the repetition of two or more consonant sounds located within a series of words. SEE *ALLITERATION; ASSONANCE*.

> "Splish splash, I was taking a bath..."
>
> This well-known line from Bobby Darin's song *Splish Splash* (1958) utilizes this form of initial rhyming by repeating the "sp" sound in the first two words.

Coordinating Conjunction: (Grammatical) From the Latin *conjungere* ('join together'), coordinating conjunctions (*for, and, nor but, or, yet, so*) are words that provide a loose link among items that are equal in rank.

> Compound subject: "Joe *and* I fished today."
>
> Compound verb: "We fished *and* relaxed today."
>
> Compound sentence: "We fished today *but* we will work tomorrow."

Deduction: (Rhetorical Mode/Pattern of Organization) From the Latin *deductio* ('leading away'), deduction is the process of reasoning from a general claim to the specific cases. This mode of logic is most clearly seen in the *SYLLOGISM*. SEE *INDUCTION*.

Denotation: From the Latin *de* ('apart') and *notationis* ('marking'), denotation refers to the direct relationship between a term and the object, idea, or action it signifies. OPPOSITE of *CONNOTATION*.

> The denotation of the word "fox" is "a small woodland creature."

Dependent Clause: (Grammatical) A clause that cannot stand alone as a sentence; it requires an independent clause to give it meaning. SEE *INDEPENDENT CLAUSE.*

> "Because I could not stop for death, he kindly stopped for me."

> This line from American poet Emily Dickinson contains both a dependent clause and an independent clause. "Because I could not stop for death" is the *dependent* because its meaning depends upon the main clause "He kindly stopped for me" for its complete meaning. The first clause cannot stand by itself as a sentence: "Because I could not stop for Death" expresses and incomplete thought. Because, what? The second clause, an independent clause, can stand by itself as a sentence: "He kindly stopped for me." It expresses a complete thought; it is understandable, alone.

Description: (Rhetorical Mode/Pattern of Organization) From the Latin *descriptionem* ('representation, copy'), description is one of the four primary modes of writing in composition courses (exposition, narration, and analysis are the others). Descriptions can be either objective or subjective:

> Objective: This form of description reports evidence factually and dispassionately.

> Subjective: This form of description reports evidence using figurative language and figures of speech.

Dialogue: (Rhetorical) From the Latin *dialogus* ('conversation, debate'), dialogue is spoken words, either real or imagined, that are recorded in a piece of writing. Through dialogue, writers reveal important aspects of characters' personalities as well as events in the narrative. SEE *COLLOQUIALISM.*

> "Music is a good thing; and after all that soul-butter and hogwash I never see it freshen up things so, and sound so honest and bully."

> Mark Twain's title character from the novel *The Adventures of Huckleberry Finn* (1885) is one of the first characters in American

literature to utilize vernacular dialogue, or the specific language of a region. By doing this, Twain is able to reveal much about southern American culture without having to resort to lengthy descriptions in the prose.

Diction: (Rhetorical) From the Latin *dictio* ('speech, word'), diction refers to the choice of words in a piece of speech or writing. Diction is often closely linked to a text's tone.

Informal diction: "That dude was pissed!"

Formal diction: "The elder gentleman was noticeably bothered."

Sarcastic diction: "Yeah, he wasn't angry at all."

Didactic: (Literary) From the Greek *didaktikos* ('apt to teaching'), didactic writing attempts to teach a moral or lesson in a work of fiction or non-fiction.

"An old man on the point of death summoned his sons around him to give them some parting advice. He ordered his servants to bring in a bundle of sticks, and said to his eldest son: 'Break it.' The son strained and strained, but with all his efforts was unable to break the bundle. The other sons also tried, but none of them was successful. 'Untie the bundles,' said the father, 'and each of you take a stick.' When they had done so, he called out to them: 'Now, break,' and each stick was easily broken. 'You see my meaning,' said their father."

This short didactic story, drawn from Aesop's collection of fables from 5th century B.C. Greece, illustrates the lesson "unity gives strength." The lesson, here, is implied although didactic stories can explicitly state their lessons as well.

Digression: (Rhetorical) From the Latin *digressio* ('a going away'), a digression is a movement away from the main focus in speech or writing. This can be intentional or unintentional.

Intentional: Authors may move away from the main plot to focus on subplots or minor issues that are peripheral to the central ideas.

Unintentional: Authors may wander in the writing because of a lack of focus/anchoring idea.

Direct Object: (Grammatical) From unknown etymological origins, a direct object is a person or thing affected by the action of a transitive verb (a verb that requires a direct object).

"James fought his nemesis behind Wal-Mart."

The verb "fought" requires an object. Who did he fight? The direct object "nemesis" answers this question.

Dysphemism: (Rhetorical) From the Greek *dys* ('not') and *euphemismos* ('speaking well'), a dysphemism is a disparaging expression used to describe someone or something. Dysphemisms are typically used to emphasize defects, shortcomings, or failings. OPPOSITE of *EUPHEMISM.*

"I hate your stupid, ugly, monster face" instead of "I think you're unattractive."

The verb in the dysphemism ("hate") is a far stronger emotion than the word for which it's substituting ("think"). Similarly, the more neutral "unattractive" is replaced with the harsher, more specific "stupid, ugly, monster face" in order to emphasize the negative qualities of the physical appearance.

Ellipses: (Grammatical) From the Greek *elleipsis* ('coming short'), ellipses are three successive periods (...) that indicate the intentional omission of words in a thought or quotation.

According to the American Cancer Society, "Cancer can be reduced by 50% by regulating your daily intake of known carcinogens... cigarettes are known to contain the most cancer-causing agents" (ACS 2).

Ellipses are used here to show that, during the transcription of the quotation, some words have been omitted and that this is not a verbatim recreation of the information from the source text.

Elliptical Construction: (Rhetorical) From the Greek *elleipsis* ('coming short') and Latin *struere* ('to build'), elliptical construction is the deliberate omission of words from a sentence for rhetorical effect.

> "Junior year was tough and senior year the same."

> The sentence omits the auxiliary verb "was" from the second clause for an effect of conciseness and brevity.

Emphasis: (Rhetorical) From the Latin *emphasis* ('showing, seeming'), emphasis is the placement of important ideas and words within sentences and longer units of writing so that they have the greatest impact. It is achieved by any means that highlights a syllable, word, phrase, idea, event, etc. In general, the end has the most impact and the beginning has nearly as much; the middle often has the least.

> "Get to your room, *now!*"

> Two features of the text, italics and exclamation point, emphasize the increase in vocal intensity and change in expression.

Epigram: (Rhetorical) SEE *APHORISM*.

Epistle: (Literary) From the Latin *epistola* ('letter'), an epistle is a work of poetry or prose that is presented as a series of letters.

> The *Letters of Abelard and Heloise* is a medieval example of a story told through letters. In the story, Abelard, seduces a nun, Heloise, into a passionate, lustful relationship. Heloise's father, the abbot, has Abelard castrated as punishment. This action is meant to be understood before the letters begin; the passion of their love burns on through the letters and the reader comes to understand their love through the correspondence.

Epistrophe: (Rhetorical) From the Greek *epistrophe* ('a turning about'), epistrophe is a figure of speech where successive phrases or clauses all end with the same word. OPPOSITE of *ANAPHORA*.

> "When I was a child, I spoke as a child, I understood as a child, I thought as a child."

Drawn from 1 Corinthians 13:11, the apostle Paul heavily utilizes epistrophe in this quotation, with the each of the four clauses all ending with the same word, "child."

"For no government is better than the men who compose it, and I want the best, and we need the best, and we deserve the best."

President John F. Kennedy delivered this line on October 17, 1960 and, similarly to Paul, the final three clauses each end with an identical word, "best."

Epithet: (Rhetorical) From the Greek *epithetos* ('put or added on'), an epithet is a word or phrase which is attached to a character for the purposes of description in a work of literature or non-fiction.

Literary epithet: In Homer's *Iliad*, the character Achilles is referred to repeatedly as "swift footed Achilles" and "lion-hearted Achilles."

Although these terms were used, in part, to fit the metrical pattern of the Homeric poetic line (dactylic hexameter), they also function to give modifying information about the character as he is being introduced. Epithets are light, quick ways to signal qualities of a character which quickly become synonymous with how the reader understands that person.

Non-fiction epithet: Many historical figures are known, almost exclusively, with their epithets: "Alexander the Great," "Vlad the Impaler," "William the Conqueror."

Each of these epithets, like literary ones, give a quick characteristic of the person under examination.

Eponymous: (Literary) From the Greek *eponumos* ('named on'), an eponymous character is a person in a work of fiction whose name is derived from the title, or vice versa.

Eponymous characters are common in Shakespearean play titles. All twelve of Shakespeare's tragedies (*Troilus and Cressida, Coriolanus, Titus Andronicus, Romeo and Juliet, Timon of Athens, Julius Caesar, Macbeth, Hamlet, King Lear, Othello, Antony and Cleopatra, Cymbeline*) and all ten of his history plays (*King John, Richard II,*

Henry IV Part I, Henry IV Part II, Henry V, Henry VI Part I, Henry VI Part II, Henry VI Part III, Richard III, Henry VIII) use this device.

Ethos: (Rhetorical) From the Greek *ethikos* ('showing moral character'), ethos is the characteristic spirit or ideal that informs a work. Ethos also refers more generally to the ethics or values of the arguer: honesty, trustworthiness, and morality.

> "My 10 years of experience as a military general should indicate that I am ready to lead the country as President of the United States"
>
> Here, the speaker is emphasizing his trustworthiness in the form of his personal credentials. In other words, since he has this experience, he is an authority on the subject at hand and his arguments should be trusted.

Euphemism: (Rhetorical) From the Greek *euphemismos* ('speaking well'), a euphemism is a mild or pleasant-sounding expression that substitutes for a harsh, indelicate, or simply less pleasant idea. Euphemisms are often used to soften the impact of what is being discussed and can be effective when dealing with sensitive issues or shocking news. OPPOSITE of *DYSPHEMISM*.

> "We put Fido to sleep" is a euphemism for "We euthanized the dog."
>
> "Gil has passed away" is a euphemism for "He died of a crippling heart-attack."
>
> In each of these examples, the speaker has substituted the nouns and verbs to make the language softer and more abstract, something a sensitive audience may need in the moment.

Evidence: (Argumentative) From the Latin *evidentia* ('distinction, clearness'), evidence is the grounds upon which a judgment or argument is based or by which proof or probability is established.

Figures of Speech: (Rhetorical) From unknown etymological origins, figures of speech are comparisons that highlight the similarities between things that are basically dissimilar. Similar to an *ANALOGY*. The following are the most common figures of speech:

Simile: An implicit comparison introduced by like or as: "The boxer is like a lion."

Metaphor: An implied comparison that uses one thing as the equivalent of another: "The wrestler is an animal."

Personification: A special kind of simile or metaphor in which human traits are assigned to an inanimate object: "I knew my calculator would malfunction on test day. It is out to get me!"

Figurative Language: (Rhetorical) From the Latin *figurativus* ('a form, shape'), figurative language is a categorical term for all uses of language that imply an imaginative comparison. Often, this term refers to language that appeals to sensory experience.

> "I felt the sunshine on my skin, hearing the buzzing of the bees, while gazing at the gentle babble of the brook in the distance."

> Gina is appealing to three senses: sight ("gazing"), hearing ("buzzing," "babble"), and touch ("felt") in her figurative description.

Foreshadowing: (Literary) From the Old English *fore* ('before') and *sceadwe* ('imitation'), foreshadowing is a purposeful hint placed in a work of literature to suggest what may occur later in the narrative.

> At the beginning of a baseball novel, a scene in which the young protagonist is shown throwing rocks into glass bottles could foreshadow his eventual career as a pitcher in the Major Leagues.

Gobbledygook: (Rhetorical) From the Scottish slang *gob* ('mouth'), and *gook* ('a speaker of gibberish'), gobbledygook is a mode of speech where the language is completely unintelligible, either because of extreme *JARGON* or overblown diction that overwhelms the reader, a combination of *BOMBAST* and *CIRCUMLOCUTION*. The term is onomatopoeic, derived from the sounds a turkey makes.

> "It's time to realize our strategic growth mindset and use operational mindfulness to make our presence known in the industry with quality implementation methodologies."

At once, this quotation says a lot and nothing at all. Coming in at a hefty 22 words, it is almost unintelligible to the average listener given the high degree of corporate jargon and needless wordiness.

Harangue: (Rhetorical) From the Old Italian *aringo* ('pulpit'), a harangue is an emotionally based speech meant to spur an audience into action.

> "This that you have heard is the case of every one of you that are out of Christ. That world of misery, that lake of burning brimstone is extended abroad under you. There is the dreadful pit of the glowing flames of the wrath of God; there is hell's wide gaping mouth open; and you have nothing to stand upon, nor anything to take hold of: there is nothing between you and hell but the air; 'tis only the power and mere pleasure of God that holds you up."

These are the opening lines to Jonathan Edwards' *Sinners in the Hands of an Angry God* (1741), a pathos-laden sermon in which he attempts to frighten or coerce the congregation into agreement with his position. The imagery ("world of misery," "lake of burning brimstone," "dreadful pit," "glowing flames") and diction ("nothing," "anything," "power," "misery") clearly indicate the haranguing tone of this sermon.

Hyphaersis: (Rhetorical) From the Greek *huphaersis* ('small removal'), hyphaersis is the omission of a letter from a word, usually to condense the number of syllables.

> "O'er the ramparts we watched, were so gallantly streaming? And the rockets' red glare, the bombs bursting in air, gave proof through the night that our flag was still there. O say, does that star-spangled banner yet wave o'er the land of the free and the home of the brave?"

This well-known passage, the lyrics to Francis Scott Key's *The Star-Spangled Banner* (1814), has two examples of hyphaersis, "o'er" substituting (in the first and second to last line) as a single syllable version of the word "over."

Hyperbole: (Rhetorical) From the Greek *huperbole* ('flung too far'), hyperbole is a figure of speech in which exaggeration is used to achieve emphasis, usually for comical effect. Hyperboles ought to be understood as overstatement rather than literal representation. OPPOSITE of *UNDERSTATEMENT*.

"You really drive me up the wall!"

"The lunch line is a thousand people long!"

In both cases, neither speaker intends to communicate the literal meaning of their words, but rather uses hyperbole to express the idea in a lighthearted, comical way.

Hypostatization: (Rhetorical) From the Greek *hypo* ('under') and *stasis* ('foundation'), hypostatization is a form of *PERSONIFICATION* in which an abstract concept takes on living qualities. Sometimes, hypostatization is considered a logical fallacy, since the speaker addresses an *ABSTRACT* entity as if it were *CONCRETE*.

"Guilt forced me to confess."

"Justice is the leader of this country."

In both cases, the abstract concepts of "guilt" and "justice" – things which have no physical reality – are described as being able to force another person to confess, or be a leader of a society, respectively.

Idiom: (Rhetorical) From the Latin *idioma* ('special phrasing'), an idiom is a word or phrase that is used habitually. Idioms are often difficult for non-native speakers to understand since meaning is suggested by conventional use, not denotation.

"Time to rise and shine!"

"If I stay outside, I'm going to catch a cold. I can already feel my nose running."

The meaning of these expressions is clear to native speaking English speakers who know that the first expression means to "get up and start the day with energy" and the second expression means that "remaining outside during bad weather will lead to a cold symptomized by nasal discharge." The literal meanings of the words "rise and shine," "catch a cold," and "nose running," however, are confusing to non-native speakers who may only be applying the denotative, not connotative, definitions.

Imagery: (Rhetorical) From the Latin *imagines* ('likeness, picture'), imagery is a mental picture that is conjured by specific words and associations, though there can be auditory and sensory components to imagery as well. Nearly all writing depends on imagery to be effective and interesting. SEE *FIGURATIVE LANGUAGE; METAPHOR; PERSONIFICATION; SIMILE; SYMBOL.*

Independent Clause: (Grammatical) A clause that can stand alone as a sentence; it can be paired with dependent clauses but does not require them for meaning. SEE *DEPENDENT CLAUSE.*

> "Because I could not stop for death, he kindly stopped for me."
>
> "Because I could not stop for Death" expresses an incomplete thought. Because, what? The second clause, an independent clause, can stand by itself as a sentence: "He kindly stopped for me." It expresses a complete thought; it is understandable, alone.

Induction: (Rhetorical Mode/Pattern of Organization) From the Latin *inductio* ('leading towards'), induction is the logical process of arriving at conclusions based off of the experience of specific cases/scenarios. This form of reasoning, typically found in the sciences, moves from the particular to the general. SEE *DEDUCTION.*

Inference: (Rhetorical) From the Latin *inferentia* ('a bringing-in'), inference is the process of arriving at a conclusion based on a hint, clue, or implication.

> Todd can infer that Richard is an angry man because of his knotted eyebrows and clenched fists. He does not need to be directly told, but rather it can be inferred through non-verbal cues.

Irony: (Literary) From the Greek *eiron* ('a dissembler'), irony is a mode of expression in which an intended outcome is substituted with the reverse of what is expected. This is often done for humor or ridicule.

"The day Chris decided on sobriety, he got run over by a Bud Light truck and died."

The obvious irony here is what Chris thought would save his life, abstinence from alcohol, ending up killing him in another form, death from a truck carrying alcohol.

Jargon: (Rhetorical) SEE *TECHNICAL LANGUAGE; GOBBLEDY GOOK.*

Juxtaposition: (Rhetorical) From the Latin *iuxta* ('beside, near') and *positio* ('placing'), juxtaposition occurs when two contrasting things – ideas, words, or sentence elements – are placed next to each other for comparison.

A writer may choose to juxtapose the coldness of one room with the warmth of another, or one person's honesty with another's duplicity. Juxtaposition sheds light on both elements in the comparison.

Litote: (Rhetorical) From the Greek *litotes* ('meagerness'), a litote is a form of *UNDERSTATEMENT* in which the opposite is used to achieve emphasis.

"She's not a bad hockey player."

The negated statement here actually represents a positive sentiment. To say that "she's not bad" really means that "she is good," the opposite.

Logical Reasoning: (Rhetorical Mode/Pattern of Organization) SEE *INDUCTION; DEDUCTION.*

Logos: (Rhetorical) From the Greek *logos* ('word, reason'), logos is the use of reason as a controlling principle in an argument. In argumentation, authors often attempt to persuade readers by appealing to their sense of logos, or reason, by using data, evidence, factual information, or patterns of organization.

"We need the addition of a traffic light at the corner of 1st and 34th. Traffic lights are shown to reduce traffic accidents by up to 30 percent at busy intersections."

The speaker uses relevant, measured data to prove the legitimacy of his claim: to install traffic lights at the intersection of two busy roads.

Loose Syntax: (Rhetorical) A sentence in which the main clause is presented first followed by a series of dependent clauses. The most important information is frontloaded, and following phrases or clauses merely modify this main idea. OPPOSITE of *PERIODIC SYNTAX*.

> "The corpse was stuffed in the trunk as drove the car carefully, his shaggy hair whipped by the wind, his eyes hidden behind wraparound mirror shades, his mouth set in a grim smile, a .38 Police Special on the seat beside him."

In this sentence, drawn from Brook Landon's *Building Great Sentences*, there is no suspense; the reader knows from the first clause ("The corpse was stuffed in the trunk") that some suspect activity has taken place. The descriptive information ("drove carefully," "shaggy hair," "eyes hidden," "grim smile," ".38 Police Special") modifies and supplements the main clause.

Malapropism: (Rhetorical) From the French *mal-a-propos* ('inappropriate'), a malapropism is the substitution of a word for a word with a similar sound in which the resulting phrase makes no sense and often creates a comic effect.

> "Let's create a little dysentery among the ranks."

Drawn from the HBO series, *The Sopranos*, the above quotation's humor rests on the word "dysentery." The speaker, Christopher Moltisanti, does not mean that he wants to create intestinal inflammation among the ranks of his adversaries; he means to say "dissention" which means "disagreement" or "disharmony." The malapropism is used to show him as a foolish character.

Metaphor: (Literary) From the Greek *metaphora* ('carry over, transfer'), a metaphor is any figure of speech in which two unlike things are compared directly, usually for emphasis or dramatic effect. Metaphors can come in a variety of forms:

Standard: A figure of speech that makes a connection between two unlike things.

"My heart is a rose."

Extended: A metaphor that extends over several lines, verses, or chapters.

"Writing this research paper is a grind. My brain is not operating. I am running out of steam." (Each sentence extends the metaphor that the mind is a machine)

Implied: A less direct metaphor.

"The boxer pecked away at his opponent."

Dead: A metaphor that has become so common that we no longer notice it as a figure of speech.

"My sister drives me out of my mind."

Metonymy: A figure of speech in which something closely related to a thing is substituted for the thing itself.

"Here comes the crown." (The crown stands in for the king himself)

Mixed: A faulty metaphor that switches the terms of comparison before it finishes.

"We are at the crossroads of an enormous precipice."

Synecdoche: A substitution of a part for a whole (or vice versa).

"Five hundred hands were needed to build the bridge." (The manual laborers are represented by their hands, the instrument of their labor)

Mood: (Literary) From the Latin *modus* ('form, manner'), mood is the audience's attitude or feelings towards a subject. SEE *ATMOSPHERE; TONE.*

Narration: (Rhetorical Mode/Pattern of Organization) From the Latin *narrationis* ('telling, recounting'), narration is one of the four primary modes of writing in composition courses (description, exposition, and analysis are the others). To narrate is to tell a story, to tell what happened.

Although narration is most often used in fiction, it is also important in nonfiction, either by itself or in conjunction with other types of prose.

Neologism: (Rhetorical) From the Latin *neo* ('new') and *logos* ('word'), a neologism is a newly invented, or coined, word. Neologisms can be altogether new, an addition to a previous word, or an existing word which has been given new meaning.

> Shakespeare, writing in the Renaissance, a time which saw a return to Classical Greek and Roman languages, has been credited with inventing nearly 2000 words including: "accommodation," "countless," "dishearten," "dwindle," "submerge," and "suspicious." But neologisms are not reserved for older authors; in 2010 more than 200 words, most of which reflect the dominating technology of the internet and pop-culture, were added to the Oxford English Dictionary including: "overthink," "bromance," "buzzkill," "frenemy," and "exit strategy."

Onomatopoeia: (Rhetorical) From the Greek *onomatopoiia* ('making a name'), onomatopoeia is a word that captures the essence of what it describes or stands for.

> "The bees buzzed and zoomed around my head. I screeched in horror."

> "Buzz," "zoom," and "screeched" are onomatopoeic because they mirror the sounds that they represent.

Oxymoron: (Rhetorical) From the Greek *oxumoros* ('sharp and dull'), an oxymoron is a pair of contradictory words or ideas joined together in one expression. SEE *PARADOX*.

> Love is a "cold fire."

> Oxymorons are often paradoxical, but they usually serve to illustrate a deeper truth that is not readily apparent. In this quotation from *Romeo & Juliet* (1597), Romeo describes the dual effect love has on him throughout the play in the domain of two words.

Pacing: (Rhetorical) From the Latin *pandere* ('to spread'), pacing is the speed of a story's action, dialogue, or narration. Some stories are told slowly, some more quickly. Events happen fast or are dragged out according to the narrator's purpose. Pacing is often dictated by how time elapses in a story:

> Flashforward: The story begins at the end and works to fill in the gaps.
>
> Flashback: The story begins in the present and flashes to past events for clarification.
>
> En Medias Res: The story begins in the middle of the action and works outward.

Panoramic Method: (Literary) From the Greek *pan* ('all') and *horama* ('sight, spectacle'), panoramic method is a term derived from the film/photography technique of a wide angle shot. In writing, this term refers to an omniscient, or all knowing, narrator in a work of fiction or non-fiction.

> J.R.R. Tolkien's trilogy *The Lord of the Rings* (1950) features the panoramic method of narration from beginning to end. Throughout, the narrator knows the thoughts, feelings, motivations and ideas for all of the characters present in the story.

Paradox: (Rhetorical) From the Greek *paradoxos* ('contrary to expectation'), a paradox is a seeming contradiction that in fact reveals some truth. SEE *OXYMORON*.

> "You are the daughter of your son. You are most humble, most exalted."
>
> In Dante Alighieri's 14th century poem *Paradise*, he describes the Virgin Mary in the language of paradox. When describing the relationship between Mary and Jesus, it is logically impossible to be a daughter of your son or be most exalted and most humble simultaneously, but this is the only type of language that can render the idea he is attempting to convey. To Dante, this seemingly contradictory

language reveals a truth about the divine nature of the Virgin Mary. Paradox is often used to communicate mystical experiences.

"War is peace, freedom is slavery, and ignorance is strength."

This governmental slogan from George Orwell's 1949 dystopian novel, *1984*, captures the tyranny of an absolute government with series of paradoxical expressions.

Paragraph: (Rhetorical Mode/Pattern of Organization) From the Greek *paragraphos* ('at the side of writing'), a paragraph is a series of closely related sentences and is the single most important unit of thought in an essay. In expository writing, a paragraph's sentences work in conjunction to develop a central or controlling idea, usually stated in a topic sentence, that is related to the purpose of the whole composition. A well-written paragraph has several distinguishing characteristics: a clearly stated or implied topic sentence, adequate development, unity, coherence, and an appropriate organizational strategy.

Parallelism: (Rhetorical) From the Greek *para* ('beside') and *allelois* ('each other'), parallelism is a technique that relies on the use of the same syntactical structures, (phrases, clauses, sentences) in a series to develop an argument or emphasize an idea. As a rhetorical device, parallelism can aid coherence and add emphasis. Coordinate ideas, compared and contrasted ideas, or correlative constructions call for parallel structure.

"At sea, on land, in the air, we will be loyal to the very end."

This line from Thomas Jefferson's *The Declaration of Independence* (1776) uses parallelism in the opening prepositional phrases to emphasize the level of loyalty held by the people.

"I came, I saw, I conquered."

This famous saying, attributed to the 1st century Roman emperor, Julius Caesar, uses parallelism in the repetition of the subject-verb pairs to communicate the sure-footed confidence of the emperor.

Parody: (Rhetorical) From the Greek *paroidia* ('something sung alongside'), a parody is an imitation of a work meant to ridicule its style and subject.

The Naked Gun films parody Film Noir detective movies.

Scary Movie films parody horror movies.

Participle: (Grammatical) From the Latin *participium* ('a part-taking'), a participle is an expression built from a verb that can function as a verb, an adjective, or noun. Participles can be in present, past, or infinitive forms.

Past participle as verb: "Julie has *tried* to finish the problem a dozen times."

Present participle as verb: "Julie is *trying* to finish her lengthy homework assignment."

Past participle as adjective: "An *embarrassed* Julie came to class empty handed."

Present participle as adjective: "*Crying*, Julie came to class without her homework."

Present participle as subject: "*Sobbing* is the only thing that gives Julie comfort."

Infinitive participle as subject: "*To earn* an A would solve Julie's problems."

Passive Voice: (Grammatical) From the Latin *passivus* ('capable of suffering, being affected'), passive voice is a syntactical term for a sentence where the subject is the receiver of the action. Contemporary style guides often urge writers to avoid passive voice since it often is wordier and more confusing than active voice constructions. OPPOSITE of *ACTIVE VOICE*.

"The missiles were fired at the city."

In this sentence, the main subject, "missiles," is written in what's known as an "agentless" form (i.e. it is unclear who was responsible for firing the missiles.) Sentences like this are why the passive voice is sometimes associated with evasiveness or deception.

Pathos: (Rhetorical) From the Greek *pathos* ('feeling, suffering'), pathos is the feelings or emotions evoked by an artistic work. In argument, authors often attempt to persuade readers by appealing to their sense of pathos, or emotions, often by using sentimental language, connotative diction, or appeals to certain values.

> "We should get rid of cigarettes because my grandmother, who raised me by herself, was slowly overtaken by the illness."

> The speaker is relying on the emotional content of his own story to change the minds of the audience instead of making a moral argument against their sale (ethos) or presenting quantifiable data that illustrates cigarettes to be a health risk (logos).

Periodic Syntax: (Rhetorical) From unknown etymological origins, periodic syntax describes a sentence that delays the most important information until the very end, creating a sense of suspense that demands the reader's attention, sometimes to that very last word. OPPOSITE of *LOOSE SYNTAX.*

> "He drove the car carefully, his shaggy hair whipped by the wind, his eyes hidden behind wraparound mirror shades, his mouth set in a grim smile, a .38 Police Special on the seat beside him, the corpse stuffed in the trunk."

> Adapted from Brooks Landon's *Building Great Sentences* (2008), the speaker builds the information, and the suspense, by saving the most important bit of information for the final clause.

Persona: (Rhetorical) From the Latin *persona* ('mask'), persona is the character created in the voice and narration by the speaker of a text. The term "persona" implies a fictional representation or an act of disguise (i.e. the speaker is not the author, but a created character).

> "What I want to say, and it is difficult to say, is that had you not read a single piece except for, maybe, the novels of C.S. Lewis, *The Lord of the Rings*, *Treasure Island*, or Flannery O'Connor, you would not need this advice. You would have already learned, without intending it, the strong cadences of English prose; and you already would have in your mind's ear the "sounds" of thought, its swift attacks, its stately progresses, its cuts and turns, its imposing stands."

Here, the writer is highly allusive to other authors and works and assumes that the reader *has* in fact been reading lesser literature. The accompanying explanation is full of English jargon in an attempt to distance the material from the audience, rather than, ironically, demonstrate clear writing through simple, yet effective, expressions to make the ideas more accessible.

Personification: (Rhetorical) From the Latin *personificatio* ('making a person'), personification is a figure of speech in which ideas or objects are described as having human qualities or personalities.

> "When I was taking my Calculus final, my calculator shorted out on me. I knew it just wanted to embarrass me in front of my teacher."

> The calculator is presented as being capable of human emotion.

Pleonasm: (Rhetorical) From the Latin *pleonasmus* ('excess, redundancy'), a pleonasm occurs when speaker's word choice is redundant or tautological. SEE *CIRCUMLOCATION*.

> "This is a new innovation that is more superior than the competitor's product."

> In this example, "innovation" carries with it the idea of something being "new" and "superior" already implies "more" than what's under comparison. Both "new" and "more" in this sentence are pleonastic.

Point of View: (Rhetorical Mode/Pattern of Organization) From unknown etymological origins, point of view is the perspective from which a story is told. Stories may be told from the point of view of specific characters or from a detached narrator. SEE *PANORAMIC METHOD, PERSON*.

> Subjective: The narrator relays individual experiences and may or may not be involved in the story.

> Objective: The narrator relays only what can be empirically observed.

> Omniscient: The narrator knows the thoughts and feelings of every character.
> Limited: The narrator knows the thoughts and feelings of only a few characters.

Some literary works blend different points of view for emphasis and experimentation. For example, a first-person point of view uses the pronoun *I* and is commonly found in autobiographies and personal essays; a third-person point of view uses the pronouns *he, she*, or *it* and is commonly found in expository writing.

Polysyndeton: (Rhetorical) From the Greek *polysyndetos* ('many connections'), polysyndeton occurs when coordinating conjunctions (*for, and, nor, but, or, yet, so*) that would normally connect a string of words, phrases, or clauses are intentionally overused. This is done to emphasize the number of objects in a sequence or to convey enthusiasm in the speaker's voice. OPPOSITE of *ASYNDETON*.

> "The injustices we have suffered are many. The brainwashing of our children and the eroding of our rights and the segregations of our schools must end!"

> The use of polysyndeton here emphasizes the amount of injustices. A series offset by commas would diminish the effect.

> "The first day of school was awesome! We colored, and played, and laughed, and learned math, and saw a play!"

> Polysyndeton can also be used to display enthusiasm or excitement, as if the speaker just keeps interjecting new words into their existing string of thoughts as they come.

Preposition: (Grammatical) From the Greek *prothesis* ('putting before'), a preposition is a word that indicates a relationship between words or ideas. Common prepositions include:

aboard	atop	excepting	on top of	times
about	before	following	onto	to
above	behind	for	opposite	toward
across	below	from	out of	towards
after	beneath	in	outside	under
against	beside	in front	over	unlike
along	besides	inside	past	until
alongside	between	instead of	per	up
amid	beyond	into	plus	upon
amidst	but	like	round	versus
among	by	near	save	via
anti	despite	next	since	with
around	down	of	than	within
as	during	off	through	without
at	except	on	till	

Proverb: (Rhetorical) SEE *APHORISM, EPIGRAM.*

Pun: (Rhetorical) From the Italian *puntiglio* ('a quibble'), a pun is a play on words. A pun is created by using a word that has two different meanings, or using two different words with similar meanings, for a playful effect. SEE *AMBIGUITY.*

"Time flies like an arrow. Fruit flies like a banana."

This pun plays on the definition of "flies." In the first sentence, "flies" is used in the sense of "moving quickly." In the second sentence, "flies" is used in reference to the small insect. The syntax – the word number and simile sentence style – of the two sentences are identical which contributes to the effectiveness of the pun as well.

Repetition: (Rhetorical) SEE *ANAPHORA, CHIASMUS, EPISTROPHE, PARALLELISM.*

Rhetoric: (Rhetorical) From the Greek *rhetorike tekhne* ('the craft of speaking'), rhetoric is the art of using language to achieve a particular purpose or goal.

The term "rhetoric" is most commonly understood via Aristotle in *The Art of Rhetoric* (4th Century B.C.) where it is defined as, "the faculty of observing in any given case the available means of persuasion."

Rhetorical Question: (Rhetorical) From unknown etymological origins, a rhetorical question is an inquiry that is asked for the sake of argument.

Jorge: "How much longer will we have to tolerate this injustice?"

No direct answer is expected. Rhetorical questions have the appearance of an interrogative statement, but function as a declarative one. Writers often use rhetorical questions to introduce topics they plan to discuss or to emphasize important points.

Sarcasm: (Rhetorical) From the Greek *sarkasamos* ('tearing flesh'), sarcasm is a form of verbal irony in which apparent compliments are bitter or nasty.

(*As her partner trips and falls to the ground on the dance floor*) "Wow, you're real graceful!"

The sharp and caustic response, in its denotation, appears to be a compliment, but the context of the situation reveals it as a jibe or taunt.

Satire: (Rhetorical Mode/Pattern of Organization) From the Greek *saturos* ('satyr'), satire is a mode of expression that ridicules ideas, persons, events, or doctrines in order to make fun of human foibles or weaknesses. SEE *PARODY.*

> *A Modest Proposal* (1729) by Jonathan Swift is a satire of the "logic-driven" mentality of the Enlightenment. In this essay, he proposes to rid Ireland of its social ills by selling and eating newborn babies. The idea is economically sound, but it ignores the human element intentionally to illustrate the dangers of Enlightenment thinking.

Semicolon: (Grammatical) From the Latin *semi* ('half') and *colon* ('part of a verse'), a semicolon (;) is a form of punctuation typically used to join independent clauses.

> "I could not prevent him from stabbing Caesar; he shall not prevent me from taking my revenge."

> The semicolon joins the two independent clauses on either side of it. Each statement can stand alone as its own sentence.

Sequence: (Rhetorical Mode/Pattern of Organization) From the Latin *sequi* ('to follow'), sequence refers to the order in which a writer presents information. Writers commonly select the following orders:

> Chronological: Points are organized in a temporal relationship.

> Spatial: Points begin at one location to logically move forward.

> Importance: Points progress from least to most important.

> Complexity: Points progress from simple to complex.

Sic: (Grammatical) From the Latin *sic* ('intentionally so written'), sic is a notation (often used in journalism) made during the transcription process to indicate that an apparent error was made in the source document, not in the transference. The notation usually appears in brackets or parenthesis.

"The House of Representatives shall chuse [sic] their Speaker..."

The author, reproducing this quotation from the *U.S. Constitution* (1787), indicates that the spelling of "chuse," which appears to be incorrectly formed to 21st century readers, was made in the original document, not during the transcription.

Simile: (Rhetorical) From the Latin *similis* ('like'), a simile is a figure of speech that compares two things using the words "like" or "as."

"Ricardo ran like a gazelle at the track meet."

"Ran like a gazelle" is a simile that compares the speed and grace of a gazelle to that of Ricardo at the track meet.

Slang: (Rhetorical) From unknown etymological origins (though scholars believe it to be a derivation of the word 'sling'), slang is the unconventional, informal language of particular sub-groups of a culture. SEE *COLLO-QUIALISM; DICTION.*

"Let's split. I've had enough of this joint even though it was off the hook."

Like other forms of informal expression, the acceptable use of slang is context dependent. Formal writing typically discourages this level of informality, though if a writer is trying to capture the cadence of everyday language use for a specific reason, it is acceptable to include this mode of speech.

Speaker: (Rhetorical) From the Middle English *spekan* ('to speak'), a speaker is the narrator of a story, poem, or drama. The speaker should not be confused with the author, the creator of the speaker's voice. SEE *PERSONA.*

Specific/General: (Rhetorical) General words name groups or classes of objects, qualities, or actions. Specific words, in contrast, name individual objects, qualities, or actions within a class or group. SEE *ABSRACT; CONCRETE.*

> General: *Dinner* is a class of things.
>
> Specific: *Pasta* is more specific than *dinner*, but more general than *fettuccine alfredo* or *muscles marinara*.
>
> Skillful writing judiciously balances the general with the specific. Writing with too many general words is likely to be dull and lifeless. General words do not create vivid responses in the reader's mind as concrete, specific words can. However, writing that relies exclusively on specific words may lack focus and direction – the control that more general statements provide.

Stream of Consciousness: (Literary) Coined by William James in the *Principles of Psychology* (1890), stream of consciousness is a narrative technique meant to mirror the continuous, and often disjointed and disconnected, flow of information through a speaker's mind with little to no regard for traditional narrative coherence.

> "The Vances lived in number seven. They had a different father and mother. They were Eileen's mother and father. When they were grown up he was going to marry Eileen. He hid under the table. His mother said – O, Stephen will apologise. Dante said – O, if not, the eagles will come and pull out his eyes. *Pull out his eyes, apologise, apologise, pull out his eyes. Apologise, pull out his eyes, pull out his eyes, apologise.*"
>
> James Joyce's novel *A Portrait of the Artist as a Young Man* (1915) attempts to show the evolution of the main character, Stephen Dedalus, from birth to adulthood. In the quotation, Joyce tries to capture the mind of the artist as a young child. He jumps from observations ("the Vances lived in number seven"), to emotional feelings ("When they were grown up he was going to marry Eileen. He hid under the table") to musical associations made from scold-

ing comments ("*Pull out his eyes, apologise, apologise, pull out his eyes. Apologise, pull out his eyes, pull out his eyes, apologise*") with no signaling of these transitions of changeovers in the narrative.

Style: (Rhetorical) From the Latin *stilus* ('a stake'), style is the manner in which an author uses and arranges words, phrases, and ideas to express his or her ideas. The classical definition of style from Cicero, a 1st century B.C. Roman orator, can be broken down into three primary categories:

> The ornamental style: Ceremonial or exhortative. Suitable for formal speeches, arguments and legal proceedings.
>
> The middle style: Conversational and amiable. Suitable for everyday interactions and expressions.
>
> The low, plain style: Unadorned. Suitable for simple explanations and teaching.

Style is not always understood in Cicero's three-part taxonomy. It can also be thought of as a way to more informally define diction within a work. For example, an author may use:

> Tough style: "You better believe I like hamburgers."
>
> Sweet style: "Don't you just think hamburgers are fabulous?"
>
> Pretentious style: "My gastronomic preferences include, but are not limited to, that peculiarly American version of a sandwich known as a hamburger."

Syllogism: (Argumentative) From the Greek *sullogismos* ('a thinking out'), a syllogism is an argument that utilizes deductive reasoning and consists of a major premise, a minor premise, and a conclusion.

> All bachelors are unmarried men. (Major premise)
>
> Joseph is an unmarried. (Minor premise)
>
> Therefore, Joseph is a bachelor. (Conclusion)

In Aristotelean syllogisms, there are four types of categorical propositions which can be used to advance an argumentative position: "all," "none," "some are," "some are not."

Symbol	Form of the proposition	Example
A	All *S* is *P*.	All cheese pizza is delicious.
E	No *S* is *P*.	No dogs are scaly creatures.
I	Some *S* is *P*.	Some men have brown hair.
O	Some *S* is not *P*.	Some women are not left-handed.

Below is a standard-form syllogism, accompanied by its symbolic notations. For a more detailed look at syllogisms, consult Ch. 8.

Stage of syllogism	Linguistic proposition	Symbol
Major Premise	All mammals have hair.	A
Minor Premise	Some mammals are cats.	I
Conclusion	All cats have hair.	A

Symbol: (Rhetorical) From the Greek *sumbolon* ('mark, sign'), a symbol is a person, place, or thing that evokes ideas and associations that are not literally part of the original object.

> To a teacher, a stick of chalk may represent education.

> To a U.S. citizen, the flag may represent freedom and the American way of life.

Syntax: (Rhetorical) From the Greek *suntaxis* ('arranged in order'), syntax is the manner in which words are arranged in a sentence.

> "The big blue sky beckoned her."

> "She was beckoned by the big blue sky."

> These two sentences share a similar meaning, but have different syntax, or word order. Essentially, each sentence says the same thing

except the syntactical arrangement for each has been slightly altered, resulting in the same image expressed in active and passive styles.

Technical Language: (Rhetorical) From the Greek *tekhnikos* ('of art, skill'), technical language is the special vocabulary of a trade or profession. Writers who use technical language should do so with an awareness of their audience. SEE *DICTION, GOBBLEDYGOOK, JARGON.*

> If the audience is a group of peers, technical language may be used freely.
>
> If the audience is a more general one, technical language should be used sparingly and carefully so as not to sacrifice clarity.

Theme: (Literary) From the Greek *thema* ('something put down, proposition'), a theme is the central idea, usually an abstract concept, upon which a written piece, fiction or non-fiction, is built. There can be several themes in a single work.

> In *Hamlet* (1609), Shakespeare includes loyalty, bravery, duty, revenge, and sanity as themes which are variously treated and dramatized in the action and characters.

Thesis: (Argumentative) From the Greek *thesis* ('put in place'), a thesis is a statement of the main idea or argument in a work of speech of writing. Also known as the controlling idea, a thesis may sometimes be implied rather than stated directly.

Tone: (Literary) From the Greek *tonos* ('tension, sound'), tone is the author's attitude towards a subject or scenario. An author's tone can be serious, scholarly, humorous, mournful, ironic, etc. SEE *ATMOSPHERE; MOOD.*

> A particular tone results from a writer's diction, sentence structure, purpose and attitude toward the subject. A correct perception of the author's tone is essential to understanding a particular literary work. Misreading an ironic tone as a serious one, for instance, could lead a reader to miss the humor in a description or situation.

Transitions: (Rhetorical) From the Latin *transitio* ('a going across'), transitions are words that bring unity and coherence to a piece of writing by drawing connections between paragraphed ideas. Authors use these words according to purpose.

Connection	Contrast	Sequence	Indication
And	But	First... second	This
Or	Yet	And then	That
Nor	However	Before	There
Therefore	Despite	After	For Example
Moreover	Still	Until	In this case
Hence	Although	Next	For

Understatement: (Rhetorical) From unknown etymological origins in 19th century English, understatement occurs when an author assigns less significance to an event or thing than it deserves. SEE *HYPERBOLE; SARCASM*.

> A foot-deep flood in a basement referred to as "a few drops of water" deliberately understates the seriousness of the situation.

Vernacular: (Rhetorical) SEE *COLLOQUIALISM*.

Voice: (Rhetorical) From the Latin *vox* ('voice, word, saying'), voice is the manner in which a speaker of a literary work presents himself or herself to the reader. Voice can refer to either *TONE* or *ACTIVE/PASSIVE VOICE*.

> Tone: A speaker's voice can be loud or soft, personal or cold, strident or gentle, authoritative or hesitant, or any manner or combination of characteristics.

> Verb tense: Voice is also a grammatical term. A sentence can be written in either active or passive voice. A simple way to tell the difference is to consider how action is performed in a sentence. For example: "I sent the letter" contains an active voice. When the subject is acted upon, the voice is passive: "The letter was sent by me."

Zeugma: (Rhetorical) From the Greek *zeugma* ('yoking'), zeugma is a figure of speech in which the same word is applied to two other words in the same sentence with different meanings.

"She looked at the dictionary with curiosity and a magnifying glass."

The past tense verb "looked" is referring to the separate ways that she read the dictionary. The first way, "with curiosity," describes the emotional content of the look while the second, "with…a magnifying glass," explains the tools she used while performing this look. Each of these ways hinge on the sentence's main verb.

ACKNOWLEDGMENTS

Ashbery, John. "Paradoxes and Oxymorons" from SHADOW TRAIN. Copyright © 1980, 1981 by John Ashbery. Reprinted by permission of Georges Borchardt, Inc., for the author.

Adams, Eddie. "South Vietnamese Gen. Nguyen Ngoc Loan, chief of the National Police, fires his pistol into the head of suspected Viet Cong officer Nguyen Van Lem (also known as Bay Lop) on a Saigon street Feb. 1, 1968, early in the Tet Offensive." Reprinted by permission of AP Photos/Eddie Adams.

Barthes, Roland. Excerpt/s from "Rhetoric of the Image" from IMAGE-MUSIC-TEXT, translated by Stephen Heath. Translation Copyright © 1977 by Stephen Heath. Reprinted by permission of Hill and Wang, a division of Farrar, Straus and Giroux.

Bartholomae, David. "The Study of Error." *The Writing Teacher's Sourcebook*, edited by Gary Tate and Edward P. J. Corbett, Oxford UP, 1999. Reprinted with the permission of the author.

Barthes, Roland. Excerpt/s from "Rhetoric of the Image" from IMAGE-MUSIC-TEXT, translated by Stephen Heath. Translation Copyright © 1977 by Stephen Heath. Reprinted by permission of Hill and Wang, a division of Farrar, Straus and Giroux.

Bazerman, Charles. *The Informed Writer*. Houghton-Mifflin, 1994. Reprinted with the permission of the author.

Bertoff, Ann. Forming, Thinking, Writing. New York: Boynton/Cook Publishers, 1989. Reprinted with the permission of the author.

Bialostosky, Donald. "Liberal Education, Writing, and the Dialogic Self." *Contending with Words*. New York: Modern Language Association of America. 1991. Reprinted with the permission of the author.

Birkerts, Sven. "Into the Electronic Millennium." *Boston Review: A Literary and Political Forum*. October 1991. Reprinted with the permission of the author.

Block, Cathy, and Gerald Duffy. "Research on Teaching Comprehension: Where We've Been and Where We're Going." *Comprehension Instruction*, edited by Cathy Collins Block and Sheri R. Parris. New York: Guilford Press, 2011. Reprinted by permission of Guilford Press, Inc.

Cahir, Linda. *Literature into Film: Theory and Practical Approaches*. McFarland & Company, 2009. Reprinted by permission of McFarland & Company.

Charney, Davida. "Teaching Writing as Process." *Strategies for Teaching First-Year Composition*. NCTE: National Council of Teachers of English. Urbana, IL, 2002. Reprinted with the permission of the author and by permission of NCTE.

Cowen, Tyler. *Creative Destruction: How Globalization is Changing the World's Cultures*. New Jersey: Princeton University Press. Reprinted with the permission of the author.

Crowley, Sharon. "Teaching Invention." *Strategies for Teaching First-Year Composition*. NCTE: National Council of Teachers of English. Urbana, IL, 2002. Reprinted with the permission of the author and by permission of NCTE.

Didion, Joan. "Los Angeles Notebook" from SLOUCHING TOWARDS BETHLEHEM. Copyright © 1966, 1968, renewed 1996 by Joan Didion. Reprinted by permission of Farrar, Straus and Giroux.

Dillard, Anne. Brief quote from p. 131 ["A weasel is wild .... obedient to instinct."] from TEACHING A STONE TO TALK: EXPEDITIONS AND ENCOUNTERS BY ANNIE DILLARD. © 1982 by Annie Dillard. Reprinted by permission of HarperCollins Publishers.

Elbow, Peter. *Writing Without Teachers*. New York: Oxford University Press, 2007. Reprinted with the permission of the author.

Esolen, Anthony. "Dog Eared Pursuits." *Touchstone Magazine* March 2005. Reprinted by permission of the editor.

Fagles, Robert. Translator's Postscript by Robert Fagles; from THE AENEID by Virgil, translated by Robert Fagles, translation copyright © 2006 by Robert Fagles. Used by permission of Viking Books, an imprint of Penguin Publishing Group, a division of Penguin Random House LLC. All rights reserved.

Faigley, Lester, Diana George, Anna Palchik, and Cynthia Selfe. *Picturing Texts*. W.W. Norton & Co, 2004. Reprinted by permission of W.W. Norton & Co. Publishers.

Foster, Harold. *The New Literacy*. NCTE: National Council of Teachers of English. Urbana, IL, 1979. Reprinted by permission of NCTE.

Halasek, Kay. *A Pedagogy of Possibility: Bakhtinian Perspectives on Composition Studies*. Southern Illinois UP, 1999. Reprinted with the permission of the author.

Harris, Joseph. *Rewriting*. Salt Lake City: Utah State University Press. 2006. Reprinted with the permission of the author.

Hielker, Paul. *The Essay: Theory and Pedagogy for an Active Form*. National Council of Teachers. 1996. Reprinted with the permission of the author.

Haas, Christina, and Linda Flower. "Rhetorical Reading Strategies and the Construction of Meaning." *College Composition and Communication*, vol. 39, no. 2, May 1988. Reprinted with the permission of the author.

Karoly, David. "Climate Science Change Misinformation." ABC News. August 4, 2008. Reprinted with the permission of the author.

Kroll, Barry. "Arguing Differently." Pedagogy, vol. 5, no. 1, Winter 2005. Reprinted with the permission of the author.

Lakoff, George, and Mark Johnson. *Metaphors We Live by*. Chicago: University of Chicago Press, 2003. Reprinted by permission of University of Chicago Press.

Landis, John, dir. *Animal House*. Universal, 1978. Reprinted by permission of Universal Studios Licensing, LLC.

Levinson, Matthew. "Letter to the Editor" in response to "How Google Conquered the American Classroom." *The New York Times*. May 20, 2017. Used with the permission of the author.

MacManus, Doyle. "Are Businessmen Better Presidents?" *The Los Angeles Times*. September 12, 2012. Used by permission of *The Los Angeles Times* Rights & Permissions Office.

Murray, Donald. "The Stranger in the Photo is Me." Originally published in *The Boston Globe* August 27, 1991. Reprinted with permission of The Rosenberg Group.

Norberg-Hodge, Helena. "Consumer Monoculture: The Destruction of Tradition" *Global Dialogue*, vol. 1, no. 1, 1999. Used by permission of Local Futures.

Ochiltree, Scott. "Letter to the Editor" in response to "How Google Conquered the American Classroom." *The New York Times*. May 20, 2017. Used with the permission of the author.

Petrosky, Anthony. "From Story to Essay: Reading and Writing." *College Composition and Communication*, vol. 33, no 1, 1982. Reprinted by permission of NCTE.

Rex, Lesley A., Ebony Elizabeth Thomas, and Steven Engel. "Applying Toulmin: Teaching Logical Reasoning and Argumentative Writing." *English Journal* vol. 99, no. 6, 2010. Reprinted by permission of NCTE.

Roskelly, Hephzibah. *Breaking (into) the Circle: Group Work for Change in the English Classroom*. Portsmouth, NH: Boynton/Cook Heinemann, 2003. Used with the permission of the author.

Speigel, Alix. "How Politicians Get Away Without Answering the Question." *NPR.org* October 3, 2012. Reprinted by permission of NPR Permissions Office.

Toulmin, Stephen. *Introduction to Reasoning*, 2nd Ed., © 1984. Reprinted by permission of Pearson Education, Inc., New York, New York.

Van Tholen, James. "Surprised by Death." *Where All Hope Lies*. Grand Rapids, MI: Wm. B. Eerdmans Publishing Company. Reprinted by permission of Eerdmans Rights Department.

CPSIA information can be obtained
at www.ICGtesting.com
Printed in the USA
BVHW041338080222
628089BV00010B/777